Cover: After Hieronymus
Bosch, Central panel of the
*Triptych of the Temptation
of Saint Anthony* (detail).
15th century.
Panel, 131.5 x 53 cm.
Koninklijke musea voor
Schone Kunsten, Brussels.

Published by th

13

**Published by
the Flemish-Netherlands
Foundation
Stichting Ons Erfdeel**

Contents

Chronicle

Next page:
Adriaen Coorte, *Still Life with Asparagus.* 1697.
Oil on paper mounted on panel, 25 x 20,5 cm.
Rijksmuseum, Amsterdam.

What's Cooking?

A carefully prepared and fittingly revered asparagus adorns the cover of this book. Adriaen Coorte's raw asparagus from the Rijksmuseum in Amsterdam accompany this foreword. White asparagus grow underground and thus in the dark, so that they stay white. Green asparagus are cultivated above ground. Rub two asparagus stalks together. If they make a chirping or squeaking sound, they're fresh. Fresh asparagus can also be recognised by its fine white colour, its tip is firm to the touch, the base of the stem is not woody and does not yield when pinched. The stems of green asparagus are not fleshy but they retain a fresh tenderness. *Le bon Dieu est dans le détail.*

11

Tell me what you eat and I'll tell you who you are. According to the cliché Flanders is torn between sensuality and mysticism, dithers between fat and piety: it masks its angst with Breugelian guzzling and desperately fills the emptiness of existence with the materiality of food. It's all very well to say that in Flanders people devote a great deal of attention to eating well. You'll find good restaurants everywhere in the world, but culinary culture is measured by the average quality of all that's on offer.

Then again, the Netherlands is said to have been long devoid of any real culinary culture. Was it a Calvinist contempt for the body, that eventually led to the rissole in the automat, the greasy simplicity of the meatball? After the Second World War and its notorious hunger winter the Netherlands was branded a culinary desert. 'The smell of boiled sprouts' evokes all that is petit bourgeois, greasy gravy and gruel the depressing back kitchen. Luckily there was always the Indonesian *rijsttafel*. By now, though, that desert really has been made to blossom. These days the Dutch are enjoying their food more and more, and it plays an increasingly important part in their lives.

If cooking and eating don't yet quite rate as art, art has always fed on food; so in this yearbook you will find pillars plastered with ham; an installation that consists of newly crossbred kinds of chicken; a work of art that consists of …smells and a machine which replicates the process of digestion in the human body. Think of them as *amuse-gueules.*

For the thirteenth time this yearbook offers you, along with the themed section on eating and drinking, an *hors d'œuvre*. To stay with the eating metaphor, then, the essays by Ian Buruma and Martin Conway are about problems of digestion: how is Belgium digesting the collaboration that went on in World War II, and how did the young Buruma and the country where he grew up digest the Holocaust?

Also on the menu are Utrecht, the Dutch trade union movement and a war photo from Kosovo. And how does America go down in the Netherlands? Eat your fill from the laden tables of the Low Countries, and for dessert take another look at Coorte's asparagus: he is fascinated by surfaces, by shining, glistening skin. His asparagus stems, rudely torn from the dark earth, have resolved to stay together, like tree-trunks floating downstream, like papyrus scrolls from the Library of Alexandria – and like the articles from this yearbook.

We wish you a tasty and spicy Low Countries and good digestion for body and soul, for heart and mind. And for the drinkers among you a glass of the noble barley brew (from Heineken to Duvel and Geuze): *Santé, proost, prosit, here's to you, iechyd da, sláinte, cheers.*

Cooking is not a Hobby

And why peeling things is undeniably erotic

[MARJOLEINE DE VOS]

Do gardeners get it too, I sometimes wonder, that urge to dash off and do something they've just been reading about? I wonder whether they think: yes, I'm going to order those seeds right away, I'm going to prune things now, I'm going to take cuttings and plant things – in the same way as I, when I see certain fish at the market or when I read about shoulder of lamb with kidneys, immediately think: yes, I'm going to cook that! That desire for action. I can't actually imagine that there's any other activity that so frequently and so persistently spurs you to get busy. Cooking is so much richer than all other pleasures. Of course it's wonderful to smell the scent of the earth in the garden, but you can't change anything about that scent. However, if I take a pan, it immediately smells different if I melt butter in it than if I heat up olive oil in it. And that's just the fat. I haven't yet even started to talk about the smell of fried bacon, the smell of fried bacon with onions, the smell of beef roasted in fat in which bacon and onions have been fried... A rose smells wonderful, but there's nothing else you can do with it.

That said, I have once eaten deep-fried rose. It had been briefly dipped in batter, then deep-fried and sprinkled with icing sugar. Very nice, and very flowery. But then we're practically in the allotment already, and that means that gardening has become just a reason for more cooking. And when all's said and done, as a cook you don't have to compete with hobbies such as fishing and doing puzzles and knitting and tinkering with old motorbikes, because cooking is not a hobby. At any rate, I don't think much of people using that word for it. Cooking is something that you have to get really involved in. Cooking is necessary; it is essential and eternal and has nothing to do with pastimes.

That's the great thing about it.

You don't have to set aside free time for it, because you have to do it anyway, otherwise you don't have anything to eat.

Now I know very well that there are arguments against that last point – lots of people buy a pizza covered with rubbish like pineapple and taco sauce and pop it in the oven and call that cooking. Disturbing articles regularly appear in the newspapers about the disappearance of elementary cooking skills amongst 'young people'. Young people are only able to cook with pre-prepared products, the articles say; young people no longer have any idea what a raw beetroot looks like, let alone what to do with one; young people 'assemble' their meal with the

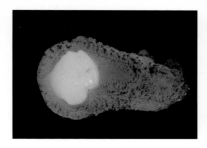

aid of a pair of scissors and a microwave, and cooking no longer gets a look-in.

There may well be something to that. I recently saw an Iglo advert for steamed vegetables. Now, I eat steamed vegetables very often. In fact, I'm inclined to steam all my vegetables nowadays. It may just be a phase, but it might be here to stay: vegetables are so much tastier when they're steamed. They get less soft and mushy, they retain more flavour (if they had any flavour in the first place, but that's another story), they keep their colour better, and they also cook more quickly. Not that I'm permanently in a tearing rush in the kitchen – which everyone else seems to be, if you go by the endless series of quick recipes and quick products – but it can be rather nice when things don't take too long. But anyway, Iglo had gone and cut up all sorts of vegetables very small and made carrots into little round balls, put them in a plastic bag and you could stick that in the oven or who knows where, and a little later you had steamed vegetables. When I saw that, my jaw dropped. The world has had steaming baskets for centuries – in the Netherlands they're usually those handy little stainless-steel ones that open out and fit into any size pan – and then the frozen-food company Iglo comes along and invents steaming. As it is, all you have to do is put your steaming basket and vegetables in a pan of boiling water and the steaming starts. No cellophane packets are involved and there's no way you could call it complicated or time-consuming. But apparently it is.

No, it's best that we just don't talk about that large new non-cooking sector of the population. It's depressing. Mainly because of all the things these people are depriving themselves of: the anticipation, the tactile pleasure, the scents, the little licks and nibbles, the pleasure of cutting through tender meat with a sharp knife – that sort of thing. I've always wanted to do a course with a butcher on how to bone meat, and learn how to transform half a cow or a whole pig into slices, sausages, cutlets, rump, marrowbone, washed intestines, ready-to-cook cheeks. There's a delight in using an elegant, slender knife to cut loose a layer of fat and membranes from a piece of meat, or in stripping kidneys, or in peeling a cooked tongue. Peeling a tongue is a completely different thing from the act of cutting. All the same, peeling is also one of the most enjoyable tasks to be carried out in the kitchen.

So number one in the peeling top ten, now that we're talking about it, is the cooked ox tongue, which you have to leave to cool for a while after cooking or you'll burn your fingers. Then, while it's still warm, you make a long incision on the underside of the tongue, after which you can just strip the hard skin from the velvety tongue. When you're doing this it's very difficult to control yourself and not chop off the tip of the tongue straightaway and gobble it up – the tip is so wonderfully soft and appetising. But it really does look pathetic if you were intending to serve up the whole tongue and its tip is missing.

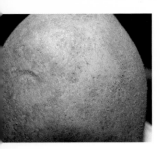

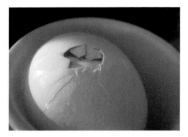

Peeling boiled new potatoes also scores high, I think, particularly when the skin comes off with a couple of tugs and the potato beneath is completely smooth – every crumb of potato that sticks to it spoils the pleasure. And almonds, brown almonds that you've blanched for a moment in boiling water and which you then pop straight out of their skins. There's something undeniably erotic about peeling, because it's always a form of laying bare. A peeled shrimp is considerably more naked than one in its little suit of armour; a grapefruit is defenceless after its thick rind has been removed; an egg is transformed from a fortress into a thing of gleaming loveliness. This is less true for the removal of skins than it is for peeling. Probably because skins are generally softer, they conceal less. As soon as a skin becomes thick, like that of a banana, you can talk about peeling again. Bananas are of course notorious for their naked, half-peeled appearance.

All these, then, are things that non-cooks don't enjoy; or they think that they don't enjoy them because they never do them.

Just picking up a leftover bit from the plate with your fork

Now, it's true to say that not everything is enjoyable. Cutting through tender meat is wonderful, filleting a fish so that you can stuff it is satisfying, but having to chop three carrots into small pieces, having to take a kilo of tomatoes and peel them (although that bit is nice), remove the seeds (hmm) and chop them small is not particularly something to look forward to. It's not something to dread either, for that matter, it's just the way it's done. And you're doing it for a higher purpose, after all, namely the meal. And the meal is for eaters. And the eaters are your family, your sweetheart, your friends. Preferably. Because one of the nicest things a person can do has always been to give a dinner party. For friends.

Even the prospect is nice. Anyone who's got a bit of time generally begins planning ahead at an early stage – for that matter, anyone who doesn't have

much time is also better off doing that: planning ahead frees up more time. But you can plan ahead in different ways, by putting together a dinner in a quick and practical fashion, maybe with the help of a carefully selected cookery book, or by treating yourself and exploring different possibilities.

The last option is the most pleasurable. For that, you lay out far too many cookbooks on the table and you begin leafing through them. Preferably in a book that you love and that contains many possibilities. After a lengthy North African/Mediterranean period, I have now found my way back to mainly French with light-hearted excursions. For French cuisine, you take Bocuse or Elizabeth David and you leaf through and then you think: hey, how witty, poached eggs on fried onions, shall I try that? Or shall I finally get round to making *oeufs en gelée* again, and then I can go and buy a calf's foot – they make such nice jelly – and I'll put some leaves of tarragon in as Elizabeth David suggests, and not, as I usually do, leaves of watercress – just for a change. Very nice. Or a terrine, with a mallard in it, or... no, brains! Yes, poached brains in brown butter, as Bocuse recommends – but perhaps not all of them like brains. And don't forget the danger of BSE! Next thing you know, our brains will be looking as soft as the poached ones on the plates, so maybe not, then. Oh, look here, *cardons à la moelle* – that looks wonderful – I recently saw cardoons at a Moroccan greengrocer's, yes!

Anyway, you can quite easily spend a whole evening tasting endless dishes in your mind without ever arriving at anything approaching a plan for dinner. But it's not a waste of time, because it's fun, and because you learn a lot from reading cookery books.

Another evening follows when you get down to business. The following meal is decided upon: the *oeufs en gelée* after all, because a little of what you fancy does you good. Then sauerkraut soup from Kaatje bij de Sluis, a soup that consists of sauerkraut that has disappeared and sausage that has remained and which has the robust flavour of a sauerkraut dish and, at the same time, the refinement of a clear soup. Then smoked salmon from our own smoking oven – a present which for years now I've been constantly and profoundly grateful to

Father Christmas for. It is a metal box that you put on the gas. You scatter smoking sawdust in the bottom, then you put a cover plate on top, and on top of that there's a little grille with whatever you want to smoke; the whole thing is closed with a sliding metal lid. You heat the box, and after about ten, twelve minutes the salmon comes out, warm and smoky and still orange inside, but opaquely pink on the outside. And you sometimes hear grumbles about modern farmed salmon that is supposed to taste like chickenfeed, but salmon cooked like this really does taste good every time.

Of course, it needs some sauce, so we're going to make a fish fumet and turn it into a sauce with dry vermouth and cold butter – that kind of sauce is always wonderfully tasty. And insanely laborious of course, because first you've got your entire work surface covered with ingredients for the fumet, with fish bones and leeks and fish heads and carrots and bay leaves and onions and so on, and then you've got a pan of fish stock, and you reduce that, and then you cook shallots in the Noilly Prat and then you reduce it further and finally whisk in the butter. So, from that whole surface covered with ingredients, all that remains is a small bowl of sauce. And that's typically French. Economy doesn't come into it. Precisely the reason why everyone has gone over to Italian and Thai food and the like, because that works the other way round: on your work surface you've got half a kilo of green beans and a piece of chicken, and an hour later a copious meal appears on the table thanks to a cunning use of herbs.

Anyway, to the salmon and the sauce we add steamed broccoli (without cellophane, just out of the pan) and tagliatelle, also bearing in mind how things will look on the plate: the pink of the salmon looks good next to the green of the broccoli, the creamy yellow of the sauce and the tagliatelle. Anyone who wants to make a really big impact goes for black tagliatelle, but you've got to be very sure that you won't look like a poseur.

Maybe just a small piece of cheese if we really feel like it, and then a nice lemon tart, with a tangy filling and sweet, hard pastry.

A fantastic plan – all that remains now is to carry it out. The best idea is to do this kind of thing for six to eight people – the ideal number for a dinner party. It

has to be six nice people that you ask, too, people who get on with each other and people who take pleasure in eating. Of course, you don't have to talk about food all evening – God forbid – but it's not satisfying to expend all that effort preparing a meal for those types who keep waving the wine bottle around and slurring their words as they swill down the food.

Of course, you don't cook for the compliments, but, all the same, some of the pleasure beforehand is the agreeable knowledge that the guests are soon going to be enjoying themselves. And guests who just swill stuff down aren't enjoying it. At least they're not enjoying what the cook has made – maybe they're enjoying the wine, I've no problem with that, that's important too, but even so. I like to see a guest just picking up a leftover bit from the plate with their fork – that sort of guest enjoys their food. Listless guests who turn over everything on their plate three times and then declare that they've had a wonderful meal are not favourite dinner companions, however suitable they may be in other respects. Not every friend is the ideal eater. Which doesn't matter, but for a non-ideal eater you have to make other things. Not *oeufs en gelée*. More like meatballs in tomato sauce. Or a roast chicken with lemon. Or paella, everyone loves that, or something very spicy, Thai prawn soup, for example, or something with melted cheese, aubergines and tomatoes baked in the oven, or potatoes cooked with rosemary and – but we were talking about something else.

So, everything is as it should be, the dinner has been put together, the guests have been invited. You can begin, so you do. You can have two days of fun with this dinner, because you have to prepare all sorts of things in advance. That said, it's cleverly thought out, though I do say so myself, because once the guests have arrived you've actually got nothing to worry about. The complicated work is all in the preparation, which means that the cook doesn't have to trot back and forth with a red face and frayed nerves.

There's even time to lay the table. With care. The appearance of the table is half the work. A dinner party is the occasion for getting out the table-cloth and the dinner service and maybe the silverware – but on no account should you overdo it , because the guests shouldn't have to wonder whether they're really

worth all this and whether they shouldn't have dressed differently and whether they should be having different conversations. However much the hosts are putting themselves out, the effort must remain inconspicuous. Otherwise the glasses, knives and plates suddenly start to play the main role, or the food does, and that should just be present at the table in a silent supporting role.

With a more Mediterranean meal there isn't much laying of tables to be done anyway; the starters serve as the table decoration then. That's the nice thing about making lots of little dishes; you put them straight on the table and they give lots of colour and aroma and zest. It's also very pleasant to make lots of little dishes; you're always finishing off another one; you see the number of dishes and bowls growing; and, full of anticipation, you just have the occasional nibble now and then to check whether that aubergine in honey sauce still tastes so nice and spicy, whether the baby beets with walnuts really are so surprising, whether the carrot and orange salad really is as nutty, tart and earthy as you remembered from previous occasions. And yes, everything tastes as it should. A few colourful plates to put it on and Bob's your uncle.

And then the bell goes and they arrive, your friends.

Translated by Laura Watkinson

And nowadays people seem mad keen to swap all that for a bag of dried-up salad with dressing out of a bottle and a packet of powder that swears it's actually a Spanish fish dish if you just throw in a bit of deep-frozen fish yourself.

But that's an extremely unlikely story. Nobody believes it. ∎

Marjoleine de Vos (1957-)

The Urge to Cook

With greedy breasts desire stands at the work-top
slurps seed out of tomatoes, watches the swelling
of batter under its damp cloth. Her hand fondles
the sirloin of prime young beef, its searching tongue
is made for hers, enraptured she slides its
meaty balls into the pan. Passion
is a kitchen princess with touchable skin,
downy as dough, fragrant as butter, a defenceless
duck freed of its bones that wants to be naked
as an olive in oil, a peach in its juice.
She wants to be dismembered on the chopping block,
touched by gluttonous fingers and guzzled piping-hot.
To be a fish, swimming in creamy sauce
cradled, known, craved, enjoyed.

Kooklust

Met gretige borsten staat begeerte aan het aanrecht
zoent het zaad uit tomaten, kijkt naar het zwellen
van beslag onder vochtig doek. Haar hand liefkoost
de haas van een jonge stier, zijn zoekende tong
is gemaakt voor de hare, verzaligd streelt ze
zijn ballen de pan in. Hartstocht
is een keukenprinses met aanraakbare huid,
donzig als deeg, geurig als boter, een weerloze
van bot bevrijde eend die naakt wil zijn
als een olijf in olie, een perzik op sap.
Ze wil zich ontleden op het hakblok, betast worden
door gulzige vingers en gloeiend verslonden.
Een vis zijn, zwemmend in roomsaus
gewiegd, gekend, begeerd, genoten.

Translated by John Irons

From *A Seal Please* (Zeehond graag). Amsterdam: G.A. van Oorschot, 2000.

Peter Theunynck (1960-)

Translated by John Irons

Game

the hare had lingered long in wine-vinegar marinade
wild marjoram and thyme the barest touch of lips sufficed
to savour it, so obligingly the meat slipped from the bone
after hours of patient simmering in game stock on the stove

chanterelles picked in the woods received from butter
that which makes mortals happy on a rainy day

when sheer delight had just descended over all the tables
and everyone was chewing with bulging cheeks, nodding, laughing,
swallowing, it arrived after a long wait on a serving dish,
the laurel-wreathed head of a still young fox

Wild

de haas was lekker lang gemarineerd in wijnazijn
en tijm en wilde marjolein hem proeven volstonden
lippen, zo inschikkelijk glipte het vlees van het been
van uren lijdzaam op het vuur te garen in wildfond

in het bos geplukte cantharellen kregen van boter
dat wat stervelingen op een regendag gelukkig maakt

net toen verrukking over alle tafelen was neergedaald
en iedereen met bolle kaken kauwde, knikte, lachte,
slikte, kwam hij na lang wachten op een dienblad aan,
de met laurier omkranste kop van de nog jonge vos

From *Raster*, no. 105. Amsterdam: De Bezige Bij, March 2004

An Enticing Taste of the Past

Art in Food and Food in Art

[PETER G. ROSE]

Paintings by the seventeenth-century Dutch Masters portraying food and drink give an insight in the period's food practices and shed light on their relevance to the American kitchen today. Every day Americans eat dishes that can be traced back to the foodways brought to New Netherland by the early Dutch settlers, who planted fruit trees, among them apples, pears and peaches, vegetables such as lettuces, cabbages, parsnips, carrots and beets and herbs like parsley, rosemary, chives and tarragon. Farm animals such as horses, pigs and cows were among the most valuable imported commodities.

While the Dutch period of New Netherland (the present-day states of New York, New Jersey, Delaware and parts of Pennsylvania and Connecticut) only lasted officially from 1609 to 1664, the Dutch influence, particularly the culinary influence, persists to this day. From eighteenth- and nineteenth-century hand-written cookbooks belonging to the descendants of the early settlers, we know that they continued to cook in the manner of their forebears. Many of the recipes not only indicate the method of preparation but reveal that Dutch social customs continued as well, as is clear for example from a recipe for *doot koeckjes* (literally: death cookies), biscuits served as funeral refreshments. Or from a recipe for *kandeel*, a special drink served at births. Agricultural practices and horticultural introductions are attributable to the Dutch colonial past of America, but so also are cookies, doughnuts and coleslaw, to mention only a very few examples. The Dutch touch left a lasting mark on the American kitchen.

I chose a small sampling of Dutch and Flemish paintings from collections in the Netherlands and America that will demonstrate how these artworks give an insight into seventeenth-century Dutch food practices and bring a new understanding of the colonial diet.

Job Berckheyde
(1630-1693), *The Baker*.
c.1681. Canvas.
Worcester Art Museum,
Worcester, MA.

A baker blows his horn to alert his customers that his wares are ready. In the Netherlands bread was generally baked by the town's bakers rather than at home, so it was important for him to let them know when it was available. The custom continued in New Netherland, as we know from a court case in which a baker was fined for blowing his horn and selling white bread in a time of grain scarcity.

Bread was the mainstay of the diet. It was consumed with butter or cheese for breakfast, paired with meat or *hutsepot* (a one-pot dish of meats and vegetables) for the midday main meal, and served with, or as a part of, the porridge at night.

In the seventeenth century the poor and working class ate rye, or coarse wheat bread, while daily consumption of white bread was a symbol of affluence. Rye and wheat were the main grain ingredients for bread baking. Rye, grown in the drier eastern and southern provinces, produced a dark (black) bread. Wheat, mostly imported, produced a lighter bread with softer crumb, or, when finely sifted, a finely textured white bread. In the workroom, often behind his shop, the baker mixed the flour, salt, yeast and water into dough, which was then kneaded to the right consistency. Bread dough was shaped in various ways, as we see in this painting with large loaves and various kinds of rolls. It was sometimes flavoured with nutmeg, cloves and especially cinnamon, or filled with dried fruits and decorated with sugar, or even gold leaf.

The local municipal government regulated the size and weight of bread by appointing inspectors to oversee its production, and it also set the price of both wheat and rye bread.

Peeters portrays a table laden with shellfish, cheeses, butter (far left), eggs, including plovers' eggs, and breads. A large wheat loaf is shown behind the salt stand and a coarse, dark rye loaf is displayed in the background on the right. The baked goods in the foreground on the left are called *zotinnekoecken* and are akin to rusks. On the right we see hardtack, the mainstay of seafarers. A New Amsterdam ordinance of 1647 set the weekly rations for ships of the West India Company at '*31/2 pounds of hard tack*'. A dinner roll is presented on the plate under the napkin, as was the custom at the time.

The crabmeat would be prepared in its shell with butter, herbs and spices. Shrimp were often cooked in seawater and eaten on the spot. Many Americans erroneously assume that European lobsters do not have claws, but actually the lobsters on both sides of the Atlantic are very similar. However, slight variations have led to their classification as two different species with the American lobster (*Homarus Americanus*) being the larger of the two.

The yellow cheeses in the stack are made from cow's milk, either whole milk (with cream), or skimmed evening milk and whole morning milk, or skimmed milk only. The dark cheese in the stack might be sheep's cheese, coloured with sheep's faeces. Cheeses get their names from the town where they are made, e.g. Gouda or Leiden.

Clara Peeters (1594-c.1640), *Still Life with Crab, Shrimps and Lobster*. c.1635. Canvas, 70.8 x 108.9 cm. The Museum of Fine Arts, Houston, TX. Gift of the Enthoven Foundation.

Adriaen van Utrecht
(1592-1652),
A Fishmonger's Stall.
Canvas, 215 x 298 cm.
Museum voor Schone
Kunsten, Ghent.

Fish markets were divided into two parts. One area was for the sale of saltwater fish, in another freshwater fish was sold. In this painting, Adriaen van Utrecht follows that custom by carefully separating the freshwater fish and arranging them on the small table on the right, among them flounder, roach, northern pike, tub gurnard and garfish. Freshwater fish were used in a typical period dish known as *doopvis* (fish for dunking). The freshly caught fish were cooked in salted water to which parsley was added. The cooking broth was then used for dunking the fish and the bread that was served with it.

The saltwater fish include salmon, cod, sturgeon, herring, tench, and thornback ray. Salmon was typically slowly stewed, seasoned with pepper, nutmeg, and mace and topped with breadcrumbs and butter, according to *De Verstandige Kock*, the definitive Dutch cookbook of the seventeenth century. As was the case with other important foodstuffs, such as bread and meat, in both the Netherlands and New Netherland the processing and marketing of fish was strictly regulated by the government, thereby ensuring a superior product.

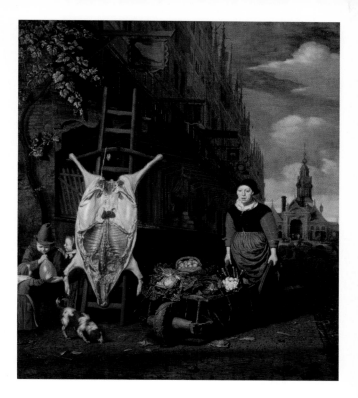

A woman selling autumn vegetables from her wooden wheelbarrow is passing a pig hanging on a ladder. It was customary to hang the animal in this manner for 24 hours to drain its blood. Those who could afford it would purchase half a cow and a whole pig for winter in the slaughter month of November. An appendix to *De Verstandige Kock* gives instructions on how to process the meat. It is stored in brine, where hams and shoulders remain for 9 to 10 days before being hung in the chimney to be smoked. The back, sides and feet were used in stews or soups.

Pigs feature prominently in New Netherland lore. They roamed free, causing damage to public and private property, as is clear from many court cases involving pigs. Period records show that pigs even uprooted the walls of the fort in New Amsterdam.

Michiel van Musscher
(1645-1705),
The Pig on the Ladder.
Canvas, 87 x 75.5 cm.
Amsterdams
Historisch Museum.

Pieter Cornelisz van Rijck
(c.1568 - c.1635),
Market Scene. 1622.
Canvas, 126.4 x 148.6 cm.
North Carolina Museum of
Art, Raleigh, NC.

This painting seems to be a quintessential document of food history. Dutch market vegetables are mixed with New World foodstuffs such as pumpkins and cucurbites, Jerusalem artichokes, and a turkey, all brought to Europe as the result of the exploration of Christopher Columbus and subsequent expeditions.

New and exotic plants were found in the gardens of Dutch country houses. Botanist Pieter Hondius, for example, describes in a long poem his garden's 'artisocken onder de aert' or Jerusalem artichokes. A native of the Americas, it got its name from the girasole or sunflower and from the fact that it was thought to taste like artichoke hearts. By the seventeenth century turkeys had long been domesticated in the Netherlands and feature in several recipes in *De Verstandige Kock*. Large-headed cabbage, like the one on the right, was often referred to as Leiden cabbage, presumably because it was grown there. Correspondence of the period indicates that seed for these cabbages was ordered from the homeland by New Netherland settlers. White, yellow and red carrots were available in the seventeenth century. Orange carrots, so popular today, were developed from the yellow and red types, probably in the city of Hoorn, because they were often referred to as 'Hoorn carrots'. Together with turnips and parsnips, carrots were the root vegetables most frequently eaten, either as side dishes or in stews. Large-scale horticultural experimentation for commercial purposes and private pleasure took place at this time in the Leiden and Amsterdam botanical gardens and in the gardens of the country houses owned by the wealthy upper classes.

A woman, seated by the fire in a low chair, is frying pancakes in a long-handled frying pan. A batter pot is standing beside her. She only needs a small knife to loosen the edges of the pancake, which she will then turn flap-jack style.

Recipes for pancakes already appear in medieval manuscripts. Since one needed only a few implements and inexpensive ingredients – flour, liquid in the form of milk or water, eggs, and butter – to prepare them, their popularity with the lower classes was ensured, although they were equally favoured by the affluent middle class. Since it was such a popular food, it is no wonder that when the Dutch settled in New Netherland, they adapted local foodstuffs to a familiar preparation. For example they mashed cooked pumpkin and mixed it with cornmeal to make pancakes.

Pancakes, waffles, wafers, and *olie-koecken* (deep-fried balls of dough with raisins, apples, and almonds that became a fore-runner of the American doughnut) were some of the celebratory foods both prepared at home and sold on the streets, as contemporary artists portray.

Jan Steen (1626-1679),
The Feast of Saint Nicholas.
c.1665-1668.
Canvas, 82 x 70.5 cm.
Rijksmuseum, Amsterdam.

This seventeenth-century scene is familiar to any twenty-first-century Dutch person. A family is celebrating the feast of Saint Nicholas. The children have placed their shoes by the chimney the night before. During the night Saint Nicholas has passed by, and on the morning of December 6 they have found toys and all sorts of good things to eat. But only if they have been good like the little girl in the foreground, who clutches a new doll. Her brother, standing behind her crying, apparently was not so well-behaved because his shoe contained only a *roe*, a bunch of twigs used for spanking. Three other siblings stand by the fireplace and sing a song of thanks to the Saint.

Virtually nothing is certain about the real Saint Nicholas. According to tradition, he was a fourth-century Catholic bishop of Myra in Asia Minor, who became associated with anonymous gift-giving and is worshipped as the patron saint of sailors. He was often the main character in the miracle plays performed in town squares. This made him less of a venerated saint and more of a popular folk hero. He was and is so much part of yearly family celebrations that even during the Reformation his holiday could not be eradicated by government or Protestant church officials.

The Dutch feast's traditions became absorbed into the American Christmas festivities when American novelist Washington Irving borrowed its central figure and changed the tall, thin, stern, but just bishop into the short, rotund and jolly Santa Claus (*A History of New York from the Beginning of the World to the End of the Dutch Dynasty*, published on St. Nicholas Day, December 6, 1809). Nineteenth-century illustrators created further embellishments to his appearance, while different ethnic groups added their own traditions, and the result is the secular component of the American Christmas celebration.

The seven paintings I have discussed are only a minute part of the estimated 6,000,000 produced by the Dutch Masters during the seventeenth century. All of us marvel at their beauty and the skilful ways in which foodstuffs, objects, animals and people are portrayed after being carefully arranged by the painter. Many wonder about the hidden implications. Some art historians find religious and other meanings, based on study of period literature; others feel that more attention should be directed to the techniques and beauty and the paintings should be enjoyed for what they are, exquisite works of art. I approach them in a very pragmatic way and see them as visual documents, which, in addition to their beauty, also give us insight into aspects of seventeenth-century daily life, not only in the Netherlands, but in New Netherland as well, thereby affording us an intriguing and enticing taste of the past. ■

NOTE

Peter G. Rose is the author of *Matters of Taste: Food and Drink in Dutch 17th-century Art and Life* (Syracuse University Press, 2002), *The Sensible Cook: Dutch Foodways in the Old and the New World* (Syracuse University Press, 1998) and *Foods of the Hudson* (Overlook Press, 2000). Visit her website at www.peterrose.com

Lucebert (1924-1994)

Translated by Les Murray

Peace is Eating to Music

peaceful eating is good eating
because tasty food is eaten only in quiet and peace
good digestion requires a person
to chew each mouthful at least fifteen times
thus it's best to eat to music
since happy notes make the jaws move by themselves
harmoniously and with the jaws the oesophagus
and thereafter the further thirty metres
of working intestine that wind through the body

peace is good eating to pleasant music
martial music is better for tramping than for meals
so long as you tramp peaceably
and don't march with squads of soldiers
going to fight other soldiers
in that case marching music is as dangerous
as botulin in foodstuffs

dance music however is perfectly good to eat to
since dancing isn't fighting
a dancer keeps in time with other dancers
just as at the table you don't gobble
all the best bits but share them around
with other people with your fellow diners

Vrede is eten met muziek

vredig eten is goed eten
want lekker eten doet men alleen in rust en vrede
voor een goede spijsvertering is het een vereiste
dat men elk hapje minstens vijftienmaal kauwt
daarom eet men met muziek ook beter
want onder vrolijke tonen bewegen de kaken vanzelf
harmonieus en met de kaken ook de slokdarm
en later zelfs de overige dertig meter
lange darmen in de buik

vrede is goed eten met goede muziek
met marsmuziek kan men beter lopen dan eten
als men dan ook maar vredig loopt
en niet meemarcheert met een troep soldaten
tegen andere soldaten
dan is marsmuziek net zo bedorven
als besmet voedsel

maar bij dansmuziek is het zeker goed eten
want dansen is geen vechten
wie danst houdt rekening met andere dansers
zoals men onder het eten niet alle
lekkere hapjes alleen verorbert maar die deelt
met de overigen de disgenoten

From *Collected Poems* (Verzamelde gedichten). Amsterdam: De Bezige Bij, 2002.

Erik Menkveld (1959-)
The New Fish

Already when the specimen was being served
adjoining tables stopped the digging
of further trenches in the chestnut purée,

the spading of curled-up lettuce leaves
stagnates, wines linger in lifted glasses:
this fish is not the usual feast

of the deep. A revelation,
hauled it would seem from primordial
waters. Though head and tail-fin gone,

seasoned fishermen blinked back their tears
at the sight of breasts, the rudiments
of limbs. How many species had had to

perish for this peerless creature? Or
in it had their origin? But the time
has come for consumption. Uncertain moment:

the chef was faced with a culinary enigma.
How to prepare what's never been prepared
and in itself is seemingly complete?

Poach, braise or marinate? Superfluous,
an insult. And what then? Do you keep things
simple with seaweed and slivers on toast

or does this call for a complex brandade
for the more demanding stomach? Raw, unsliced
it became, with ostrich egg and shoveller roulade.

Even the sploshing ice-cube water
halts at the point of pouring.
Then the first elected eater places

the first forkful in his mouth. He chews
in silence and unparalleled abandonment. Then
starts to utter ghastly screams. Revulsion,

ecstasy perhaps? He dances round for minutes,
subsiding into baffled staring. Even
after the babas he can't speak about it.

De nieuwe vis

Al bij opserveren van het exemplaar
staken belendende tafels het graven
van verdere greppels in de kastanjepuree,

het afplaggen van de verruigde salades
stagneert, wijnen talmen in geheven glazen:
de gebruikelijke gezelligheid uit zee

is deze vis niet. Een openbaring,
opgehaald uit wateren van aanvang
lijkt ze. Al ontbraken kop en staartvin,

ervaren vissers verbeten hun tranen
bij het zien van de borsten, de aanzet
tot ledematen. Hoeveel soorten moesten

vergaan voor deze ongeëvenaarde? Of
zijn eruit ontstaan? Maar het ogenblik
van nuttigen is daar. Ongewis moment:

de kok stond voor een culinair raadsel.
Hoe bereid je wat niet eerder bereid is
en ogenschijnlijk in zichzelf volmaakt?

Pocheren, braden, marineren? Overbodig,
een belediging. En daarna? Hou je het
simpel met zeewier en mootjes op toast

of vraagt dit om een complexe brandade
voor de meereisende maag? Rauw, ongesneden
werd het, met struisvogelei en slobeendrollade.

Zelfs het plonzend ijsklontenwater
onderbreekt zich nu op het uitstroompunt.
Daar steekt de uitverkoren eerste eter

de eerste hap in zijn mond. Hij kauwt
in stilte en ongekende overgave. Begint
dan ijselijke kreten te slaken. Uit afkeer

of extase? Minutenlang danst hij rond
en bedaart tot verbijsterd staren. Zelfs
na de soesjes kan hij er niet over praten.

Translated by John Irons

From *Raster*, no. 105. Amsterdam: De Bezige Bij, March 2004

The Dutch and their Appetites

Changes in Eating Habits in the Nineteenth and Twentieth Centuries

[ANNEKE H. VAN OTTERLOO]

Café *Mille Colonnes*
on Rembrandtplein,
Amsterdam,
painted by G.H. Grauss
in 1918.

In the opinion of foreigners the Dutch, unlike the Belgians, have never progressed very far in the culinary arts. There's nothing new about this observation; it's been almost a cliché since the seventeenth century. In that celebrated and prosperous era the Dutch made a name for themselves as a people with robust appetites, a great capacity for drink and a weakness for smoking tobacco-pipes. At the same time they also earned a reputation for their lack of refinement and appreciation of culinary pleasure. That impression is partly based on the group paintings of civic guards popular at the time, in which all these excesses are depicted. But paintings are not always a reliable source of information when it comes to daily life, where eating habits play a central role. Travel records are another source. How did Dutch appetites fare two centuries later? Here our informant is Ortigão, a Portuguese journalist who visited the country in 1883. He recounts what he saw in a restaurant called *De Karseboom* in Kalverstraat in Amsterdam: *'Most*

Somewhere in the
Netherlands, 1949.

*of the guests order a bowl of soup, a meat dish and vegetables. They put the meat
and the vegetables on a plate and mix them together, spread themselves out com-
fortably, cut everything up into little bits, drench the whole lot in the gravy left on
the serving dish, then wolf it all down, forkful by forkful, with mechanical voracity,
exhibiting a fierce appetite and an even greater lack of gastronomic sensitivity. Few
of the customers eat bread, even fewer take dessert and almost no one drinks with
their meal. Once the dish is empty they hastily settle the bill.*[1]

Senhor Ortigão was in the Netherlands at this particular time for the Amsterdam World's Fair, a badge of modernisation and progress. In the last decades of
the nineteenth century factory production made huge strides in the Netherlands
and the big cities grew proportionately. Commercial traffic became livelier, restaurants and other eating establishments appeared, and it would not be long
before department stores such as *De Bijenkorf* were established. Coffee houses opened near the harbours and factories. In the cities, busy centres evolved
where businessmen, office workers, ladies out for a day's shopping and people
with the day off would make their way and become the 'guests' of the new ea-
teries. But unlike the restaurants of Brussels, for example, our Portuguese
visitor's observations suggest that these were not places to see and be seen
or to flaunt one's refined style or manners, to say nothing of the quality of the
meal itself. Restaurants did exist, but they often functioned merely as places
where people could fill their stomachs if they couldn't do so at home. It would
be more than a century before the first Dutch restaurant finally earned foreign
recognition in the shape of a three-star rating (from the authoritative French
Michelin guide). That was in 2001, and it was awarded to chef Cees Helder of the
Parkheuvel restaurant in Rotterdam.

This remarkable event may signify that a fundamental change has taken
place in the way the Dutch relate to their cooking and their stomachs. This piece
will consider the questions *what* changed, *how* it happened and *what brought it
about*, and *who* made the major contributions.[2] Dishes will be dealt with as well,
and the location where the cooking occurs will not be limited to the exclusive
restaurant alone. Everyone has to eat, lofty and humble, from the countryside to
the city, from east to west and from north to south – in the Netherlands, too.

Bread with no chalk or sand:
modernisation, industrialisation and urbanisation

Eating habits are bound up with society as a whole in a variety of ways. Changes in the economic, social and cultural sectors are directly reflected in what people can and want to eat, and how they do it. At the end of the nineteenth century, the Netherlands was busily engaged in industrialisation. This affected the living conditions and way of life of the population at large, most of whom lived in the countryside and worked on the land. The existing cities continued to grow and new cities sprang up; they offered newcomers the opportunity to build a new life for themselves. This brought with it a profound change in cooking and eating habits, for factory workers, office personnel and factory owners alike – in short, for people from every walk of life. Living in cities meant that the women of the house or their domestic staff had to buy the ingredients for the household's daily meals instead of getting them from the potato field, the kitchen garden or the pickle vat, as was usual in the countryside. At the end of the nineteenth century, food was still a major item in the housekeeping books

In 1920 bread factories had been around for more than sixty years, but home baking was still done in the country side.

of most of the 'working class'. More than half of a worker's wage had to be spent on potatoes and bread, supplemented by very small amounts of butter, sugar, milk, vegetables and a very occasional bit of bacon or meat. Households also had to buy fuel to cook with and to heat the room they lived in (usually it wasn't much more than that). Many low-paid urban workers' households found it hard to make ends meet. The more well-to-do groups from the middle class, however, could live quite well and eat a varied diet. The contrasts in lifestyle and eating habits between families ranked higher or lower on the social ladder were considerable.

Yet by around 1890 the largest and least fortunate segment of the Dutch population had a better chance of being able to obtain adequate food, both quantitatively and qualitatively, than fifty years before. Back then, in the 'black forties', there were serious shortages and even talk of famine due to the high price of grain and the failure of the potato harvest. In 1847 deaths outnumbered

Vincent van Gogh,
The Potato Eaters. 1885.
Canvas. Rijksmuseum,
Amsterdam.

births, but that was the last year that the figures produced such a result. An uncertain pre-industrial rhythm would turn into a modern industrial tempo. The food supply slowly became more stable and less precarious with the advent of steam navigation and mass production. In 1856 the country's first bread factory was established in Amsterdam by Samuel Sarphati, a physician with a social conscience and an urban reformer who also built the Amstel Hotel. Bread, the staple food of the masses, was expensive and was often adulterated with sand and chalk. Sarphati's aim was to improve the quality of the bread and lower its price by means of factory production.

There were other basic items whose production moved from the household and the small producer to the factory. Some were completely new – margarine, for instance, the first 100% industrially manufactured article, which would replace butter, and especially lard, after 1871. Lard had to be rendered from fat in the kitchen (the traditional 'pot of lard') before it could be used. Margarine, or 'artificial butter', was half the price of real butter and originally consisted of a combination of skimmed milk and fats derived from offal. Two Dutch butter merchants from Oss in Brabant, Sam van den Bergh and the brothers Anton and Jan Jurgens, were the first margarine manufacturers. Margarine manufacturing, which at that time was still a by-product of the emerging meat industry, spread quickly during the last decades of the nineteenth century and in around 1930 would form part of the basis for the food giant Unilever.

Dutch dairy:
Gouda cheeses.

Other new discoveries also made it possible to extract and process sugar from beet instead of sugar cane, flour and syrup from potatoes, powder and fats from cocoa and to produce other new luxury products such as jam, custard powder and chocolate products. In the second half of the nineteenth century the Netherlands built up a major food industry.[3] Some of these products were initially exported, such as margarine and meat to England, but others were aimed directly at the emerging urban middle classes.

With industrialisation and urbanisation came the need for new sanitary facilities and other utilities in the new urban districts. This was not immediately apparent to the city councils, and it took several decades before all homes were hooked up to the local or provincial sewage, water, gas and, from the 1920s, electricity networks. Among well-to-do housewives at that time it was also considered modern (in connection with ideas about hygiene and the shortage of domestic help) to prepare meals on an electric cooker with four rings. Modernisation in food production was also reflected in the increasing amount of research, the growing knowledge about food and the desire to disseminate these new insights through education.

Cookery teachers: a typical Dutch taste?

By around 1890 Dutch workers did indeed enjoy a somewhat better and more varied diet than in earlier decades, but it was only then that the middle class became aware of a dietary problem among the working class. Morality played a greater role in this than taste. The middle classes were convinced that working men wasted their wages on drink, and that their wives had no notion of how to provide nutritious meals for their families. As a result, disease and debility were far from uncommon on the shop floor. It was the birth of the 'social question'. Living and working conditions were even made the subject of a Parliamentary

Inquiry in 1887. The progressive journal *Sociaal Weekblad*, printed menus devised with consideration for nutritional value and cost, and these were served up in the *Volks- en Kinderkeuken* (the People's and Children's Kitchen). In this new philanthropic establishment, families could come to eat or collect their meals for 7 cents a portion. The dishes consisted of pea soup and marrowfat beans several times a week, and stockfish with potatoes and vegetables once a week. The discussion in the journal had to do with the editors' decision to give pride of place in the working man's menu to the nutritious stockfish. A critical reader noted that stockfish only tasted good when served with butter (too expensive for the working class), but the editors stood firm. The reason *'most of our working-class population eats so poorly'* had less to do with taste and expense than with *'habit and prejudice'*. It was a matter of urgent necessity to improve the working man's lifestyle and educate him in self-control and orderliness. Eating habits were an important means to this end.

Various groups from the middle classes as well as factory owners, philanthropists, doctors and well-to-do ladies joined forces in the campaign to set up courses in cooking and housekeeping for the *'working-class woman and*

Albert Heijn outlet,
Den Bosch, 1907.

her daughters'. The schools were duly established, but they never reached the target group. The first was the Hague Cooking School, later the posh Laan van Meerdervoort School of Domestic Science, started in 1888. In its early days young ladies from the moneyed middle class and their domestic servants profited from the lessons; working-class girls were not admitted until decades later. The most progressive training came from the New Amsterdam School of Domestic Science, with which famous teachers such as Martine Wittop Koning and, later, Riek Lotgering-Hillebrand were connected. The first cookery teachers acquired their practical knowledge of haute cuisine from (French) hotel cooks. In upper-middle-class circles, French cuisine was regarded as setting the standard . For simpler dishes they took field trips to comparable institu-

Innovations of the 1960s and 1970s: supermarkets and shopping trolleys.

tions in England and Germany. The theoretical basis for their recipes, however, came mainly from doctors and other experts in the field of nutrition and health.

The newly developed science of dietetics provided insights into what nutrients human beings needed to ingest each day in order to function well. Housewives at both ends of the social ladder, so the teachers believed, ought to apply this science of nutrition. For this reason they should serve nutritious, varied and economical meals instead of an exaggerated number of dishes or merely potatoes with fatty bacon or boiled *stamppot* (a traditional simple Dutch dish consisting of potatoes mashed with vegetables and sometimes meat). Ideally meals should consist of potatoes, vegetables and meat in varying combinations: nutritious, but simple. Traditional Dutch virtues such as moderation (neither too much nor too little), neatness and orderliness took on an entirely new meaning here. Tastiness, atmosphere and snug conviviality were also emphasised, but not always to the same extent . The teaching of domestic science also made its way into the countryside and thus attained national significance. According to Alan Davidson, the culinary historian who was awarded the Erasmus Prize in 2003, that significance was not terribly positive when measured by the criterion of taste, however. Davidson lays the blame for the underdeveloped Dutch culinary merits directly on the typical Dutch tradition of cookery teachers: '*The conservatism of the Dutch in their kitchens was instilled in the female population by means of the popular cooking schools, which were prominent in the first half of the twentieth century (...) The teachers developed a scientific approach in their courses, in which nutritional values were dominant and questions of palatability and pleasure were considered to be of secondary importance (...).*'[4]

Be that as it may, the teachers of domestic science produced a torrent of frequently reprinted basic cookery books and thus continued to be highly influential in the Dutch kitchen until at least 1960.[5] In this way they made an important contribution to the modernisation and uniform composition of the Dutch meal. By as early as 1850 these changes had begun to occur in well-to-do middle-class circles, and over a century later they had penetrated to every level of so-

ciety.[6] Dutch families in every geographic region and all social strata ate three meals a day. Breakfast and lunch consisted simply of sandwiches with cheese, meat or a sweet spread (the popular *hagelslag*, or chocolate sprinkles, jam and peanut butter) washed down with coffee, tea or milk. The hot meal at that time normally consisted of potatoes, vegetables and meat, sometimes preceded by soup and (more often) followed by a sweet dessert of porridge or pudding. As in 1883, it was still not customary to serve any drink with the hot meal. But things can change, as the next section will show .

Eating out ... of the wall

The breakthrough
of the refrigerator
in the 1960s.

Up until 1960 eating out was not a common custom in the Netherlands. There were eating establishments for business dinners and hotels for foreign and domestic guests. Well-to-do families would also often eat in a restaurant or have meals sent in, but the average family could not afford such luxury. Eating at home and home-cooked meals was the rule. In 1960, most Dutch people (85%) said they seldom or never ate in a restaurant, but two decades later that figure had dropped to only a quarter. A 'culinary breakthrough' was what food writer Wina Born called this and other remarkable changes in the Dutch eating culture since the sixties.[7] How could this happen? The national history of 'eating out' gives us part of the answer.

Going to restaurants for pleasure is one aspect of this many-sided phenomenon. Taken literally, eating out even includes the sandwich you make at home to eat in your lunch break, a Dutch custom that continued well into the eighties. It also includes street food: sweet and hearty snacks such as ice cream, herring, rissoles, *frikadels* (a kind of spicy frankfurter) and chips. Patisseries and butchers broke into this market early on and were the first to sell homemade sandwiches and true Dutch beef rissoles. Rissoles themselves were not unknown as lunch fare in bourgeois circles, but the time and place in which they were consumed were both new. After 1920 the downtown areas in the big cities

Eating out of the wall
in the 1950s.

and improved public transport by rail and tram opened up new opportunities for small entrepreneurs in the dynamic catering and restaurant sector. The successful sandwich shops were joined by milk parlours, lunch rooms and later – after the crash of 1929 – by the more soberly furnished cafeterias. Some had nothing but standing room at high tables. These eating establishments in the city downtown areas developed alongside the established coffee houses. Here customers could buy and eat warm and cold snacks or order milk, soup, chocolate or coffee to accompany the sandwiches they brought with them. In short, the interbellum period produced a great variety of places where hurried travellers, office clerks and café, cinema or theatre-goers could eat quick, cheap and informal lunches or snacks.

In the thirties, a new arrival on the eating scene was the automat: little cubby-

holes in the wall with locked doors that were filled with salads, croquettes and meatballs by the staff on the cafeteria side and opened at the front by hungry visitors after inserting a coin. Between 1945 and 1960, eating out of the wall became increasingly popular, especially among young people when the consumption of chips made its way from the southern part of the country and became fashionable north of the great rivers as well. These and other hearty snacks were available at snack bars equipped with automats that were hugely popular until the end of the seventies. These were meeting places for young people, who hung out there and were known as 'nozems'. Rissoles, *frikadels* and other street food functioned as outside supplements to the three meals served at home. They were informal, cheap and filling, but they were not a gastronomic breakthrough.

The true Dutch rissoles sandwich

...and the equally true Dutch meatball

The Dutch go Chinese: globalisation and international cuisine

For many years the popularity of the typical Dutch automats and snack bars formed a barrier to the advance of fast food restaurants from the United States. Hamburgers and tempting snacks did not become really successful until after 1980, despite the speedy service and low price. Globalisation from the West was a long time coming. Oriental cuisine, on the other hand, had already been available for decades in simple, informal and cheap restaurants and had be-

come very popular. Chinese, Indonesian and Chinese-Indonesian dishes such as nasi, bami, shrimp foo yung omelette, babi pangang and *rijsttafel* became increasingly familiar, partly as a result of the post-war decolonisation of the former Dutch East Indies and the spirit of enterprise among Chinese immigrants. Foreigners came to eat *rijsttafel* and even came to regard this attractive dish, with its numerous spicy side-dishes, as typically Dutch. The restaurants offered large portions for little money, giving customers the choice of eating the food there or letting them take it home – precisely the features that the Dutch valued so highly in their snack bars. Nasi balls, egg rolls and saté were delicious, and they very soon appeared in the automat cubby-holes.

But there more was to come when the sixties arrived. A cultural revolution took place, in which established living habits and power relationships went out of the window. The Dutch had more money in their pockets. They bought cars and went on trips to France, Spain, Italy, Greece and Yugoslavia. Migrants came from the same Mediterranean countries to make up the shortages in the overstretched job market. The newcomers brought their own eating habits with them. Both developments resulted in the sudden appearance in ordinary supermarkets of foreign ingredients for experimental cookery and in the opening of a whole range of simple foreign restaurants. A great many Dutch people gradually began eating at such places. The period between 1960 and 1990 was one of vast changes in Dutch eating habits, both inside and outside the home. The food industry also took advantage of the demand for convenience, luxury and variety. International cuisine had conquered the Netherlands, but without the disappearance of pea soup and *stamppot* with kale (also now available in packets or tins). Changing trends were in, with something for everyone – and all available and accessible. The contrasts between social groups from days gone by had given way to small variations.

The development of a gastronomic sector

In the meantime there had been a sharp increase in interest in cooking and eating as an art form, and as the mark of a joyous and hospitable lifestyle. This manifested itself in many ways in the media. Cookery books, culinary magazines, recipes featured in daily newspapers and television chefs showed how healthy, low-calorie, fresh and more refined cooking and eating could be. Wine-drinking became widespread and commonplace. This custom had never been so popular before, something that supermarket giant Albert Heijn had a hand in with its special offers and in-house magazine *Allerhande*. A new culinary discourse emerged, which included the establishment of the Alliance Gastronomique Néerlandaise in 1967. The aim of this organisation was to promote an exclusive culinary culture in the Netherlands by putting the emphasis on taste and quality, offering cookery lessons, cookery contests and prizes and encouraging the professionalisation of chefs and other restaurant staff. From then on, more organisations and persons came to demand a place in the 'gastronomic sector', and there were more openings for exclusive restaurants. A consensus developed concerning quality criteria, evaluative bodies and the determination to overcome the Netherlands' poor position in the international world of top restaurants. Finally there came recognition in the form of the three Michelin stars with which this article began.

Not all social distinctions have faded. Wealthy diners in around the year 2000 can satisfy their appetites in Dutch restaurants, too, with a bit of refined cooking. The 'typically Dutch' quality of meals and manners has disappeared from the ambiance, however, as it has in almost every other facet of life. To find that, a present-day Ortigão would probably have to visit the Febo automat in Amsterdam's Kalverstraat. ■

NOTES

1. Ramalho Ortigão, *Holland 1883*. Utrecht: Spectrum, 1964, p. 37.

2. Partly based on: Anneke H. van Otterloo, *Eten en eetlust in Nederland 1840-1990. Een historisch-sociologische studie.* Amsterdam: Bert Bakker, 1990.

3. Harry W. Lintsen (ed.), *Techniek in Nederland. De wording van een moderne samenleving 1800-1890*, vol. I.: Zutphen: SHT/Walburgpers 1992; Johan W. Schot *et al.* (ed.), *Techniek in Nederland in de twintigste eeuw*, vol. III. Zutphen: SHT/ Walburgpers 2000.

4. Alan Davidson, *The Oxford Companion to Food.* Oxford: Oxford University Press, 1999, p. 264.

5. *Recepten van de Huishoudschool Laan van Meerdervoort (het Haagse Kookboek)* and *Het Kookboek van de Amsterdamse Huishoudschool (het Wannéekookboek)* were still being reprinted throughout the twentieth century. Martine Wittop Koning's *Eenvoudige berekende recepten* went through a considerable number of reprints between 1901 and 1951.

6. Jozien Jobse-van Putten, *Eenvoudig, maar voedzaam. Cultuurgeschiedenis van de dagelijkse maaltijd in Nederland.* Nijmegen: Sun, 1995.

7. Wina Born, *Culinaire herinneringen*. Utrecht: Het Spectrum, 1999, p. 62.

Translated by Nancy Forest-Flier

Patty Scholten (1946-)

Translated by John Irons

DUTCH SINGLE-PRICE COMPANY AMSTERDAM

As truly Dutch as pea soup with diced bacon.
One nation all, though school children are at
their texting, foursomes at the chat.
And down my neck pink Fristi some child's shaken.

The oldies here consume their daily ration
of mishmash, kale and sausage, on their plate
a paper serviette to keep things straight.
And porridge with brown sugar's quite in fashion.

The Kitchen is the restaurant's swish name,
with lots of tiles to imitate the same.
They've nine or so fruit teas in fine array.

Marie and Fientje changed to Marthe, Fini
and a long roll is now called a panini.
It's time we tackled the saucisse fumée.

HOLLANDSE EENHEIDSPRIJZEN MAATSCHAPPIJ AMSTERDAM

Zo Hollands als de erwtensoep met spek.
Het volk is één, al zitten er scholieren
te SMS'en, kletsen met z'n vieren.
Een kind sproeit roze Fristi in mijn nek.

Bejaarden hebben hier hun vaste stek
voor stamppot, boerenkool met worst, papieren
servetje in hun boord tegen het klieren.
Ook havermout met basterd is in trek.

Het restaurant heet nu joyeus De Keuken,
met tegels om de keuken op te leuken.
Er zijn wel negen soorten vruchtenthee.

Marie en Fientje werden Marthe, Fini
en een kadetje noemt men een panini.
Straks moeten we aan de saucisse fumée.

From *Unequalled Sleeping* (Slapen zonder weerga). Amsterdam: Atlas, 2002.

Manuel Kneepkens (1942-)

Garden of Appetites

On cool summer evenings when the family noisily consumed
green herring, followed by choice asparagus in butter sauce
a steak, salad, french fries, topped off with
strawberries and cream, mocha and vanilla

they then bobbed, the aunts, like peonies, like gas-brimful
balloons on their sticks, on the swell of their eruptive laughter
in every tender breast Wagner audibly cooed

they then drank glass after glass of wine
until each head resembled Pope Pius XII in the Holy Year
so pale!

finally uncle after uncle, drunk as a lord, said goodbye
and the creamy derriere of every aunt swayed away
leaving only the night, that ancient lady
that peacock-blue fan for the lonely smile
of the universe
god of the butterflies, then you slept!
the windows open, a prey to precious dreams

Tuin van Eetlust

Op koele zomeravonden als de familie smakkend tot zich nam
groene haring, gevolgd door slierasperges in botersaus
biefstuk, salade, pommes frites, en toe
aardbeien, slagroom, mocca en vanille

dan deinden zij, de tantes, als pioenrozen, als zwaargassige
ballonnen op hun steel, op de golfslag van hun lacherigheid
in alle malse borsten koerde hoorbaar Wagner

zo dronken ze wijn na wijn
tot elk hoofd paus pius twaalf leek in het Heilig Jaar
zo bleek!

tenslotte nam dan oom na oom, stomdronken, afscheid
en van elke tante wiegde het romig achterwerk weg
alleen de nacht bleef over, die hele oude dame
die pauwblauwe waaier voor de eenzame glimlach
van het heelal
god van de vlinders, dan sliep je!
de ramen open, kostbare dromen ten prooi

Translated by John Irons

From *Garden of Appetites* (Tuin van eetlust). Amsterdam: De Bezige Bij, 1976.

The Added Flavour of Art

[DAVID STROBAND]

When I was asked to write an article about 'art and food', I was a little confused at first. What was I supposed to take into consideration? The art of eating? In these days of the continuing onwards march of fast food, many people have forgotten, or have never even learnt, how to handle their cutlery skilfully and they're incapable of transporting a morsel of food to their mouths in an elegant manner.

On the other hand, images also loomed up of self-service restaurants in department stores, where all sorts of delicacies are displayed in dishes and bowls in very aesthetically pleasing combinations, in a way that almost borders on the art of painting. *Food should be pleasing to the eye as well as to the stomach,* a large number of caterers seem to have thought over the past fifteen years. And indeed the visual stimulus seems to be almost as important as the taste buds. It just makes me think of all the food colourings there are on the market, which are even used to lend a bright blue or purple glow to whole dishes at many a dinner party. The result is that colour and smell enter into a relationship where they are at odds with each other, supposedly offering a new adventure for the consumer. Is this an experience that might perhaps also come within the scope of the visual arts?

Sensuality and technical ingenuity

When you look at the role that food and related articles such as cooking utensils (pots, pans and cauldrons) and cutlery have always played in the visual arts, then you see that there have been a great many applications. In the sixteenth century there were already painters in the Low Countries who would, for example, take a festive meal or food itself as the subject matter for their paintings. For instance, Pieter Bruegel the Elder shows us a festive gathering of rustic types in his *Peasant Wedding* (c.1565). The people are sitting at a long table and in between them you can just about make out dishes with food and bread. Two stout cooks are carrying a door that has been lifted off its hinges and which has innumerable plates of food on it. In the bottom left-hand corner of the painting is a collection of jugs that a man is filling with drink. Bruegel the Elder did

easel paintings for the market, which often had a crude or rustic theme. Eating, drinking and related pleasures were, of course, very popular subjects within this genre. Bruegel was praised for his true-to-life painting. The tradition of this 'genre painting' was continued in the seventeenth century by artists such as Adriaan van Ostade and Jan Steen.

In 1551 Pieter Aertsen painted *The Butcher's Stall*. We see a stall displaying carcasses, severed cow and pig heads, slices of meat, fish and a great many sausages. This large-format painting (123 x 150 cm) offers us a very sensual experience in a 'basic' state. This is no would-be aesthetic presentation of food-stuffs but a functional accumulation, a mountain of meat and fish that almost hurts the eyes. Pieter Aertsen also did a great deal of work for the private market, so this example of a 'display of everyday pleasures' would not have looked out of place in a respectable aristocratic home.

Food also featured now and then in paintings of biblical scenes. In another painting by Pieter Aertsen (*Christ in the House of Mary and Martha*), an image of Jesus in the company of Mary and Martha is visible in the background. The viewer's eye is guided to this scene through the kitchen of the house. In this room, some people are hovering around a table full of delicacies (bundles of vegetables, lots of fruit and a piglet). The food is displayed in a very neat and

Pieter Bruegel the Elder, *Peasant Wedding*. c.1565. Panel, 114 x 164 cm. Kunsthistorisches Museum, Vienna.

tidy fashion. Art historians sometimes interpret this biblical scene as having a moralising purpose. An exemplary scene from the Bible is combined with an everyday, worldly situation. Interpreters say that the message could be that the attention devoted in this painting to culinary delicacies, in connection with the pious historical tableau in the background, is intended to inspire the viewer to absolute virtue. In this context, food is interpreted as earthly and alluring, and

Pieter Claesz,
Still Life with Fish. 1647.
Panel, 64 x 82 cm.
Rijksmuseum, Amsterdam.

therefore as tempting the viewer to carry out sinful and impure acts. The immediate presence of the 'holy' in the background appears to weaken the force of the temptation.

The seventeenth century was a time when Dutch art for the private market flourished, and the genre of the still life was a very popular element of this. A *Still Life with Fish* by Pieter Claesz (1647), another still life by Willem Claesz Heda (ca. 1636) and a 'pronk-stilleven' (still life of ostentation) by Abraham van Beyeren (1654) all show brilliant painted arrangements of tarts, peeled fruit, pieces of fish, shellfish, jugs, dishes and glasses. Against the background of a light, monochrome wall, the various elements are arranged on a table in a most meticulous way. The lighting gives the whole scene a certain theatricality. The depictions have a strongly sensual feeling. In the late 1980s art historians engaged in a war of words about the interpretation of this sort of work. A generally accepted point of view was that worldly pleasures, including food, could lead people astray. Seen in this light, the peeled fruit stands for the transience of life: '*Memento Mori*' or '*All is vanity*'.

'*Too much of aught is good for naught* 'and '*Enjoy in moderation*' would have been popular expressions in this environment, influenced as it was by Calvinist thinking. Other art historians, however, deny the existence of these supposed moralistic messages in art. In their view, the artist is concerned only with demonstrating his virtuosity. The still lifes, in terms of form, colour combination, composition and tactile appearance, had to capture a world of artistic beauty. According to this way of thinking, a painted peeled fruit is nothing more or less than an example of pictorial ingenuity and skill.

A new reality

In short: the presence of food and kitchen utensils in the works of the old masters will always find very diverse interpretations. The remains of a sumptuous meal, half-filled glasses, a goblet that has fallen over, pieces of bread, oyster shells, crumpled napkins and a lemon that has been cut into could be an exhortation to moderation. Although it must be said that the semantic power of all this is a little less strong than that of the books, skulls, hour-glasses and burnt-down candles in the Vanitas paintings, which are supposed to make us aware of our mortality. And so people sometimes also think that the artists, by arranging and presenting costly fare, silver jugs and crystal glasses superbly lighted, just want to demonstrate their technique in the best possible way.

So, what's the situation in modern art? In the twentieth century, and particularly in its second half, the use of food in the visual arts can no longer be interpreted according to a handful of models. In the late nineteenth and early twentieth century, food was indeed still being painted, but it was now material to be used in the development of a new artistic language. I'm thinking here of Paul Cézanne's still lifes, where, for example, apples and peaches form artistic elements within a quest for a new depiction of 'reality'.

In the second half of the twentieth century, the depiction of reality was exchanged in a number of cases for the direct display of reality, and food and drink can also play a large role in this. So, food and utensils are sometimes assigned a surprising symbolic role, but eating as a physical activity and eating as a social ritual also receive attention from the visual arts. And the sequel to the eating and drinking, the inevitable excretion, has also been allocated a generous place within more contemporary art.

Everything is egg...or mussel

The Italian artist Piero Manzoni is one of those artists who have broadened the concept of the visual arts. In the late 1950s and early 1960s, he utilised everything he worked with to confirm his status as a visual artist. In a playful fashion, he wanted to make an absolute truth out of the aura of genius that artists have been credited with since the early fifteenth century (together with the ideal of the *Uomo universale*). One of his materials was the egg. Manzoni would sit in a studio at a table full of hard-boiled eggs. The visitor would receive an egg from him that had on it the artist's fingerprint in ink. That meant that the egg had been signed by Manzoni, so it increased considerably in value. Of course, there's a game being played here with the symbolism of the egg as the source of all life. In this way, Manzoni gives his artistic skill an almost all-embracing and timeless character, an intangible and universal aura. The visitor could eat the egg and so, in a way, become a parasite on the brilliant consciousness of the artist Piero Manzoni. Incidentally, another of his works had the same intention. Manzoni had his own excreta canned and then put these cans on the art market. A photo shows the artist standing with an open can next to the toilet bowl. His cans were adorned with a label with the words *Merda d'Artista*. They already cost a pretty penny at the time, and now they fetch astronomical prices on the art market.

Another artist who worked with eggs, but who gave them a somewhat different philosophical and poetic significance, was the Belgian Marcel Broodthaers. He did not so much use the whole egg, but the shell. These shells were specially kept for him by the chef at *La Boue*, a restaurant in Brussels, who could break eggs more beautifully than anyone else. Broodthaers installed thousands of egg shells in rhythmic designs on various materials: arranged on the seat of a lilac-painted chair, piled up in a doctor's bag or placed in a wooden cart. Broodthaers says of this: '*Everything is egg. The world is egg. The world originated*

Marcel Broodthaers,
*Grand panneau au
moules*. 1965.
Mussels on panel,
173 x 120 cm.
Communauté Française
de Belgique, Brussels.
© SABAM Belgium 2005.

in that large yolk, the sun. Our mother, the moon, is made of slivers. The moon is nothing but mashed-up slivers of egg. The stars are egg. Everything is dead and lost eggs. Empty. Empty eggs.'[1]

For Marcel Broodthaers in the 1960s, eggshells were carriers of meaning-full emptiness, as were mussel shells. They are husks and therefore contain emptiness, the void. The void into which everyone can place his own truth, his own meaning. No single truth is unequivocal, it is ambiguous by definition. During his exhibitions, Broodthaers also presented black pans with a mountain of mussels as their contents. The lid danced on the mussels, which were rising up out of the pan. *'Moule'* has a double meaning here: 'mussel', but also the 'mould' in which something is cast. And there are also sexual connotations to consider. Broodthaers: *'Mussels, eggs, objects with no contents but air, and without charm. Their shells alone of necessity emphasise emptiness. It's the base you have to look at. Actually, my work presents you with reality.'*

And, finally, a poem by Broodthaers: *'The mussel: this crafty devil eluded the mould of society. It used its own self to cast itself. Others of its kind share with it the anti-sea. It is perfect.'* Within this framework, for Broodthaers, eggs and mussels were instruments for relativising the value of everything that smelt of institutions, such as 'the museum'. Their inherent ambiguity lent itself admirably to this purpose.

The exploration of borders

In the 1960s, food increasingly became a consumer commodity. Affluence was increasing, new food was coming onto the market (fast food) and the rich supply of different foods and stimulants was increasingly communicated blanket-fashion via new media such as television.

The American artist Robert Rauschenberg placed three empty Coca-Cola bottles in a box-like construction that was adorned on both sides with angel's wings. In this way, the work *Coca-Cola Plan* (1958) functions as a sort of altar for consumer goods. And this presentation transforms the Coca-Cola bottle into a fetish. This idea was elaborated upon by many American artists in the 1960s. Jasper Johns made two bronze cans on which he painted a label for a brand of beer (*Painted Bronze*, 1960). He then placed the cans on a minimal plinth. In the 1960s, Andy Warhol worked with the depiction of a can of Campbell's soup. Claes Oldenburg made enormous sculptural blow-ups of hamburgers, lollies and sandwiches (including *Bacon, Lettuce and Tomato*, 1963) from, among other things, linen filled with kapok and wood. These objects were then painted in bright colours. These artists celebrated new, typically American food, but at the same time also gave it a slightly critical and anti-consumerist commentary.

Whilst the consumption of food was taken to a higher level in the American art scene, it was the phase following the consumption that was ritualised in a particular way in the Vienna of the time. The Wiener Aktionisten, a group of artists who took the human body and the borders of its functions as the starting point for their work, were active there in the 1960s. Many of the works they created had something of religious ritual about them. It was all about demolishing borders within body and spirit. So, for example, there was Gunter Brus, who urinated in a bottle and then drank it or who literally rolled around in his own excrement so that he could feel completely at one with his own body. The work of these artists created a lot of freedom for artists in the 1970s and 1980s to choose the physical and spiritual exploration of their borders (and eating and drinking naturally played a role in this) as the basis for their work.

Films often provide an important visual source of inspiration for artists. I would like to cite two films from the 1970s that, in a very stimulating way, demonstrate how food and the rituals around eating can play a major role within a story.

Firstly, there is *La grande Bouffe* (1973) by the Italian Marco Ferreri. In this film we see a group of people who, in marathon style, so overindulge themselves with food that some of them literally collapse . Four middle-aged friends meet up at a lonely villa in order to literally gorge themselves to death on exquisite dishes. But first the director Marco Ferreri shows the viewer in all sorts of rather unsavoury ways that the meal isn't going down well. The consumption of food forms the main action in this spectacular film, and the ultimate pig-outs and orgies of the bourgeoisie in a French villa may be seen as an expression of Ferreri's subversive, apocalyptic vision of society and capitalism.

Eating as a social ritual is central to *Le charme discret de la bourgeoisie* (1972) by Luis Buñuel. This film is about six people's endless and arbitrarily interrupted series of attempts to have a meal together. But all sorts of unforeseen circumstances conspire to get in the way of the meal. There's a dead body in the restaurant and the host and his wife escape via the drainpipe and dive into the bushes. Then a wall hanging opens up and the diners suddenly turn out to be sitting on a stage in front of a hissing audience, where it emerges that they don't know their parts in the play. The meal is further disturbed by a mob of cavalrymen, by a raid by the police, who arrest all the guests, and even by terrorists who shoot them down.

Good art should stink

In the 1990s, the visual arts were injected with a healthy dose of everyday context and the viewer often played an active part in completing the work. Many ideas were drawn into the domain of the visual arts, simply by being shown in a visual arts context or because they were conceived by professional artists. Once again, as in the 1960s and 1970s, the visual arts concept was given much more elbow room and so received a shot of new energy.

The theme of 'eating' in the visual arts of the 1990s had a wide range of applications. In her short video films the British artist Maria Pask, who lives in Amsterdam, seems to draw her inspiration from the Body Art of the late 1960s and 1970s. Here too the exploration of the borders of body and spirit are central. For example, there is a short film in which Pask eats cake, spits it out and then eats it again. She does the same with spaghetti in another short film. The slow spooning out of a pot of spicy sambal is the theme of a third work. The viewer directly witnesses the physical (and probably also mental) suffering that accompanies the act of consuming food. Pask's reward is a dreadful stomachache. In these short films, she seems to be referring to the eating disorders that are inextricably linked with our consumer society.

The Antwerp theatre director and visual artist Jan Fabre has demonstrated that the nature of food also has its dark side. During the visual arts event *Over The Edges* (2000), which was held in Ghent, he plastered the pillars of the uni-

versity auditorium with slices of Ganda ham. Back in 1978, Fabre made a sculpture in which meat was one of the materials. The sculpture shows a man sitting at a table and studying something through a microscope. Both his legs and those of the table are covered with large pieces of meat, packed in clingfilm. Fabre wanted to do something similar on a large scale with the auditorium. The building's columns reminded him of limbs, real giant legs. Fabre said, '*By wrapping them up in this way, I wanted to create the illusion that they had been stripped of their skin. In the same way as the university, with its academic research, has uncovered so much over the years.*' And: '*I didn't care what sort of meat it was, as long as it was red meat, with a nice white edge. I wanted to create a sort of marbled effect, you see. That's why I stuck the slices on top of each other and then wrapped them up tightly in transparent film: I wanted a beautifully mottled and even surface. The meat will also keep longer because little or no air can get at it. Although, as far as I'm concerned, it can rot a little. Only when you see and smell that there's life in the pillars is it really complete. Good art should stink. The ham is only replaced if it really does get too mucky.*'[2]

The artist Eveline Mooibroek, who lived in Groningen until her recent move to Berlin, has also used meat as the basic material for a work of art. As her graduation presentation piece in Groningen (Academie Minerva, 1995) she arranged seven 'meat teddies', teddy bears made from pork, on a concrete floor in a separate room. The 'animals' looked soft and cute, but after a few days

Eveline Mooibroek,
Meat Teddies. 1995.
Mixed media.
Photo courtesy of the artist
(www.emooibroek.nl).
© SABAM Belgium 2005.

they began to go a rather unsavoury colour. This, however, was not the most challenging element of the work: after three days the whole exhibition space was filled with an almost unbearable stench of putrefaction and the room itself could only be entered with a hand pressed tightly over one's nose and mouth. Mooibroek had, of course, anticipated this, but after an emergency discussion the work had to be cleaned up immediately. Beauty and almost barbaric transience go hand in hand here.

Smells are fundamental to culinary enjoyment: there's no taste without smell. The Belgian artist Peter de Cupere has used this fact in a gently poetic way. Smell is an essential component of De Cupere's work. For example, he designed a number of clowns' noses for a children's hospital in Brussels, which would give off a gentle smell of strawberries when the children put them on their noses. In addition to this, he has produced such things as a perfume-based

Peter de Cupere's model
(in chocolate, started in 1998)
for his *Shit Toilet*, to be made
out of human faeces.
Photo courtesy of the artist
(www.peterdecupere.com).

on chicken droppings, a scented mask with dried red wine and a design for a toilet made of chocolate and shit.

The nose also has a hard time of it with *Cloaca* by the Flemish Wim Delvoye. The *Cloaca* (2000) is a machine that perfectly imitates the human digestive mechanism. The twelve-metre-long device has been set up at various sites including the MUHKA in Antwerp. It consists of six transparent laboratory flasks that sim-

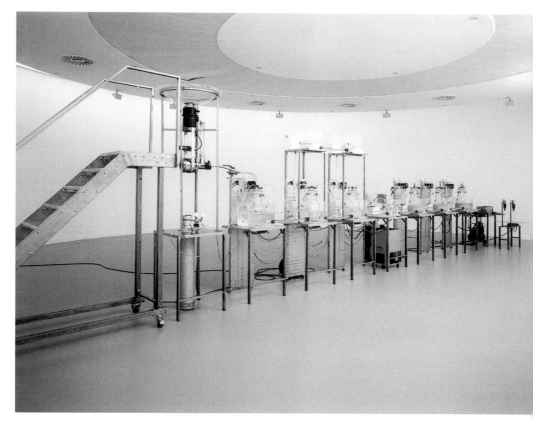

ulate the function of the stomach, the pancreas and the intestines, and which are linked by a complex network of tubes and computers. The half-digested remains of the exclusive meals that are created for the work of art by one of the best caterers in Belgium bubble away in the reactors. The equipment looks very futuristic, is fed three times a day and squeezes out a very realistic turd once a day (which, for the benefit of the art lover, is sealed in airtight packaging, signed and sold). Delvoye, in collaboration with engineers and scientists, worked for two years on the machine. In 2000, the prototype was found to still have quite a number of teething problems. Or as Delvoye described it: 'The methane gas that is released, or the farts, smell so bad that we have to remove them via the ceiling. Cloaca also proved to be incapable of coping with some foods. Last week it had constipation because it had eaten too much mashed potato. And it turned out to handle alcohol badly.'[3]

Wim Delvoye, *Cloaca*. Installation in MUHKA, Antwerp, 2000. This machine imitates the human digestive mechanism.

The Dutch Atelier van Lieshout designed a toilet that immediately turns excreta into compost. This, along with the equipment for a complete abattoir and distillery, formed one of the components of the self-sufficient state AVL-Ville.

This autonomous free state in the Rotterdam harbour area (with an abortion boat, a hospital, spaces for free sex, and a workshop for making weapons) operated for only a short period in 2001. The authorities closed it down because various of its activities were against the law. At the beginning of the 1990s, Joep van Lieshout (later Atelier Van Lieshout) mass-produced all manner of kitchen accessories and a lavatory pan in brightly coloured polyester. In this way, utensils (unlike Marcel Duchamp's ready-mades, these were actually usable) made their entrance into the world of the visual arts.

At the table

In the 1990s many artists were occupied with small-scale social processes. Artist and observer became more closely involved with each other, and so, at the beginning of the 1990s, it was possible for the cooking of a meal and its subsequent consumption to be seen as a work of art.

In 1992, the Thai artist Rirkrit Tiravanija introduced the concept of the 'eet-tentoonstelling' (eating exhibition). Tiravanija had grown up in the kitchen of his grandmother, who ran a restaurant in Bangkok. Among other things he set up a gallery in New York as a restaurant with an open kitchen. The visitors sat on folding chairs at camping tables and then ate hot curry and vermicelli soup. A Thai chef prepared all of this, whilst Tiravanija restricted himself to chopping and slicing the vegetables. He explained these cooking performances in terms of his Buddhist background, in which the emphasis lies not on the divine, but on a more everyday, practical attitude to life. You can bring about a better world through more individual interaction with your fellow human beings. In the Thai culture, cooking, serving, eating and talking are bound up with hospitality to family and friends. Tirvanija extended this to the art-loving public.

Accounts of the visual arts in the 1990s sometimes regard the event *Chambres d'Amis in Gent* (1986) as setting a standard for a number of new trends within the visual arts. Curator Jan Hoet asked artists to create work in a number of houses and apartments in Ghent. He was struck by the large number of tables that eventually featured in the different works. Hoet saw the table as an instrument for promoting a meaningful dialogue between artist and observer or between observers themselves. In numerous art initiatives in the 1990s, this model resulted in dinners with artistic aims. For example, in the early 1990s the Dutch Jeanne van Heeswijk invited artists to come to her house and talk about their work, particularly those whose work Van Heeswijk could not completely fathom. The table represented a forum where they could give an explanation of their work to an invited audience. Van Heeswijk prepared the dinner but stayed out of the conversation around the table because she was playing the part of butler. The meal and the discussion about art took over the role of the material art object, literally becoming the work of art. Here, the visual arts celebrate the social ritual of the meal.

The mother of all kitchens

Theatre director Sjoerd Wagenaar sees a clear connection between food and power. According to him, all the important negotiations in world politics are

accompanied by a good meal. The real negotiations don't take place in the conference room, but over the restaurant menu. *Klepperrek* brings to light the connections between food and power in a number of theatrical scenes between
two important politicians, who are not identified any more clearly than that. As
politicians, the two are opponents; as people, they share a great passion: the
art of cooking. Vital to the shape of the second performance of *Klepperrek* was
an installation of hundreds of pots and pans, together forming an imaginary
square kitchen that cooks for all mankind: the mother of all kitchens. At the
same time, the installation is a music and smells machine. The pots and pans
simmer away on gas rings. Together they make a set of chimes that clatters,
taps and shakes, producing a multitude of sounds. Alongside the pan composition, stirring, baking and bubbling noises and hissing gas rings can be heard,
and the audience can inhale the scents of popcorn, baked potatoes, peanut butter, oranges and sprouts.

In the summer of 2000, the *Chiko & Toko Cooking!* project took place at the
Stedelijk Museum Bureau Amsterdam. The Japanese Chicako Watanabe and
Tomoko Take, who live in Amsterdam, give shape to their artistic skills in collaboration with other artists, photographers, designers and musicians. They, in
turn, were asked to record songs for the music producers Arling & Cameron.
Chiko & Toko, the happy Japanese cartoon characters that Take designed for
this session, took on lives of their own during their subsequent projects. During
the summer months of 2000, Chiko & Toko organised a series of cookery workshops with Amsterdam children between the ages of eight and twelve. Together
with Chiko & Toko and with head chefs from Amsterdam restaurants, the children prepared a five-course menu in the series of workshops, which included
a fruit and vegetable salad in the shape of a sports car. At the end of the project
the tasty, unconventional menu was served to the public at *Our Restaurant*. The
group of children who, during the project, worked in the hexagonal mobile kitch-
en (with its musical doors) were put into chefs' outfits, and the walls of Bureau
Amsterdam were covered with menus, illustrations and photos showing the
culinary adventures of Chiko & Toko and the children. While they cooked, Arling

Sjoerd Wagenaar's *Klepperrek*.
Photos courtesy of the artist.

Chiko & Toko Cooking! project at the Stedelijk Museum Bureau, Amsterdam. Photos by Tomoko Take & Chicako Watanabe. Courtesy of Martijn van Nieuwenhuyzen.

& Cameron's 'Chiko & Toko Song' was played. In an accompanying text, Martijn van Nieuwenhuyzen writes: *'Putting a sophisticated dish on the table requires the same "intuition, imagination, enthusiasm and great organisational skills" as the making of art and architecture. The children who take part in Chiko & Toko Cooking! will certainly come to understand something of artistic and gastronomic inspiration this summer. Whether this will make them better people or artists in the future, though, remains to be seen. At least they will have learned to cook.'*[4]

Portrait of Elvis as an ice-lolly

Food and art. Eating is a daily necessity; it literally keeps you alive. Art has everything to do with reflection, with pondering things. And therefore also, indirectly, with the idea of death.

At the beginning of this account, I wrote about particular interpretations of seventeenth-century still-life paintings. They were supposed to have a moralising message and remind those who contemplate the work of art that they are

Job Koelewijn's lollies in Galerie Fons Welters, Amsterdam, 2003 (www.fonswelters.nl).

mortal and must live in moderation. In the contemporary visual arts, there are indeed also works dealing with the 'All is worldly vanity' theme, often in a playful manner. The Dutch artist Job Koelewijn, as part of his *One Taste* installation (2000), had visitors eat ice-lollies that were coloured and flavoured with mint. These goodies, which lay waiting in a large freezer, were modelled on historical greats, such as the Buddha, Karl Marx, Elvis Presley and Marilyn Monroe. These historical figures with all their inspiration were quickly washed away via the stomach. And so sophistication dissolves in the blink of an eye, but is still carried around in the body for a while.

The Groningen-based artist Dineke Oosting once created a town based on archetypical modern architecture in a German host atelier (Bad Ems). *Bad Suss* (2001) was situated on a sturdy rectangular table. The work consisted entirely of

Dineke Oosting,
Bad Suss. 2001.
Installation,
28 x 240 x 60 cm.

sweet things. All sorts of buildings were constructed out of biscuits, cake, chocolates, marzipan and sweets. One attack of the human appetite could wreck *Bad Suss*. The sweet town would, in its entirety, perish in an organic fashion and the idyll of its existence would therefore be short. The same applied to *Ein Berg zum Essen*. This work was shaped like a mountain and consisted solely of chocolate, cake and icing sugar. It was made especially for a meeting of regional dignitaries. After an hour the mountain had been completely levelled. The beautiful reality of Oosting's miniature worlds proved to be very transitory.

The American artist Stephen Shanabrook, who trained at the Rijksacademie in Amsterdam, has designed chocolates in many forms. His series *Morgue Chocolates* (1993/1994) comprises three sections: *Unidentified*, *Evisceration of Waited Moments* and *Halcyon Nest*. The works *Unidentified* and *Evisceration of Waited Moments* are chocolate boxes containing parts of the human body made from chocolate, each one wrapped in colourful, shiny foil. They are body parts cast in chocolate, originating in the mortuary, displaying wounds and scars that have been cut open by a pathologist and sewn up again with large stitches. The *Halcyon Nest* boxes contain thirty-two identical eyes. Half of them are wrapped in purple foil. In one box the eyelids are closed; in the other they're wide open.

A set of Stephen Shanabrook's
Morgue Chocolates.
Photo courtesy of the artist
and deSchoneKunsten,
Haarlem.

Translated by Laura Watkinson

The eyes also come from dead people laid out in mortuaries in Russia and America. Shanabrook was given access to them and cast all his 'materials' in chocolate. For years he worked in a chocolate factory and so he knows the manufacturing process inside out. Shanabrook: *'Chocolate is more than food, it is totally unnecessary food; unnecessary, but desirable. It transforms something terrifying into something peaceful and desirable. The eyes and the mind say no; the nose and the mouth say yes.'*

In conclusion: my answer to the question that I put forward at the beginning of this article, whether beautifully designed meals are also art, has to be a resounding 'No'. In my opinion, Shanabrook has made it clear that food can only belong to the world of the visual arts if a moment of reflection precedes the bite or the gulp. Why is that food there? What am I eating? Why am I eating? These are the essential questions that can be raised precisely through the experience of an artistic context. Shanabrook's *Morgue Chocolates* make it apparent that contemplation of the important things in life (or in this case: death) can be very meaningful: it is that added flavour of reflection that makes art into art. ■

NOTES

1. Anna Hakkens (ed.), *Marcel Broodthaers aan het woord*. Ghent-Amsterdam: Ludion, 1998, p. 35 & p. 49.
2. Koen Sonck, 'Redelijkheid gestroopt'. In: *Gent Universiteit*, 14, no. 7, April-May 2000.
3. Sandra Smallenburg, '"Ik verkoop stront omdat de vraag er is". Kunstenaar Wim Delvoye over zijn "spijsverteringsmachine" Cloaca'. In: *NRC Handelsblad*, 3 October 2000.
4. Martijn Van Nieuwenhuyzen, 'Chico & Toko cooking'. In: *SMBA (StedelijkMuseumBureau-Amsterdam)*, no. 54.

FURTHER READING

Anja Krabben, 'Morgue Chocolates'. In: *Doodgewoon* anthology (Doodscultuur en uitvaartmanieren). Zutphen: Walburg Pers, 2001.
Rutger Pontzen, *'Nice!' Over nieuw engagement in de hedendaagse kunst*. Rotterdam: NAi Publishers, 2000.

Charles Ducal (1952-)

Refectory

Coercion feeds the soul. In the lowness
of cold cellars the food has been
laid out. On gleaming dishes
the cold meat shivers. Take and eat.

A bony hand blesses the gifts.
Thick as a slug the blood slides
down the throat. The child, skinny,
licks his lips, prepared to foot the bill.

For his taste is never attended to.
Aversion lies like gruel in his gut,
untranslated, material for the soul.
Thus it is one learns the hunger

for poetry.

Refectorium

Dwang voedt de ziel. In de laagte
van koude kelders staat de spijs
opgediend. Op blinkende schalen
huivert het vlees. Neemt en eet.

Een knookhand zegent de gaven.
Dik als een slak glijdt het bloed
door de keel. Het kind slikt,
mager, bereid het gelag te betalen.

Want zijn smaak wordt nooit bediend.
Tegenzin ligt als een pap op de maag,
onvertaald, materiaal voor de ziel.
Op deze wijze leert men de honger

naar poëzie.

Translated by John Irons

From *To the Earth* (Naar de aarde). Amsterdam: Atlas, 1998.

Ida Gerhardt (1905-1997)

Translated by Rina Vergano

The Prayer

Three times a day, according to the iron rule,
they each take their own place,
and sit down around the table;
unified by hate: the family.

The father has whetted the knife,
the children wait, white and still,
The mother grips her plate
as if to pulverise it with her will.

A growl: and then they fold their hands,
those at table in the house
from table's edge to table's edge
together form an unseen cross.

Het gebed

Drie maal per dag, naar vaste wetten,
nemen zij de eigen plaatsen in,
en gaan zich rond de tafel zetten;
van haat eendrachtig: het gezin.

De vader heeft het mes geslepen,
de kinderen wachten, wit en stil.
De moeder houdt haar bord omgrepen
alsof zij het vergruizelen wil.

Een grauw: dan vouwen zij de handen,
de disgenoten in het huis:
van tafelrand tot tafelranden
geschikt tot een onzichtbaar kruis.

From *Collected Poems* (Verzamelde gedichten). Amsterdam: Athenaeum/Polak & Van Gennep, 1995.

Crossing Chickens with Art

Koen Vanmechelen's Cosmopolitan Chicken Project

'I feel like a lost egg on a quest for the 38° that will enable me to hatch out.'
(Koen Vanmechelen)

Three words are sufficient to introduce the artist Koen Vanmechelen: the chicken, the cage and the egg. You might call them the obsessive foundations of his life and work. Since his childhood Vanmechelen has been obsessed by everything that has wings and lays eggs: poultry scratched around at the back of the home where he grew up – so we have the chicken; to house them the young Koen sawed planks of wood and built henhouses – the cage; in his room he had an incubator to raise his own birds – the egg.

Vanmechelen's professional life started in a kitchen. He caused aromatic vapours to waft from the stoves of renowned restaurants, but what he liked best was to work with baking ingredients – he considers it an art to create something that stands upright out of formless materials. And when he closed the kitchen door behind him, he went to his own studio to give shape to all the things that arose in his artist's mind while cooking – and at any other time. These were initially large wooden structures in which he laid such things as big white eggs (as in an installation at the Museum of Contemporary Art in Antwerp in the late nineties), and also sculptures which from a distance looked more like prehistoric bipeds than anything else. But there was more going on here than an artist creating sculptures. The 'philosopher' Jan Kenis, who met a premature death, pointed out to Vanmechelen that his bipeds – sculptures made of wooden slats (skeletons in other words) – were in fact cages. Vanmechelen understood that in this way he was setting something free by simply letting it be what it was.

As his work evolved it gradually led him to a series of new materials – after the initial wood, wire, clay, steel reinforcing bars and glass all made their appearance in his constructions. These sculptures were compared to *'primitive prototypes for the well-known moving chickens/birds by Panamarenko, (...) monsters inspired by constructivism, the virtuosity of whose creation gives way to the depiction of bitter despair'* (Luk Lambrecht, *De Morgen*). Sentiment and aesthetics have no place here. *'Art'*, says Vanmechelen, *'is what is hard outside and soft inside.'* Even so, *'bitter despair'* is the last thing he himself is attempting to express in his work.

In his artistic quest for the right cage for the right chicken – which is what it is really all about – Vanmechelen finds it more and more difficult to avoid the call of philosophy and science and becomes aware that the place they claim in his art increasingly determines its direction. Big glass eggs, blown on Murano, are given metal legs – no eyes – and, answering to the name 'Walking Eggs', begin to lead what at first sight looks like a life of their own. They give rise to a new understanding: the world is shaped like an egg; the egg is the potential of and a metaphor for life; it refers to fertility, but at the same time it is the most beautiful of cages. What will come out of each egg is always an open question.

The literary world was also pleased to make Koen Vanmechelen's acquaintance. In 1996, 1997 and 1998 he collaborated with the writer Gregie de Maeyer on three 'children's books' which, although they play around with the definition of the genre, were warmly received by the publishers Altiora Averbode. *Juul* tells the story of a child made of wood, who is horribly bullied but for whom there is ultimately a healing. *The Cage* is an epic account of this subject as the two

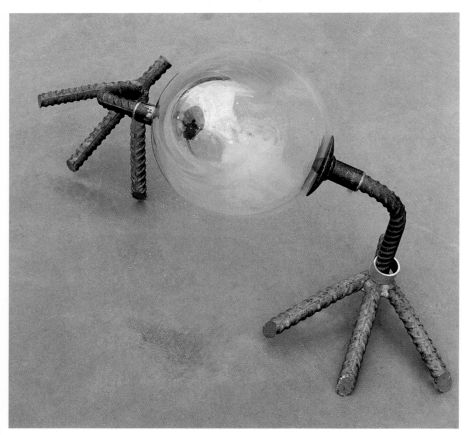

Koen Vanmechelen,
The Walking Egg.
Sculpture 1997,
installation 1998,
magazine 1999.
Photo by Rudi Vanbeek.

authors saw it, at a time when, together with the philosopher Richard Anthone, they were developing programmes in which to philosophise and hypothesise with children. Lastly, *Little Glass Man* is a delicate and complex story about an unfulfilled childhood wish, a covert illustration of the way the fertility issue and the related scientific research infiltrates Vanmechelen's work. In 1999, together with the gynaecologist Willem Ombelet, head of the Genk Fertility Centre, the artist founded the publication *The Walking Egg*, an English-language periodical in which ethicists, philosophers and scientists discuss all manner of issues relating to reproduction. Vanmechelen provides artistic comments.

There came a moment when the cook-cum-sculptor became a farmer and his art transcended the material from which it was made. Far removed from all his brooding on materials, Vanmechelen realised that the cage he was looking for was nothing other than the living chicken running around in his back garden. Like the wooden sculptures, the chicken carries its own cage inside it. The chicken is the cage. The chicken is the work of art that has to be continued.

Breeding project

And then things really took off. The starting point was the Mechelse Koekoek – *nomen est omen* – and the Poulet de Bresse, two varieties of chicken that have from time immemorial been subject to manipulation, breeding and refinement, but which in Vanmechelen's view have never reached their full potential: the Koekoek is too fat and the Bresse slightly too tough. Yet Flanders continues to swear by the former and France claims that nothing ever created has come as close to perfection as the latter. Trying, in the midst of all this, to distinguish between sense and nonsense, Vanmechelen could only observe that it was all very limiting and smacked of navel-gazing. After all, today's Fleming is not the same as yesterday's, is he? An evolution has taken place between the two moments in time. There has been a mixing of breeds and cultures, enriching the line. The artist-cook launched a new concept: the Mechelse Bresse. It was to be a breeding programme, a hybridisation, an artistic enterprise. He would create a new chicken, a chicken as a work of art. In the middle of the woods, Emile Craeghs and Marianne Dirkx, proprietors of the restaurant *La Feuille d'Or* – where Vanmechelen was then working in the kitchen – offered time and space for henhouses. They believed in the project. Brooding pens were installed and runs for the chickens were built in the cellars under the restaurant. Vanmechelen noted everything down. There were sketches, plans and doodles... There had to be scientific supervision too. Things started to get complicated. Biology, philosophy, statistics, copyright and patents all came into it. But it was decided from the beginning that the Mechelse Bresse, the cross between the Mechelse Koekoek and the Poulet de Bresse, was first and foremost an artistic project.

The objective was achieved. A new variety of chicken was produced. But the breeder has not stopped brooding. On what to do next with the Mechelse Bresse, for instance. The bird had hardly seen the light of day when its creator decided that this was not the end, but the beginning of something totally new: a 'Cosmopolitan Chicken Project'.

The call of the chicken

Koen Vanmechelen did some research and came up with a new starting point: the Red Jungle Fowl, otherwise known as the hen of hens. It is still found at the foot of the Himalaya, somewhere on the boundary between the woods and the village, in the vast border areas of India and Nepal. It originally lived only in the wild, where it led a quiet, monogamous existence. But about 7,500 years ago it left the safety of the forest to go out into the world. This brings us straight to one of the basic questions in the philosophy of Vanmechelen's project: did man

Koen Vanmechelen,
Mechelse Koekoek.
'In de ban van de ring', 1999.
Provinciaal Museum, Hasselt.

Koen Vanmechelen, *Mechelse Bresse*.
Storm Centres,
Watou, 2000.

Koen Vanmechelen,
Mechelse Giant.
Museum Dhondt-Dhaenens,
Deurle, 2002.

set out to catch the chicken, or did it come to him of its own accord? Either way, what had been a wild species was from that time on subject to domestication. Looking for means of providing for his own needs, man put the chicken through an endless series of mutations and hybrids with one main aim in mind: the production of meat and eggs. Lack of communication between continents and countries has resulted in different varieties occurring in various places, no

Koen Vanmechelen, *Genetic Genius*. Secret Gardens, Rekkem, 2001. Photo by Alex Deyaert.

two of which look the same. In the course of time the qualities of the country that raised them can be clearly seen in all these chickens: proof of a sense of nationhood. On top of that, domestication and forcing growth for consumption has changed their behaviour patterns: they have become polygamous.

The Red Jungle Fowl was a starting point, the Mechelse Koekoek and the Poulet de Bresse and all the other national varieties of chicken were finishing points. Vanmechelen is now turning them into starting points again and in his Cosmopolitan Chicken Project is working towards a completely new climax. With the image of the mother hen of all Red Jungle Fowl in mind he will 'combine' all the scattered national varieties of chicken by means of crossbreeding, which means bringing them back to a single cosmopolitan, transparent 'super-hybrid'. He will even out all the individual characteristics achieved over the centuries by manipulation for purposes of commercialisation and consumption and then patented; he will channel the genetic diversity of the different varieties, while retaining random traces of biological individuality.

To begin with he selected fourteen varieties at random – there will be more: the project will take several decades, perhaps fifty years, perhaps a hundred. He will then crossbreed these varieties in the most 'natural' possible way: this is genetic manipulation in the sense that he is always the one to bring two varieties together. He will release the creations thus produced. At no time will he determine in advance how the result should look: the call of the chicken is all-important. The artist will never stake a claim to the end-product. But he will bring order to the chaos that has arisen over the centuries. He will act on behalf of a certain form of globalisation by working, as an instrument of something bigger than himself, on the creation of a new and strong variety of chicken, with fresh blood, and traces and characteristics of all the varieties it carries within it. The Cosmopolitan Chicken Project is a *perpetuum mobile*. The work in progress will nevertheless raise a multitude of questions, and set people thinking about where we and our world are going. Isn't the chicken a good metaphor for man? Koen Vanmechelen's 'active art' – distributed over meadows and exhibition halls – will raise a great many fascinating questions. How and in what order this will happen is at the start of the project still a puzzle to the creator. He plays a subservient role in the whole business: he will respond to the call of the chicken.

Philosophical incubator

Drawings on paper and on canvas, in charcoal, coffee, eggshells, egg yolks and so on; collages, montages, installations, models and video pieces; works in glass and carpet and stuffed chickens; talks, debates and discussions with people who are for or against – each and every one is the product of the unceasing twists and turns of the breeder's brain, results hatched from the artist's daily sojourns in his own philosophical incubator, indispensable parts of the never-ending genesis of this project. For all that, the project is chiefly sustained by the 'Installations' and the 'Interpretations'. The former are actual presentations for the public, showing intermediate stages, milestones in the growing work of art. The latter can best be described as the materialisation of the accompanying thought processes in the form of digital prints of drawings or – why not? – the 'breeder's philosophical incubator'.

The Cosmopolitan Chicken Project is essentially a story, a family story. About a series of new varieties of chicken that fertilise others. In each chapter a new country takes the stage in the form of a national variety of chicken. The nesting place is very often an installation on location. Preferably in the country where

the newly introduced variety originates. (In the absence of an invitation from that country, the meadows behind Vanmechelen's house, the nesting places in his garden and cellar serve the same purpose.) Despite several recurring ingredients – an incubator, portraits of chickens, living animals, a video presentation – each installation is still a new part of the story. What happens during the presentation is always a sequence that not even the artist can predict. Countless surprises create unplanned chapters. About the birth of a black chick, for example, or a variety that unexpectedly turns out to be monogamous, or another, virtually infertile, which appears to regain its potency through the combination with fresh blood. This is what takes place in the mainstream of activity, in the main installations. In addition there are smaller installations with a smaller story, a chapter on the side or just a marginal note or footnote.[1] Curators in many museums and galleries both in Belgium and abroad included (part of) the project in their programmes and so helped to write the story: Jan Hoet in Watou and later in Herford, Jo Coucke in Otegem, Jill Silvermann in London, Adriano Berengo in Miami and various places in Europe, Wim van Krimpen in Amsterdam. All these people are like coaches on the sidelines, godfathers and godmothers to countless hens and chicks, mentors of their keeper.

There is no better all-round summary of the Cosmopolitan Chicken Project than Koen Vanmechelen's combined 'Interpretation' *Pyramid of Time & Pyramid of Brains.* For several reasons the *Pyramid of Time* and the *Pyramid of Brains* may well be the philosophical backbone of the whole project. The aim of crossing the chickens is to create a transparent super-hybrid or a new chicken whose internal characteristics will be more important than the external. Equivalent in man to the mental being more important than the physical. In addition, what happens to any particular individual (human time) is essentially no different from

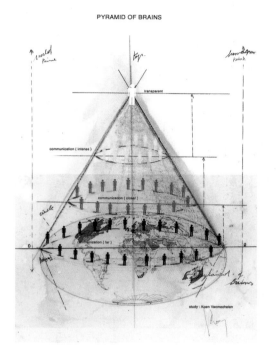

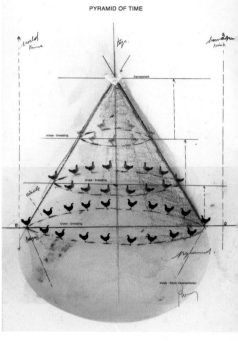

what happens on a larger scale in the world as a whole (world time). The desire to understand oneself and the world, to be aware of existence and its meaning, are characteristic of the human species. Self-knowledge is important to those who seek wisdom. *'Gnoti seauton'*, 'know yourself'. This adage was already to be found above the oracle in Delphi.

Koen Vanmechelen,
Pyramid of Brains/
Pyramid of Time.
Deweer Art Gallery,
Otegem, 2001

The *Pyramid of Time* study compares the world to an egg. The art is to break through the shell and emerge from the egg. In the *Pyramid of Brains* the chicken metaphor, as it evolves in Koen Vanmechelen's work, is transposed to human thinking.

Crossing borders, the need for communication, the importance of evolution, longing, freedom, globalisation, cosmopolitanism, anti-racism, tackling surfeit, these are all incorporated into the pyramids. All these topics have come up more or less explicitly in the cross-breeding that has taken place so far. Beneath the surface of the *Pyramid of Time* – like a mirror-image pyramid – lies the story of the 'primal chicken' from which purebred chickens were bred, the primal hen that was raised to the level of a commodity.

In the same reading, it may not be so odd to see the *Pyramid of Brains* as the reflection of God's reaction to the building of the Tower of Babel: spreading confusion among people, scattering them across the whole surface of the globe . In any case, Koen Vanmechelen's Cosmopolitan Chicken Project brings everyone

Koen Vanmechelen,
New Brood.
Deweer Art Gallery,
Transfo Zwevegem, 2004.
Photo by the artist.

Translated by Gregory Ball

the promise of healing. Though one must not ignore the question 'what next?'. After all, what happens when the top of both pyramids has been reached? What is the value of an individual standing transparently at the top, but seeing no one anywhere around to communicate with, to oppose, to match himself against? No other identities to enrich himself with, none to react against? Despite that, the *perpetuum mobile* will demand yet another new reflection. It may well be that in order to achieve this we shall need a different universe.

The following work was published on the occasion of the exhibition *The Desire of the Mechelse Dresdner* at De Brakke Grond in Amsterdam (11 April – end of June 2003): Barbara Simons & Wouter Keirse, *Koen Vanmechelen. Cosmopolitan Chicken Project.* Ghent/Amsterdam: Ludion, 96 pp. ∎

Six generations have so far been crossed. It would take too long to explain all the details, so here is a brief overview:

Mechelse Koekoek + Poulet de Bresse = Mechelse Bresse
(The name of each new generation begins with 'Mechelse', followed by the last word in the name of the latest addition).
Installations in Hasselt (Provincial Museum, *In de ban van de ring*, 1999) and Watou (Poëziezomer 2000, *Storm Centers*, 2000) were used as breeding-places. The same generation later enjoyed the hospitality of Bourbourg, France (ESPACES RENCONTRE AVEC L'OEUVRE D'ART, *The Cosmopolitan Chicken*, 2004), Hasselt (Anouk Vilain Art Gallery, *Mechelse Bresse First Generation*, 2004) and Otegem (Deweer Art Gallery, *Second Generation: Mechelse Bresse – Sex and Mortality*, 2004).

Mechelse Bresse + English Redcap = Mechelse Redcap
This variety first made its appearance in London (Lisson Gallery, *A Shot in the Head*, 2000) and this was repeated in Otegem (Deweer Art Gallery, *Between Natural Breeding and Genetic Engineering*, 2001).

Mechelse Redcap + Jersey Giant = Mechelse Giant
In late 2001, when the artist wanted to involve America in the story, things became more complicated. 11 September 2001 made the world a rather less safe place and Vanmechelen thought it would be decidedly inadvisable to take live animals to the States for cross-breeding so soon afterwards. At the time it was very much the question whether the cross-breeding *could* still go ahead, and whether he *would* still proceed with it. He responded to an invitation from Berengo Fine Arts to build an installation at the Miami Art Fair (2002) by sending a work that is a fusion of the Mechelse Redcap with an abstract glass model of the same animal. It was called *Artificial Cross-Breeding*. The actual cross-breeding took place 'in exile', at Vanmechelen's home in Meeuwen. The public was able to see the new chicken in Deurle (Museum Dhondt-Dhaenens, *FEB.3.2002*, 2002).

Mechelse Giant + Dresdner Huhn = Mechelse Dresdner
The cross-breeding took place in Meeuwen; not until later was there the offer of a German 'breeding place' (K4 Gallery München, *Mechelse Dresdner*, 2004).

Mechelse Dresdner + Nederlandse Uilebaard = Mechelse Uilebaard
The story of the fifth generation began in April 2003 when Vanmechelen showed an installation entitled *The Desire of the Mechelse Dresdner* at the Flemish-Dutch cultural centre De Brakke Grond in Amsterdam. It was an appeal to Dutch museums and galleries to allow the bird to mate with the Nederlandse Uilebaard on Dutch soil. The appeal was answered by the then newly opened Museum of Current Art in The Hague, with a presentation during the KunstRAI in Amsterdam (GEM, *Glass Crossing Project*, May 2003).

Mechelse Uilebaard + Mexicaanse Louisiana = Mechelse Louisiana
Having reached this point in his cross-breeding, Vanmechelen has so far organised two major overviews of the project: one in Hasselt (Museum Z33, *Red Jungle Fowl: Genus XY*, 2004) and another in Zwevegem, where the New Brought Installation added lustre to the jubilee exhibition honouring 25 years of the Deweer Art Gallery (*Eclips*, 2004).

www.koen-vanmechelen.be

Poetry from the Pantry
A vulgar yet cheerful plant

Ben Cami (1920-2004)

Translated by John Irons

To the Potato	Aan de aardappel
I do love the potato since	De aardappel heb ik lief daar hij,
Striving for perfect roundness	Strevend naar volkomen rondheid,
It is always differently round,	Altijd ànders rond is,
And has small eyes	En oogjes heeft
Like an animal blind at birth.	Als van een blindgeboren diertje.
I'm fond of it since, so delicious,	Ik heb hem lief daar hij, zo lekker,
It is misjudged by those in power;	Door de Groten wordt miskend;
Because its leaves are so ugly	Daar zijn kruid zo lelijk
And its flower so unpretentious.	En zijn bloem zo onaanzienlijk is.
And most of all since	En vooral daar hij
(As if it knew it will land up in	(Alsof hij wist dat hij in vrouwenhand
A woman's hand)	Belandt)
It is bashful and abashed	Bescheiden en beschaamd
Keeping its nodules	Zijn klootjes
Hidden beneath the sand.	Verborgen houdt onder het zand.

From *Poems 1959-1983* (Gedichten 1959-1983). Antwerpen: Manteau, 1984.

H.H. ter Balkt (1938-)

Potatoes

More vulgar and yet more cheerful plant
hardly lives in this gloomy land.
The potato's so Dutch: it dances, dumb,
into the basket and much later the mouth.
The brown of old much-used ball bags
and extremely exhausted brides it joins
with porkish roundness, *Grand Moguldom*,
and the look on its face of rolling coins.
In the ballroom of god's acre it merrily shags
and keeps its savings bank under the ground.

Aardappelen

Platvloerser en toch blijmoediger plant
leeft er bijna niet in dit sombere land.
De aardappel is zo Hollands: hij danst dom
de aardappelmand in en veel later de mond.
Het bruin van oude veelgebruikte balzakken
en van wel zeer versleten bruiden paart hij
aan varkensachtige rondheid, *Grootmogoldom*
en de gezichtsuitdrukking van rollende munt.
Op de balzaal van gods akker wiegelt hij blij
en zijn spaarbank heeft hij onder de grond.

Translated by James S Holmes

From *In the Water-Collection Areas* (In de waterwingebieden). Amsterdam: De Bezige Bij, 2000.

Alphabet Soup

Thoughts on Food and Food for Thought, with a Flemish Twist

Ask not what you can do for your country. Ask what's for lunch.
(Orson Welles)

[FILIP MATTHIJS]

Kitchen

The place in the home where it all begins. The place where the Fleming can get stuck into his rich culinary tradition, his cookery books by Antonio Carlucci and Jamie Oliver, and the recipes of countless television chefs. The place the Fleming spends less and less time. But more of that later. And is 'his' really the right pronoun to use? More of that, too, later (and if you can't wait, go straight to W).

Typical

'*Foodie nation*'. Flanders is not a country, although it's labelled as such in 'Flanders: a gastronomic guide', a special supplement in *The Guardian* in 2004. At www.visitflanders.co.uk there is a sequence of animated gif images of chocolate, beer, mussels and other delicacies forming a loop to make your mouth water. A look at the cultural calendar informs us that in 2004 we could, among other things, go to *Spots and Crumbs*, an archaeological and culinary exploration of Aalst. In Ostend there was *Dinner with Art*. From 17 September 2004 to 20 March 2005, the culinary delights of twelve renowned Ostend restaurants went hand in hand with exclusive art. A number of Flemish artists designed special table-mats for the occasion that restaurant guests were free to take home after

Jan Toorop, *Café Mille Colonnes, Brussels*. 1885. Canvas, 99 x 89 cm. Private collection.

the meal. A dream come true for those who can never resist the temptation to slip hotel towels and soap into their suitcases. At the golden 50th parade of Flemish fashion designer Dries van Noten in Paris in early October 2004, the plates had a golden rim – though you were not allowed to take those home with you. Instead, after a lavish meal served by 250 waiters, you were treated to Van Nooten's latest creations in a fashion show on the 149-metre-long table, turned into a catwalk for the occasion.

So we can safely start from an anything but premature conclusion: Flanders means food. Or rather: Belgium means food. For after 175 years of Belgian weal and woe, and a sweeping process of federalisation, the unitary state is perhaps nowhere as functional as in the culinary area. And, like so many other things in Belgium, the culinary melting pot is Brussels. Or, to use a somewhat unimaginative metaphor from *The Independent*: '*Belgium's capital is a tasty cocktail of French and Flemish ingredients with a sprinkling of other influences.*' Though shouldn't it be 'Walloon' rather than 'French'? Or does the French-speaking part of Belgium not have any typical cuisine, unlike Flanders? And what, then, does that 'typically' Flemish consist of? Is it waiters shrouded in monk's habits serving such dishes as 'salad liégoise', 'asparagus hollandaise', 'green Thai mussels' and *stoemp*' (a Dutch – and thus 'Flemish' – word which is translated in the menu as 'Belgian mash') in Belgo-restaurants in London? Or is the 'typical' to be found in 'Flemish' chip stands in Amsterdam, where an extra-large bag of chips (or *French* Fries, but we'll touch upon this sore spot later on) goes by the name 'Vlaamse Reus' ('Flemish Giant')? Whereas every right-minded Fleming knows that a 'Vlaamse Reus' is a kind of large rabbit. Even greater confusion: according to *The Independent* of 8 November 2003, the Vietnamese chef of the Ghent restaurant *The 3 Little Pigs* serves 'Flemish dishes with an oriental touch'. Although according to a gastronomic expert of the Flemish weekly *Knack*, we are dealing here with *French* dishes with the occasional exotic tinge.

The Guardian, in its special Flemish culinary supplement, doesn't avoid the trap, either: *'But what is Flemish cooking, exactly? Or Belgian cuisine, come to that? Belgians tell you that their food is cooked with French finesse and served with German generosity – you can go on a diet in Paris, they snigger.'* And thus the discourse silently slides from Flemish to Belgian. And in a supplement *'produced in association with Tourism Flanders-Brussels'*, to boot!

Chocolate

So let us deal with something that nobody would call 'Flemish': Belgian chocolates. Brussels is regarded as the chocolate capital of the world, though it's Bruges that has the world's greatest concentration of chocolate shops. And recently a new chocolate museum opened in Bruges, Choco-Story, whose mission is *'to make known the story of the transformation of cocoa into chocolate and to promote the health and quality values of Belgian chocolate'*. Even in Bruges, now more medieval than the Middle Ages ever were in Flanders, the praline remains Belgian, in the good old unitarian spirit of the nineteenth century. It is even becoming a politically correct delicacy, for Choco-Story uses as its signboard the 'chocolate fairy' – a painted exotic beauty who presumably symbolises the multicultural origins of cocoa.

Apologies to the poor massacred Mayas and Aztecs, then, but the truth must out: when it comes to pralines, Belgium rules. The British may have established the first club for chocolate devotees in 1746; a Swiss may have produced the first milk chocolate in 1875; and Mars may have seen the light of day in Chicago in 1911 – but we still have the best chocolate in the world. For the Belgian chocolate manufacturers select the very best ingredients, always keep the cocoa percentage well above the legal requirements and grind their beans finer than anyone else. In addition, the Belgians have turned chocolate into a present. Countless foreigners have gladdened the hearts of their wives and/or mistresses with Belgian pralines. James Wadworth (1768-1844) already knew the aphrodisiac power of chocolate. In *A History of the Nature and Quality of Chocolate* he writes: *'She makes old women young and fresh, / rushes renewed quivering through their flesh. / Let them yearn for you know what... / As soon as they have tasted chocolate.'*

So forget about the famous *'Mama always said life was like a box a chocolates, never know what you're gonna get.'* Not when it comes to a box of Belgian chocolates. Eat that, Forrest Gump!

With comfort food like chocolate we have arrived at the fact that for a long time now we haven't been eating in order to live. *'Belgium is not a low-calorie nation,'* writes *The Guardian*. Chips, beer and chocolate are indeed extremely waistband-stretching. But 'plenty' is apparently also Belgian. A true Dutchman wields a cheese-slicer in order to produce wafer-thin slivers, but in Belgium portions are generous. We are all familiar with the Bruegel feastings and the sumptuous female flesh of Rubens and Jordaens – and this reputation for surplus if not surfeit continues to dog the Fleming. *'Is this perhaps a typically Flemish book?'* the Dutch reviewer Kees 't Hart asks himself when looking at *The Black Stone* (De zwarte steen, 2003) by Geert van Istendael. He finds this

a frightful question, but even so has to conclude that no book has appeared in the Netherlands over the past thirty years like this novel, *'containing this sustained metaphor of eating and this voluptuous pathos of writing'*. So, yes: whoever eats plenty, eats Belgian. Or vice versa.

Jacob Jordaens,
Eating Man.
17th century. Canvas.
Staatliche Museen, Kassel.

Health

A greedy person doesn't always have to be a fat person – but it definitely helps. The Belgian zest for eating leaves its merciless mark on the average Body Mass Index. Between 1993 and 2000 the problem of overweight or obesity increased, except among the youngest members of the population. But for this latter group as well, fat is very much lying in wait. While the French-speaking Belgian schools will not be allowed to offer any sweets, soft drinks and fast food for sale, the Flemish authorities have not yet considered restricting the unhealthy eating habits of young people in this way.

But there is hope. At the end of 2004, the Belgian Food Industry Federation (Fevia) published the study *A Hundred Years of Appetite: 1925–2025* (Honderd jaar appetijt: 1925-2025), which suggests that the Belgian anno 2005 is no longer prepared to be torn between good health and pleasure. Food has to be tasty, but preferably also healthy. In addition, one out of every two Belgians has at some point bought cholesterol-lowering food or drink. *Light* products and vitamins are also doing well. Not for slimming purposes, but so as not to put on weight. Blow-outs are apparently *out*; the sublimation of gastronomic pleasure and 'functional food' with ingredients designed to cleanse the body of undesirable substances are *in*. Eat well and still live to be a hundred or more – that seems to be the message.

Slow food

In the beginning there was Fast Food, and it would seem that the age of Slow Food has now dawned. In the Flemish newspaper *De Morgen*, Johan Vande Lanotte, Minister of the Budget and Public Enterprises, proudly claims that his way of eating reflects what he is: quick and impatient. In the evening he sometimes eats pancakes. A dozen, usually, until he gets a bit of a stomach ache – which he describes as a wonderful feeling.

That is no longer on. If you are to enjoy your food, you will have to stick to one pancake. And you can't enjoy properly if you just chuck something in the frying pan and then wolf it down, standing up in the kitchen. Savouring food is also a sin in such fast-food classics as McDonalds and Pizza Hut. In 1986, the Italian culinary journalist Carlo Petrini was so horrified at the opening of an American hamburger stall on the Piazza di Spagna in Rome that he got together a number of gourmet friends in order to spread the art of enjoyment and the philosophy of savouring food. At the end of 1989, the International Slow Food Movement was established, with a genuine Slow Food Manifesto. The emphasis here is not only on quality of life but also on combating the blurring of taste: on upholding local culinary traditions, supporting traditionally prepared and natural products and, in general, venerating quality of life.

Dirk Lambrechts, one of the prominent figures of the Flemish Slow Food scene, published in 2003 with *The Taste of Nostalgia* (De smaak van heimwee) an ode to the amazing richness of traditional European popular cuisine, making a passionate plea for retaining diversity. No sloppy nostalgia, but a longing for distinctive tastes and smells. In his chapter on Belgium he talks about soup that was green with chervil, asparagus that wasn't just four scrawny stems on a plate, and garlic that still tasted bitter. He praises a gastronomic culture that often seems anarchistic to the outside world. Lambrechts lures the reader to a café in Anderlecht. Five tables, plastic table cloths, naturally fermented Brussels Gueuze beer as an apéritif, and half a kilo of juicy, rare entrecôte that has had only a fleeting acquaintance with the frying pan. Afterwards the author continues to savour it, but his heart misses a beat when he hears talk of large-scale urban clearance and new rules and regulations for restaurants.

Quality control

In an opinion column in the *NRC Handelsblad* of 24–25 April 2004, Dirk Lambrechts declares war on 'the bureaucratic grand inquisitors from Brussels'.

According to him, the European Union's preoccupation with hygiene is as great a threat to traditional popular cuisine as the impoverishment of the consumer's capacity to taste. *'What they'd really like is to see butchers and chefs perform-ing in moon-suits in germ-free operating theatres,'* he snarls. Their obsessive search for bacteria is treated with scorn. This is followed by a eulogy on moulds and other micro-organisms as providers of such delicacies as Belgian Herve cheese and authentic Brussels Gueuze beer.

Food safeguards are, of course, hardly unnecessary at a time when mad cow disease and swine fever are still fresh in people's memory. Sterilised vegeta-bles and pasteurised milk do not perhaps do justice to the full, distinct flavour of these products – but are we really nostalgic about tuberculosis? Or would we perhaps rather have European hygiene guidelines to which all industries ought to conform?

There is also the fact that our present-day food culture can only be guaran-teed by industrial production and processing. As a result of the contamination of several consignments of cattle feed with dioxin, one of the biggest food scan-dals of recent years broke out in Belgium at the end of May 1999. Numerous products were removed from shelves, the supply of chicken, pork and beef was halted, and the production of meats, biscuits and pralines was stopped. Belgians, used to abundance, suddenly found themselves faced with scantily stocked shops. The reaction to this came in 2000, with the establishment of the Federal Agency for the Safety of the Food Chain. It grouped together the seven existing inspectorates that until that time had been fragmented in the various depart-ments of Agriculture and Public Health, and thus enabled an eye to be kept on the entire production process and the statutory hygiene regulations relating to it.

Despite this increased control of food safety – the most rigorous and thus the best in the world, according to some people – the Belgian debate on food and health is a very serene affair, according to Michel Delbaere, the chairman of Fevia. Unlike in Great Britain, where, according to Delbaere's address dur-ing the annual meeting in 2004, the food industry is being *'diabolised as an un-*

scrupulous money machine that tries to gets consumers to eat more and more and thus boost profits at the expense of public health', Delbaere prefers the path of freedom with responsibility, and what has happened: without all that much cavilling, Belgian consumers have opted for health and natural taste. What a lucky break for an entrepreneur who gives us a quick peek at his soul when he says: 'This proves yet again that the best driving force for progress is consumers and their complaints.' Subtext: the powers that be should not stick their unwelcome noses in too far.

Meat

Our Cookbook
(Ons Kookboek, 1955),
the Flemish housewife's
gastronomic bible

On the other hand, sometimes people are only too willing to appeal to authority. In a press release from the beginning of 2004, the Bond Beter Leefmilieu (Better Living Environment Federation) calls for policy initiatives to reduce the excessive consumption of meat in the interests of public health. This concern about overconsumption of meat is not new. In a 1955 edition of the Flanders gastronomic bible and bestseller, *Our Cookbook* (Ons kookboek), we can already read: 'Excessive use of meat leads to an accumulation of nitrogenous waste products that produce disturbances in the body.'. The Flemish writer Louis Paul Boon, however, takes a different view in his *Eating Flemish Style* (Eten op zijn Vlaams): 'Chapter III, then, deals with never-sufficiently-praised meat, that gives us stamina and enables us to bear with fortitude the vicissitudes of life.' In 1872, the British economist Brassey decided that British industry had nothing to fear from Belgian competition because the Belgian worker was underfed. He ate lots of potatoes, but that only develops a paunch, not muscles. In Dr Meynne's *Topographie médicale de la Belgique* from as early as 1865, it was also stated that the vegetarian diet of the Belgian worker provided him with a full stomach but not much strength. In productivity's name, therefore, the worker ought to have more meat on the table. Gradually, the democratisation of meat consumption became a reality. Livestock was farmed on a large scale and 'fashioned' to fit human requirements – with all that this entailed.

As early as 1930, though, the culinary lady's magazine *The Kitchen* (De Keuken) praised a meat-free diet, for 'such a diet calms the nerves and is diuretic (...) and prevents constipation.' It is not, however, until the 1970s that the interest in meat begins to decline in Belgian cookery books. It now appears from a recent survey that the average Belgian is consuming less and less meat. Such traditional meat dishes as spare ribs and roast joints, especially, have been dealt a heavy blow. Nowadays, the Belgian buys more mixed meat products such as gyros, kebabs or cordon bleu. And he is apparently eating less meat than before. Apparently, because the above conclusions were made on the basis of what the Belgian buys for consumption in the home. But it would appear that more eating is now taking place outside the home: at least 39% of one's total consumption. The Belgian is seldom to be found at his stove.

Restaurant

One evening when Paul Verlaine and Arthur Rimbaud wanted to go out to dine at the *Richer de Canale* restaurant in Antwerp, they hit a nasty snag. Although the

Sign outside a restaurant in Bruges.

poets had a considerable amount of money on them, they were too informally dressed for the establishment and were promptly shown the door. At that time, the more expensive restaurants were very much the places where the new and the old élites used to meet each other – and the company of shabbily clad bohemians was not something that was greatly appreciated.

The first restaurants in the major Belgian towns were still modelled very much along French lines, with superb cuisine and wines to match. Portions were exceptionally large, so that around 1900 Baedeker's guide advised travellers to order one portion for two people and two portions for three.

Quite soon, regional dishes also began to appear on the menu of more popular restaurants. *Chez Georges* was one such restaurant: established in 1926 with a capital of F2000 in the till and 48 bottles of wine in the cellar. There guests could eat a portion of mussels with chips for F1.25 – and it was so cosy a place that one regular customer used to tell the *patron* that you could eat there '*comme chez soi*'. Today, the *Comme chez soi* is a gastronomic Valhalla, where you can eat more deliciously and – above all – more expensively than '*chez soi*'.

Today's Belgian restaurants are most certainly emancipated restaurants. From time immemorial France has dictated what is allowable in the field of gastronomy, but Belgian chefs have fought their way out of the French stranglehold. The former masters have been overtaken; the inferiority complex is a thing of the past. '*The capital no longer feels like a second-rate version of Paris*', a gastronomic expert concludes in *The Bulletin* of 18 November 2004.

Brussels restaurants were praised as far back as 1965 in the French *Guide Julliard*, although their eulogy is tinged with the odd jarring note. No matter what the dish, Belgians insist on eating soggy, lukewarm chips... *'even with lobster!'*.

Paul Ilegem's
The Complete Chip Book
(Het volkomen frietboek,
2002)

That brings us to what, according to many, is the culinary zenith of Belgium: chips, or French fries. Forget that 'French' in front of the 'fries'. They are *ours*. And they are everywhere. Settle yourself at a small table in the brasserie *Aux vieux Bruxelles* and you'll see a surrealistic-type painting depicting a row of nuns shuffling past with bags of chips in their hands. In an advertisement for a bank that welcomes foreigners to Belgium a beaming gentleman is offering a cornet of chips to an even more beaming lady. Gillis Houben has been painting chip stalls in a Hopperesque style for a decade already. He calls it future nostalgia and even ventures to portray fictitious chip stalls, as on a canvas where one has been placed in the garden of the royal palace. With *The Complete Chip Book* (Het volkomen frietboek, 2002) the art historian Paul Ilegems is already on his fourth publication about potato strips, this time with the subtitle 'A story of Belgian cultural history', since: *'Belgium and chips are one. The country has, as it were, been sculpted out of deep-fry fat, and public life has the same slippery smoothness and the same golden crispy coating as the national popular food.'* The battered caravans and converted mini-buses that serve as chip stalls are an illustration of the anarchistic urge to improvise that is characteristic of the Belgian. In the coffee table book *Chip Stall = Baraques à frites* (Fritkot = Baraques à frites, 2002) the Flemish writer Koen Peeters explains tongue-in-cheek why chip stalls are of vital importance to the Belgian state. For it is fairly unstable, a kind of invisible volcano with its crater silted up. The chip stalls appear to be dispersed haphazardly along the roads, but this appearance is deceptive. In actual fact, they are small people's chapels that stand on important lava veins and are thus crucially important for the country: *'Do not in any way underestimate what takes place in the chip stall. These simple people manage the fire and the chaos like vestal virgins.'*

At present, the chip stalls are suffering increasingly from the competition of snack bars, hamburger chains and Turkish pita bars, but despite that they are proudly holding their heads above water. They are more and more acquiring a sedentary character, and on their spacious premises the chip-friers are constantly professionalising and diversifying: they now also serve rolls and sandwiches, spaghetti – or even ox tongue in madeira sauce. But the chips are still their staple product: fried twice to give them that extra crispiness, and preferably in beef fat. For, as the owner of the Antwerp chip museum says: *'Fries are fun. You don't eat them for your health'*.

Potato

Underground tubers that give maximum yields on the relatively meagre agricultural land of the densely populated Low Countries. Suppliers of chips. According to Louis Paul Boon *'the prime, most important ingredient of Flemish cuisine (...) because over the years – the years of war and of hunger – they were the main commodity you could use to feed yourself.'*

There are the potatoes in onion sauce of the nineteenth-century workers, the *pommes de terre soufflées* that their king used to consume, the new potatoes that give you delightful intestinal convulsions, the gently boiled and mashed old potatoes in the purée. And then, top of the line, there are the French fries. There are all sorts of potatoes, and small new potatoes sooner or later become old and wrinkly, but as Boon says, *'whatever may happen to them, as chips they retain their excellence and merits.'* Whatever form they should happen to assume, potatoes stand for vitamins and, even more, calories. In a word – basic food.

Famine

But when in less globalised times that basic food was not available, it led to famine, popular uprisings and emigration. Just ask the O'Reillys and the O'Haras in the US. The same thing also happened to Belgium. The name of the scourge of God was *Phytophtora Infestans* and it took up its hateful residence in Belgian fields. In 1845, the price of potatoes doubled within a short space of time. Not only did the crop fail; the fungal infection caused what potatoes had been harvested to rot in no time.

Then came pesticides and import regulations, since when Belgium has not known any large-scale famine. At the beginning of the twenty-first century, famine as a feeding problem has given way to eating disorders: from an acute shortage to an oppressive surplus.

Daily bread

To make matters worse, the production of rye also fell to an all-time low in 1846. Wheat bread was a luxury item. So this meant that the worker also lost his daily rye bread with dripping. *'Never has famine claimed so many victims in our fertile fatherland!'* says a pamphlet published by the Friends of the People

of Flanders in 1846. Bakeries were stormed, and even the mayor of Ghent was injured during bread riots.

Today you can find bread in all shapes, sizes and weights at Belgian baker's shops. But the bakers themselves are busy doing quite other things. On 8 July 2004, a Belgian team of confectioners won first prize in the 'chocolate showpiece' category of the World Pastry Team Championship in Las Vegas. This sweet work of art had as its theme the four elements 'earth, air, fire and water'. This is somewhat different from what Louis Paul Boon sought for in vain in the modern baker: *just try to buy a good loaf, one baked with unadulterated wheat flour, in an oven heated by wood.*

Vegetables

Belgian chocolates, Belgian waffles and now a prize-winning Belgian chocolate showpiece. All very delicious, but as children we were only allowed to taste any of it if we had finished all our sprouts.

That vegetables (and fruit, too) are healthy is something no one in his right mind would deny. In a survey conducted in 1996, 97% and 92% respectively of the Flemings asked confirmed that they thought it important for their health to eat vegetables and fresh fruit every day. But the road to an imbalanced diet is paved with good intentions. That there is a difference between what they 'knew' and what they 'chewed' was soon revealed by the selfsame survey: only 22% ate sufficient quantities of fresh fruit and a mere 5% ate enough vegetables. Not tasty enough, too many pesticides, one helluva job to clean and to prepare – we all know the excuses.

And all that while Ardo, the European market leader when it comes to frozen vegetables, is located in the heart of West Flanders. The area around Roeselare, where such companies as Dujardin Foods and Pinguin are based, is known as 'Flanders' Vegetable Valley'. A vegetable was once even invented in Brussels. In the first half of the nineteenth century, experiments with the chicory root were

carried out in a botanical garden there. It transpired that if you stuck those roots into some soil, white, edible leaves began to grow. The temperature in the greenhouses was raised, the roots were left in the dark and fine, firm bodies of white foliage appeared. Scarcely one year after its birth, chicory (endive) had already found its way to America. But the chef at the Ancienne Belgique concert hall in Brussels nevertheless said recently that she cannot get British and American artists to touch braised chicory. Too bitter. So *no* dessert for you, gentlemen musicians!

Yoghurt

Dairy products are also problematic. Milk can undergo 1001 changes of appearance. Yoghurt, for example, first appeared in France in 1542 in an attempt to cure King François I of a spell of deep apathy. Another fermented personality milk assumes is cheese, and Belgium has roughly as many varieties, relatively speaking, as the cheese meccas of France, Switzerland and the Netherlands put together. The Dutchman may have the renowned Gouda cheeses (Defoe's Robinson Crusoe managed to save three such cheeses from his shipwreck), but with his 17 kg a year the average Belgian consumes quite a bit more cheese than his northern counterpart. Even so, the Flemish protagonist of Willem Elsschot's marvellous novella *Cheese* (Kaas, 1933) has more Dutch cheeses foisted onto him that he can possibly deal with. In this gentle, satirical fable of capitalism and wealth a clerk in Antwerp suddenly becomes the chief agent in Belgium and Luxembourg for this red-rinded Dutch delight and is saddled with 370 cases containing ten thousand full-cream cheeses.

Things are not going so well as far as consumption of the straight stuff is concerned. In Europe, milk began to give way to coffee from the eighteenth century onwards. While milk and fruit are the main constituents of snacks in primary schools in Belgium, in lower secondary education this changes to sweets and soft drinks. The admonishment *'you were raised on it at any rate'* seems to be to no avail.

Jean Fouquet,
*Mary and Jesus surrounded
by Serpahim and Cherubim.*
Panel, 91 x 81 cm.
Koninklijk Museum voor
Schone Kunsten, Antwerp.

Breast

I stand corrected. *This* is ultimately the place where it all begins. Not the kitchen. Except, of course, for bottle-fed children – but we all know that they are push-overs. Moreover, a team of investigators from the University of Chicago recently discovered that substances released when a woman breastfeeds her child arouse the desire to have sex in other women and stimulate sexual fantasies. After which, when the man returns home everything is surely going to be swept off the kitchen table at one go – and the kitchen will then in a sense once more become the place where it all begins.

Love

'The way to a man's heart is through his stomach,' Flemish mothers used to impress upon their daughters in times gone by. Again, look at the letter W. It's not far now.

Joy

Candlelight dinners, the slow, sensual feeding of the loved one: the eroticising pleasure of an intimate meal is just one aspect of the joy of eating together.

Belgians love life, but Belgians love eating most of all. They are known far beyond their national borders for their zest. As the Flemish writer Felix Timmermans once wrote: *'Pious people here love Our Lord, but with a piece of pork in their mouths.'* It is a terrible cliché to say that a cliché contains a germ of truth, but in this case it really does. Not for nothing are we a people that was forbidden by the Austrian Emperor Joseph II from organising funeral repasts that lasted longer than ten full days.

The company with which you share a meal intensifies the gastronomic pleasure. For the Slow Food movement, too, culinary togetherness is a central tenet. Johan Vande Lanotte, the minister who eats pancakes until he gets a stomach ache, says of his youth: *'At home nobody said anything during meals. Eat up and belt up was the message.'* He readily admits that such behaviour is anything but conducive to enhancing culinary culture. Any more than the development signalled by Fevia in *A Hundred Years of Appetite*, namely the advance of one-person meals in Belgium. Ideal for the hip one-person family, admittedly. But in families too, eating whatever-you-feel-like is becoming more important than the-same-for-everyone.

Woman

Things used to be different. In the preface to the 1955 edition of *Our Cookbook* we read that it has been published *'so that the woman of the house may be able, through her culinary skills, to contribute to domesticity and to the life of family*

David Teniers the Younger,
Kitchen Interior (detail).
1644. Canvas. Mauritshuis,
The Hague.

and friends.' Apart from the fact that the joys of eating together are important, we also learn here that the woman's place is in the kitchen. In the preface to Boon's *Eating Flemish Style* there is the ominous remark: *'But did you know that every year just in our own small country over twenty thousand husbands leave their wives? (...) Quite possibly because of those cold meat leftover dishes or that vol-au-vent.'* So Boon advises his female readers not to skimp on either trouble or cost when it comes to cooking: *'Buy a couple of pairs of tights less, or don't wear any – and in exchange get half a pound of real farm butter.'*

From way back, the woman of the house had to ensure that the breadwinner had enough to eat. That also led to a kind of 'eating hierarchy'. The head of the family ate first. Later, during the early industrial period, the children who were old enough to bring home a wage came second. Last came the wife and young children. The older daughters, who used to help mother with the housekeeping, often came off worst of all, with just a few leftovers.

The first domestic science schools were in fact established by the middle classes with this family model at the back of their minds. A working-class girl who knew all about housekeeping would be sure to marry a man who was eager to come home. Such a man would keep his hands off other women and also avoid drinking... and thus be quite a bit more productive for the factory owner. In that way, the little housewives, force-fed with domestic skills, would be able to ensure a 'Flemish domestic culture'.

In 1931, the magazine The Kitchen writes that feminism is guaranteed to lead to neglect of the art of cooking. And there are also moans that the kitchen is, after all, a domain that ought to remain in female hands. Admittedly, men want to conquer a great deal, but the kitchen remains unpopular territory. After the Second World War there was a tidal wave of kitchen gadgets designed to lighten the workload. Advertisements for them were invariably aimed at a female audience. Today, the prospect of a Brave New World is held up to us in TV commercials where we see men doing the cooking. Here, though, what a Flemish female chef said in a recent newspaper interview about the numerical supremacy of male chefs applies: 'I sometimes get the impression that female chefs care a lot more about what they prepare, while the men would prefer to have the best restaurant that is in the spotlight everywhere.' So the few men who cook for their families regularly (i.e. not just at parties, to impress friends with their unworldly exploits with the wok) undoubtedly also want to 'contribute to domesticity', but the male models in the ads and commercials normally have ulterior motives that would be better placed under the letter L in this article: 'cooking gets you laid', the message would appear to be. It is, by the way, striking how few men you ever see washing up or polishing in ads and commercials. And if this actually does happen, then a good (and sexy) fairy invariably arrives with a wonder product that is demonstrated while the guy looks on with sheepish gaze. In Flanders too, the New Man is a hazy hero who only exists in commercials.

One male Belgian out of two hasn't got a heroic physique anyway: the sagging paunch is gradually becoming a national curse. That's what comes of centuries of men flaunting their appetite as proof of their virility. Just as 'real' ladies were once assumed to peck at their food like young sparrows and above all never to reveal that they liked eating. Once... for now there is nothing less than an ideal of beauty that ensures that 10% of Belgian women are underweight. Perhaps that is also the reason why I myself saw the waiters at a solid old-fashioned Flemish wedding party systematically serve the male guests with four and the ladies present with three croquettes.

Etiquette

All right. I have to admit that I saw that because I was not looking at my own plate, as I really should have been doing.

Washing your hands, eating with obvious pleasure though with moderation, eating with a knife and fork while gazing at your own plate, not speaking with your mouth full, turning away if you have to cough, not (audibly) breaking wind... In his impressive standard work *Eating and Drinking in Europe* Leo Moulin claims that we owe our table manners to the medieval monastic orders, for *'they lived in a state of great intimacy'* and strict rules were designed to prevent domestic tensions.

In the meantime, these table manners, as with all other strict rituals from the past, have been subjected to considerable wear and tear. Fortunately, we now also have *gay cooking*, which produced the small book *Cuisine Italienne Gay*. In it, Antonio Lapipa and Davide della Rondella also provide us with a number of commandments: being well-dressed at table, no sending or reading of text messages, but also this: *'do not start to shriek hysterically if one of your false eyelashes falls in the soup. Fish it out quickly and discreetly.'* Camp... it's one of the last bastions of conventionality.

Unsavoury

'Should a dish appear that someone does not like, he should still attempt to eat some of it,' is one of the guidelines in *Our Cookbook*. But what to do with food that we genuinely find nasty and repulsive? Are those horrible flowerets on our plate edible? Why is the squid in that pasta so visibly *squid*, with that tiny head and likewise tentacles? Who wants to eat food that *stares* at you?

It's all a matter of taste, of course. And taste varies from one area to the next. As early as the nineteenth century, there were people who insisted that locusts were healthier than pork, but they never became a gastronomic smasheroo in Europe. Flemings eat horsemeat without flinching, but the horse-mad Irish find it revolting. In 2004, Bo Derek actually joined in a protest campaign against the Belgian companies that operate the only two slaughterhouses that exist in the US for horsemeat.

Preferences also vary over time. Once, the nobility of the Low Countries used to consume with relish both larks and thrushes, provided that they were *'so crunchy'* that they could be devoured bones 'n all. Roman patricians used to feast from time to time on dolphin balls or stuffed sow's uterus. And what Belgian would ever have thought in 1970 that in 2004 ostrich and kangaroo steaks would be readily available in his local supermarket? *The menus...they are a'changing.*

By the way, to answer a pressing question from many Americans and Brits: we do *indeed* eat those French fries with mayonnaise. Because – do I really need to repeat this? – they're actually *Belgian* fries.

Offal

*De gustibus...*One man's offal is another man's meat. What, for example, is one to think about Dendermond's headmeat? After they have been thoroughly cleaned, the pig's heads are cooked in a heady stock until tender. Then the meat is removed from the bones and minced really fine. It is then reheated in a little stock and herbs are added. After that, it is poured into moulds. Delicious? Not to everyone, without a doubt. In *Eating Flemish style*, Boon breaks a lance for hot slices of udder with puréed potatoes: *'You can taste something of the meat of a cow in it, but also something of the milk that once flowed out of it. Enfin, something really special that you naturally have to fancy, as the Marquis de Sade put it.'*

Xenomania

Going to the Chinese restaurant in Lieven Debrauwer's film *Jam* (Confituur, 2004).

The same Boon, however, is somewhat more conservative when it comes to non-native dishes. Nasi Goreng is a bit of rice *'with some leftover vegetables and, if you look really carefully, something that resembles meat,'*; a spring roll *'a fried roll with soya bean sprouts they cannot get rid of in their own country.'*

On the other hand, Leo Moulin calls Belgium a gastronomically ecumenical country, *'uniquely open to foreign flavours'*. As far back as 1932 we find recipes for *'Creole soup, Hungarian goulash and Russian vegetable soup'* in *The Complete Flemish Kitchen Maid* (De Volmaakte Vlaamsche Keukenmeid). While in the early 1970s people were just summoning up the courage to visit the first Italian and Chinese restaurants, you can now enjoy Thai, Japanese, Russian and Ethiopian cuisine with no trouble at all. There is even a fusion going on in the people's chapel. In an article in *Eating out in the Low Countries since 1800* (2002), the author is surprised at the choice her son makes when visiting a chip stall: a *mitraillette*, which comprises a baguette with small merguez sausages, lettuce and the indispensable fries. Other people prefer a small Lebanese pita bread with meat, vegetables and fries. And if you do not want to feel completely displaced in your own country, why not simply wash it down with a glass of beer?

Alcohol

Belgian beer: an inexhaustible subject. Let us at this late stage in the article not get lost in drink. Just try and *google* with the following: Michael Jackson (the – naturally – fair-skinned one), Tim Webb, and whatever you do, don't forget Interbrew (now InBev). Or just type in 'Belgian beer'. After that, it may be

Tony Michels, *Modern Primitive Branding* beer mug, with a knuckle-duster as a handle. 2002.

a good idea to visit www.beerandhealth.com, a four-language Belgian site where, among other things, you can find hangover cures. And *'anyone who hasn't woken up with workmen in his head deserves to be beatified'*, as you can read there. Any saints or near-saints here? No...? Thought as much...

Night

Hangovers and food are often bad companions, but seeing that the average Belgian is becoming less and less interested in breakfast, the painful confrontation can be postponed until lunch. Or even much longer, for in *A Hundred Years of Appetite* we read that the new eaters are night birds. A late evening meal around 10pm is becoming increasingly common, especially among young Belgians. With night comes hunger. Just ask any old vampire.

Rich Fare, engraving by Hieronymus Cock (c.1507-1570) after Pieter Bruegel the Elder.

Indigestion

Cornucopia. In Flanders fields Belgian waffles and Ghent chicken casserole are being served. Too much is never enough. First comes the eating, then the recipes, Mr Brecht. Well, in this case at least.

So read on, you hungry ones. Come and get it, as Mae West once shouted. ∎

Translated by John Irons

Do Try this at Home

Home Cooking from the Low Countries

Soup as a main dish
Ghent chicken casserole (*Gentse waterzooi*)

It has been claimed that this is a Hungarian dish. But people make so many claims. This chicken casserole (which was originally made with fish!) is intended as a main dish and is served in soup plates, with a spoon (for the broth) and a knife and fork for the chicken and vegetables. People often eat a boiled potato with the dish, or some bread with a generous layer of butter. In *Eating Flemish Style*, Louis Paul Boon notes that this dish is famous all over the world and he is therefore reluctant to feature it: *'many Americans come here to see the Minnewater in Bruges and to eat 'waterzooi' in Ghent – so I was afraid the specialists would be telling me: Good grief, man, you haven't the faintest idea.'*

Ingredients
1 oven-ready chicken cut into pieces, 1 pack soup vegetables, 100g (4oz) butter, 1 bouquet garni, salt, freshly ground white pepper, 2 stalks of celery, 2 leeks, 3 carrots, 8 non-floury potatoes, 1 pinch freshly chopped parsley, 200ml (7 fl.oz) fresh cream, 1 egg yolk

Preparation
Sauté the coarsely-chopped soup vegetables in half the butter in a large pan. Place the chicken pieces on top, season with pepper and salt, add the bouquet garni and cover with water. Bring to the boil, cover and simmer until the chicken is tender.

Take the chicken out of the pan and remove the skin. Strain the broth into a bowl and reserve. Cut the rest of the vegetables and the potatoes into large pieces, put them in the same pan and braise them quickly in the remaining butter. Arrange the chicken pieces on top of the vegetables. Mix the broth with the cream, pour over the chicken and vegetables and allow to simmer over a low heat for a further 15 minutes. Thicken with the egg yolk mixed with some cream or broth, and remove from the heat. Sprinkle with parsley and serve in a soup tureen or soup plates.

For enthusiasts: according to Boon, the neck and the feet, stomach and liver of the chicken may also be cooked along with the other ingredients. When everything is ready, the pot is placed on the table and everyone takes what they want from it. According to Boon, this can make for some tense moments: *'The only drawback – according to my wife – is that one person may end up with a thigh and the next have to make do with a bony bit of the carcass. And what she means by this, my wife, is that she is the one who ends up with the carcass and I get the two chicken thighs.'*

A naturalised Spanish dish
Leiden hotchpotch (or mishmash?) (*Leidse hutspot*)

Hotchpotches first appeared in the Netherlands at the end of the seventeenth century, when the potato became *the* staple food of the population. The Dutch hotchpotch tradition probably has its origins in the Eighty Years' War. During that conflict Leiden was besieged by the Spanish for a long period. Shortly after the city had been relieved on 3 October 1574, the hungry citizens found in the hastily abandoned Spanish camp an unfamiliar dish consisting of parsnips, carrots and meat. They liked it so much that it stayed on the menu. When, many years later, the potato had become popular, it was added to the dish. This is how the popular hotchpotch came into being. Every year on 3 October some Leiden people eat a hotchpotch based on the Spanish stew of 1574 to commemorate the relief of the city.

Ingredients
1kg (2lb) parsnips, 500g (1lb) large carrots, 500g (1lb) rib of beef, 1.5kg (3lb) potatoes, 500g (1lb) onions, 300g (10oz) haricot beans, butter or lard, salt and pepper to taste, vinegar

Preparation
Soak the haricot beans overnight, drain and discard the liquid. Simmer the beef in water with a little salt for two hours until tender. Remove the meat and put in the potatoes cut into pieces and the coarsely chopped carrots and parsnips. Cover with the onions, sliced into rings. Simmer for 20 minutes until tender.

   Then place the drained haricot beans and the beef on top of the onions and cook for a further 10 minutes. Remove the beef, pour off the liquid into a bowl, then mash the vegetables, adding some of the cooking liquid until you have a smooth consistency. Add the butter or lard, salt, pepper and vinegar, according to taste. Finally, cut the rib of beef into slices. Serve with a slice of rye bread.

   Important note: in many recipes for Leiden hotchpotch it is claimed that mashing is a sin – everything should be thoroughly stirred but certainly not mashed. Herein lies the subtle difference between a hotchpotch and a mishmash...

The rib of beef used (thin flank) in this dish is really only known from Leiden hotchpotch. The meat, taken from the chest of the animal, has the reputation of being rather fatty. This conception, however, dates from the time when cattle were slaughtered at quite an advanced age and were much fatter than today's animals. And thus do calories fall by the wayside, even in traditional cookery.

Big, square, light...and definitely not for breakfast
Brussels waffles (*Brusselse wafels* or *gauffres de Bruxelles*)

Waffles are a Belgian culinary speciality that is eaten straight, or covered with sugar, whipped cream, chocolate,... Every part of Belgium has its own recipe, though the basic ingredients (flour, milk, sugar and eggs) are the same everywhere.

The word 'waffle' comes from the Frankish and actually means 'honeycomb'. Nowadays, it is the term used for every kind of mixture baked in a waffle-iron. The most famous Belgian waffle is, without a doubt, the Brussels waffle. It is big, square and very light – and it is eaten hot.

Ingredients
250g (9 oz) butter, 10 eggs, 500ml (1pt) water, 500ml (1pt) milk, 50g (2oz) yeast, 1kg (2¼lb) flour, salt

Preparation
Melt the butter without allowing it to brown. Then allow it to cool slightly. Break the eggs and separate the yolks from the whites. Gently beat the yolks into the warm butter. Warm the water and milk together. Dissolve the yeast in some lukewarm milk and stir well. Mix the egg-yolk and butter mixture with the water and milk. Then add the flour, along with a pinch of salt. Mix all together to form an elastic dough and then add the dissolved yeast. Leave the dough in a warm place to rise for about 30 minutes. Whip the egg whites until stiff and fold into the risen dough. Heat the waffle-iron until it is really hot. Smear it with butter before baking the first waffle, spoon a portion of dough into it and bake on both sides. The waffles can be sprinkled with powdered sugar, or spread with whipped cream, butter or jam.

The Brussels waffle is not only prepared in the home but is also available 'on the hoof'. The shopping-streets of the big cities, and the Belgian coast as well, are swarming with waffle-sellers. Some Americans even eat Belgian waffles for breakfast. When in the run-up to the American-British invasion of Iraq in 2003 *French fries* suddenly became *freedom fries* in various places, Francis Deblauwe – a Fleming who lives and works in the US – wrote 'a satirical elaboration on the anti-French backlash on Capitol Hill as it would pertain to Belgian foods': '*Citizens, I beseech you! Due to the unfortunate disagreement between your and my governments regarding Saddam Hussein Murder Inc., my native country's reputation is on the line. Yes, I admit it: I am a native of the smallest member of what some of the greatest minds in this country call the "Axis of Weasel," a.k.a. France, Russia, Germany & Belgium. But let me give you some concrete examples of the unfortunate turn of events that pains me so. Consumption of Belgian waffles is at risk, potentially dooming breakfast to the drudgery of chasing cereal flakes in your milk. Of course, real Belgian waffles' dough is prepared with yeast so that the waffle bits enter your mouth fluffy and light. They are eaten as a dessert, with powdered sugar, whipped cream or strawberries.*'

Translated by John Irons

A dish best served cold
Rusk with aniseed comfits (*beschuit met muisjes*)

As early as the seventeenth century, rusks with aniseed comfits were given to people visiting new mothers in the Netherlands. Pink comfits for a girl and white for a boy. Later, the white seeds were replaced by blue ones. The rusks used are round, flat rolls that have been baked twice, which makes them crispy and somewhat fragile. The sugared aniseed comfits are called 'little mice' (*muisjes*) in Dutch.

Ingredients
1 roll rusks, 1 packet (dairy) butter, 1 packet aniseed comfits

Preparation
Spread the rusks liberally with butter. Sprinkle the comfits on them and serve on attractive small plates.

Even the most hamfisted cook can manage a rusk with comfits. And anyone who after a couple of tries is ready for a challenge can even try out a variant – the big rusk with marshmallow mice. To do this you need a pastry flan case, butter and a packet of sweets shaped like real mice. Spread a little butter on the flan case and sprinkle with the comfits. Result: a very big rusk with comfits. Then lay the marshmallow mice on this big rusk with their noses pointing inwards. One has to admit that this looks a lot more sophisticated than a run-of-the-mill rusk with comfits!

It's a Matter of Awareness

An Extract from Hermans Brusselmans' *Diary of a Weary Egoist*

Today I smoked about sixty cigarettes, I think – well, probably a few more.
Exactly how many, I don't know. Since the day I smoked exactly sixty-four (the
seventh of January 1987), I've given up counting.

I don't count the drink any more either. I've no trouble remembering that.

For instance, today I've drunk six pils, three Trappists and four whiskies –
a really moderate amount, all told.

And besides, a nephew of mine knocked over one of the Trappists when the
glass was still more than half full. The kid looked at me in panic after he'd done
it but I persuaded him, and so did his father (he's my brother), that it really
wasn't a major disaster.

Someone who's only just started his Hundred Years' War should be caused as
little panic as possible.

Later on they'll get a rifle butt on the back of the head or a bayonet in the guts
for a lot less than a spilled Trappist.

(...)

I inherited all that boozin' from my grandfather, I guess.

Or maybe not. What has my old grandfather got to do with my boozin'? Besides, he died when I was seven – drank himself to death. He used to come home
legless and my grandmother (they lived at our place – they had two little rooms
of their own) would take off his boots sweet as pie. Then she'd whack him over
the head with them, furious that he'd come home drunk yet again. I'll never
forget the scene, especially because of the boots. I wrote all about it in that story
'When I'm drunk, I meditate'. One day my grandmother stuck his footwear in
the oven and then turned it up full blast. I can still vividly recall those burning
boots – particularly the smell .

My grandfather would sit there smiling and nodding away in his armchair, even
that time when the smoke from the burning leather began seeping through the
cracks in the oven casing.

He never got aggressive when he was drunk, like I do. I think that he boozed
because he liked the taste of it and not because he wanted to smother angst or
some such murderous feeling about life.

To those other murderous feelings about life we can also add, as you well know: an awareness of the pointlessness of everything that exists, an awareness of the pointlessness of everything that doesn't exist but could have existed (an awareness of the pointlessness of the reasons, in so far as they are thinkable, why they don't exist), an awareness of the certainty that we consist of 80% water and 19% chance. An awareness of the fact that, after all is said and done, that 19% chance has nothing, zero, nix to do with who in the world your grandfather was or whether, in the event that you are or are not one yourself – whether he was a boozer too, to mention just one thing for starters.

It's a matter of awareness – that much is clear. It's a matter of questions (that should never have been asked in the first place because the answers are already known in advance, and despite that they make no difference to the pointlessness of the questions, among other things) and it's a matter of answers (which are in much the same sorry state, as far as I can tell)

(...)

Pukin' – now that's something I can tell you a story or two about. All my life I've been a puker of the purest water. Of other substances as well, but what I mean is even if there's nothing else but pure water in my body, the chances are I'll puke it up .

As a child, when I ate two eggs and my father flew into a temper, I'd puke up the eggs. 'It's the eggs that caused it', said the doctor, 'that child has a weak liver.' Of course it was because of all those eggs and my liver. Have you ever heard me claiming it was my father's bouts of rage that caused it? They never made me puke; they made me hide under the table, and not always even that. (Sometimes he'd already thrown the table out into the farmyard).

The importance of my father's wrath is lost on me, particularly when it comes to puking and eggs and chocolate. (Oranges didn't agree with me either, despite all those vitamins). Anyway, my father sometimes forgot his temper when one of his kids started puking – especially when my brother puked, because, Jesus, he was a dab hand at it too. He had an even weaker liver than me. Even today, he sometimes turns all yellow after a night on the booze. Not long ago I saw him stretched out on the sofa nursing a hangover the size of a house, furious with himself and the whole world beside. His son – my nephew – went over and stroked his hair gently. My brother smiled. The picture – I was part of that still life – reminded me of how my father used to stroke his sons' hair when they were sick, which was their own fault (an egg too many), and of how we too would smile. The pictures don't match exactly, I know. It's a comparison taken from a side street of 'the child is father to the man' or something of that order – such a beautiful phrase but for the rest total bullshit.

Yeah, in retrospect it's all just literature.

From *Diary of a Weary Egoist* (Dagboek van een vermoeide egoïst).
Originally published in 1989 by Bert Bakker. To be republished by Prometheus, Amsterdam. (here taken from *Cold of You* (Koud van jou, Amsterdam: Ooievaar, 1999; pp. 305-317)).
Translated by Peter Flynn

Miriam Van hee (1952-)

The Frugal Meal

Under the dining-table lamp
we eat in silence, our hands
toing and froing like white spots;
our ringed fingers playing
aimlessly with the familiar bread.

No joy nothing unusual
is there in the sound of
our knives and forks.

And naturally we know nothing
of the happiness of travellers
in an evening train.

Het karige maal

Onder de lamp aan tafel
zwijgend eten wij; onze handen
als witte vlekken komen en gaan;
onze beringde vingers achteloos
met het vertrouwde brood spelend.

Geen vreugde niets ongewoons
is er in de klank van onze
messen en vorken.

En natuurlijk weten we niets
van het geluk van reizigers
in een avondtrein.

Translated by John Irons

From *The Link between the Days* (Het verband tussen de dagen). Amsterdam: De Bezige Bij, 1998.

Luuk Gruwez (1953-)

Translated by Ria Loohuizen

Fat People II

They can play such silly games with their flesh
that preys on cotton candy or on gingerbread,
up to their last kilo of ridicule
searching for all the sweets of love.

Their body is not their own.
Each small surplus is a great lack.
But if they strip the rind off of their soul,
they remain wrapped up in their fat

that they can never do without:
as if with belly and with buttocks
they are not more than normally endowed
and want to keep it that way.

For each farewell weighs heavily.
Who will be there with generous applause
when later on they go posthaste
down the slide into the grave?

From *Riotous Poems* (Bandeloze gedichten).
Amsterdam: De Arbeiderspers, 2000.

Dikke mensen II

Zij kunnen zich zo dwaas vermaken met hun vlees
dat aast op suikerspin of speculaas,
tot in hun laatste kilo ridicuul
op zoek naar al het zoets der liefde.

Hun lichaam is het hunne niet.
Elk klein teveel is groot gemis.
Maar stropen zij het zwoerd af van hun ziel,
zij blijven ingeduffeld in hun vet

dat zij nooit ontberen kunnen:
alsof zij slechts van buik en billen
niet al te onbemiddeld willen zijn
en enkel dat behouden willen.

Want ieder afscheid weegt hun zwaar.
Wie staat er klaar met gul applaus
wanneer zij straks in aller ijl
de glijbaan naar het graf afgaan?

*All poems were lifted from
the pantry by Anton Korteweg*

Attributed to Carel Fabritius,
The Slaughtered Ox. c.1642-1643.
Panel, 73,5 x 51,4 cm.
Glasgow Museums: Kelvingrove
Art Gallery and Museum,
Mrs. John Graham-Gilbert Bequest, 1877.

I didn't know about the Holocaust then

Growing Up in Holland

[IAN BURUMA]

This is the text of the second *Ons Erfdeel* lecture, given by writer Ian Buruma at De Balie in Amsterdam on 16 September 2004.

I cannot remember the first time I became aware of the Holocaust, but it was certainly before I ever heard, let alone used that word. There must have been hints, snippets of overheard adult conversation that could have alerted me as a child to the Jewish catastrophe. But since I knew little of such things, indeed barely knew what a Jew was, I did not pick up on any of this until later.

Any vague awareness I might have had of the Nazi genocide was suddenly sharpened in the mid-1960s, when I took a book about the Eichmann trial from my father's shelf; it was *The 40/61 Case* (De zaak 40/61, 1962), by Harry Mulisch. I remember the shock of reading about hitherto unimaginable cruelty. I also remember a certain pornographic *frisson*, which is the disturbing by-product of this kind of literature. Perhaps I was a little late in my Holocaust-awareness, but I don't think so. Before the Eichmann trial, the Holocaust was not much discussed. The stunned but also guilty silence had taken time to break. There was Anne Frank, of course, whose diary came out in the 1950s, but the full impact of her story took a little longer to be universally felt.

The war, however, was omnipresent when I grew up. I was born at the end of 1951, too late to experience the war, but too soon to escape from its shadows. At my primary school, a private institution in The Hague, I became aware of certain taboos concerning the recent past. Without quite explaining why, our headmaster impressed on us that we were never to draw a swastika. Since I enjoyed drawing pictures of war, and most of the wartime pictures I had seen included swastikas, this didn't make a lot of sense. The fact that the swastika was 'very bad' and would make people 'feel very sad' only made it more alluring. Perhaps there was mention of the Jews. If so, I don't remember. In any case, I was reprimanded on several occasions for defying the headmaster's prohibition.

The headmaster was rather an ineffectual man with a taste for feeble jokes. But the war, for whatever reason, had left a great mark on him. On the 4th of May he invariably made a solemn speech, and then marched at the head of the silent procession into the dunes of Scheveningen – the former Nazi execution

Photo by Cas Oorthuys.

ground. The war, for me, will always be associated with those dunes, and the three-minute silence that still in those days turned the whole country mute. (Hapless German tourists, unaware of this annual occasion, were often treated harshly; there were stories of German cars being overturned. I rather suspect that we were supposed to feel proud of these belated acts of anti-German re-sistance.)

There were other taboos. We knew where not to buy our meat. The butcher nearest to our house was rumoured to have been a member of the Dutch Nazi party, the NSB. And the rather sour-faced, buxom lady who ran the chemist's on the corner of our street was also shunned. She had 'gone out' with German soldiers. Or so it was whispered in the neighbourhood.

If our headmaster was discreet about his role during the German occupation, other adults, including most of our teachers, were less reticent. Almost everyone had a story about some petty gesture of defiance, always recounted with a proud grin: sending a German soldier the wrong way, and other things of that kind. We were taught anti-German songs and anti-German jokes, which had circulated for so long that they were creaking with age. And then there were the books, the adventure stories.

I devoured them, those fictional chronicles of brave young resistance heroes who crossed the North Sea to England in rowing boats or fought the Gestapo with Sten-guns dropped from Allied planes. Much was made of the Hunger Winter of 1944, of making do with barely edible tulip bulbs and stinging-nettle soup. We got the impression that no people could possibly have suffered so terribly under the Nazi heel as the Dutch, and no people resisted so bravely. That was the picture drawn in the stories of K. Norel and others who specialised in this genre.

A cartoon by Heiko Sakurai (1998), showing a German couple on a Dutch beach. The sign says: 'This section is German-occupied'. The woman remarks: 'And you think that this won't be misinterpreted?' To which her husband replies: 'Hell! Even the Dutchies have some sense of humour'.

It is often said that the Dutch like to make absolute distinctions between those who were 'goed' or 'fout', between goodies and baddies. This may no longer be true. It was certainly the case when I grew up. All the people I knew were, as far as I was told, goed. Later, when I knew more, various shades of grey crept into this rather hard-edged picture. The other thing I was made aware of early on was an element of commercially inspired opportunism in my fellow countrymen, often coupled with self-righteousness. My mother, who was British, would get annoyed with the ubiquitous signs saying 'Zimmer frei', rooms vacant, which hung by the doors of cheap boarding houses along the coast, trying to attract the German tourists who would often be treated rudely by the same people who were fleecing them.

All this, however, as far as my own consciousness was concerned, was pre-Holocaust. Jews were not mentioned in my favourite books by K. Norel. In fact,

I later found out that he did mention them in at least one of his works, entitled *To Drive out Tyranny* (De tyrannie verdrijven), published in 1947: *'The Jews did nothing to resist the pogroms. This lack of resistance is not surprising. The Jews may be no heroes, but they are certainly crafty. Not until the Nazis began to stretch grasping hands towards their money and personal property did they wake up. And with a vengeance. With enormous cunning and at a cost of countless millions they removed themselves from the enemy's clutches.'* According to Chris van der Heijden, in whose book *Grey Past* (Grijs verleden, 2001) the quote appears, this kind of thing was not at all unusual in the early post-war years, when a disturbing amount of Nazi propaganda had stuck to the Dutch, as it were.

It is easy, however, to exaggerate this for the sake of polemics. It is true that the small number of Jews who returned to Holland from the Nazi death camps, were sometimes less than welcome. Some found their old homes occupied by strangers who refused to move out. Many found that their possessions, given to friends or neighbours for safekeeping, had disappeared. And as Van der Heijden writes: *'Not only was there little or no concern for the suffering of the Jews, they were even criticised for complaining. A classic example is the bicycle comparison: the Jewish tale of the concentration or extermination camp interrupted by the comment that the Germans had taken the hearer's bike, that badge of Dutch citizenship. "Think yourself lucky you weren't here", Rita Koopman was told when she went to fetch her fur coat. And she did actually get it back, which wasn't always the case – far from it.'*

But this kind of thing happened in every European country that had been occupied by the Germans. In France, the unique nature of Jewish victimhood was disguised by General de Gaulle' s official pretence that all French had been equal in their suffering under and resistance to the Nazis. In Holland, it must be emphasised, anti-semitism was never murderous, and was indeed less vicious and less wide-spread than in France, for example. That nonetheless far more Dutch Jews, relatively speaking, were murdered than Belgian, French, or even German Jews does require explanation, but Dutch anti-semitism cannot have been the main reason.

Various theories have been put forward. One is the lack of mountainous regions in Holland, where people could be more easily hidden. It is indeed difficult to hide in a small, flat country, but this did not prevent a large number of non-Jewish men from going underground to avoid the *Arbeitseinsatz* in Germany. Another possible reason is the fact that Holland was put under German civil administration. There was no Dutch government or monarchy that could have tempered German policies, as happened in Denmark. The Queen was in London. There was not much she could have done to save her Jewish subjects, to be sure, but she hardly even mentioned their plight.

Perhaps it was the peculiarly law-abiding nature of the Dutch population, including the Jews, characteristic of a very bourgeois society which had been spared the terrors of war and revolution for hundreds of years. This is van der Heijden's main explanation, and I find it plausible. People were used to following rules, doing what they were told by the authorities, even when those authorities wore German uniforms. Adolf Eichmann remarked to a Dutch SS man: *'In the Netherlands the transports ran so smoothly that it was pleasure to see.'* And it must be said that Dutch officialdom, not for reasons of anti-semitism but out of a sheer sense of bureaucratic duty, did everything to assist the German in their murderous endeavour.

Given that 75% of Dutch Jews failed to survive the war, there was a surprisingly large number of Jews in my school. Some had Sephardic names, such as Mendes de Leon. The reason why my rather snooty private school should have had more Jewish pupils than, say, less privileged state schools in Amsterdam, was a direct result of the Holocaust. Poor Jews, with no connections in the Gentile world, had almost all perished. The survivors would tend to have been assimilated, well off, even in some cases rather grand; the kind of people, in other words, who would have sent their children to snooty private schools in The Hague.

As a sideline to this it might be mentioned that the Dutch tendency to form clubs had something to do with the fate of the Jews as well. Simon Kuper, in *Football against the Enemy* (2003), his superb study of the top football club Ajax during and after the war, points out that the primary social identification for most Dutch citizens before and during the war was with clubs or associations of one kind or another. The club, often with a religious affiliation, was where one grew up, met one's marriage partner, sent one's own children, and so forth. For example, middle-class Jews who were members of Ajax were regarded first and foremost as 'Ajacieden' and were sometimes able to survive because of that.

As a further sideline, I would like to mention a story I heard not long ago from a friend in London, who ran into a uneducated youth whose opinion on the Jews was as crude as it was uninformed. You should know that Tottenham Hotspur, or Spurs, the famous club in North London, is commonly known as the Jewish club, or the Yids. When the young lout spouted some stupid anti-semitic cliché, my friend told him that before he went on, he ought to know that he, my friend, happened to be Jewish. 'But that's impossible', cried the football fan, 'you' re not a Spurs supporter.'

Even though I can't recall precisely when I became aware of the Holocaust, I do have a distinct memory of becoming aware of my own provenance. I must have been about nine or ten. Behind our block of houses lived a family named Bloch. There were two sons, who kept to themselves, but were physically rather intimidating; large and with the sturdy build of rugby players or boxers. They were a few years older than me. One day a boy who lived next door to us, and knew a little more of the world than the rest of us, whispered, as though it were some sexual secret, that the Blochs were 'Jews'. At home that evening, I relayed this piece of adult information to my parents. My mother smiled and said: 'But don't you know that I am Jewish too?'

It was like learning a new word, which then suddenly turns up on every page. Now old family conversations came back to me and began to make sense. My British grandmother's fondness for 'Jewish geography': Is he...? Is she...? My uncle's obsession with Nazi crimes. My aunt's conversations about being an 'outsider' and 'feeling inferior.' The family stories about twelve Jewish children from Berlin rescued at the last minute by my grandfather who brought them to London and established a home for them. The presence of Dick Levy, a distant German relative, who came over to England as a child during the 1930s, and was bullied at school – not because he was Jewish, but because he was German. The story of Martin, another relative who lived in Holland, whose yearly birthday greetings to my uncle suddenly stopped in 1943. Martin was crippled, but he, too, had disappeared in his wheelchair into the night and fog of the death camps.

My mother's family was much like the families of my Jewish classmates, that is, as assimilated as they could possibly manage. Religion and tradition played no part in my mother's life. Jewishness was a private matter, of family jokes and coded insecurities. A sign of their assimilated Jewishness was the zeal with which they celebrated Christmas. Of solid bourgeois Anglo-German-Jewish stock, my family were such committed Wagnerians that, despite everything that had happened, despite all the relations lost, despite the hostel children, despite Martin, when Bayreuth reopened for business for the first time after the war, the Schlesingers were there.

The irony here is that Wagner's music could not be publicly performed in Holland until much later. It is probably true to say that Dutch Gentile feelings about Germany were at least as complicated as Jewish sentiments about that country, if not more so. The Jews in occupied Holland, like everywhere else in Europe, were victims pure and simple. In the case of Dutch Gentiles reality was a bit more ambiguous, something with which many have yet to come to terms.

My mother, despite her love of Wagner's operas, was not keen on Germany. My father, who had been forced to work in a German factory in the *Arbeitseinsatz*, and lived through the Battle of Berlin to be liberated by the Soviet Red Army, was no Germanophile either. We did not go to Germany for family holidays, and neither did any of my classmates. This was partly a matter of climate. In the 1960s, the Dutch upper-middle class headed south. It was also a matter of class. The Dutch bourgeoisie, especially in the coastal cities, tended to be anglophile. Men wore blue blazers and club ties. Some even played cricket.

The lower-middle classes in Holland, to the extent they could afford it, were more likely to choose Germany as a holiday destination. This was particularly true of those who lived in the east, near the German border. And before the Beatles swept all that away, the appeal of German pop songs and German movie stars lingered among the less anglophile, or indeed anglophone Dutch. In fact, even I can remember the sugary voice of Connie Froboess in my own childhood. These regional and class distinctions had a history which the Nazi propagandists had tried to exploit.

Curing the Dutch

Some years ago I picked up a book in a second-hand bookshop in Amsterdam. Entitled *Face of the Netherlands* (Das Gesicht der Niederlände), it was published in 1940 and had been commissioned by Arthur Seyss-Inquart, Reichskommisar of the Netherlands during the German occupation. This picture book, filled with illustrations of industrious farmers in traditional clothes, of canals and churches, cheese markets and the like, was meant to entertain and enlighten Germans serving in the Netherlands. The text, written by Ernst Leutheusser, an SS officer, is interesting because it conforms to certain Dutch as well as German prejudices of the time.

The Netherlands, says Leutheusser, was traditionally an agrarian country, whose Germanic people were firmly rooted in European soil; in terms of culture and customs they looked east, towards their racial brethren in Germany. Alas, however, in the course of the seventeenth century Holland became gradually estranged from its roots. Merchants in the coastal cities, in their hunger for profit, began to look west, towards England and beyond. This deracinated part of the Netherlands became, as the author put it, 'Jewified' (*verjudet*). The meaning was not just literal, in the sense of 'Jewish power', or some such myth. Jewified Holland was poisoned by alien ideas, such as liberalism and democracy. These, as much as the actual presence of Jews, were the sources of rootless

The thin line between Dutch and German, Hollywood-style: the son of a celebrated Dutch actor and a French countess, John van Dreelen (foreground; 1922-1992) was reported to have escaped a concentration camp in Nazi-occupied Holland by disguising himself as one of the German officers he would later play so often on both big and small screens. Here, in *Von Ryan's express* (1965) he is a German colonel hot on the tail of escaped POW Frank Sinatra.

cosmopolitanism. It was the task of the German occupiers to cure the Dutch of these ills and take them back to their true roots.

This kind of stuff from an SS propagandist was hardly surprising. What many Dutch people chose to forget, however, until young historians began to dig deeper into the past, is that such views were shared by a surprising number of Dutch intellectuals who cannot simply be dismissed as opportunists or thugs. Few Dutchmen were infected by murderous anti-semitism, to be sure, and unlike France the Netherlands did not have a tradition of reactionary extremism. But mild anti-semitism coupled to a deep distrust of liberal democracy was not uncommon. 'Americanism' was the usual phrase to describe what such people detested. Some even viewed the German occupation as an opportunity to cleanse the stables, as it were, and establish a more authoritarian, more 'European' order.

The NSB leader, Anton Mussert, was a patriot of this kind. To accuse him of opportunism is to miss the point. He was an idealist, who wanted the Netherlands to be an autonomous fascist state in a new European order dominated by Germany. Although doubtless no friend of the Jews, his mission certainly did not include their extermination. He regarded 'the Jewish question' as a peculiarly German affair.

Mussert, though quite well-educated, could not be described as an intellectual. But such figures as Hendrik Krekel and the professor of archeology G.A.S. Snijder certainly were. Their pro-German fascistic opinions may not have been in the mainstream, but in the 1930s they were highly regarded figures, who wrote for respectable publications. What they believed was not far removed from Leutheusser's crude thesis. Krekel blamed the merchant spirit of the Dutch bourgeoisie for destroying the 'higher vision' of a Germanic community bound together by blood. Erasmus, as the despicable promoter of humanism, was a villain. Internationalism had sapped not just the Netherlands but Germany too of their vital racial energy. Open societies are decadent and weak, and so on and on.

Professor Snijder drew a straight line from the ancient Greeks to the Germanic race. The rot set in with the French Revolution, and then Americanism, with its machine-like materialism and soulless individualism, destroyed all sense of community in Europe. The Netherlands could only regain its vitality by becoming part of the German Reich. Again, these were not mainstream ideas even in the 1930s. But they played into the widespread disillusion with democracy, shared by prominent pre-war politicians and other notables.

The cool of Jewishness

I grew up in what Leutheusser would no doubt have described as Jewified circles. The Hague was very much part of the liberal western seaboard. And though the anglophile liberalism of the Dutch bourgeoisie was not new, bad memories of authoritarian, Germanic race theories must surely have strengthened it. Britain, France, and America were hugely admired. Germany was not. Most Dutch people were not anglophile liberals, however. The Netherlands in the 1950s was still a very provincial society, whose obedient citizens' main loyalties lay with their religious affiliations. This began to change in the 1960s, along with the increasing willingness to examine the recent past. Not everything about the past, to be sure. And not everyone was equally willing. I remember the fury of my history teacher when the socialist broadcasting organisation VARA broadcast a programme exposing Dutch brutality in colonial Indonesia. But then he was not exactly in the mainstream himself. A former NSB man, he had become an ardent admirer of South Africa's Apartheid system and distributed journals with such titles as *Suid Afrika* in the classroom. Still, the fact that he was able to do so, even in the 1960s, shows how much Holland has changed since then.

By the mid-1960s the Eichmann Trial, Anne Frank, The Beatles, and the emergence of a less obedient, more secular post-war generation had changed the cultural and intellectual climate of the Netherlands profoundly. In a sense, the whole country became more anglicised, or Americanised, and more libertarian. Anti-German attitudes merged with youth rebellion against the paternalism, or what was known as the 'repressive tolerance', of the Dutch authorities. Amsterdam was the centre of protest and the most symbolic event was the marriage, in 1965, of Princess Beatrix to Claus von Amsberg, who was said to have been in the Hitler Youth. This provoked street riots that shrouded the royal Golden Coach and much of the city centre in smoke. It was puerile, and deeply unfair to Prince Claus, who was anything but a Nazi, but it was symptomatic of the general climate of rebellion.

The 1974 World Cup final
in Munich: old enemies
meet again.
Photo by Cor Mooij.

And that, too, was precisely the time when the fate of the Jews was finally discussed in detail. Jacques Presser's book *Destruction* (De ondergang) came out in 1965 and became a huge bestseller. In a peculiar way, the fate of the Jews in Holland began to be associated more and more with the fate of the whole country during the war. Jewish victimhood was Dutch victimhood. Anne Frank might be said to have let the Dutch, who mostly looked the other way when she and roughly one hundred thousand other Jews were loaded into the cattle trucks bound for the east, off the hook.

It became rather fashionable to be Jewish or associated with Jewishness. The Dutch cultivated their somewhat fraudulent image of brave philosemitism. This image went down well in Israel, and for many years Israel could count the Netherlands as its greatest friend. Philosemitism could take some peculiar forms. Ajax fans wrapped themselves in the Star of David, harking back to pre-war Amsterdam when many middle-class Jews had been members of Ajax. Even some of the players, including Gentiles, took pride in a Jewish identification. These were the days of Johan Cruyff, Johan Neeskens, and Bennie Muller.

The culmination of this was the 1974 World Cup final in Munich, when Holland played Germany. To many people in the Netherlands, and indeed in Israel, this was more than a football game. It was as though the Dutch finally had their chance to do what they had failed to do more than thirty years earlier: beat the Germans. But it was not only a test of national virility, a show of a quiet bourgeois people being uncharacteristically brave and combative. In the Dutch media, and among the fans, the contest was presented as one between a liberal, tolerant, cosmopolitan nation, and a rigid, authoritarian, racist one. There was a distinct echo of Ernst Leutheusser's *Gesicht der Niederlande*: the Jewified Dutch against the blood-and-soil Germans. Holland lost. But this clash of civilisations could still be described as the victory of ruthless German efficiency over the liberated artistry of the plucky Dutch.

Much has changed since 1974. The Germans were finally beaten at soccer in 1988, unleashing one of the greatest national celebrations since liberation in 1945. And even though fewer and fewer Dutch people bother to learn German (there are more German students of Dutch literature than Dutch students of German – an astonishing and rather shameful statistic), the old Nazi image of Germany is beginning to be replaced by something more positive. It used to be true – and to some extent perhaps still is – that most Dutch people had an image of Germany that was, in the words of M.C. Brands, *'the negative'* of *'the image that the Dutch cherish of themselves'*. *'Typical German'* was used for *'qualities... with which the Dutch do not wish to be associated'*.

Brands might have mentioned the opposite phenomenon in Germany, where Dutch writers have enjoyed huge success over the last ten years or so; partly, I suspect, because many Germans had the illusion that Holland represented a kind of better version of Germany – basically the same culture, but more liberal, more liberated. But in Holland at least these stereotypes might be fading. Berlin is 'cooler' now than Amsterdam. At the same time open manifestations of Dutch discrimination – against Turks, blacks, and Moroccans – and the sudden popularity of Pim Fortuyn, have somewhat dented the flattering self-image of world-beating tolerance.

Philosemitism and the love of Israel have also gone out of fashion, though Ajax fans still take pride in being identified by their opponents as 'the Jews'. Anne Frank, from being a Jewish, and then a Dutch symbol of victimhood, has now become a patron saint of all victims, a sacred symbol of universal oppression and discrimination, used in schools as a parable in teaching social studies. This is what her father, Otto, would have wanted. It also suits those who would prefer to forget the Dutch role in what happened to the Jews. It is, however, at the very least ahistorical.

We all carry our background with us, wherever we go. I am still an Ajax fan, and proud to be Jewified. Yet I like to think that the anti-German prejudices I grew up with have worn away with time. And although I am sure anti-semitism will never go away completely, I did not see much of it in Germany. The rawest echoes of the murderous language that turned millions of innocent people into victims did not reach me in Munich or Berlin but in Amsterdam, one afternoon in the 1990s, at the Olympic Stadium, where Ajax was playing Feyenoord.

On the Ajax side of the stadium was a sea of Israeli flags. On the other side, a sea of red and white. By some hideous mistake, I had been given tickets for the wrong side, and found myself in the midst of men screaming 'filthy Jewish scum!' I do not believe there was one Jew playing in the Ajax team. Nonetheless, every time an Ajax player – as like as not a black from Suriname – touched the ball, he would be taunted with cries of 'dirty Jew!' or 'Jewish swine!' It was all very, very unpleasant. The worst thing was the venomous hissing of people mimicking the sound of gas. I thought of myself, in the first form of primary school in the mid-1950s, and of my compulsion to draw swastikas because I knew it annoyed my headmaster. I didn't know about the Holocaust then. I looked around me at the screaming fans, baying for Jewish blood in the stadium, and did not know whether it was a comfort to believe that neither did they. ∎

Problems of Digestion

The Memory of the Second World War in Flanders

[MARTIN CONWAY]

The Second World War in Flanders, in the influential formulation of the Leuven sociologist Luc Huyse, is *'an undigested past'*. The metaphor of digestion is a seductive one. In particular, it captures the sense in which the events of the war and its aftermath have seemed doomed to recur in public life and politics in Flanders over the sixty years which have elapsed since the events themselves. The war is indeed a very long way away. As far, for example, as were the revolutions of 1848 when the First World War broke out in 1914. Flanders, moreover, has been transformed in the intervening decades. Almost nowhere else in north-western Europe was the pace of economic, political and above all cultural change so rapid during the second half of the twentieth century. The traditional Flanders of bell-towers, small farms and predominantly Catholic values idealised by innumerable writers and painters of the early twentieth century has almost literally disappeared under the concrete and tarmac of technological industries, new roads and out-of-town shopping centres. In that sense, the war years *ought* to be as distant from the secular, pluralist and multi-cultural Flanders of today as, say, the civil war tangibly is from the politics of twenty-first-century Spain.

The public and private worlds of memory

But at almost every turn in the uncertain political evolution of Flanders over recent decades, issues associated with the war have reasserted themselves. The campaigns for an amnesty for those convicted of acts of wartime collaboration have been joined by disputes over the responsibility of the communal police of Antwerp in Jewish deportations and, more bizarrely, by the posthumous retrial in 1995-1996 of a Flemish woman, Irma Laplasse, executed after the war after having been found guilty by a Belgian military court of having denounced local Resistance fighters to the German army in the final moments of the Occupation. These and other issues have ensured that the war, and more especially its legacies in terms of the stern penalties imposed by the post-war Belgian authorities for acts of collaboration, has retained its centrality in public debate and private memory. It is perhaps this double-edged character of the war that provides part

German propaganda
photo taken after the
capitulation of the
Belgian army in
May 1940.

of the explanation of its durability. The war was never solely the subject matter of political campaigns and newspaper articles. Instead it rapidly became, and despite all the intervening upheavals has remained, the central point of reference for the private world of family memory. Perhaps teenage children do occasionally ask their parents (as indeed they should) what they did in the Marches on Brussels for linguistic equality during the 1960s or the student demonstrations in Leuven of the late 1960s and early 1970s. But one suspects that much more frequently the question asked is what more distant generations (the large majority of whom are, of course, now dead) did in the war. Flanders is, in that sense, a society well equipped to maintain long memories. The obstinate rootedness of Flemish life which manifests itself in the lack of geographical mobility and the consequent durability of local memories makes it easy for most Flemish people to retain a coherent sense of what their family did, and more especially which side they were on, during the war.

Belgium as history

HET NATIONAALSOCIALISTISCHE ZWAARD
BESCHERMT ONS TEGEN HET BOLSJEVISME

A poster promoting fascist bliss to the Flemish population: the Sword of National Socialism protects against Bolshevism.

And yet this cannot be the whole explanation. The Second World War is not a ghost that haunts the minds of most contemporary Europeans. In almost every European society, including in recent years those that have emerged from the constraints of Communist rule, there have been a plethora of discussions and re-examinations of wartime issues. The age of individual silence and the collective taboo has in this sense long since passed. But in most of these societies there is a clear sense that what is being discussed is indeed the past. In Belgium, in contrast, the war and its immediate aftermath remains an element of the present. Much of the reason for this difference lies in the particular nature of the Belgian war experience. The Second World War in Belgium was, in the contemporary European *lingua franca* of football, a draw, but a high-scoring one. All sides scored goals (and own goals), but the deeply complex outcome of the conflict left few clear winners and losers. Between 1940 and 1950, the swings and roundabouts of political fortunes lurched this way and that with disorienting rapidity. The heroes of 1940 were the villains of 1944, and *vice versa*. The parties of the extreme right and the somewhat motley collection of New Order figures who replaced the pre-war political elite in 1940 were, four years later, the vilified objects of patriotic hostility. The Communists, persecuted by Belgian and German authorities alike between 1939 and 1944, emerged triumphant after the liberation as the self-proclaimed 'party of the resistance' but by 1947 had once again been thrust to the margins of the political landscape. King Leopold III, the perceived saviour of the martyred nation in the aftermath of the German invasion in 1940, was obliged to promise to abdicate in the summer of 1950 despite winning a passionately contested referendum on his position a few months earlier. The three 'historic' parties, the Catholics, Socialists and Liberals, appeared to have been the principal losers of the war. Discredited by their responsibility for the military defeat in 1940 and dislodged from their positions of power and patronage within occupied Belgium, the government-in-exile they established in London won them Allied backing but only limited public support at home. In the months following the liberation of September 1944 political collapse or even civil war seemed possible. But, through a mixture of Allied intervention, good fortune and sheer political determination, the

Catholic, Socialist and Liberal parties, purged of their more discredited figures, gradually regained their control of national life. By 1950, Belgium appeared to have been restored to its pre-war shape. Major constitutional, political or economic upheavals had been prevented and its slightly dull but conventionally democratic politicians could take their place among their West European colleagues in the similarly dull but democratic institutions of NATO and the EEC.

This strangely immobile outcome to the upheavals of the preceding decade lies at the heart of the gradual unravelling of the Belgian nation-state over the subsequent half-century. Political order had been restored, but the amalgam of political, social and regional conflicts that had driven the conflicts of the 1940s had neither disappeared nor been resolved. Consequently, unlike in most European states, the era of the Second World War is not merely a source of awkward memories; it remains a major focus for debates about the historical reality that was, and more tentatively is, Belgium. Indeed, as the nascent federal governments of Wallonia and Flanders and the structures of the European Union have erased the frontiers and institutions of the Belgian nation-state, so debates about Belgium have become inescapably concentrated on the past. The country may or may not have a present and a future, but it emphatically has a history. Therefore, to deplore, as professional historians are occasionally prone to do, the 'politicisation' of contemporary history is perhaps to invert the nature of the problem. The real issue is the way in which politics in Belgium, or more accurately politics about Belgium, have become historicised.

Sympathy for the devil

This inter-penetration of past and present, of history and politics, has followed different paths in francophone Belgium and in Flanders. In Wallonia the memory of the war years has become integrated in recent decades into a rather simplistic story of the making of a Walloon identity through resistance to the Germans, the Flemish majority and ultimately Leopold III. Thus the more awkward elements of the wartime history of southern Belgium, such as the extreme collaborationism of Léon Degrelle and his Rexist movement or the involvement of much of the administrative and economic elite in a politics of accommodation with the German occupier, have little place in the public memory. In Flanders the situation could scarcely have been more different. The engagement of a substantial proportion of the pre-war Flemish nationalist intelligentsia in the policy of pro-German collaboration espoused by the principal Flemish nationalist party, the Vlaams Nationaal Verbond (VNV), was too important to be denied. Flanders, or at least those who regarded themselves as the vanguard of the Flemish nation-in-making, had been on the 'wrong' side in the war. This awkward reality posed a particular challenge to those who, once the immediate moment of retribution at the liberation had passed, sought to rebuild a nationalist movement to carry forward Flemish demands for national, linguistic and cultural emancipation. The peculiar consequence was that the memory of the war in Flanders came to be dominated not by the victors but by the defeated. Flemish nationalism, and still more pro-German collaboration, had actively involved only a small minority within the Flemish population. Yet the experience of the war from the 1950s onwards came to be written predominantly in terms of the actions and choices of that minority. The original sins (and many others besides) in this account

VNV leader Hendrik Elias.

were Belgian, not Flemish. Denied linguistic or cultural equality by Belgium's francophone elite, the leaders of the Flemish cause had opted to work with the German occupiers after the invasion of 1940, just as some of their predecessors had chosen to do during the first German occupation of 1914-1918. In doing so, however, their motives were patriotic not treasonable. Loyalty to the Flemish nation was more important than imposed citizenship of an 'artificial' Belgian state. Moreover, once it became clear that the German occupiers were not sincere about granting independence to Flanders, the VNV led by Hendrik Elias had attempted to disengage from active collaboration. Nevertheless, after the liberation the authorities of the restored Belgian state seized upon the wartime 'crimes' of the nationalists to carry out a ruthless repression of all movements and individuals associated with the Flemish cause.

The many inadequacies of this version of the Flemish wartime experience are not difficult to demonstrate. As Bruno de Wever has documented in convincing detail in his authoritative account of the VNV, the engagement of the Flemish nationalist movement with the German cause was as much ideological as it was nationalist. The VNV, in common with many other such nationalist movements in 1930s Europe, evolved markedly towards sympathy for Nazism and espoused many of its ideological and political goals. Far from being the almost imposed consequence of Belgian oppression, the choice of collaboration was therefore the logical continuation of the party's pre-war evolution towards fascism. Definitions of fascism are notoriously flexible, and what is most important is not whether the wartime VNV with all its residual nationalist and Catholic characteristics can be fitted into an abstract template of fascism, but the local and daily reality of its collaboration with the Nazi occupier. On the Eastern Front in the armies of the *Wehrmacht* or at home in the administrative organisations and the paramilitary and police forces that worked with the German occupiers, the engagement of the Flemish nationalist movement behind the German cause was emphatic and often bloody in its consequences. Though some of course withdrew from collaboration as the fortunes of war changed, many other Flemish nationalists adopted a more extreme pro-German stance, rejecting the nationalist mentality of the VNV in favour of the pan-German extremism of its collaborationist rival DeVlag (the Duits-Vlaamse Arbeidsgemeenschap). The local mayors who had been appointed by German *Diktat* as the rulers of many Flemish villages and towns increasingly came to see themselves as an armed elite destined to impose liberation on an unwilling and uncomprehending Flemish population. Collaborators and resisters became embroiled in a cycle of violence and reprisals that in some areas such as Limburg gained a momentum of its own, largely independent of the German authorities. The global war had also become a Flemish-Flemish war. This radicalisation was as much social as it was political. Though the leadership remained dominated by the intellectuals and professional intelligentsia who had provided the historic basis of Flemish nationalism, the military and police organisations of the later war years were staffed overwhelmingly by young Flemish men (and some women) with little discernible political commitment. For these men, collaboration was a material choice imposed more by desperation than by any higher ideal.

Members of the Flemish 'Sturmbrigade Langermark' celebrating July 11 (the Flemish national holiday) at the Eastern Front.

The very partial way in which wartime collaboration came to be presented in post-war Flanders also denied a voice to those who had not followed that course. The dichotomy which developed in popular memory between a 'resistance' Wallonia and a 'collaborationist' Flanders has little basis in historical fact, and has served to disguise the fact that pro-German collaboration in Flanders was the choice of a small minority. This should not be surprising. Flanders was always a much more pluralistic society than nationalist stereotypes might suggest. The Socialist trade unions, particularly in the major industrial centres of Ghent and Antwerp, were as much an element of the fabric of the region as the Catholic youth movements of the countryside and the intellectual cadres

An ode to the Flemish *Feldfrau*. On the set of *The Vlaschaard*, a film after the well-known novel by Flemish writer Stijn Streuvels, the German photographer Otto Kropf used some local extras to make this picture.

of cultural nationalism. So too, it must be stressed, was that minority of the population of Flanders which was French-speaking. The way in which Flemish nationalism and the part-civic, part-political struggle for Dutch language rights within Belgium became fused for much of the twentieth century has created a particular difficulty in recovering the historical reality of a Flanders that encompassed not merely immigrant groups, such as the rapidly expanding Jewish community in Antwerp, but also a bourgeoisie that was Flemish in origin but francophone in language. Resistance in Flanders during the Second World War often had its origins in this minority, but support for it soon spread into large areas of Flemish society. The individual motives behind engagement in acts of resistance were complex, but the mentality was often uncomplicatedly patriotic. For most Flemish people, there was no tension between being Belgian and being Flemish; indeed, the war years and the decades that followed were in many respects the high point of a sense of 'Belgianness' that transcended linguistic and ideological frontiers.

History and the Flemish cause

The way in which the memory of the war came to be dominated by the actions of what was in many respects an unrepresentative minority owed much to the political balance of power in Flanders during the post-war era. The campaigns over Dutch language rights and the bilingual status of Brussels which gathered pace from the late 1950s onwards gave a new and more inclusive social and political character to the Flemish movement. The authoritarian and largely Catholic mentality of the 1930s and 1940s that had been focused on the achievement of an independent Flemish state was replaced by a new language of civil rights and a more flexible goal of Flemish autonomy within Belgium. Alongside this change in political ideology, however, the campaigners' definition of the legitimacy of the Flemish cause remained couched in essentially historical terms. In opposition to the language of individual freedom adopted by francophone activists in Brussels, the Flemish campaigns of the post-war decades drew heavily on history. Campaigners for the Flemish cause saw themselves as the heirs to the struggle of the Flemish people since the late nineteenth century to achieve linguistic and political equality within Belgium. The Flemish nationalism of the era before and during the Second World War formed an essential link in this 'long march' towards freedom. Thus, although there was an increasing willingness to acknowledge the crimes committed by those Flemish militants who allied themselves with Germany, this often stopped short (with a few exceptions) of a critical examination of the ideological affinities which had led those Flemish nationalists not merely to work with the German occupiers but to espouse large elements of Nazi ideology.

A new awareness

In the polarised linguistic and regional politics of the 1970s and 1980s, this essentially nationalist vision of the war experience had an evident plausibility. As Flemish politicians mobilised to demand federal devolution within the Belgian state and resist francophone pressure for changes in the language laws, it seemed all too easy to provide a historical legitimation for their cause by invoking the struggles of the past. However, with the abatement of the Belgo-Belgian constitutional wars during the 1990s the political context and consequently the perception of the war experience have changed. Concepts of Flemish 'victimhood' have lost credence and plausibility. Both economically and politically Flanders occupies a dominant position within Belgium. This change has also been reflected in the writing of contemporary history. A new generation of energetic Flemish historians unconnected personally to the events of the war years have laid the basis of a much more critical history of the Flemish movement during the twentieth century. Awkward questions have been posed and dark corners explored, while public projects such as the proposed Holocaust Museum in Mechelen demonstrate a new political will to bring a more complex history of Flanders to a wider audience.

If therefore the events of the war years have remained at the forefront of public debate over the past decade, it has been for largely new reasons. Invocations of the historic struggles of the Flemish people have been replaced by a more problematic awareness of the way that the war raises questions about attitudes

Drastic measures for collaborators: after the Liberation this 'Flemish House' was ransacked and destroyed.

within Flanders. Above all, this change has been provoked by the rapid and disconcerting rise of the Vlaams Blok in Antwerp and latterly in other Flemish cities. There are many reasons for the electoral success of this extreme-right party, most of which have absolutely nothing to do with history. Well-meaning efforts to use the events of the 1930s and 1940s to demonstrate the dangers of xenophobic rhetoric or simplistic attacks on political elites have had little impact on the Blok's basis of support. Indeed, far from demonstrating the continuity of fascist politics in Flanders, the rise of the Blok (which, after a legal dispute, changed its name to Vlaams Belang (Flemish Interest) in 2004) has served as confirmation of how profoundly Flanders has changed since the 1940s. Whatever the public, and more especially the semi-private, declarations of leading members of the party about wartime collaboration or Nazism, the sources of the party's appeal are emphatically contemporary rather than historical. But the Blok or Belang has provoked a much wider debate about the historic character of Flemish nationalism. Rather than seeing nationalism as the vehicle for the collective emancipation of the Flemish people, a new awareness has developed of how ethnic or linguistic nationalism, be it in Flanders or the Balkans, can justify intolerance in the name of a homogeneous nation.

The present's invasion of the past

Do these changes indicate that Huyse's concept of an undigested past, first formulated almost fifteen years ago, is no longer relevant? Wartime anniversaries continue to be commemorated and politicians still make intermittent and generally unwise comments on the events of the 1940s. But it is difficult to avoid the sense that the war and its legacies no longer generate the same passion. Old men do die, and in so far as the war was the central experience of a generation now reaching the end of their natural lives, so the events of that war pass from direct experience into something less tangible. Yet it would be premature to suggest that the Second World War is about to pass peacefully into history. In so far as its conflicts remain intertwined with the unfinished business of the Belgian state, they can never be far from the surface of public debate. Moreover, within Flanders there has been a shift in the terms of de-bates about the war years. What retained for a long time a burning topicality has become more a means of using the past to talk about the present. The war, and more especially the political choices made by Flemish nationalists, has become the focus for wider civic debates about the inter-relationships between nation-alism, tolerance and democratic values. The war may not have lost its promi-nence, therefore; but rather than the past invading the present, the present is now influencing perceptions of the past. ■

BIBLIOGRAPHY

The concept of an 'undigested past' is discussed in L. Huyse and S. Dhondt, *Onverwerkt verleden. Collaboratie en repressie in België 1942-1952* Leuven: Kritak, 1991. The indispensable study of the VNV is B. de Wever, *Greep naar de macht. Vlaamse nationalisme en Nieuwe Orde. Het VNV 1933-1945*. Tielt/Ghent: Lannoo/Perspectief Uitgaven, 1994. The changing patterns of Belgian national identity are discussed from different perspectives in L. Wils, *Van Clovis tot Happart. De lange weg van de naties in de Lage Landen*. Leuven/Apeldoorn: Garant, 1995, K. Deprez and L. Vos (eds.) *Nationalism in Belgium. Shifting Identities 1780-1995*. Basingstoke: Macmillan, 1998 and A. Morelli (ed.), *Les grands mythes de l'histoire de Belgique, de Flandre et de Wallonie*. Brussels: Editions Vie Ouvrière, 1995. The evolution in post-war approaches to the wartime past is analysed in J. Gotovitch and C. Kesteloot (eds.), *Het gewicht van het oorlogsverleden*. Ghent: Academia Press, 2002. The bilingual journal *Bijdragen tot de eigentijdse geschiedenis/Cahiers d'histoire du temps présent* is the principal forum for the discussion of the twentieth-century history of Belgium).

Photo by Stephan
Vanfleteren.

America: from Example to Exasperation?

[MARC DIERIKX]

'America? Miserica!' (America means misery) That, according to my family, is what Uncle William always said, though no-one wanted to believe it. Uncle William, who departed for Chicago in the early 1920s, was speaking from experience. His was a most unusual view in the Low Countries before the Second World War. America, the land of endless opportunities, far beyond the horizon, had always had a magical ring to it, the stuff of dreams. You could work your way up the ladder *'from newspaper boy to millionaire'*; or so it was claimed. How could one criticise such a society?

A recipe for success

Perceptions of America suddenly became more concrete at the end of the Second World War, when American soldiers played the leading role in the liberation of Western Europe. In just four years the United States had turned itself from a rather isolated, introverted country into a world power. Better dressed, better fed and better armed than their opponents and allies alike, in 1945 the American GI's epitomised in large numbers the perceived image of a country where everything was better.

In the quiet that followed victory on the battlefield a thick blanket of American military, political, economic, technological and cultural supremacy spread across Europe. This 'instant imperialism' was largely unintentional. And for the first time in history it was not literally enforced with weapons, though its effect was no less because of that. For those who welcomed the liberators in the Low Countries, practically everything the Americans brought with them seemed better than the local equivalent. This began at the most basic level with food and drink: for people accustomed to rationing and shortages the food packages of the American military represented luxury, the instant products they contained were symbols of progress. Those who wanted to be 'really American' went along with the imperative displayed on the huge new billboards: *'Drink Coca Cola'*. This brown beverage, first introduced to the Netherlands on the occasion of the 1928 Olympic Games in Amsterdam, acquired an almost magical aura after 1945. In May 1955 '25 years of Coca Cola in

Queen Juliana of the
Netherlands addressing
the US Congress on
3 April 1952.

Liberation, 1945: *'How to
recognise the American
soldier'*.

the Netherlands' drew large crowds to a whole parade of automobiles through Amsterdam.

America, in the second half of the forties, was the new Utopia where average income was some 15 times higher than in Europe. Between 1948 and 1952 this almost unimaginable prosperity was further underlined by the Marshall Plan, by which the United States helped to get its impoverished allies back on their feet when European reconstruction was grinding to a halt for want of dollars. In this singularly ingenious plan Washington combined generosity with self-interest. Apart from a major boost to Western European reconstruction, it also provided an important stimulus to the American export industry and strengthened American hegemony in the world. For the Netherlands and Belgium it meant that in international politics supporting America – guardian of the free Western world – was seen as a matter of course in a time of increasing tension between the new superpowers.

America emerged as a model and a fount of wisdom in many fields, the cornerstone of a society in the process of rebuilding itself. While American town planning concepts were all the rage during the reconstruction and subsequent expansion of cities, industry embraced the rational American management system. In agriculture it was the same story. Productivity became a magic word from across the Atlantic. For those who wanted to find out at first hand about all these new developments, special Washington-sponsored courses and study trips to the United States were organised. The report *Recipes from the American Industrial Kitchen* (Recepten uit de Amerikaanse industriële keuken), published in 1954 by the Contact Group for Improved Productivity (Contactgroep Opvoering Productiviteit) and comprising a synopsis of the findings of 31 study trips to the United States, set out the most important reasons for America's exemplary labour productivity. The lack of formality and encouragement of a sense of community within the company were the most important factors, followed by the higher salaries and greater range of salaries, educational standards and career opportunities. American companies offered more opportunities for social mobility. The colleague of today could be the boss of tomorrow. As a result of

Esther Williams advertising
Lux Soap to Dutch women.

the study travel programme a report finally appeared in February 1958 entitled *What will tomorrow bring? People and business in the new world* (Hoe morgen hier? Mens en bedrijf in de nieuwe wereld). It seemed obvious to everyone
which direction to take.

Rock around the clock...in silence

This sudden American dominance did not confine itself to the social sector; in
the fifties it even reached into the nursery in the family home. There *the* expert
in caring for babies and toddlers was the American paediatrician and educa-
tionalist Benjamin Spock. The first American edition of his book *The Common
Sense Book of Baby and Child Care* came out in 1946; only four years later the
Dutch translation appeared, and remained the bible of modern child-rearing
in the Netherlands and Flanders for a good two decades. America acquired an
enduring hold over the young. Through toys – even in the fifties the toy police
cars and tanks little boys chased round the living-room floor were modelled on
American types, as were the dolls and kitchen equipment girls played with – and
translated children's books and comic strips, children grew up surrounded by
American symbols. For those a little older, from the mid-fifties onwards there
was the new forceful rhythmic sound of American pop music, heralding an
American-style youth culture which quickly became more and more universal.
Variations on the originally 'black' rhythm and blues style, in which emotional
and sexual connotations went hand in hand, rose spectacularly in popularity.
And in their wake relationships among young people also underwent a radical
change. The second half of the fifties was characterised by an incredible surge
in pop music in general and rock-'n'-roll in particular. Record sales of those
musicians who made it to the top ran into millions. The undisputed winner in
the popularity stakes was Elvis Presley, who from 1956 on, curiously enough,
was managed – and kept away from the Low Countries – by the Breda-born
Dutchman Dries van Kuyk as Presley's legendary manager 'Colonel Parker'.

Parker, who had no passport and had entered the US as an illegal immigrant, kept Presley (and himself) well away from international appearances.

Parents – and adults in general – had considerable trouble with the newly imported forms of music and the enthusiasm with which the youth of the day embraced them. At the première of the musical film *Rock around the Clock* in 1956 the mayor of the Dutch town of Gouda ordered the local cinema to show the film without sound! For all that, the film industry played a significant role in the Americanisation of youth. Stars such as Jane Russell, Rita Hayworth and of course Marilyn Monroe represented the emergence of a new image of woman with a self-confident, physical aura that went well beyond the old-fashioned and outdated approach of *How to Marry a Millionaire* (1953). Hollywood presented America as exciting, dynamic. A new generation of American filmmakers succeeded in expressing their own dissatisfaction with the traditional, material interpretation of *The American Dream* to an audience of millions. New stars such as James Dean and Marlon Brando provided cinema-going youth with American role models for their rebellion against existing social norms and attitudes. In one of Brando's first box office successes, *The Wild One* from 1953, he appeared as a member of a motorcycle club clad in jeans and leather jacket, the new style in youth fashion. One crucial piece of dialogue encapsulated resistance to established norms and values. Asked *'What are you rebelling against?'* Brando snapped back: *'Wha' d'ya got?'* European youth happily embraced such examples, though there were limits to how far they could copy their American role models: for motorbikes they had at best mopeds, while in the fifties jeans were sold only as *Boys' denim trousers*. Still, the universal fascination with all things American prompted the British dramatist John Osborne to write in 1957 *'I must say it's pretty dreary living in the American Age – unless you're an American of course. Perhaps all our children will be Americans. That's a thought, isn't it?'*

The Dutch edition of Dr Spock's *Common Sense Book of Baby and Child Care* (1946).

Law and order

But things would never go quite that far. During the sixties the American image began to crumble. It didn't look like that to start with, because the rise and spread of television from the late fifties on initially brought America even closer. In the Netherlands and Flanders, money-conscious television makers embraced the relatively cheap series shown five to ten years previously in the United States. In the mid-sixties no evening of television was complete without a programme originating from America, and imported series were the most popular among the television offerings. In this way the growing numbers of television viewers had a daily portion of America served up to them via their television screens. American television imagery with its stereotyping became standard fare. Along with an informal spreading of the ideals and lifestyle of middle-class America, television had another standard-setting effect. From the early stages it was clear that American television makers were masters in the portrayal of the eternal struggle between good and evil.

'Law and order' programmes on television were subtle translations of the issues of 'good' and 'evil' being played out on the world stage and which reached a climax in October 1962 during the Cuban missile crisis. The Americans proved that they would indeed stand by their stated ideals – and also that they were *almost* able to impose their will (and their language) on their opponents all the way up to the UN Security Council. In the words of the American UN ambassador Adlai Stevenson: *'All right, sir, let me ask you one simple question: Do you, Ambassador Zorin, deny that the USSR has placed and is placing medium- and intermediate-range missiles and sites in Cuba? Yes or no – don't wait for the translation – yes or no?'* At the time Valerian Zorin declined to answer, but two weeks later the Soviet Union withdrew its missiles. People in the Low Countries too heaved a sigh of relief that the 'Pax Americana' had held. President John F. Kennedy was elevated to hero status. When he was murdered a year later on 22 November 1963 in Dallas, even citizens living 7,000 kilometres away were deeply shocked. As a martyr for peace Kennedy was immediately honoured in practically every Dutch and Flemish town and village by having a street or a square named after him.

The defoliation of an image

Nonetheless, Cuba proved a turning point for the spread of Americanisation in Europe. Kennedy might be immortalised in the names of streets and squares as the man who had kept his promise that *'we shall pay any price, bear any burden, meet any hardship, support any friend, oppose any foes, in order to assure the survival and success of liberty'*; but he was also the man who escalated American military involvement in the internal conflict in the former French colony of Vietnam. And that war in all its horror then featured daily on television in the Low Countries. This was a new development, and one with far-reaching consequences. Never before had such shocking, up-to-the-minute images of the violence of war been so powerfully presented to the general public. Time and again television pointedly presented Vietnamese civilians as victims of modern warfare. Was it any wonder, then, that an increasing section of public opinion, in reaction to these constantly repeated images of violence, turned against the militarism of the United States? In the second half of the sixties the international press had made Vietnam into the yardstick by which to judge America,

A coffee shop in
Amsterdam.

and with every bomb that fell on Vietnam the image of the United States as a beacon to the world was further undermined. At a time when the younger generation was becoming increasingly critical of society the use of napalm, fragmentation bombs and chemical defoliants which destroyed wildlife and crops came to symbolise a deteriorating America. The pro-American authorities in the Low Countries found this acutely embarrassing. To the government's severe irritation, anti-Vietnam War demonstrators kept shouting over and over again *'Johnson: murderer!'* referring to a friendly head of state. In the international relations of the time diplomacy was one of the few areas in which 'Vietnam' seemed to have no influence.

'Johnson the War Criminal'.
An Aktiegroep Vietnam
poster, 1967

Despite that, the war also ensured that Europeans began to take a much more critical view of America. Perceptions of the United States changed, and cracks and fissures in American society came under serious scrutiny. Controversial subjects such as the struggle for civil rights in the United States received particular attention. Reports on the black population's struggle for emancipation increasingly evoked a sympathetic response. With the rapid advances in news-gathering technology the message of Martin Luther King's dream could be spread just as quickly in Europe as in the United States itself. What in 1958 was described as 'a race problem', was called 'a racist society' five years later. Other negative features of American society such as the high crime rate and the concomitant violence also received a great deal of attention. And thanks to the international success of American singers such as Bob Dylan the entire post-war generation knew that the answer to many social and moral questions in the United States was 'blowing in the wind'. At the end of the sixties it seemed that in many areas America's role as the great exemplar had come to an end.

Rumble in the global shopping mall

But was that really the case? With all their interest in and imitating of the United States, by around 1970 the Netherlands and Flanders were sufficiently 'Americanised' for the 'second phase' of what the American political philosopher Allan Bloom described in 1987 as *'the American moment in world history, the one for which we shall forever be judged'*. At the heart of this second phase was the embracing of *commercial* America. This first manifested itself, as a result of strong economic growth, in the appearance of covered shopping centres modelled on American shopping malls, in which almost every conceivable product could be found in ever more varieties. The street scene too changed in line with the American model. From the seventies onwards there was a marked increase in the number of large, multi-coloured advertisements. In the cities, neon signs flashed on every street corner. Despite an – un-American – political belief in the achievability of a more collectivist society in which knowledge, skill, money and power would be more fairly distributed, consumption rose dramatically in the Low Countries. It was no accident that from 1971 on McDonald's and its hamburgers did very good business here. Even those who turned away from America to follow Marx and Engels still could not resist taking a curious look

What nobody noticed, because of the focus on commercial America, was that the United States was itself undergoing a change: there was a new emphasis on religious faith as a counter-balance to an increasingly materialistic culture. Piety had always been a characteristic of American society, but at a time when large numbers of Europeans attended church this had gone largely un-noticed. While the Low Countries becoming were strongly secularised, which was accepted as one of the achievements of a material welfare- and knowledge-based culture, in the United States there was a counter-movement which would have considerable consequences for relations between the countries. With the rural areas of the American Mid-West and Southern states in the vanguard, strict Christian views on life and society based on a literal interpretation of the Bible gained in strength and influence. At the highest level this was first expressed by presidents such as Jimmy Carter and Ronald Reagan, who spoke openly of the Christian inspiration that fired their politics. Reagan went so far as to describe the struggle with the atheistic Soviet Union in semi-religious terms as a battle against an Evil Empire. As Reagan put it in a speech in July 1983: *'Two visions of the world remain locked in dispute. The first believes all men are created equal by a loving God who has blessed us with freedom. Abraham Lincoln spoke for us... The second vision believes that religion is opium for the masses. It believes that eternal principles like truth, liberty, and democracy have no meaning beyond the whim of the state. And Lenin spoke for them.'*

Washington DC,
9 June 1991.
Photo by Marc Dierikx.

Amsterdam, 2003.
Banner against war in Iraq.

Many Europeans thought that was going too far. The American preoccupation with the struggle against communism as something like a religious mission, in which every possible means had to be tried, formed the basis for a rapid-ly-growing 'Hollanditis', a wide-spread resistance to the updating of NATO's American-controlled nuclear arsenal in Western Europe. In the Netherlands and in Belgium hundreds of thousands took to the streets to protest against the siting of new nuclear weapons on their soil. With the international situation as it was around 1980 there was no practical alternative, however, though the Belgian government appeared more receptive to the criticism than its Dutch counterpart. The latter adhered firmly to a pro-American course of action – and was able to do so because opinion polls showed that when it came down to it around 75 percent of the Dutch were pro-American and supported NATO. The result was predictable: the missiles arrived, in Belgium too.

Criticism of American policies during the Cold War did nothing to reduce the dominance of America and American culture in the Low Countries. Quite the reverse, in fact; with the turning economic tide of the eighties the spirit of entrepreneurship and 'market forces' were rediscovered and American-style management was embraced as a highly desirable social good. At the same time the march of consumerism accelerated, most pervasively perhaps on television, where the most popular channels copied the American commercial model. And so post-war America's all-encompassing exemplary role was effectively reduced to the everyday living of a consumer's dream – which in the United States too was the most immediately apparent form of 'the American way of life'. After the end of the Cold War this became even more the case. Now it was virtually impossible to get away from it. Those who could not keep up saw the welfare safety-net shrinking and, as in America, were thrown back more and more on their own resources.

America's extreme make-over?

America's influence has declined in recent years, however. What triggered this process may well have been the American presidential election of November 2000, which for the first time cast a harsh light on the weaknesses in the American democratic system and put into the White House a president tainted by irregularities in the vote-counting system. On top of that, all was not well with the American economy; the economic growth of the nineties was levelling off, and America's position as role model was damaged by a number of corporate scandals. Under George W. Bush the country projected an image not seen since 1945: that of an isolationist superpower which cared little for events outside the United States and viewed the world primarily in terms of relative military strength.

The alarming and tragic events of 11 September 2001 and the consequences that followed only reinforced this attitude. In reaction to 9/11 Washington shook the world with an explosion of political and military violence. But if the war in Afghanistan could still count on broad moral support from America's allies, for most people in the Low Countries the invasion of Iraq that followed in March 2003 was going too far. With (certainly in hindsight) no other justification than its own determination and military might, in full view of international public opinion America turned away from the objectives of peace, order and justice in the world for which it had stood for decades. In doing so, Washington seemed to regard the agreement of its allies as a minor matter. They were confronted with a simple choice: you were either for the American action, or against it. This attitude, probably even more than the American action itself, was seen as extremely disturbing in Europe and provoked a storm of criticism of a stubborn and arbitrary America. The moral reputation of America crumbled. And although the Dutch authorities hesitantly joined the 'coalition of the willing', America's public image began to slide. Increasingly, 'Miserica' became the tone in news reporting.

Meanwhile, events in the world arena acted as a catalyst for the revitalisation of the ancient Christian roots of the American nation. Almost unnoticed by a Europe focused on secular, urban America, the advance of conservative, Christian-inspired ideas continued in the United States. Where at the beginning of the nineties around 47 percent of Americans said their Christian faith was very important to them, opinion polls in October 2004 indicated that this percentage had risen to almost 60 percent. The Republican Party was able to

capitalise on this and project itself as the champion of conservative, Christian principles. Right up to the election in November 2004, in the Low Countries as elsewhere there was little understanding of just how fundamental these changes were. Suddenly evidence struck that a conservative revolution had taken place in America, and that under George Bush America now had a different face. It turned out that it was precisely these pious folk, most of them living in the rural heartland of the United States, who had ensured Bush's re-election.

'Four more years!' What seems like a promise to Bush supporters is for most Europeans, including the inhabitants of the Low Countries, a depressing thought. The new cocktail of Christian fundamentalism, patriotism and militarism served up in November 2004 has caused many in the Low Countries – particularly the intellectuals – seriously to doubt whether America in the twenty-first century still stands for the same values as it did in the previous century. ∎

Dutch NATO Secretary-General Jaap de Hoop Scheffer and George W. Bush at the White House, 10 November 2004.

Translated by Joy Kearney

The Structure of Shame

Stephan van Fleteren's Portrait of the Kosovo War

1.

I don't even need to look at the photo any more – gentle hills and the small lake on the left (Ireland, you think, clouds and all); two fifths of the picture generously endowed with peace; on the right a pick-up truck. There are neither wheels nor cab, but you know they are sitting in a truck – the wooden sides, the hinge, the tarpaulin. Peace shattered now. Three women, a cascade of wool and felt and velvet; three women, one pair of eyes; folds of fabric, folds of skin; a gaze I hardly dare return. I don't need to look at the photo any more, but I do anyway.

2.

The photo was taken in the spring of 1999, close to the Albanian town of Kükes. The women are Albanian Kosovars, fleeing from the violence that has hit their province so severely since the start of the air attacks. On 24 March 1999, NATO began to bomb Serbian targets, military ones first, then civilian ones as well. For the first time in its fifty-year existence the most powerful military alliance in the world attacks a sovereign country, the Federal Republic of Yugoslavia. The reason given was that it was to prevent – or put an end to? – a new humanitarian catastrophe in the Balkans. President Slobodan Milošević's regime is suspected of yet another series of crimes against humanity, this time directed at the rebellious province of Kosovo. Once Slovenia, Croatia, Bosnia and Macedonia have split away there is not much left of Tito's unitary Yugoslavia save Serbia, the adjacent constituent republic of Montenegro and the province of Kosovo. From 1995 on the (mainly Albanian-speaking) Kosovars' struggle for autonomy has become an ever greater thorn in Serbian flesh. Once a small-scale ethnic Albanian guerrilla group, the Kosovo Liberation Army (KLA), has overtaken the informally elected President Ibrahim Rugova's pacifist nationalism, the behaviour of the Serbian militias has become more and more violent. International observers watch the murderous attacks and reprisals with eagle eyes. After the civil wars, ethnic cleansing and genocides in Croatia and Bosnia, the West no longer wants to stand by impotently and watch as human rights are flagrantly

and systematically violated on the eve of the third millennium. The international community arrived too late in Rwanda and pulled out of Srebrenica too soon. It was not going to happen this time. The NATO bombardments were supposed to persuade Milošević to accept the Rambouillet peace initiative (which gave Kosovo more autonomy, but no independence for the time being). In practice, however, the air attacks gave the Serbian army carte blanche to plunder and murder with impunity in Kosovo. As a result, in the first few weeks of the war more than nine hundred thousand Kosovars fled, half the then population of Kosovo. It was the biggest exodus since the Second World War.

Photo by Stephan Vanfleteren.

3.

All of this happened six years ago, but the illustrated supplement is engraved on my memory. It was published on 24 April 1999, exactly one month after the first bombs, as a special section to the Flemish newspaper *De Morgen*. The design was sober and serene, semi-matte paper, quarto format, black and white photos, framed only by the edges of the negative. In-house photographer Stephan Vanfleteren had been to cover the refugee camps in Albania and his poignant photos told the whole story. There was hardly any text. Apart from a brief introduction by Koen Vidal the photos were accompanied only by a handful of short quotes from the refugees themselves – gruesome stories of Serbian abuses, missing family members and endless despair. An international observer was also quoted, his neutrality a guarantee of objectivity: *'Right now the Serbs are doing what they're good at.'*

The photo was on the centrefold, spread across two pages. I do not know how long I looked at it, but what I do remember is disillusion, so immense, so furious that it had to be masking a deeper sorrow.

On the back of the page, as some kind of relief, was an account number for the Help Kosovo campaign.

4.

I have meant to write about that photo for several years, about its disturbing composition, that eerie landscape, that still life with sorrow. I was going to write about Vanfleterens' overexposure and how it sculpts the foreground, about his ingenious use of depth-of-field (just look at the edge of the tailboard, I would say, and notice how narrow the zone is where the photo is sharp); and about how that draws your gaze from the handkerchief and fine wrinkles of the woman in the middle to the paler eyes on the right in front, to end on that one razor-sharp earring. I would write about dignity and how it is epitomised by an elderly lady who wears mother-of-pearl earrings even as she flees. That is what I was going to write, that is still what I would like to write, but the longer I wait, the harder it becomes. Not that the photo has lost any of its effect, far from it, but because something else has changed: the world, the way I look at it – my appreciation of beauty, what moves me, touches me.

The photo hangs on my wall. Over the last few years I have not only looked at it every day, I have also started to look at it differently. If I can no longer report on what I experienced when I first saw it, without a feeling of perversion, then perhaps I can still try to chronicle the changing way I view it. In doing so, photographic analysis and pictorial aesthetics give way to retrospection and international politics.

5.

I remember how I viewed the war then – as a moral dilemma. Was it justified to attack a sovereign nation for the sake of human rights? Was it justified to use massive and indisputable military superiority against a vicious, but inferior army? Was it legitimate to use violence to enforce human rights? Could a military intervention have humanitarian motives? I remember exhaustive discussions with friends and colleagues about it, but the answer to these questions often came close to a hesitant 'yes'. We chided an older colleague who invoked territorial integrity and the right of the nation state to self-determination, with arguments about post-national Europe, the intolerableness of tribal violence and the need for a new, international, moral order. *'Wouldn't just a little bit of war be better?'* sang Flemish rock singer Stijn Meuris.

No, we were not in favour of violence and our lofty ideals certainly did not include a readiness to die, but somehow or other we agreed with the Dutch Minister Van Aartsen when, during a hastily summoned emergency debate, he informed the Second Chamber *'with the greatest possible regret'* that the war had begun. With the exception of the far left-wing SP fraction the whole Chamber endorsed the campaign. GroenLinks (the left-wing environmental party) called it *'the most difficult decision of the past year'*.[1] The Netherlands and Belgium would supply a combined squadron of 26 fighter aircraft for the air offensive. The Belgian Federal Government kept its promises as a NATO ally with few complaints. The then Minister of Foreign Affairs, Derycke, said: *'We are a member of NATO, the most solid alliance which everyone wants to join and which is wanted by all. That entails obligations. I am fairly optimistic that the population understands the theory of rights and obligations and can accept it."*[2] Derycke was right about public opinion. Only days after the outbreak of war an editorial in *De Morgen* warned against *'an endless spiral of violence'*, but the legitimacy of NATO's action was not questioned.[3] The leader-writer of the more conservative newspaper, *De Standaard*, went a step further and stated frankly: *'Occasionally, very occasionally, military aggression is all that we have left to defend legitimate collective interests.'*[4] A moral dilemma, yes, a struggle to resolve, but eventually we got there.

Those were the nineties; the decade that didn't belong to any particular century because the twentieth century was over and the twenty-first had yet to begin; that remarkable period between 1989 and 2001, between the fall of the Wall and the fall of the Twin Towers, between the end of the Cold War and the start of the War on Terror; the decade in which 'the end of history' was prematurely announced because the combination of parliamentary democracy and free-market economics had surfaced as the best, definitive type of state; the decade of the Third Way in Britain, the active welfare state in Belgium, the Dutch *poldermodel*, the French *cohabitation*, the German *neue Mitte* and other appealing attempts at reconciliation between socialism and neo-liberalism that have since been exposed as fake marriages. With the Twenties and the Sixties, the Nineties were undoubtedly amongst the gayest decades of the twentieth century – they too came shortly after the end of a war, albeit a cold one. This time too, everything would be different. Economics would become social, politics consensual, and war humanitarian.

6.

How very different from the present state of affairs! Compared to the moral and political complexity of the war in Kosovo, the Second Gulf War seems like a piece of cake as far as ethics are concerned. The blatant economic and geo-political interests, the flimsy and contrived *casus belli*, the unabashed imperialism, the boundless unilateral arrogance, the voluntaristic religious discourse – it is all a very long way from what happened in Kosovo five years ago. The NATO intervention was a lot of things, but certainly not a struggle for oil and minerals. The Serbian army did commit humanitarian crimes (though the extent of them is unclear, and yes, so did Saddam, and on a much larger scale, but that was not Bush and Co.'s motive for war). At the time, the military coalition was considerably larger than the present 'coalition of the willing' (although there was no UN mandate then either) and the motivation was universal humanism, not sectarian religion. To put it cynically, since March 2003 you might look at Vanfleteren's photo almost with nostalgia. Those women belong to another era now. The woman on the right – she must have been eighty or ninety even then – was experiencing her third war and has, in all probability, passed on in the meantime. However great her suffering, you could say it still took place within the framework of a humanitarian intervention. Today the world in which that photo was taken no longer exists; that world order seems gone forever. I still look at her, but she doesn't very often look back now. The moral dilemma of those days seems to have been surpassed by the absurd stupidity of today.

7.

On 24 March 1999 there was a meeting of the American Senate. On the agenda was a small but important point – compensation for the victims of the ski lift accident in Cavalese.

At about exactly the same moment, around seven local time, forty fighter planes and bombers took off from Aviano, in Northern Italy, heading for Kosovo. Aviano is NATO's most important European air force base. North Africa, the Middle East and Eastern Europe are within easy reach by plane. It is less than half an hour's flight to the Balkans. American Air Force pilots serving with the SFOR operations in Bosnia even use the Italian Alps as a training ground for the mountainous Balkans. A year earlier, however, things had gone wrong. During an exercise, on 3 February 1998, an American reconnaissance plane from Aviano cut through the cables of a large ski lift in the nearby town of Cavalese. The crew were ten kilometres off course, at extremely low altitude, and had just executed a number of unscheduled stunts. For years the inhabitants of Cavalese had been complaining about the cowboy antics of fighter pilots who would dive under the cable for a laugh – but to no avail. On 3 February the ski lift's gondola tumbled a hundred metres to the ground. All twenty passengers were killed .

To great consternation in Europe, a year later the pilot of the plane was acquitted by an American military tribunal. That was one month before the start of the war in Kosovo. So great was the sense of outrage that President Clinton had to try and smooth things over in continental Europe. It is not insignificant that all the victims came from NATO member states (Germany, Austria, Italy, the Netherlands and Belgium) or would-be members (Poland).

On the day the Aviano air base served as the take-off point for the war in Kosovo, the day the US fully grasped the importance of a military presence on the continent of Europe, the day the US had every reason to want a good relationship with its NATO allies, on that day the American Senate met to vote on a sum of 40 million dollars as compensation for the relatives of the Cavalese accident victims.[5] For months there had been haggling about who should pay,

Italy or the US, and how much. Now, suddenly, it was all wrapped up, and the size of the settlement was described in the evening news on Flemish television as *'an absurd amount for an absurd accident'*. Absurd, yes, unless one assumes a link between the exorbitant amount of compensation and the importance the US attaches to transatlantic cohesion.

No, the war in Kosovo was not directly about economic interests, but to draw the conclusion that the deployment *must* therefore have been strictly humanitarian is categorically wrong.[6] Since the fall of communism, in 1989, the military alliance between the US and Western Europe had been stripped of its primary raison d'être. *'New military humanism'*, as Noam Chomsky called it, offered NATO a new reason to carry on, regardless of the integrity of some of its convinced supporters.[7] A successful, highly technological intervention, without victims on NATO's side, would be the best recommendation for a renewed mission – and for America to continue to keep a foot in the European door. The opposite was true, too, and was strikingly summarised by White House advisor Zbigniew Brzezinski: *'The failure of NATO (in Kosovo) would mean the end of the Alliance's credibility, as well as a weakening of American leadership in the world.'*[8] For that credibility and leadership, the American Senate was quite willing to hand out some compensation.

8.

Stephan Vanfleteren's photos left us in no doubt. In the context of the discourse about the horror of ethnic violence, they confirmed precisely the motivation for going to war: *'Right now the Serbs are doing what they're good at.'* We regarded those women with cool compassion. It was dreadful, but it would turn out all right.

I'm afraid it was only slowly beginning to dawn on us[9] that the NATO attacks were at least indirectly responsible for the exodus; that the bombing would last not several days, but several months; that the NATO planes flew five kilometres high to stay out of reach of the Serbian air defences; that because of that only fourteen tanks and twenty pieces of artillery were destroyed, compared to 300 factories, 190 schools and 50 clinics; that there were at least 2000 civilian victims and 6000 wounded; that the 'collateral damage' to the civilian population and infrastructure, if it had not yet begun to look like a deliberate tactic, was at least intolerably high; and that NATO's actions went against every form of international law of war.[10]

9.

I look back at the photo, and more particularly at the least important part – those clouds. With Stephan Vanfleteren the skies are never clear blue. Like many black and white photographers he hates bright light. It is only amateurs who get their cameras out on summer days. But there is more to it than that. Like his seventeenth-century predecessor Jan van Goyen, who painted more sky than land, Vanfleteren's clouds already contain everything. They are the canvas against which he portrays his world, and it is not a pretty one. The heavy cloud cover is pure threat, the strip of light above the hills full of foreboding.

His sky is reminiscent of the eclipse of the sun that passed over Europe that same war year. It went dark for three minutes that day, from Cornwall to Syria, as if someone was using a strange torch to project not a beam of light but a beam of shadow across the brightly lit world. In Kosovo the eclipse lasted three months, not three minutes – seventy-nine days of bombing .

Was the war in Kosovo really so different from the Second Gulf War? Was it really the high point of a short, ethical period in international politics? Was it the first but, because of the changed world after 9.11, also the last manifestation of a new type of logic for war, that of military humanism?

Now, six years later, we know better. Diplomatic means were far from being exhausted at the peace negotiations in Rambouillet. NATO's secret, but last-minute demand that the peace agreement should guarantee it free and unlimited access to the whole of Yugoslav territory was absurd and rightly unacceptable to the Serbs. It would have amounted to de facto acceptance of a foreign occupying force in their country.[11] The accusation of genocide levelled against the Serbs was badly documented and later turned out to be unfounded. There was no question of a systematic and planned extermination of a particular population group.[12] If genocide was the motive for going to war, the world had many 'better' and more likely candidates for a NATO intervention. By acting without a specific UN mandate, NATO did serious damage to international law and paved the way for the recent, much more flagrant travesties of multilateral politics. NATO's military hegemony and invulnerability were so disproportionate that, according to international lawyer Richard Falk, the balance of power was like torture, whereby one party inflicts damage on another arbitrarily and at its own discretion, without retribution.[13] NATO's reluctance to deploy ground troops forced the international alliance to cooperate with the local KLA, an organisation which the US had only recently described as terrorist. But the KLA's political language was just as ethnically nationalistic as the Serbs'. In an ethnic conflict it was not very advisable to support the nationalistic claims of one of the warring parties.[14] Today, the bombing raids and their consequences have still not eliminated the ethnic tensions in Yugoslavia but have actually complicated them, with the Serbian Kosovars (the minority within the minority) as the main victims. In March 2004, exactly five years after the start of the war, Kosovo was the scene of the worst ethnic violence in years, despite the presence of UN and NATO troops.[15] And in December 2004, former KLA leader and notoriously brutal political figure Ramush Haradinaj was elected Prime Minister of Kosovo. To be continued, alas.

How do you look at those women once you know that? With anger? Yes, absolutely; but belated anger is also embarrassment.

10.

It is not that I was *moved*, that assumes some measure of resolve, steadfastness, even superiority. Being moved is the melancholic counterpart of a smile, it is being briefly but superficially affected by an incident in the outside world. Being moved is also the empathetic side of pity. The door of sympathy stands ajar, the account number is noted down, the purse opened. But that is not the point. So what is it?

It is not indignation either, which is yet another of those good-hearted senti-

ments, and definitely not melancholy. Anger? Yes, there's anger perhaps, but most of all there's *shame*; shame for the limited depth-of-field with which I used to look at it; shame for the over-exposure of the foreground at the expense of the background, the clouds.

Those out-of-focus eyes again. Shame brings her gaze back to life, makes it disconcertingly alive, even if she is dead. How can I return it? She looks out mildly, yes, full of compassion, without reproach. The look of an owl in a cage, lost but superior, aware but resigned. I look away, but it is no use, even the earrings make me shrink.

No, I am not moved by that photo, but shaken. And it gets worse. ■

NOTES

1. *NRC Handelsblad*, 23 March 1999

2. *De Standaard*, 15 April 1999

3. Frank Schlömer, *De Morgen*, 25 March 1999

4. Axel Buyse, *De Standaard*, 25 March 1999

5. *De Morgen*, 25 March 1999

6. See: Tzvetan Todorov, *Hope And Memory: Lessons From The Twentieth Century* (Tr. David Bellos). Princeton: Princeton University Press, 2004, chapter 6, for a brilliant analysis.

7. Noam Chomsky,*The New Military Humanism: Lessons from Kosovo*. London: Pluto, 1999.

8. Quoted in Todorov, op.cit., 369

9. Edward Said, 'The Treason Of The Intellectuals'. In: *Al-Ahram Weekly*, 24-30 June 1999. (weekly.ahram.org.eg)

10. 'Some Ethical Aspects of Nato's Intervention in Kosovo'. The Transnational Foundation for Peace and Future Research, 14 July 1999, www.transnational.org/pressinf/pf73.html

11. Noam Chomsky, 'Another Way For Kosovo?'. In: *Le Monde diplomatique*, 14 March 2000 (www.commondreams.org)

12. Noam Chomsky interviewed by Patrick Cain. In: *The Activist*, June 1999. (www.chomsky.info)

13. Richard Falk, 'Reflections on the War'. In: *The Nation*, 28 June 1999. (www.thenation.com)

14. Todorov, op.cit., 344-56.

15. 'Collapse in Kosovo', International Crisis Group, 22 April 2004 (www.icg.org); 'Serbia and Montenegro (Kosovo/Kosova): The March Violence: KFOR and UNMIK's failure to protect the rights of the minority communities', Amnesty International, 8 July 2004 (web.amnesty.org).

Translated by Lindsay Edwards

Tear Down This House

The Poetry of Tonnus Oosterhoff

Where the origins of modern poetry lie is something that you can philosophise about for a long time, but few would dispute that the compact oeuvre of Stéphane Mallarmé constitutes a benchmark. He was not the first poet to apply himself to writing largely incomprehensible poems, but he attracted more of a following than anyone else in the nineteenth century. While Rimbaud sometimes gives you the feeling that he is just messing around, Mallarmé's poems are firmly and solidly constructed, so that every interpretation – no matter how ingenious – simply glances off their superior impassivity. There is no way of shifting them.

In his collected poems there are three poems about fans: 'Éventail', of which the poet has stated that it has to do with a fan belonging to his wife, 'Autre éventail', this time about one of his daughter's, and lastly 'Éventail', dedicated to his friend Méry Laurent. The first and last of these were written by the poet on an actual fan, which he presented to the dedicatee. They are extremely complex poems, but one thing is clear: in each case the fan is an image of the poem. This is the first verse of the wife's fan: *'Avec comme pour langage/Rien qu'un battement aux cieux/Le futur vers se dégage/Du logis très précieux'*. Poetry is no more than the displacement of air. Precisely this comparison of poems that stand immovable as houses with the most volatile object imaginable is one of the great paradoxes of modern literature.

Derailment

Where does modern poetry end? You can discuss this for a long time too, but I suspect that if we look back in 2050, we shall find that modern poetry in the Netherlands ends with Tonnus Oosterhoff (1953-). Ever since his debut in 1990 he has gone his own way with steely consistency, which has resulted in the strangest and wittiest poetry of the past decade. And he has also published prose that testifies to the same wilfulness.

His collection *We saw ourselves turn into a small group of people* (Wij zagen ons in een kleine groep mensen veranderen, 2002), contains the poem 'Possibly' ('Eventuele'), which begins as follows: *'Isn't that the amazed Madame sitting there on the deep-red tub chair?/How does red ink write on silver paper? Is a New Year fan/*

a useful present?' In the last verse we see Mallarmé standing opposite Madame. *'Has he brought something/ into motion, into being, to a standstill?'* Anyone who looks at the poetry of the last century will answer in the affirmative. Mallarmé has set something in motion, he has brought something into being, but his poetry is certainly also that of stasis. His poems are things. And it is possible, with a slight exaggeration, to describe modern poetry as a collection of things.

Over the past ten years it has become increasingly clear that Tonnus Oosterhoff takes a less static view of poetry. When you read his work, the first thing that strikes you is that he never gives you anything to get hold of. On one occasion he writes a melodious gem, the next time a crazy tale, and the third time a typographical experiment. Some of his poems are mysterious and unsettling in an elusive way, others excel in Alzheimeresque ellipses, and yet others seem to be constructed like Bach fugues. Many poems contain dialogue and in a great many poems language seems to derail in a way that can be compared with what happens when a poorly educated madman translates an instruction manual. Whereas the poetics of such consistent poets as Baudelaire, Brodsky and Szymborska can be reconstructed from their published work without much

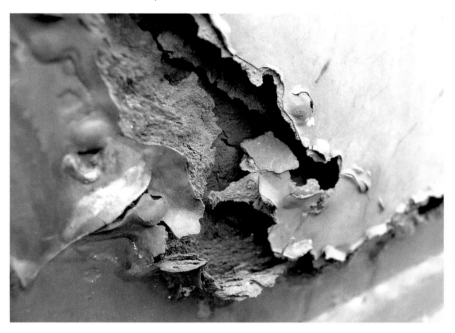

trouble, in Oosterhoff's case that is a hopeless task, since each time he does something different. He wants to surprise not only the reader but also himself.

In his debut collection *Country Tiger* (Boerentijger, 1990) we see how just under the thin veneer of civilisation and rationality that makes us human an animal madness crouches waiting to pounce on us. This is how the very first poem begins: *'The leopard at the brainstem/listens to the radio wind/knowing, not knowing.'* Man is a beast, but has forgotten that fact. It is typical of Oosterhoff that in the very first line of his oeuvre he makes a play on words: 'brainstem'. (Dutch *'stam'* = stock, race, clan, but also trunk). Plays on words have the disadvantage that, apart from being usually untranslatable, they seem to result from chance and therefore do not say much for the poet's inventiveness . But the core feature of Oosterhoff's work is derailment, dislocation, and in that context the short-circuiting caused by word-play can work miracles. Oosterhoff makes effective use of coincidences of sound and tugs – sometimes subtly, sometimes destructively – at Dutch syntax. No surprise, then, that Oosterhoff's poems abound in madmen, deranged artists, people whose powers of speech have been destroyed by a tumour.

The poet's pneumatic drill

One of the great philosophical questions of the twentieth century concerns the exact nature of our identity. Rimbaud already stated that the I is another person; nowadays it is even claimed that the I comprises an enormous collection of others. That is grist to Oosterhoff's mill, since he has no desire to write a consistent, monolithic oeuvre but has raised the lack of identity to a programme. Not only does he seem to formulate a new poetics with each poem; the poems themselves are as multi-voiced as a schizophrenic's brain. Oosterhoff gains that effect by quoting from newspapers, ads, world literature – but also by making frequent use of dialogue. A poem from *(Robust Reed Stops,) A Brilliant Assemblage* ((Robuuste tongwerken,) een stralend plenum, 1997) – the title is a quotation from an article about a church organ – begins with a question within quotation marks: *'Wally, may we write/about what you look like? Completely, that is?'* Wally approves, until 'we' write: *'Wally is really well-stacked. She stands/naked in front of the window. Indisposed for the last time.'* That was not the intention, of course, and Wally then insists that her name is changed. This is the last verse: *'We do what she says; it's no longer concocted./Wally's dead-honest face lights up once more. She finds/this poem good, to-the-point, personal.'* The poem is as artful as the paradox of the lying Cretan, for if what it says is true, the woman's name cannot be Wally. The poem makes itself impossible.

For Oosterhoff, then, the poem is not a static construction but a continuous process. That is why for years now he has been experimenting on his website with changing poems. His latest collection is accompanied by a CD-rom on which the reader can see how the poems gradually blur and dissolve , even to the extent that sentences turn into their opposites. The collection too constantly contradicts itself, for Oosterhoff deploys all manner of typographical means to emphasise the multi-voicedness of his poems – he has even written over the typed texts in his own handwriting. While we tend to regard someone's handwriting as inalienably personal to them, its purpose here is precisely to problematise the identity of the poet.

Who is Tonnus Oosterhoff? In *The Landholder* (De ingeland, 1993) he had already written:

'You're so incorruptible, so modest.'
'For the fun of it.'
It is a pleasure
to be Tonnus Oosterhoff.
'I'd like to be that too.'
Of course, but that's not on!

That's not on.

Because even the poet himself doesn't quite know how you set about being Tonnus Oosterhoff.

New poetry always calls for new metaphors that can characterise it. In 23 BC, Horace ended his three books called *Carmina* with the proud – or ironic? – conclusion that he had built a monument that would survive the centuries. The last poem in Oosterhoff's most recent collection begins as follows:

> *tear down this house*
> *pneumatic drill*
> *The ornamental well goes down metres*
> *six tons of granite*

In the poet's handwriting the open space at the beginning of the first line has been filled with the word *'Do'*, in front of the second line there is *'Use my'*. The word *'ton'* probably refers to the first name of the poet. Oosterhoff has not built a monument, but torn down a house. We shall await with curiosity the ultimate consequences of the demolition process with which Oosterhoff has held us spellbound for more than a decade. ∎

www.tonnusoosterhoff.nl

Translated by John Irons

Four Poems
by Tonnus Oosterhoff

The seed had the colour of old lamp-light
The fruit was a yellow-white vapour.
On it they performed tasks.
There were complications.
Man was the intention.
At night windows steamed up;
during the day it smelled of rubber and Mickey Mouse.
In sunny water albumens flaked.

Het zaad had de kleur van oud lamplicht.
De vrucht was een geelwitte damp.
Daaraan verrichtten ze taken.
Verwikkelingen kwamen.
Man was de bedoeling.
Des nachts besloegen ramen;
daags rook het naar gummi en Mickey Mouse.
In zonnig water vlokten eiwitten.

From *Country Tiger* (Boerentijger). Amsterdam: De Bezige Bij, 1990.

A good person is something quite simple,
but if you drop him, you can just as well throw him away.
Once the connection's lost, not even
the best technicians can ever put it back in.
You can throw him away, he's not worth anything any more.

Een goed mens is iets heel eenvoudigs,
maar laat je hem vallen, dan kun je hem weggooien.
Als het verband eruit is, krijgen
de knapste vaklui dat er nooit meer in.
Je kunt hem weggooien, hij is niets meer waard.

Cows when they have forcibly drunk
each other's marrow and head
are put to the sword by the thousand:
for just once one expensive, unique was allowed...!

Koeien worden als ze gedwongen
elkaars merg en kop hebben gedronken
bij duizenden over de kling gejaagd:
want er mocht eens één zo'n kostbaar, uniek...!

A human being however is as replaceable as a light-bulb.
Screw a new good person into the fitting
of a burnt-out good person and you have light.

Een mens is echter zo vervangbaar als een gloeilamp.
Draai in de fitting van een kapot goed mens
een nieuw goed mens en je hebt licht.

A good poem is also simple.

Ook een goed gedicht is eenvoudig.

Noneofthatyourverygoodhealth

Nooitvanzijnlangzalhijleven

I keep a spare handy.

Ik houd een onderdeel over

From *We saw ourselves turn into a small group of people*
(Wij zagen ons in een kleine groep veranderen).
Amsterdam: De Bezige Bij, 2002.

The water began to feel ashamed
of what it was and had always done.
On behalf of everyone a fish came to the land
to come to an arrangement.

The fish straightened its back:
'Folks: three wishes.'

The shore was empty, only the shells
had the form of caps with ear-flaps under them.
The crafty creature had to stop itself from laughing.

I can promise what I like, it thought.
This won't cost me a farthing. History hasn't even begun yet.
I ought to be getting back through the breakers.

Or shall I stay here for a bit? After all, I'm dry now.
I mean it's great, that sea breeze.

From *The Landholder* (De ingeland). Amsterdam: De Bezige Bij, 1993.

Het water begon zich te schamen
voor wat het was en altijd gedaan had.
Namens iedereen kwam een vis aan land
om een regeling te treffen.

De vis rechtte zijn rug:
'Mensen: drie wensen.'

Het strand was leeg, alleen de schelpen
hadden de vorm van mutsen met oren eronder.
Het uitgekookte dier moest zijn lachen inhouden.

Ik kan beloven wat ik wil, dacht het.
Dit kost me geen stuiver. De geschiedenis is ja nog niet begonnen.
Ik moest maar eens gaan teruglopen door de branding.

Of zal ik hier nog wat blijven? Droog ben ik nu toch.
Het is wel heerlijk, die zeewind.

Three juggling balls, four shades
of softly peeled skin.
One, two, three. One, two, three, four.
Green, yellow, blue, red.

Summer morning: puss is resting on the balcony
imagining a black redstart to itself.
But the hospital round the corner is below still.
And sporting couples in Randenbroek Park are playing
winter evening tennis, laughing puffs of steam.
It is only three, four hundred metres
from here to right over there.

The set of instructions claims:
'And you're juggling. Well done!'

My brother is in Australia. Up and gone.

From *(Robust Reed Stops,) A Brilliant Full Organ*
((Robuuste tongwerken,) een stralend plenum).
Amsterdam: De Bezige Bij, 1997.

Drie jongleerballen, vier kleuren
van zachtgeschilde huid.
Een, twee, drie. Een, twee, drie, vier.
Groen, geel, blauw, rood.

Zomerochtend; poes rust op 't balkon
zich een zwart roodstaartje voorstellend.
Maar het ziekenhuis om de hoek is nog onder.
En in Park Randenbroek spelen sportparen
winteravondtennis, stoomwolkjes lachend.
Drie-, vierhonderd meter is het maar
van hier tot helemaal daar.

De gebruiksaanwijzing beweert:
'En u jongleert. Gefeliciteerd!'

Mijn broer is in Australië. Geëmigreerd.

All poems translated by John Irons

Hazy Memories

Notes on the Work of Bert de Beul

[ERIC BRACKE]

No artist likes to be repeatedly compared to a more famous contemporary, but such is the fate of the Antwerp painter Bert de Beul (1961-). The successful artist he is so often likened to is his fellow-townsman Luc Tuymans (1958-). However irritating this may be for De Beul, there is no denying that there are similarities between them. For example, they both began to exhibit their work around the same time in the 1980s. Initially, they even shared the same studio for a while. Both young painters turned their backs on the prevailing tendency to furiously and lavishly apply thick, messy layers of paint, which were frequently spread with a palette knife. Rather than going in for the sharp contrasts of their neo-expressionist predecessors, De Beul and Tuymans invested small canvasses with a harmonious tonality. They shared a preference for subtle greys and sub-dued greens. They mixed copious amounts of thinner with the oil paint, applying it carefully to the still wet canvas. Both produced painted representations of a recognisable reality which because of the obscuring haze, the striking composition or an enlarged detail, came across as more alienating than realistic.

Another similarity is that before going public with their work, both painters studied history of art at university. Bert de Beul went on to work for a few years as a museum assistant at the MUHKA (Museum of Contemporary Art Antwerp), while Tuymans used his knowledge to equip himself with a shrewd and original rationale. He gained recognition as an artist with a vision, as the painter who didn't want to be a painter. And perhaps this is the key difference between them. Tuymans works mainly in series which he underpins with an ideological discourse. For his pictorial projects he usually chooses stereotyped images from our common culture which are so emotionally charged that they can unleash a polemic.

Untitled

In contrast to this programmatic approach of Tuymans, De Beul's intimate paintings are a nostalgic evocation of memories and associations from his past. The viewer should not look for an underlying message or contentious cultural symbols. In his paintings De Beul goes in search of intangible emotions and ex-

Bert de Beul, *Untitled*.
Canvas, 53 x 45 cm, 1996.
Photo by Felix Tirry
© SABAM Belgium 2005.

periences from his youth. So the real difference between the two artists is that while Tuymans formulates a discourse and looks for polemic, De Beul gropes falteringly for what is gone.

This being so, it can be no coincidence that all Bert de Beul's paintings have the same title, namely *Untitled*. It is as if what he depicts – a doll, a block of flats on the outskirts of the city, tomatoes with asparagus, an iron, a piece of white chocolate, a girl in a car – is not the real subject of his paintings. The consistency with which he fails to give his work a name was particularly apparent during a visit to the retrospective mounted at the Muhka in 2002. For this exhibition De Beul chose a hundred paintings from the previous ten years. They hung side by side without any sort of hierarchical or thematic arrangement, and yet taken together they still showed the striking coherence the artist had managed to retain in his oeuvre all those years. The themes are very diverse – all the classic genres are represented: landscape, portrait, interior, still life, even down to the flower piece – but the treatment is identical. It is not always possible for the viewer to empathise with the nostalgia which attaches to the subject. But the alienating way in which De Beul portrays cars, for example, does indeed whisk you back to the time when to youthful eyes the automobile was still far from being the everyday thing it has become.

Bert de Beul, *Untitled.*
Canvas, 74 x 62 cm, 2004.
Photo by Felix Tirry
© SABAM Belgium 2005.

There have been no real changes in Bert De Beul's oeuvre over the years; that was apparent from the exhibition at the Antwerp museum. That is also the downside of the coherence in De Beul's work; the painter gives the impression of wanting to play safe, as if he lacks the courage and determination to explore the limits of form, technique and subject matter. De Beul paints with the brakes on, as someone wrote at the time of the retrospective in Antwerp. That said, the urge to experiment is of course no guarantee of quality. As the history of art shows, repetition can even be beneficial. Giorgio Morandi painted countless comparable still lifes with bottles. In so doing Morandi – for a while regarded as an artist of the *Pittura metafisica* –, gave perfectly ordinary things a timeless quality. And just as he did not look to provide a perfect reproduction of the nature of the glass bottles, neither is Bert de Beul overly concerned to express the materiality of things. De Beul covers everything with an ashen veil which obscures the specific material of the thing depicted. His work is clearly no vitalistic ode to the actual representation and the material of earthly things, but more a meditative expression of an inner state. With Bert de Beul the backgrounds are elaborated with as much care and attention as the subject itself, so that the work as a whole becomes distant and impenetrable. Anecdotal details are blotted out, making it impossible to locate a work precisely in space or time. Thus the artist achieves a universality which stands, as if frozen, outside time. His best work leaves the spectator with the same gnawing sense of deprivation as we find in the oeuvre of Leon Spilliaert (1881-1946).

Another twentieth-century painter who succeeded in making time stand still in his work and who, like Morandi and Spilliaert, influenced De Beul, is the American painter Edward Hopper. In De Beul's paintings, too, one sometimes senses that accumulated mental charge which makes Hopper's paintings so extraordinary. Hopper was a master at reproducing light and shadow, so that in almost every painting you have a fairly good idea of the time of day. This is not the case with De Beul's paintings, which as the Muhka's former director Flor Bex writes, *'bathe in the light of dusk in which colours lose their identity'*.

At first Bert De Beul drew on his memory to produce his intimate representations charged with personal experience. Later he painted from photographs he had taken or resorted to photographic images he associated with memories. As well as Luc Tuymans, several other Flemish painters who made their names in the 1990s, such as Jan van Imschoot (1963-), took the photographic image as their point of departure. This was not really anything new, for even at the end of the nineteenth century painters were capitalising on the advantages of photography. The difference was, however, that in the second half of the twentieth century painters no longer concealed that fact. Instead of being a device for capturing reality, the photographic raster and the blurring filtered through into the art of painting. Some artists even started to paint the actual photographs. The man to whom many painters are indebted in this respect is the German artist Gerhard Richter, who even in the first half of the 1960s used illustrations from magazines and his own photographs as the basis for his paintings. And Bert de Beul was certainly influenced by Richter in his reproduction of things, in that, as in hazy photographs, there are no sharply defined contours in De Beul's paintings.

Bert de Beul, *Untitled*.
Canvas, 62 x 74 cm, 2004.
Photo by Felix Tirry
© SABAM Belgium 2005.

Browsing through Bert de Beul's oeuvre is sometimes likened to leafing through an album of old snapshots which have faded slightly with time. In the summer of 2002 the painter even reinforced this likeness to a personal photograph album when he painted relatively small representations in watercolour on large sheets of paper in the exhibition space at the Brussels office of the German federal state North Rhine-Westphalia. In fact, with that use of watercolour his career came full circle.

It may be that De Beul arrived at his characteristic thin, smooth way of painting via the watercolours he initially produced. These were rather sombre sketches in black, grey and white. Shortly after that early period, his work was noticed by Gust Hoviele of the S65 gallery. After several exhibitions at his gallery in Aalst, Hoviele brought the painter to the attention of the German art public. This he did not only via the art fairs in Basel and Cologne, but also through the gallery Hoviele opened in Cologne at the end of 2001. Bert de Beul's work has been reasonably well received in Germany, but whether this is also the beginning of a general international breakthrough remains to be seen. In the meantime, De Beul stubbornly continues sneaking up on the meaning of life via the mystery of the everyday in his paintings. ■

Translated by Alison Mouthaan-Gwillim

Shifting Sands under the 'Polder Model'

The Trial of Strength between Government and Trade Unions

Barely three years ago the Netherlands was still being overrun by foreign del-
egations eager to learn everything they could about the '*miracle Hollandais*', the
economic and industrial relations system based on consensus and referred to
as the 'polder model'. Up till then the Netherlands had succeeded in generating
considerable prosperity and maintaining employment without undue cuts in the
social security system. That was more than many other countries could boast,

[WILLEM BREEDVELD]

Mass demonstration,
October 2004.

and it explained the enormous interest in this Dutch consensus model. In 2004, however, this quintessentially Dutch model came under heavy fire from within. The sands under the polder model began to shift, and now it is not even certain whether it can survive in the longer term.

The Dutch polder model exists by the grace of the good relations between the trade unions, employers' organisations and the government. Those relations have traditionally found their expression in tripartite organisations – the Social and Economic Council and the Labour Foundation are two examples – in which representatives from all three 'social partners', employees, employers and government representatives, regularly engage in endless discussions about policy. It is a typically Dutch process which can best be described using a typically Dutch, almost untranslatable verb: 'overleggen', which can be rendered variously or simultaneously as 'discuss', 'consult', 'confer', 'liaise', 'debate', 'deliberate', etc. But now that consultative process, the magic ingredient of the polder model, has given way to conflict and a hardening of attitudes. Government and trade unions have embarked on a power struggle, a trial of strength which has so far culminated in a mass demonstration in Amsterdam on 2 October 2004 at which more than 200,000 people expressed their displeasure with government policy, followed by several 'political strikes' each lasting 24 hours or more. The once proud polder model has been shaken to its foundations. How did things get to this pass? And above all, where will things go from here?

The main protagonists

These questions are all the more interesting because right up to the last moment the polder model appeared to have worked. Like so many countries, the Netherlands has been confronted in recent years with a stagnating economy and has had to devise solutions to the problem of an ageing population. Prime Minister Balkenende's second government, a coalition consisting of Christian Democrats, Liberals and Democrats, opted for tough measures. It tabled an austerity package involving spending cuts of no less than 20 billion euros, a post-war record. Under the programme, the social security system would have to be made less generous. Not only that, but people would have to work longer and harder. The number of people in work had be increased and, partly with a view to this, the existing pension schemes would have to be radically overhauled. Entirely in the style of the polder model, however, these measures were not simply imposed but were first submitted to employers' and employees' organisations; and that appeared to work.

Until well into the spring of 2004 the parties consulted and discussed, conferred and deliberated on the basis of a shared recognition that radical measures could not be avoided. Even the trade unions did not regard pensions as sacrosanct. There was an understanding of the government's desire to scrap all manner of tax breaks which made it attractive for employees to retire before the age of 65. As an insider characterised the situation in May, the gap between the different standpoints had become so small that it would be hard to fit more than a beer mat between them. And yet the consultations broke down. And how. Since June 2004 the trade unions have refused to engage in any form of discussion and the Netherlands has succumbed to a series of demonstrations and strikes.

Given that the substantive differences were so slight, it is tempting to attribute this breakdown to a conflict of personalities. The advantage of this approach is that it enables us to concentrate entirely on the main protagonists and their specific characters and problems. There is Lodewijk de Waal, for example, who for nearly ten years now has been president of the largest trade union federation, the FNV. He is confronted with a dwindling and ageing membership. He has difficulty in convincing people that the trade union movement is an indispensable institution in today's post-modern society. For him, action – especially mass action – could seem like manna from heaven; better, in any event, than the endless combing through minutiae in The Hague, from which it appears little is to be gained. However that may be, the Netherlands has seldom heard anyone call for 'action, action, action' more enthusiastically than Lodewijk de Waal did on 2 October in Amsterdam.

Then there is Jacques Schraven, the angular president of the biggest employers' organisation, VNO/NCW. Time and again, in the spoken and the written word, he has voiced his displeasure about the polder model: it is too cumbersome, too collectivist and above all too dominated by a trade union movement which wants to keep everything the same as it has always been and appears unwilling to countenance necessary change. Schraven is also a typical representative of international big business, which sees the trade union movement as nothing more than an obstacle to progress. Where small businesses would not dare to make separate arrangements with individual employees nor to try and compete in their sector on wage costs, the large conglomerates take a different approach: the trade union movement can drop dead. The unions are hardly representative any more, and if necessary big business will simply move its operations to a low-wage country. The large corporations appear set on breaking the power of the trade unions, and the current period of economic downturn seems to them an opportune moment. 'Bring it on, Lodewijk de Waal', as Schraven said at one point; 'you won't get any support anyway.'

And then, finally, there is the Christian Democrat Minister of Social Affairs and Employment, Aart Jan de Geus. Until recently he was vice-president of the second largest trade union federation, the Christian CNV. After an intervening period in industry he was appointed a Minister in the Balkenende government. De Geus is someone who believes that the words 'own responsibility' should be written in capital letters. He has a healthy disregard for collective arrangements. Along with the Christian Democrats in the Dutch CDA party, he believes that the government should hand back many of its responsibilities to society. There is indeed a place for the trade union movement in such a vision; but less so for a trade union movement that derives its authority in part from the arrangements it makes with the government. In short, it may be that De Geus had had enough of all that consultation and conferring.

Quid pro quo

This coming together of individuals with their different personalities and problems undoubtedly goes some way towards explaining why the polder model failed in the spring of 2004. The protagonists' distaste for each other could even be seen in the television coverage. In frequently repeated footage, TV viewers saw time and time again how Lodewijk de Waal pointedly refused to shake the outstretched hand of Aart Jan de Geus. The picture encapsulated the complicated conflict perfectly in a single image. Here we had a trade union movement which was avoiding reasonable consultation. And here, it seemed, was a trade union movement which for the sake of an ageing membership, for the sake of the baby-boomers' generation, was digging in its heels and rejecting necessary change. And in the rhetoric of the government and some employers, that trade union movement was soon being denounced as ultra-conservative, as a movement which was happy for the younger generation to carry the burden of an older generation which was already enjoying such fantastic pensions.

But of course it is not as simple as that, as becomes apparent if we take the trouble to look at the substance of the conflict. Take the pensions issue, for example. Things in the Netherlands are arranged in such a way that everyone receives a minimum state retirement benefit (AOW) on reaching the age of 65. The costs of funding this benefit are borne by those in work, who pay contributions ('AOW-premie') into the system. This means that as more people retire, as the population ages, so these contributions will increase. Objectively this is a problem, although many economists believe that we should not over-dramatise it; the extra costs can simply be paid for out of economic growth.

On top of the AOW benefit comes the pension proper. In the Netherlands this pension is in reality one large savings fund, which is paid for by contributions from employees and employers. In principle, therefore, it makes no difference how many people retire: the savings have been paid into the fund, and the money is there. Here the Netherlands is in a better position than many other countries where pensions have to be funded entirely by those in work. Another typical Dutch feature is that employers and employees have equal control over this pension fund. The trade unions (together with the employers) thus administer an enormous savings fund totalling many billions of euros. The government only gets involved in the fiscal aspects, regulating things such as the tax breaks that allow employees to retire early.

So far so good, and all fairly clear. Things only started to become complicated when the Balkenende government announced that it wanted to scrap these tax breaks. In their place the government wants to introduce a 'life-span savings scheme', which is intended to enable employees to spend part of their working lives doing something else, for example looking after their families, taking a trip round the world or – also an option – retiring early. To cut a long story short, the trade unions have no objection to this revamping of the tax system. They can see some sense in it; though they do not like the abruptness with which the government wishes to switch from one system to another. But the biggest problem the trade unions have is with the fact that the choice will be left entirely to individual employees, who may decide for themselves for what purpose they wish to use the available tax facilities. The unions fear that this will remove the basis for collective agreements, something that would be disadvantageous for employees.

An outsider can of course argue that it's up to the government to decide how it spends taxpayers' money, and that it is none of the trade unions' business. But any such comment would simply demonstrate that the person uttering it has understood nothing of the Dutch polder model. The essence of that model is the joint recognition by employees, employers and government that they all need each other. For example, the Dutch government has for many years sought to keep wage costs down: that is good for international competitiveness, so the reasoning goes, and that in turn is good for the Dutch economy. For this reason the government (and not just the government) regularly calls on the trade union movement to exercise moderation. The Balkenende government has even called for wages to be frozen for several years. For its part, the trade union movement does not automatically adopt a negative stance, unlike trade unions in America, for example, who know only one principle: we want more. However, the Dutch trade unions do expect something in return, a quid pro quo: if the government wishes to keep wages down it will have to do its best to please the trade unions in other ways.

Backs to the wall

This brings us to the heart of the problem. How can the government do a deal with the unions which does not rub the employers up too much the wrong way and which also accords with the political ambitions of the ruling coalition? This compromise was achieved with immense success during the early post-war years, the period of reconstruction. Government after government succeeded in holding down wages yet keeping the trade unions happy. The economy was the great beneficiary, because the Netherlands was able to keep its costs low, which in turn was good for exports. In the late 1960s, though, this policy became untenable. The government found itself powerless in the face of a series of wage explosions. These were also the years in which the government was frantically looking for ways to rein in a trade union movement that had become virtually uncontrollable, culminating in the introduction of wage legislation which gave the government the power to freeze wages under certain circumstances.

It was not a success. Not only did it upset relations with the trade unions, it also did nothing to improve the economy. When politicians did succeed in freezing wages temporarily, the result was usually that the shortfall was promptly made up again afterwards. It was for this reason that the coalition of Christian Democrats and Liberals which took office in 1982 under Prime Minister Ruud Lubbers decided to opt for a different approach. His government was confronted with gigantic economic problems. Factory closures were the order of the day and the spectre of mass long-term unemployment was looming. The Lubbers government too saw wage moderation as the best way of escaping from the mire. Unlike previous governments, however, it avoided confrontation with the trade unions. In deepest secrecy the government attempted to do a deal with the unions, based on the quid pro quo principle: you scratch my back and I'll scratch yours. And this approach proved effective. The government offered to cooperate in all kinds of schemes to shorten working hours and in exchange the trade unions were willing to accept a freeze on wages. Less pay for less work, in other words, with the additional benefit that this would enable more people to find jobs. This deal was dubbed the 'Wassenaar Accord' (1981), and it is still regarded as forming the basis for the Dutch polder model.

And this much is true: since the Wassenaar Accord this form of consultation has enjoyed a golden age. At first it was somewhat laborious and there were regular complaints about how cumbersome the model was. But in the 1990s it was praise all round. The Dutch economy was booming as never before. For the first time in decades the Minister of Finance had money left over. The coalition governments under Prime Minister Wim Kok rolled from one windfall to the next. Nothing, it seemed, could go wrong. Until the tide turned around the turn of the millennium. In the first years of the new century the Dutch economy even showed signs of recession. Once again the Dutch reached for the tried and tested formula: wage moderation. The only problem was, how to achieve that without antagonising the unions. And more specifically, how credible is a wage freeze for employees who are confronted in their own company with a management elite who have made 'excessive self-enrichment' (to use a phrase coined by Wim Kok himself) their highest goal?

To cut a long story short, it quickly became apparent that the Balkenende government had little to offer the trade unions. Certainly, the government promised that over time it would save jobs. But what caught the attention of the trade unions was that the price for achieving this noble aim was to be radical cuts in the social security system. Moreover, the government wanted to begin dismantling the existing pension schemes immediately. And if all this was not enough, Minister De Geus announced laconically that he would not necessarily declare Collective Labour Agreements negotiated in specific sectors to be binding on the entire sector. These Agreements can be declared binding by the Minister on every employee under the terms of a law brought in in 1937, the WAVV (*Wet op het algemeen verbindend en onverbindend verklaren van bepalingen van collectieve arbeidsovereenkomsten*). For years that law had been applied as a matter of course; so De Geus' announcement that he would no longer be doing so acted like a red rag to a bull. According to the trade unions, the Minister was effectively pulling the rug from under the institution of Collective Labour Agreement negotiations.

Seen in this light, it is actually a miracle that the parties continued to negotiate for as long as they did. The reason is undoubtedly that in recent years the trade unions had forgotten how to organise industrial action. Indeed, within the trade union movement there was some anxiety as to whether they were still capable of mobilising the rank and file. The movement appeared to have lost its ability to 'fight the good fight'. The institution had been created for the forging of collective agreements and the imposing of collective schemes. But such arrangements no longer appear appropriate in a post-modern society made up of individuals who wish to be left to go their own way. To cap it all, union membership was dwindling and ageing. And so the question facing the leadership was: who or what do the trade unions still represent?

The neo-liberal forces in the government and within the employers' organisations saw their chance to push the trade union movement further on to the back foot. The union movement, they argued, is no longer of today. It is a conservative club which stands in the way of necessary reform. In their enthusiasm to model Dutch society on the American example, some ministers and employers even went so far as to seek to remove employees' protection against dismissal, halve the minimum wage and cut social security benefits to the bare minimum. Only in this way, they argued, could the Netherlands compete with the Anglo-American economy and that of emerging Asia.

In short, the trade unions had their backs to the wall. But, as is often the case in such situations, they began to fight back. At that first demonstration in September in Rotterdam, the union leaders stood nervously watching and waiting. Would anyone actually turn up? But turn up they did; more than 20,000 of them. And by 2 October the 'workers' army' had grown to more than 200,000. And so the tables were turned. The media, which until recently had been looking upon the trade unions with pity, suddenly began expressing respect for the movement once again. Lodewijk de Waal, frequently maligned as a testy, morose union man, became a hero in the space of a few days. It was the government's turn to find itself on the defensive.

At the time this article was written the trial of strength between government and trade unions was still in full swing. But it was also becoming clear that the government was making attempts to normalise relations again. The polder model had been shaken, but one thing was certain: whatever happened, it would not fall.

How polder became Rhineland

Then, at the end of this turbulent month, not long after I finished this article, the Balkenende government, the employers' organisations and the trade union movement did succeed in reaching an agreement. It is known as the Museumplein Accord, after the Amsterdam square where more than two hundred thousand people had demonstrated against the government's plans. So it seemed the polder model had triumphed after all. Later in November the grass roots of the trade union movement also agreed, so that in the coming months things can be done in the good old way. And they will need to be, for this is a decidedly vague agreement. The pension plans will be implemented, but no-one knows exactly how. In addition, the government has reached a compromise with the unions on the WAO, the reform of incapacity benefit. Most important, however, is that the government has stated that it will take no action without consulting the union movement. So it's back to the polder model, then, or more accurately the Rhineland model, since things are done in much the same way in Germany and Belgium. Those members of the government who wanted to move towards a more Anglo-Saxon method of government based on the free market have lost the battle.

The agreement came not a second too early, for on 2 November the film-maker and writer Theo van Gogh was hideously murdered in Amsterdam by a young home-grown Muslim extremist, the 27-year-old Moroccan Amsterdammer Mohammed B. His murder sent shockwaves through the Netherlands, with massive demonstrations against Muslim terrorism and for freedom of expression. In the week that followed an Islamic school was burned to the ground and there were arson attacks on more than thirteen mosques scattered throughout the country. This murder and the violent emotions it aroused are totally unconnected with events relating to the polder model. But both issues do raise urgent questions about the leadership of the Balkenende government. And consequently both issues show that the once so stable democracy of the Low Countries has come seriously unstuck. ■

Translated by Julian Ross

Any Way Tom Barman Goes

[P E T E R   V A N T Y G H E M]

Tom Barman (r.) on the set
of *Any Way the Wind Blows*.
Photo by Maarten
vanden Abeele.
Courtesy of Corridor,
Brussels.

Tom Barman isn't the sort of person who enjoys appearing on television. He doesn't like talking about his private life. Yet he is still widely perceived as an important artist and he is one of the few Flemish people to achieve the very difficult feat of being admired by pop fans while at the same time being taken seriously by artistic types.

Barman comes from Antwerp, but his roots lie a long way from there. His mother is from West Flanders; his father was a Norwegian engineer who was 62 when he fathered him. Barman came into contact with beauty in his home, partly through his parents' large collection of paintings. There were absolutely no musical influences, but there were linguistic ones. Barman grew up in a relaxed environment. The family was wealthy until his father became ill and died. Barman was 15 at the time.

For most people Barman is synonymous with dEUS, the rock group that he formed in 1991 with Stef Kamil Carlens. Initially the Antwerp group played mainly covers of American bands, but they soon began to interweave their own work with this. dEUS entered the Rock Rally, the most important Belgian talent-spotting contest, organised by the television guide *Humo*. They didn't win, but they knew that they were good. To the public that saw dEUS perform at that time, Barman's central role wasn't clear. Like that other man from Flanders, singer Arno Hintjens, Barman had the knack of gathering strong characters around himself. The result was that at least three people in the group stood out: the guitarist Rudy Trouvé, the singer Tom Barman and the co-singer and bassist Stef Kamil Carlens. The latter also had the most sex appeal. dEUS also took on Klaas Janszoons, a street musician with folk roots, and the experienced painter/drummer/roadie Jules de Borgher. Together they worked on their own numbers and slogged their way round the usual circuit for young bands: appearances in cafés, in youth clubs, attempts to secure a record contract. Not a single record company proved to be interested, so the first EP *Zea* appeared on the small, independent label Bang!

Even on this first EP, a disc with three songs, the group's ambition to be different was already apparent. The music was produced by Peter Vermeersch and Pierre Vervloesem, who were well-known from the eclectic jazz company X-Legged Sally. A jazz duo accompanying an infant rock group: *'We thought it was interesting to let someone with different ideas loose on our music,'* explained the band. *'The best songs are those that can't be slotted into a frame of reference,'* said Barman. Eventually the group was allowed to record a whole album: *Worst Case Scenario*. This proved to be an earthshaking event in Belgian rock music, and a classic on the growing European rock scene. And this time the industry did understand it. dEUS were invited to London as the supporting act for Girls against Boys, an American band that a lot of record companies were interested in at the time. But the industry representatives left the room with just one name in their heads: dEUS. Offers streamed in for the Antwerp group.

Worst Case Scenario sold 140,000 copies, an unusually large number for a Belgian debut. But what was more important was the fact that dEUS finally seemed to be a band that was also capable of making it in England. At that time, however, dEUS was an unpredictable band, with too many egos together in one place. This quickly led to tensions. Rudy Trouvé was the first one to leave. The artist Trouvé, who was also very busy with lots of smaller bands, missed his painting and hated the long tours. dEUS had become too big for him.

Worst Case Scenario is a strong album even now, sounding surprisingly mature and still progressive even ten years on. dEUS refused to make the sort of album that is meat and drink to record companies: the same song ten times, with the best one going to MTV as a single. Every song by dEUS was a microcosm, with its own dynamic. But at the same time the group still managed to have a recognisable face: songs by dEUS consistently varied between manic outbursts and subdued romance. This tension between the two extremes was sometimes masterfully rendered, giving the songs and concerts immense dramatic power.

Meanwhile the record company Island had turned out to have the most convincing arguments to persuade dEUS to sign up with them. The debut album was reissued and dEUS had to do yet more promotion and concerts, which naturally generated tension. As a result, the creative bassist Stef Kamil Carlens, regarded by some of the public as the face of dEUS, also left the band. Carlens set up his own band, Moondog Jr. (which after one album became Zita Swoon).

But dEUS continued to be successful. It was a time when British rock music, usually the trendsetter in European rock, was going through a particularly lean phase. Youth culture in England had been won over by house and techno, on the one hand , and also by the new pop music from British ethnic-minority bands. All over Europe a feeling was growing that you didn't have to come from England to be able to make good music. dEUS became one of the big names on that circuit. But right from the start dEUS showed that they had their own style, and that had a great deal to do with Tom Barman's highly-strung nature. He wrote the song 'Little Arithmetics', which had a lot of similarities with a lively country number by J.J. Cale, but he felt that he had to 'dEUS-ify' the melodic, friendly version, which meant shooting it through with a strong pulse of energy somewhere in the middle. That sort of wilfulness was not understood by the new record company, and the group had to cut out the extra piece to get the single onto the market in England.

Tom Barman also started to become active as a film director. Because the first album had done so well and dEUS were tipped to make a much more widespread breakthrough, there was money available to do rather more promotion. Barman directed the video for 'Theme from Turnpike', which he turned into *Turnpike*, a short film. The video was immediately censored, because one of the actors appeared to be parodying a handicapped person. It was clear that the tensions would develop between the commercial world of the pop industry and the artistic instincts of dEUS.

In a Bar, under the Sea, dEUS' second album, came out in September 1996. At the insistence of the record company, the group used a producer. The popular Flood was first choice, but he was tied up with U2. The choice fell upon Eric Drew Feldman, an American keyboard player who had earned his spurs with Captain Beefheart and played with P.J. Harvey. His role was to make the young group think about what they were doing and add the finishing touches to their ideas. He was actually more of a father figure than a creative stimulus.

In a Bar, under the Sea resulted in four singles. There was increased attention from Europe and England; there was no interest in the US. *Pitchfork Media* had the following to say about the CD: '*It's always nice to find an album you can't quite pigeonhole, and dEUS sheds its skin all over the place. (...) it's a smorgasbord of delights, you fool! I don't think I have to tell you that this album isn't for everybody. Some people are going to hate it outright. Some people are pretty fucking stupid.*' It was in fact a more than respectable album, but from a commercial point of view it didn't change anything for the band. Feldman had seen it coming: '*The members are all so different. They create tension and you can hear that in their music. The way they're working now can't continue. They'll change and go off in different directions.*'

In Belgium, dEUS had achieved everything that a rock band can achieve. The first two records had sold an average of 50,000 copies, dEUS commanded respect in most West European countries and had no trouble touring in largish venues and at big festivals. By 1997, five years after the group's beginning, Tom Barman had already accomplished half of his ten-year plan. How he planned to approach the second half remained to be seen.

The third album, *The Ideal Crash*, appeared in March 1999. Everything to do with this album had been well thought out. Two English 'supervisors', Dave Bedford and Nigel Coxon, were dispatched to make the unpredictable Belgian band a little more streamlined. '*The group needs to work in a more directed way,*' said Coxon. '*It used to sound a bit too arty. For my taste, there was almost too much dedication.*' Logic became the new keyword. But Tom Barman demonstrated yet again that he would far rather be an artiste than an entertainer, let alone a pop star. The aim, he says, was to make a funky summer album for once, and a lot of time was put aside for it. And because it allowed a lot of things to come to the surface, *The Ideal Crash* became a sombre album about broken relationships. A listening experience that requires real effort on the part of the listeners.

No other dEUS album reflects Tom Barman as well as *The Ideal Crash*, and the singer himself was stunned that the fans figured that out so well. He explained a thing or two to the Flemish newspaper *De Standaard*: '*I went through a psychotic phase when I was 22, and I've retained a lot of images from that episode. I had absolutely no idea what was happening to me, and I thought I was going to die. It was such an extreme state of alienation that I was too scared to go outside.*'

Barman showed greater ambition in his lyrics, proceeding from the idea that writing is a way of putting your life in order. '*In your lyrics you have the possibility of being a fascist to yourself. Through them, I can see how far I can push myself. I have the feeling that, as far as writing lyrics is concerned, I'm only just beginning. I want to work more poetically, with metaphors and magnification. Like Leonard Cohen: describing something very small in a very large way.*'

Barman had a plan. Did he really still need a group? Shouldn't he rather become a solo artist with a number of good musicians alongside him? dEUS went on tour and played large venues, but because the era of CD pirating was just beginning, this album didn't sell any more than the previous one. Barman decided that it was time for the final part of his great plan and he put dEUS on the back burner for three years.

A gently neurotic city film

Rock music was never Barman's first love. When dEUS started, he told journalists that he wanted to make three albums and a film in the following decade. The albums attracted a lot of attention , but the fact that Barman wanted to do something with film was quickly forgotten. Unfairly, because Tom Barman is much more a film person than a music person. When he was only fifteen, he wanted to go and study filmmaking in Brussels, and after leaving secondary school he did just that.

A well-known anecdote relates that in his first year at the Hoger Instituut Sint-Lucas Barman was caught cribbing in an exam and thrown out. *'My own fault,'* he later said. *'But I did pick up a few things there. But anyway, with a bit of ambition and common sense you can go far.'*

His father had died shortly before. Barman then decided to embark on a career in music. Not until 2003 would he be able to realise his dream of making a film.

In September 2002 the newspapers were able to announce *'Rock singer becomes film director.'* The film would be called *Any Way the Wind Blows*; it was actually a short film that was polished over two years, and because Barman, as an unqualified film director, did fantastically well in still managing to get the money together, the plans became firmer. A film about 24 hours in the lives of a few people. *'An awkward musical, a gently neurotic city film,'* proclaimed Barman.

Any Way the Wind Blows was not Barman's cinematographic test piece. His work with dEUS, and the popularity of the group on a European level, had allowed him to make videos. 'It's possible that I can do much more filming than most of the people I studied with who did complete their degrees,' he used to say, without gloating. Particularly in *Turnpike* (from the second album), Barman showed himself a disciple of cinephile cinema, and one of the projects he produced was *Les yeux de ma mère* for Arno.

Any Way the Wind Blows is named after a song by the American country singer J.J. Cale. He tries to capture the soul of a city, in this case Antwerp. Music and celebration are an important part of this. The critic Steven de Foer described it in *De Standaard* as *'an effervescent and original collage of eight lives in Antwerp over 24 hours, where various twists of fate lead to everyone ending up at the same party. Rather baroque, but awfully entertaining.'*

As with dEUS, Barman wanted to make something different. Up till then Flemish film had achieved little that was innovative. What it had produced was a great many screen versions of literary classics. *'I miss rock 'n' roll,'* said Barman. *'I'm looking for a contemporary feel that we already know from the theatre of Alain Platel and Arne Sierens. That's what it's about: seeing real life transformed into something that, in the best case, becomes theatre or cinema.'*

Tom Barman's first film (which was also released in England in November 2004 and is now available on DVD) had a lot in common with his first dEUS album, and Eric Feldman's words could just as easily have been intended for Barman the director: *'His ideas move more quickly than what he does with them.'* Barman was well aware of that, but wasn't at all bothered about it. *'Multiplicity was my point of departure: lots of dialects, lots of characters, lots of styles. But for my second film I want the opposite of that multiplicity: an authentic, simple story.'*

Any Way the Wind Blows (2003). Courtesy of Corridor, Brussels.

The second Ten-year plan

Whether Tom Barman will ever write an authentic, simple story or song is very much the question. During the filming of *Any Way the Wind Blows* he killed time by doing an acoustic tour with pianist Guy van Nueten. He sang his own songs, and also covers of J.J. Cale, Joni Mitchell, Captain Beefheart, Nick Drake and Serge Gainsbourg's 'Le poinçonneur des lilas'. He learned to play the guitar better and, above all, to use his voice better. The results of all this can be heard on the double CD *Live*, which came out in November 2003.

Now Tom Barman has started on his second ten-year plan, although he hasn't yet made any statements about it. In February 2004, he brought out the CD *The Body Gave You Everything* with Magnus, a side project – but definitely not a 'quickie', as Barman himself emphasised – which again turned out very different than intended. Barman wanted to explore electronic music in the company of musician/composer Peter Vermeersch and DJ CJ Bolland, but the result was ultimately more song-based than had originally been intended. The single 'Summer's here', which came out in 2003 and which could also be heard on the soundtrack of *Any Way the Wind Blows*, was already an indication of this: lazy funk with a relaxed beat, and Tom Barman sounding like J.J. Cale and, as he himself

said, not in the least bothered about that. He's rehearsing new songs with dEUS and a new album is due to be released in spring 2005. A more streamlined dEUS can be heard on 'If you don't get what you want', a new track that could already be downloaded from the group's website in summer 2004. No more forced barbs, but a more accessible sound that is anything but slick: garage rock for the twenty-first century, somewhere between the Velvet Underground and the Queens of the Stone Age. And on the eve of the tour in November 2004 that took them to France, the Netherlands, Luxembourg, Switzerland and England, dEUS once again looked completely different. Guitarist Craig Ward and bassist Danny Mommens (from Vive la Fête) have been replaced by Mauro Pawlowski (ex-Evil Superstars and now the creative axis of a number of bands including Mauro and the Grooms) and Alan Gevaert (who has played with Arno Hintjens, amongst others). So, the expectations are high. Barman himself remains calm and is brimming with self-confidence about the forthcoming CD and the subsequent international tour. And he's still living in Antwerp, in spite of his frequently repeated comment that he was fed up with the city and wanted to move to Brussels.

The story is far from over. *No More Loud Music* is the title of the 2001 dEUS compilation CD. But it certainly won't be silent either. ∎

www.deus.be
www.anywaythewindblows.com
www.magnusmusic.com

Translated by Laura Watkinson

A Plantation Turned Hotel

The Built Heritage of Suriname

[MICHEL BAKKER & OLGA VAN DER KLOOSTER]

The addition of the historic city centre of Paramaribo to the UNESCO World Heritage List was due to the exceptional value of this piece of cultural heritage. Founded by the Dutch as a trading post in 1613, the original layout of the inner city is still defined by ridges of calcified shells. Historic Paramaribo consists partly of wooden structures that have survived from the eighteenth and nineteenth centuries, and is a unique example of world heritage that should be protected. The Anglo-French war at the end of the eighteenth century and the abolition of slavery in 1863, which led to a serious labour shortage, heralded the decline of the plantations. Today, virtually nothing remains of Suriname's traditional plantation culture.

Plans are being developed to revitalise the areas that are still populated, such as the Commewijne District, to create a livelihood for the people who live there. According to Surinamese experts, there is considerable potential for reviving agriculture and horticulture on the river's right bank. This would create

ANWB sign in Paramaribo.
Photo by Michel Bakker,
2003.

Onafhankelijkheidsplein (Independence Square). The building on the left is the Court of Justice (1791, present form). The statue of Premier Pengel, who died in 1970, was the first bronze statue to be cast in Suriname. Photo by Olga van der Klooster, 2003.

a new future for the surviving historic buildings on the plantations, which would enhance the area's tourist potential. Conservation organisations in Suriname, such as the Urban Heritage Foundation Suriname (Stichting Gebouwd Erfgoed Suriname), recognise the importance of gaining international recognition for Paramaribo's heritage. They are committed not only to preserving the city, with its striking monuments such as the cathedral, but also to preserving and re-vitalising the outlying districts. The renovation and reuse of the Frederiksdorp plantation has been a spearhead project in this.

Large sections of the Surinamese population feel that these historic buildings add to the atmosphere of their country, be it as typically Surinamese or as a more general heritage. At present over 80 percent of the Surinamese considers the restoration of the historic centre of Paramaribo to be a high priority issue for policymakers. There is a general consensus that cooperation between the government and the private sector is useful in this matter.

A shared past

The Urban Heritage Foundation is housed in a former officer's residence opposite Fort Zeelandia. Guests are received in a conservatory behind the office. Hummingbirds hover and dart in the cool shade of the mahogany tree. In the distance, the mail boat sounds its horn as it departs for Baki on the Commewijne river. A man on a bicycle with a birdcage balanced on the handlebars waves to the old sentry post at the fort. Tamarind lemonade is served.

Stephen Fokké, director of the foundation, says: *'There are many different cultures in Suriname, including the Creole, Hindustani, Chinese, Javanese, Maroon and indigenous cultures. Yet everyone regards the city centre as part of their own cultural heritage, despite the fact that most of it was built by the Dutch colonists. Their ancestors helped to build this historic city, perhaps working as carpenters or tree-fellers in the forest. Although the master builders or architects were probably Dutch, the Surinamese themselves made an important contribution to the development of the city and its buildings. It is more appropriate to describe it as a "common heritage", to speak of a past shared by the Netherlands and Suriname. In general,*

most people are in favour of conservation. The growing interest is also evident on the annual Open Days and in education.'

In Suriname there are no restoration funds or special tax benefits, as there are in the Netherlands. The owners of historic buildings and monuments usually have to rely on their own resources. For companies with premises in a historic building a proportion of the restoration cost is tax-deductible, but private owners of such buildings have to fund the restoration work themselves.

Currently, 244 buildings and monuments have listed status. These are mostly large buildings such as the Fort Zeelandia complex, the Presidential Palace, the Ministry of Finance, the Roman Catholic cathedral of SS Peter and Paul, the corner house at Waterkant 2, the Weighhouse, the Reformed Church on Kerkplein, the Lutheran church and the Neve Shalom synagogue, together with a number of small traditional Surinamese homes. The Palm Garden (Palmentuin) and the Oranjetuin cemetery are also listed. The formal listing procedure is now under way for Fort Amsterdam – the first building in the Commewijne district to be listed. This will probably be followed by the Jewish Savannah (Jodensavanne) in the Para district, with the ruins of a synagogue (one of the oldest in the Western hemisphere), a Jewish cemetery and a 'Creole cemetery'. The plantation houses along the Commewijne, including Frederiksdorp, Peperpot, Spieringshoek and Mariënbosch, are also in need of attention. Apart from the Commewijne district, valuable historic buildings in the Saramacca, Coronie and Nickerie districts are also in need of preservation. However, it will be some time before listed buildings are designated outside Paramaribo.

Above all, the Surinamese were specialists in building in wood. Brickwork, using a wide range of non-standard bricks, also attests to past craftsmanship. Unfortunately, these are skills from a bygone age and considerable investment will be required to revive them. A further problem is that, sadly, a number of historic sites have been destroyed by fire. The latest victims include the Statengebouw and the adjacent Ministries (General and Foreign Affairs). The fires have left conspicuous gaps in Gravenstraat, but the most serious problem is probably neglect and lack of maintenance. This situation can only be improved by creating greater public awareness by means of management contracts, restoration funds to provide financial incentives for owners, tax benefits and a commitment to gainful reuse.

Presidential Palace at Paramaribo, formerly the Governor's residence. Photo by Olga van der Klooster, 2003.

Officer's residence at Fort Zeelandia on the Suriname river. Photo by Olga van der Klooster, 2003.

Plantation church
at Coronie.
Photo by Michel Bakker,
2003.

Noere Islam mosque of
the Surinaams Islamitische
Vereniging (SIV),
at Commissaris
Thurkowweg 744 in
Nieuw Amsterdam.
Photo by Michel Bakker,
2004.

The built heritage must be used as a catalyst for the revitalisation of the historic heart of the city. Once people see what can be achieved, a snowball effect will be created. In the past, Paramaribo was a much greener place. Gravenstraat, Jodenbreestraat and Zwartenhovenbrugstraat used to be lined with trees, but more and more of this greenery is disappearing. Mahogany trees are beautiful, but termites love them too. The Urban Heritage Foundation Suriname believes that conservation means restoring not only the buildings, but also their surroundings. Trees are an essential part of the plans to revitalise the historic city centre.

The inclusion of this historic area on the World Heritage List means, above all, that Paramaribo's heritage is considered to be of exceptional value in an international, global context. It forms an impressive combination with the Central Suriname Nature Reserve, which has been on the list since 2000. However, its inclusion has yielded little in terms of financial resources.

A cathedral in equilibrium

The *mamakerki* or mother church of Catholic Suriname, the Cathedral of SS Peter and Paul in Gravenstraat in Paramaribo, is, along with that of Georgetown, among the largest wooden churches in the world. Its predecessor was consecrated on 4 March 1826 on the same site. The cathedral used to be the theatre of a Jewish company, and was converted under the supervision of the architect W. de Vroome. A hexagonal tower denoted the building's new function. The present church (1883-1885) was built around the original structure. It was designed by the Redemptorist priest Franciscus Joseph Leonard Harmes (Venlo, 1835 – Paramaribo, 1894). In approximately 1890, the simple pavilion roofs on the towers were replaced with the current neo-Gothic spires. The cruciform basilica has a frontage of 19 metres and a central nave and two side-aisles. There is a chapel at each end of the transept. The cathedral encloses a total of 15,500 m³. The sacristy was added later and is located behind the chancel. The church building is painted in grey and yellow, a reference to the limestone and sandstone so characteristic of European architecture. Inside the building, none

of the cedarwood panelling is painted. The neo-Roman and neo-Gothic influences do not mask the fact that the building, with its light wooden structure, is
firmly rooted in the architectural traditions of Suriname.

The structure is not noted for its solidity. Maintenance was a problem from
the beginning. The building was constantly under threat from leaks and rot. By
the 1970s it was in need of a thorough restoration and in 1974 a management
foundation, STIBEKA (Stichting Beheer R.K. Kathedraal), was set up for this
purpose. Its aim was to 'conserve, protect and maintain the church'. STIBEKA
was true to its word, and the restoration began. Unfortunately, while the work
was being carried out the building began to lean so far out of true that church
services had to be stopped. The building had to be stabilised, but the expertise
and funds were not available. Help was at hand, however.

The designer of the cathedral, Father Harmes, had experience as a construction engineer but no formal training. A cathedral with a high central nave caused
a problem he could not have foreseen. If all elements of the nave are the same
height, the horizontal forces are in equilibrium. With a high central nave, the
weight of the superstructure causes the sides to buckle outwards, with consequences in the long term. In stone architecture this problem has traditionally
been solved by using buttresses and flying buttresses. A wooden building can
be stable if it has strong, continuous wooden stanchions. In this cathedral, the
stanchions are not continuous, but consist of a 'stack' of elements. Where one
element rests on another horizontal forces cannot be countered, and the point
acts as a 'hinge'.

A coffee plantation revisited

Imagine you are sailing down the Commewijne river. It is 1775. You are travelling to Paramaribo on a tent boat, but the incoming spring tide is too strong to
continue. It will soon be dark. Well, not really dark; the full moon is so bright
that you could easily read a book by it – if you weren't distracted by the fairytale swarms of fireflies, hovering above the riverbanks like tiny glowing lights.
There are no inns or lodging houses, but anyone who needs a bed for the night
will be made welcome at most of the plantations. It is an unwritten law that
people help each other. On the right bank you see the Frederiksdorp plantation, lying between the Guadeloupe and Knöffelsgift plantations. The white jetty
and copper ship's bell glint in the evening sun. The tired boat slaves, bathed in
sweat, tie up the boat. A brand-new six-oar tent boat floats in the boathouse;
the plantation manager is at home. The smell of paint from two newly painted
guardhouses lingers in the air. A negro watchman beckons to you. With its geo-
metrical flower garden and rococo stone pedestal with sundial, the plantation
evokes the stately country seat of an Amsterdam merchant by the river Vecht in
the Netherlands, or the home of a wealthy sugar-planter on the Mississippi in
Louisiana. Some plantations boast imposing, almost life-size statues in white
marble depicting the four seasons – including Winter! [1]

The tamarind trees shade the long drive leading to the grand pearl-white
plantation house with its green shutters. The steps up to the front veranda are
for guests only. The fine brickwork reveals the skill of one of the plantation's
slave bricklayers. The front veranda leads to the finest room in the house. This
is the 'best room', reserved for visitors. The room at the side is used every day,

Cathedral of ss Peter and
Paul in Gravenstraat,
the *Mamakerki* of
Catholic Paramaribo.
Photo by Olga van der
Klooster, 2003.

but most activity takes place on the veranda at the back of the house, where there is a room to which everyone comes to eat. There is always someone in the scullery, busy with pots and pans and cutlery. The stairs by the veranda at the back of the house are a hive of activity. The house-slave calls the laundry maids and gives them instructions. A young mulatto boy carries a fishing rod on his shoulder. Kwi-kwis squirm in his bucket. Everything that is consumed in the house is grown or bred on the plantation. A couple of female slaves have been given the task of cutting up the sheep, cows and poultry that have been slaughtered. In the distance you see a crop-watcher running through the vegetable garden, waving his arms wildly to scare away the birds. You walk along the veranda at the back of the house to the creaking stairs that lead to the next storey. Upstairs there are two large rooms and four small ones – some of them bedrooms – and an extra panelled room in the attic. There is a breathtaking view of the Commewijne river from the top of the house! This is where you will spend the night. You gaze out of the window for a few more moments.

A group of women squat on the stone floor in front of the coffee sheds, sorting

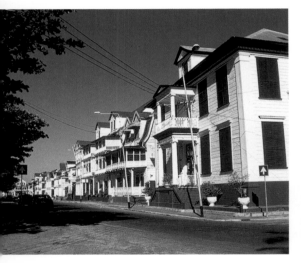 

The Waterfront in Paramaribo, with its monumental buildings. Photo by Michel Bakker, 2003.

Double-fronted official residence built on tall stilts, restored in 2004. Photo by Michel Bakker, 2004.

coffee beans. A group of slaves has gathered by the veranda stairs at the back of the manager's house. They are reporting to the manager, who is seated in a rocking chair smoking a pipe. A female slave pours out rum. Every day, when the slaves have finished their work, they are given gin or rum. They are exhausted and their skin glistens with perspiration. The slaves work from 6 o'clock in the morning to 6 o'clock at night, Monday to Saturday, with a two-hour siesta in the afternoon. The work is seasonal. Now, with the rainy season approaching, everyone is hard at work clearing out the water channels and digging holes ready to plant the young coffee bushes. The negro overseer reports on the day's activities. With the tip of his whip he points to a field slave, who shakes his head in denial and raises his hands in the air in fear. He is afraid the manager will order him to be whipped. Not every plantation treats its workers well. Slaves are regarded as working capital, the property of the plantation owner.

You close the screens to keep out the mosquitoes. Downstairs, dinner is being served: corn, mutton, vegetables, and perhaps freshwater fish. It is now

The restored 18th-century home of the plantation manager is now a hotel. Photo by Michel Bakker, 2004.

dark outside. Now and again you hear a prolonged horn blast from the jetty, where a slave keeps watch at night. In the distance, from the other side of the river, his signal is answered.[2]

A negro worth 1,200 guilders

For more than three centuries the plantations were the mainstay of the Surinamese economy. The English, Portuguese, French and Dutch settled there as colonists in the seventeenth century. During the eighteenth century they were joined by German and Scottish planters. In the nineteenth century, 40% of plantation owners were the offspring of white fathers and female slaves.

In approximately 1746 Johan Frederik Knöffel bought the Frederiksdorp plantation by lot. Knöffel was a Lutheran from Prussia. In Paramaribo he was employed as the receiver of slave monies, and lived in a house near the Knöffelsgracht, the street named after him. He had two daughters, Johanna Cornelia and Anna Dorothea, by his house-slave Grietje. After his death in 1768, they were given their freedom and the fine-sounding surname Frederiksdorff in his will.[3]

In 1768 Frederiksdorp was a large plantation with at least 200 inhabitants. Like other wealthy plantation owners, 'gentleman farmer' Johan Frederik appointed a manager to run the plantation. The manager lived in a house built specially for him: a wooden house built on stilts, with a veranda front and back. The house had a living room, an alcove and a storeroom for all manner of tools and objects such as slave branding irons, neck collars and machetes for working in the fields. The countless bottles of wine and gin stored in the cellar are still being unearthed today during excavations. Johan Knöffel probably only lived on his plantation during the holidays, when he stayed in the main house. After his death in 1768, this was replaced by an imposing two-storey wooden house with an attic and two dormers.

The Frederiksdorp plantation also had its own resident doctor, who worked in the plantation's small hospital during the day. He lived in sober wooden quarters built on stilts with a veranda, which he shared with two white overseers. Each of them had his own room with a table, bench and chair. The nine house-slaves lived in an eight-room wooden housing block, also built on stilts. Finally, there was a Negro village with 37 huts.[4]

Most of the slaves built their own huts.[5] They were usually built in a line to form small streets. Each hut had its own patch of ground, with poultry and herbs. Unlike the other buildings, these houses were not usually built on stilts but were anchored to the ground by stakes, perhaps in accordance with African tradition.

The slave force at Frederiksdorp consisted of 61 women, 16 boys, 32 girls and 67 men. Most of these slaves worked in the coffee fields. During the day, while the women were at work, the children were looked after by a 'Creole mama'. Five negro carpenters and two negro bricklayers were responsible for building and maintaining the houses, sheds and sluices. No architects were involved, but skilled craftsmen were indispensable. Following the death of Johan Frederik, one of the negro carpenters was valued at no less than f.1,200, and a slave bricklayer at f.1,000.[6] The male slaves at Frederiksdorp included four coopers and a stockman. Three crop-watchers, usually 'retired' slaves, kept watch over the vegetable garden and coffee fields. Sometimes, at night, vagrants and escaped slaves would steal from the plantation. Two male slaves at Frederiksdorp worked as (field) overseers. They were also known as *bastiaans*, and supervised the workers during the day.

Number 19, upstream on the left bank of the Commewijne River

In the seventeenth century the West India Company was trying to develop the colony of Suriname as quickly as possible, and land grants were handed out indiscriminately. Colonists could choose their own spot upriver, and allocated themselves generous plots of land. In the course of the eighteenth century, government surveyors and clerks systematically mapped the unpopulated lower reaches of the rivers. This resulted in the unique parcelisation into narrow, elongated ribbons of land. From 1744 on, the plots of land along the Commewijne river were assigned by lot.[7] In 1746, a surveyor described Frederiksdorp as *'Number 19, upstream on the left bank of the Commewijne river'*, with an area of no less than 500 acres.[8]

Here the banks of the river are waterlogged in the rainy season, and the river itself is tidal. Farming requires a specialist knowledge of water management. The Dutch were very experienced in reclaiming land from the water to create polders. The majority of eighteenth century manuals containing step-by-step instructions on how to lay out and run a plantation were written by Dutch authors.

The plantations along the lower reaches of the river were criss-crossed by a symmetrical network of dykes, dams, watercourses and channels. The water level was controlled by sluices, which kept out the salt river-water at high tide, and carried away rainwater at low tide. The difference in water level was used to power watermills. The owner's house, the 'showcase' of the plantation, stood at the front of the plantation on the central axis by the river. Nearby were the workers' homes, factory buildings and a village of slave huts. The extensive fields were located behind these buildings. Agricultural products were delivered and collected by water. To ensure the proper defence of Suriname, every plantation owner was required to maintain the communication path that ran next to the river through his property. Cast-iron cannon were located along this route. In 1768 Frederiksdorp had nine cannon.[9]

Hotel Frederiksdorp

The Hagemeyer family bought the plantation in 1975, shortly before Suriname became independent. By that time Frederiksdorp had fallen into serious dis-repair. Only one eighteenth-century plantation residence remained. The other buildings – a police post, a jail and a doctor's residence – belonged to the district commission that was established here after slavery was abolished in 1863, and date from 1922. 'The first thing I bought was a dragline to repair the dams. During the rainy season the whole plantation was flooded,' recalls Ton Hagemeyer. 'Then we started a citrus plantation and farmed some livestock.' Today the family has turned to tourism, and the buildings are restored to their former splendour.

With the help of funding from the Netherlands, the family commissioned Philip Dikland (KDV-architecten, Paramaribo) to restore the buildings. When the restoration was finished, Frederiksdorp was designated a listed monument – the first listed plantation in Suriname.

The Commandant's residence is now the home of the hotel manager, and the three double-fronted official residences have been converted into six apartments. The eighteenth-century manager's residence, now a hotel, is especially popular with guests. ■

Translated by Yvette Mead

NOTES

1. It is not known whether Frederiksdorp had a flower garden with statues, but this was usual at the time. Some of the statues were naively executed, revealing the hand of a local sculptor who was not (yet) familiar with traditional European sculpture. A statue symbolising Winter currently stands in the museum garden at *Zorg en Hoop* in Paramaribo.

2. Description of the plantation based on inventories and valuation reports from 1768, 1775 and 1863. Plantation inventories from 1768: NA Not. nr. 227, fol. 261 ev, and 1775, NA Not. nr. 242, fol. 506 ev. Inventory of the estate of A. Ferrier 1863, drawn up under the *Gouvernementsresolutie* of 10 April 1863, Building Department archive for 1863, National Archive at Paramaribo.

3. Philip Dikland, Frederiksdorp Plantation, www.surinamehelppagina.com

4. Plantation inventories from 1768: NA Not. no. 227, fol. 261 ev, and 1775, NA Not. nr. 242, fol. 506 ev.

5. E. Klinkers, *Op hoop van vrijheid, Van slavensamenleving naar Creoolse gemeenschap in Suriname 1830-1880*, thesis published by the Department of Cultural Anthropology, University of Utrecht, 1997.

6. Inventory, 1768.

7. Philip Dikland, *Het oude archief van de Dienst der Domeinen te Paramaribo*, cd-rom 2004.

8. Ibid.

9. Inventory, 1768.

10. The world market was highly competitive. In 1828, in the American state of Louisiana, steam-driven mills produced no less than 87,965 barrels of sugar and 59,874 barrels of molasses. These figures are in stark contrast to those for traditional sugar production: 1,640 barrels of sugar and 750 barrels of molasses per year.

11. A. Loor, *Suikeronderneming Mariënburg Suriname 100 Jaar, 1882 - 23 oktober 1982. (1982).*

The Mirror Image and the Question 'Is that me?'

Philip Akkerman and his Self-Absorbed Struggle with Portraiture

How is it possible, year in, year out, to engage in a harsh and unrelenting fight against life and against ageing, provoking time and torturing yourself by continually painting and drawing your own face: that head that changes, those features that wrinkle? Philip Akkerman, born in 1957 in Vaassen in the Netherlands, has painted and drawn himself in hundreds of styles and many guises. Sometimes in a funny hat, then with very bushy eyebrows, thick lips or a pointed noise. He stares into the mirror, into the canvas hanging or standing in front of him, over and over again, asking 'Is that me?' – every day that same question about 'the me', about the mystery of existence.

'There is only one thing for me to do: keep going,' Akkerman wrote in his diary at the end of May 1991. Ten years earlier he noted that, as far as his work was concerned, *'I'm now working on self-portraits (a whole series)'*. By December 1991 he had already painted 495 self-portraits, including the ones he had destroyed. A man obsessed, he has to keep on painting himself, in an 'incredible series' of self-portraits. *'No whining, no moaning. Just get to work!'* In a quarter of a century, he has made thousands of self-portraits, paintings and drawings, in an extremely determined exploration of his own face and its expressions. It is the *'result of a strategic position'*, wrote the critic and exhibition designer Jan van Adrichem when the painter was awarded the 1999 Oubourg Prize. *'A position that could only be recognised after a number of years – even by the artist himself.'* Such tenacity.

Producing the self-portrait

With 'a self-portrait a day', or thereabouts, as his motto, he has painted portraits of himself innumerable times. As though it were an obsession, he drives the art of portraiture into a corner. One time it's *en face*, the next time *trois quarts*, looking sideways with those almost-criminal eyes. Philip Akkerman started painting self-portraits around the end of February/beginning of March 1981. He is still doing so.

He had his subject matter: his own face, and a programme: the serial portrait. *'After a year or so I made a really beautiful one and I thought: I want to make* another one like that, but more red. And that's when the content gave way to the form.' More than the history of a face – for example, the ageing process – it's about the pictorial variation in each portrait. Not about time passing, but about a tightly directed programme.

His work, he often says, is not always well understood. 'A clear concept underlies my work. Of course you can paint nice pictures, a windmill or a basket of fruit. No concept, just beautiful things. With the Japanese artist On Kawara you can express in words what he does: for thirty years he's been painting "date paintings", in this colour or that, in this format or that, and the date in oil paint. In his work, the concept is more important than the form. In my work, however, the two are in balance: the execution is also important. You have to be able to see it too; words aren't sufficient.' And yet Akkerman's continuum, painting his own physiognomy day after day, resembles the conceptual projects of both On Kawara and the German Hanne Darboven. They also record the passing of time. Life is given meaning through the production of paintings.

For Akkerman, however, 'time needs a face'. The self, the painter Max Beckmann once said, is the biggest secret in the world. How do we see ourselves in

Philip Akkerman,
Self-Portrait.
1981, no. 43.
Panel, 31 x 27 cm.
Private collection.

the mirror, through the looking glass? The observer wonders: that reflection, is it me? It is the mirror's secret. The immortal principles of the Revolution gave equal rights to all people, wrote the poet Charles Baudelaire, 'So I possess the right to reflect myself, and only my conscience determines whether it is with or without satisfaction.' This is Akkerman's philosophy.

Philip Akkerman,
Self-Portrait.
1984, no. 38.
Panel, 35 x 27 cm.
Private collection.

Producing the self-portrait

Akkerman's self-portraits are reminiscent of an incident in the novel *Uno, nessuno e centomila* (One, None and a Hundred Thousand) by Luigi Pirandello. A passing remark by his wife about his nose, which she says is crooked, leads the fictional character Vitangelo Moscarda to a staggering realisation: he is not one person, but several, maybe a hundred thousand different people. Because everyone saw him in a different way; no-one saw the person that *he* knew. His nose was crooked? He'd never noticed it himself. Maybe other things about him were crooked?

The remark about his crooked nose set Moscarda thinking: *'The thought that others saw in me someone who was not the person I myself knew, someone whom*

  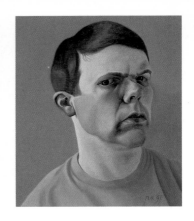

only they could know – this thought would not give me a moment's peace.' In his painting Akkerman is looking for that absolute, guided by a thought that is almost as bizarre (though not the same) as that of Moscarda. Bart Verschaffel wrote in the catalogue for his 1992 exhibition at the Witte de With in Rotterdam: 'His self-portraits show Elkerlyc, Everyman, possibly nothing more and nothing less than every banal self, each other, everyone.' Akkerman's self-portraits are about the question: is this still Akkerman, or is it, more universally, every-one?

Philip Akkerman,
Self-Portrait.
1987, no. 27.
Panel, 40 x 24 cm.
ICN collection,
Amsterdam.

'You don't understand a thing about it.' For Akkerman, reflecting himself and painting his image is 'the confirmation of his existence': I paint, therefore I live. This could be seen in the earliest art: the caveman who printed his bloody hand on the walls of a cave didn't understand anything about it either. But he *saw* that he existed. That is his motivation.

Philip Akkerman,
Self-Portrait.
1995, no. 101.
Panel, 40 x 34 cm.
Private collection.

Philip Akkerman exhibited almost all his self-portraits for the first time at the Witte de With in Rotterdam. It was a kind of stocktaking, painting next to painting, and another few hundred drawings in a filing cabinet – *le bureau d'artiste* – that could be consulted by the public. They were all panels of 40 by 34 centimetres or 50 by 43 centimetres, always those same formats that cor-respond to the dimensions of his own face. Akkerman used not to sign his pic-tures. 'My self-portraits could just as easily be painted by someone from the Golden Age.' Now he keeps records, with the date when each portrait was painted and the place where it hangs. This reinforces the conceptual element of his work: that monotony, portrait after portrait, seeking the 'indefinable absolute', as he says, 'the mystery of life'.

Philip Akkerman,
Self-Portrait.
1997, no. 48.
Panel, 40 x 34 cm.
Private collection.

The pose that Akkerman adopts is usually a three-quarter profile of the face. Over and over again. Only occasionally does he paint himself full-face. 'For me, when I'm painting, it's not about in-depth psychology, as it is for the Mexican painter Frida Kahlo, who says something along the lines of: "Hey, look, guys! I am a damaged individual." In my opinion, Otto Dix is one of the greatest painters and, together with Vincent van Gogh, one of the best portrait painters. Dix said: the less well I know people, the better I can paint a portrait of them; if I know a person, I paint what I know of that person, and it's the exterior that betrays someone, isn't it?' A true portrait.

Since the 1980s, Akkerman says, he has withdrawn from the world of glossy magazine art. He used to make modern art, he once wrote. 'I had loads of energy and enthusiasm and I'd come up with a completely new style every few

months.' After a few years he was totally worn out and he moved to The Hague. *'That was a reaction, of course, because I had become sick and tired of all those magazines and white galleries. They were doing everything wrong; they had no taste. So I literally returned to myself by concentrating exclusively on self-portraits.'*

Why painters don't paint battles anymore

As an artist he is difficult to classify. He doesn't belong to any school, trend or movement. Akkerman employs all manner of expressive idioms, both contemporary methods and those of the Old Masters. In his paintings we can spy the ghosts of other painters, echoes from other times, memories and reflections, commentaries on old and modern times. The critic David Moos wrote of him: *'In fact, we can see how since the beginning of 1981, when he consciously began his current project, Akkerman has registered, absorbed and modified the impact of different contemporary and historical modes.'* The imagery of many others resonates in Akkerman's work.

He employs a method used by the North European Renaissance painters. *'There are more and more painters utilising such Old Master techniques.'* It is a classic way of working, in three stages. *'It's not about pigments, but about composition and method. How did those artists manage to paint battles? They set about it by approaching the work in three steps: first the drawing – the composition – then the grisaille, and, after that, the colour. Since the Impressionist movement, painters have wanted to solve all those issues in one go, but that is too much for a human brain. That's why they don't paint battles anymore.'*

In the person of Akkerman, or, rather, in his work, in the hundreds and hundreds of self-portraits, the mannerist is reflected: he elaborates on and varies the features of his face, the pupils of his eyes, his cheeks, his nose, his wrinkles and the corners of his mouth. It is a hall of mirrors, sometimes hideous and then cheerful again, gloomy and on occasion mischievous.

Driving painting techniques into a corner

Is Akkerman as ruthlessly honest as Rembrandt van Rijn? Rembrandt painted dozens of portraits of himself. Those portraits form a gallery of likenesses of the young and ambitious painter, and of the old and dejected Rembrandt. It is the history of his life, of the constant fluctuations of passions and misfortunes. His self-portraits are an archive of his features, a sort of diary, a journal of his emotional life. He depicted himself with tangled and wiry curls, as a celebrated artist in a feathered cap and a gold chain, and at the end of his life as an old man with rough stubble and a bulbous nose. Like Rembrandt, Akkerman makes use of props. And like Rembrandt, Akkerman's features change, he stares into the mirror in an ever more gloomy and intense manner – and maybe just as ruthlessly. For a while he painted himself with striking sideburns, which he borrowed from Arthur Schopenhauer, a philosopher in whose pessimistic philosophy of life Akkerman recognises himself.

His self-portraits are not lacking in decorum. In his studio all kinds of headwear are neatly stacked on the shelf, theatrical props such as Rembrandt also collected in his studio. *'These are liberties that I permit myself, because otherwise it gets too boring. Maybe this will disappear too, because when you look at my work, you can see that it's becoming simpler all the time.'* Akkerman denies that his *exercices de style*, his continual stylistic exercises with the occasional touch

Philip Akkerman,
Installation at
Torch Gallery,
Amsterdam, 2003.

Philip Akkerman, Installation at Torch Gallery, Amsterdam, 2003.

of Kazimir Malevitsj, then a little Vincent van Gogh or even Charley Toorop, are meant ironically. *'No, definitely not, but it certainly is amusing. I often burst out laughing when I see my self-portraits. Those references are not something I'm striving for. But it is something that exists within me, though. If I have one talent, then it's a talent for variation. Even at school I'd write every page of my exercise books in different handwriting. It's not imitation. There are perhaps two or three portraits where I consciously wanted to paint a Van Gogh or a Poussin, just as artists used to go and make copies in museums. Then I place the drawing of my own head over a coloured print. When I was sixteen or seventeen, I looked at a tremendous number of art books and went to a lot of exhibitions. That's all there in my head; in one way or another it all comes out again.'*

'Slowly but surely, I'm driving that painting technique into a corner,' says Akkerman in his diary. *'When I get her where I want her I'll chain her up. And I'll keep her on bread and water. And I shall be her master for many a day to come.'* His reflections on his self-portraits sound heroic and intrepid: *'But we keep going. We have to keep going. A deal's a deal. No whining, no moaning. Just get to work!'* ∎

Translated by Laura Watkinson.

www.torchgallery.com

Cocooning with a View

Glocal Literature by Pol Hoste

When he's in Montreal, to him forever Montréal, his thoughts often drift back to when he was a young boy sitting with his family staring in silence at a sooty black cauldron full of pig swill. But when he's at home in his own little back garden, it's as if he's (almost) swamped by the history of the world. Pol Hoste (1947-) is a prototypical *glocal* writer, someone who continually mixes the global with the local. The world seems to be his village, something which Hoste demonstrates so eloquently in his two latest books: *The Air to Mirabel* (De lucht naar Mirabel, 1999) and *Montréal* (2003). But at the same time that village is also the world, as can be seen in his earlier work from the eighties and nineties.

A writer's goldmine

Initially Hoste projected the great themes of life onto the local backdrop of his youth, but he has since changed tack in his more recent work. His backdrop is now resolutely global but shards of his youth in Lokeren still remain visible. As the cliché has it, an unhappy childhood is a writer's goldmine; but Hoste likes clichés mainly because they are basically true, no matter how pre-digested and bland they sound. It is hard to find any other contemporary Flemish writer to whom this truism applies so totally. Hugo Claus, that *monstre sacré* of Flemish literature, didn't have it easy as a youth either, but at least his proud father still went from door to door trying to sell his son's collections of poetry. Hoste, in contrast, was locked from the day he was born in the prison of a totalitarian nuclear family lorded over by his communist father, the scourge of mother and son alike. The only beacon of light in this emotional wilderness was his grandmother, who lived with them, and his writing. Hoste has often said that it is impossible for him to imagine himself otherwise than with a pen in his hand. Caught between his father's bouts of anger and his mother's evasion, he tried to write himself an identity: *'I've always written. With my body, with the legs of letters, with the stalks of cherries, on the inside of my husk'. (Montréal)*

From the very outset, writing for Hoste has meant taking refuge in a cocoon of words. This explains why his style is somewhat autistic at times, particularly

in his two latest works where he casts himself adrift on the tide of his associations. In contrast, in his earlier work the montage of his wayward forays
is not so unrestrained. Here the autobiographical context is more than just a
pretext for writing himself away from or out of it. Hoste uses precisely this difficult childhood to construct a sandcastle full of sublime phrases, a castle he
and he alone rules over, a castle he invites the reader to visit and explore. In
his third novel, *A Lovely Life* (Een schoon bestaan, 1989), he provides us with a
masterful display of how a literary paradise can be moulded from the blood
and tears of a difficult childhood. In fact, in this work his literary isolation is
not all that pronounced. He eulogises his contact with his grandmother, and
his warm affection for her invests ordinary moments in his childhood with
a golden glow.

The writer as anti-hero

Hoste's *A Lovely Life* can be compared to the homage Leo Pleysier once paid
to his dying mother in *White is Always Nice* (Wit is altijd schoon, 1989). Pleysier
allowed his mother's dialect to speak for itself. The result was a touching montage of her words, just as they must have sounded at the time. Hoste is sparser
in portraying his grandmother. He is not as positive and lyrical as Pleysier. Hoste
is first and foremost a lucid and especially a critical prose narrator who can
never remain silent about his anti-paradise: the hell of his life and upbringing
with an authoritarian father. Some passages from *A Lovely Life* remind us of
Gerard Walschap's best prose. Walschap, the most famous exponent of Flemish
heimat literature in the period between the two world wars, also harboured
a deep distrust of those in power in his day. One of his characters proclaims
a credo of disillusionment that summarises what Hoste must have felt:
*'Ach, what is life: being born, oppressed in an educational greenhouse, making
love, marrying, having children, becoming rich or poor and always being well-behaved. Letting yourself become civilised instead of becoming a hero.'* (Adelaïde,
1929)

However, the young Hoste refused to be tamed or 'civilised' by his father or
the education system because he truly wanted to become a hero, albeit an anti-
hero. In *A Lovely Life* he relates how with his grandmother's help he succeeds
in becoming a writing anti-hero who casts a laconic eye on how hard things are
in an adult world bereft of fantasy. His indictment of the totalitarian injustice of
paternal authority and the educational establishment is telling in this respect:
*'We ourselves are not hiding anything. But it may be that our upbringing has hidden
us. Even from ourselves.'* (A Lovely Life). To this day, Hoste continues to point
out how a patriarchal education system alienated him from himself. But luckily
he had his grandmother and the magic of writing, which he never tires of talking about. Since then Hoste's life has oscillated between these two poles – a
mistrust of the existing order on the one hand, and the warmth of successful
moments of affection and creativity on the other: *'Do I keep shutting myself out
from everything, is that it? (...) I guess I'll go on distrusting everybody in this place
(...)'* But as against that: a golden reinette apple, oven-baked *'with a dollop of butter and brown sugar in winter. Dry kindling to light the fire, a shovelful of coal: tiny,
poor-quality anthracite. So we don't have to go to bed in the cold.'* (A Lovely Life).
Here ends Hoste's tribute to his grandmother.

Following on this little masterpiece, Hoste wrote *Letters to Mozart* (Brieven aan Mozart, 1991) an intriguing bit of fun addressed to Wolfgang Amadeus Mozart. He always wanted to be a musician, and he handles his words as if they were notes in a score. One day while sitting in a friend's garden reading Mozart's letters he decided to write sixteen epistles back. Hoste happened to be looking after his friend's house while he was away on holiday. The atmosphere of the work is all sunny and summery, much like the airy music of that master of eighteenth-century rococo. It was when writing these letters that Hoste began to work himself free from the mire of his childhood. Some of its gruesome contours do re-emerge every now and then in his writing, but now without their sharper and rougher edges. On the contrary, possible visions of angst from the past are now disarmed by teasing wordplay and a musicality that contains a multitude of meanings: *'I'll tease anyone who refuses to accept the multi-layeredness of his own words.'* (*Letters to Mozart*) At last the needle on the barometer began to point towards sunny. Hoste the writer had liberated himself from his local past and, with Mozart as his guide, headed off into a fully global life.

Almost at the same time as this pivotal work in Hoste's oeuvre was published, his day-to-day work and life took a drastic turn. He divorced his wife and gave up his job as a teacher. In 1994, he decided to devote himself to writing full-time. The two novellas that make up *Emotions of a Commuter* (Ontroeringen van een forens, 1993) summarise what he had been doing up until then: mulling over a difficult childhood and in so doing discovering himself as a writer (the first novella) and moving back and forth between obligatory work and writing (the second novella). Both stories take stock of one state of affairs in order to move on to something new and different. But not entirely. He now began consciously to cultivate the multi-meaning polyphonic musical language that he had already explored sporadically in *Letters to Mozart*. *High Key* (1995), a montage of monologues, dances and stories, jettisons his autobiographical writing and trades it in for a type of prose that explores all manner of issues from a variety of perspectives. The 'authoress', the 'woman dancer' and 'the speaker' take turns as the mouthpiece of the author Hoste. *Photos with the Ape* (Foto's met de aap, 1997) is a collection of unconventional views that he published following commissions for radio and the press. On more than one occasion he inveighed against the hostile climate for writers to be found in official cultural institutions. In doing so he adopted the satirical tone of a court jester, he who stands aloof and speaks the truth in jest: *'The feeling that you live in a region of speech but not in a region of writing, not in a region of reading. Why would someone want to write down what shopkeepers, clerks, delegates and the elected say? ... Doesn't he understand what this spoken culture is all about? Why can't he just repeat the stock formulations like everyone else, on his way from the baker's to the court house, from the café to the town hall, from the paint shop to the conservatoire, from the butcher's to the theatre?'* (*Photos with the Ape*)

Polyphonic Pol becomes a polyglot

A writer's grant in Canada provided the springboard for his more recent work. Hoste sees Canada as the ideal mirror of Belgium, as it is also a federal state and multilingual. When the narrator in *Montréal*, Hoste's latest book, mentions the word Montréal, a veritable language carousel of Dutch, French and English is set in motion: '*Montréal. The curtain rises. But it's Flanders! Mon réel, my realm.*' (Montréal). To be brief, polyphonic Pol has become a polyglot. In his latest works, Hoste has begun to exploit the multiple meanings and multi-linguistic nature of words more than ever before. The rich variety of narrators' voices (Ost, Oyster, Mister Tweed, Traveller, Passant) serve to provide some anchorage for the interior monologue. In fact Hoste unleashes a sea of words on the reader, a sea with very few lifebuoys. For the reader-swimmer it's all a matter of letting oneself float along fearlessly – *go with the flow!* – and in so doing bumping against sudden pearls of expression that save him. Such fragments of meaning owe their existence to the traumatic childhood that so dominated his earlier work, but here they are only used sparingly.

How far can Hoste take his acrobatic wordplay before tipping over completely into vacuity? It seems as if he has reached a limit and, for my taste, has on occasion overstepped that limit. He realises that he is balancing on the edge of what is possible in literature, and protects himself against objections in advance by firing off a salvo of rhetorical questions: '*Why don't I write about life itself, which is 'a thousand times stronger than writing?*' Or about a man from Martinique sitting on a terrace enjoying the sun setting behind the tall rushes on Kraanlei in Ghent? '*Why don't I surrender to speechless light and the innumerable details of Montréal?*' (Montréal) Hoste knows the answers all too well, but probably doesn't want to come out with them too quickly. The fact is, he suffers from a fear of turmoil – a consequence of his upbringing in an overly harsh patriarchal school: '*We have been so hardened that we never did find out what kept distancing us from everything we were made to face.*' (A Lovely Life). Ever since then, for want of anything better, Hoste can only warm himself at the icy frost-flowers of language. His grandmother, his gateway to brief moments of warmth, died some time ago. The reader who wishes to feel more than the glacial glow of wordplay would be best advised to warm himself up by reading Hoste's touching memories of her. Because *A Lovely Life* is without a doubt a masterpiece. ■

Translated by Peter Flynn

Photo by Stephan
Vanfleteren.

Three Extracts

by Pol Hoste

We dreamt of a world without people

We had an authoritarian upbringing. Were we the better for it? A totalitarian upbringing. Were other people the better for it?

A German dog-training method had made our parents dedicated adherents of behaviourism. Healthy discipline could only lead to a better organised party, family and state. A conditioned body guaranteed personal happiness. The cat (our *Choop*) was shoved in a sack and drowned.

Like fascism, socialism too was based on authority. Communism too, like national-socialism, subjected to absolute power.

Classical equalled German. French culture had oppressed the fatherland for centuries. The Truth was set in gothic script.

Our cultural education stood on ethnographic foundations. Our humanistic instruction was politically sound . To improve our race: gymnastics and marching music.

Hear the song of these our schools. This is not a call to fight. If in doubt or indecisive, sing a song of tolerance.

My brothers and myself – they wore the brown and yellow of Flemish Youth movements, I was in the garden around our villa – were educated 'for later'. For times of war. For times of peace. For some sort of hereafter which we could not comprehend, which we never did comprehend. We dreamt of a world without people.

We have been hardened. We have been so hardened that we never did find out what kept distancing us from everything we were made to face. We unlearned hunger, thirst, fatigue. We learnt to swallow pain, never mentioned our fears. After the age of five, I do not remember ever being hungry or thirsty. Not even when I did not eat or drink, and so knew all too well that I was wrong about myself.

Open up the screening shutters, to what was and is to be. Hope to live a clean existence, through the broadness of your mind.

What time we spent with people who knew nothing of our background, left them thinking we were always hiding something. That my brothers and I were hiding ourselves.

We ourselves are not hiding anything. But it may be that our upbringing has hidden us. Even from ourselves.

From *A Lovely Life* (Een schoon bestaan). Antwerp: Manteau, 1989, pp. 80-81.

Small bourgeoisie

If I build a house out of this Heap (give in to what others expect of me) – having first assembled myself like a prefab dwelling –, will I not be confronted with the poverty of the grandparents who brought me up? As a child of a new layer of society, the son of post-war minor officialdom?

We no longer eat straight out of the container, we put everything on a plate. Salted dairy butter soaks into pearly white crumb. A white tin loaf on Fridays. On the dark blue thin wooden box of processed cheese: the freckled face of a boy. Little fellow.

I may well end up just as drab as the workmen's terraces in the neighbourhood, where I played with factory workers' children. The child of an aspiring middle class, the product of a progressive white-collar Civil Servant.

Next to the bread, the dishcloth, on the white and green tiled table top, lies the bread knife. Crumbs stuck in black joins. A poorly silver-plated fork fishes herring out of a jar, vinegar drips on the glaze. Tepid ale sparkles in blue-stemmed rummers.

Isn't there some way I can get closer to the house I'm building? Do I keep shutting myself out from everything, is that it? Didn't I always just wander around in that parental villa, never really live there?

Every day the cleaning lady – her apron smells of gingerbread – cleans the mantelpiece, the windowsills, the table's edges, the door frames, the skirting boards, the floor's edges, the bluestone doorsteps in front of the house, the jugs in the basement.

What background entitles the folks bossing me about at work to speak? What county did their parents live in? What priest taught them morality?

I guess I'll go on distrusting everybody in this place: will always feel threatened here, in this Heap, this house, restless between strange city walls.

Mind you: a baked cooking apple with a dollop of butter and brown sugar in winter. Dry kindling to light the fire, a shovelful of coal: tiny, poor-quality anthracite. So we don't have to go to bed in the cold.

'Warm yourself up a bit before you go upstairs.'

From *A Lovely Life* (Een schoon bestaan). Antwerp: Manteau, 1989, pp. 119-121.

An actor's life for me

I spent the first twenty years of my life using only words that did not mean what I wanted to say. And why? I learned that man must fear himself. That's why he doesn't live in nature, but in systems.

I detested trickery or abuse of trust. I was raised on a thousand fibs. Scared is what I was. But I was by no means afraid to hang about with ghosts. Summer evenings were spent playing with the bats in the garden. Had people examined my loneliness more closely, they would have spotted this lively little lad, who loved company and mirth. Though spelling was not my pet aversion, I definitely disliked minding my p's and q's. Impossible, that's what I was!

But having to swallow the words you hear inside is sheer torture. A child might seize the opportunity to familiarise itself with the imperfections of life and unravel the commonplaces of its native tongue.

I merely made sure to blend in. Whether I liked the piece or hated the director, I was determined to play the part. So nobody bothered to ask my opinion.

That didn't stop me from finding things out for myself, though. It's still a mystery to me why people in my native town insist on using the most complex figures of speech to impose the most banal views on each other. The technique does, however, make it incredibly easy to change your opinion as soon as you've come out with it. With a bit of talent you can actually repeat everything and make it sound exactly like its opposite.

I certainly acquired an insight into verbal manipulation that way. But let me become an actor? No way. Is there anything more pleasing than making other people laugh?

I beg your pardon? Effacing myself into the part of a seductive but obnoxious extra is a female trait, is it? *Tu exagères.*

It all ends in uncertainties anyway, just like this mortal coil. I'll tease anyone who refuses to accept the multi-layeredness of his own words. Aren't we constantly being fooled by the very terms we rely upon for leading others up the garden path ?

I guess I should really be much more careful and keep quiet about the ambiguities I hear. What use is a language that fails to formulate itself? Nosy parkers! The last thing you should expect from me is that I should keep my opinion to myself: that, I leave to others.

All excerpts translated by Nadine Malfait

From *Letters to Mozart* (Brieven aan Mozart). Antwerp: Manteau, 1991, pp. 52-53.

Utrecht: A Jigsaw of Intimacy

For I cannot but mourn the loss of dream
(Kees Ouwens)

[K O E N   V E R G E E R]

The Hoog Catharijne
development in 1979.

C. 'The Utrecht'

Where shall we start? With a building that no longer exists: 'The Utrecht', the only genuine Art Nouveau building ever to grace the city. When the life assurance company 'Let op uw Einde' ('Prepare for your Demise') merged with 'The Utrecht' at the end of the nineteenth century a new headquarters was needed. This jewel of a building was completed in 1901, only to be demolished less than three quarters of a century later.

Indeed, the whole of the station area where The Utrecht's head office stood was swept away at the same time to make room for a large-scale development of offices and shops known as the Hoog Catharijne (High Catherine). The idea was to provide an improved, manageable and comfortable link between the Central Station and the city centre. Covered and warm, with houseplants and muzak, it was to be a place where one could shop without wearing a coat. Shopping without a coat? Surely everybody's dream!

The condemned buildings in the area round the old station naturally provided a wonderful source of excitement and adventure for inquisitive street urchins like us. We imagined that we were three detectives on the trail of a dark conspiracy. As indeed we were – although its scale and effrontery went far beyond our understanding. Time and again we were driven away: 'Sod off, you lot! It's not safe here; the whole place is undermined!' Precisely! But things aren't demolished so thoroughly without good reason. So we went looking for hard evidence that something fishy was afoot. And more or less by accident, via gardens, sheds and souterrains we ended up in the abandoned temple of industry that had once been 'The Utrecht'. What could we know? Caught between flower power and No Future, we were struck dumb: we could still hear the muffled tapping of typewriters, the whispers amid the opulence of wine-red carpets and grey marble walls, sandstone stairs and gleaming snakes of copper, and above them flamboyant curving ladies symbolising Trade and Industry, their cold, doom-laden gaze staring into a distant promised land. Less than a week later it had all disappeared for ever.

The Vredenburg Music
Centre, designed by
H. Hertzberger
(1973-1978)

D. Vredenburg

Crossing the Catharijnesingel (Catherine Canal), today a dual carriageway, one comes to the real heart of the city at the Vreeburg. In the sixteenth century there was a castle here, then an Exhibition Centre and now we have the Vredenburg Music Centre, neatly reflecting the city's steady climb up the cultural ladder.

A few days after the ceremonial opening of the Hoog Catharijne – the conspirators had won the day – my friends and I got hopelessly lost in Utrecht's new showpiece. We were finally chased out through a car park garage by a volley of curses from the Security's loudspeakers. But like a Titanic of affluence, 'shopping without a coat' struck disaster. Magical words like arcade, meeting points and fountains captured in glass and concrete came to mean a welcome resting place for the less fortunate in society. The shopping public warded off this perceived threat with angry glances and buttoned-up overcoats. Every attempt to revive its fortunes foundered on the game of Monopoly being played out by the council and the property tycoons. Finally the citizens received the plans for the Utrecht City Project in the post. They were even allowed to vote, with the help of colourful architectural designs that showed no rubbish, rusting bicycles and junkies. But still as large-scale as ever. In practice, it was no more than a makeshift remedy that included of all things the destruction of the only feature of any merit, the Music Centre.

'This really cannot stay as it is' sneered the developers' lackeys, by which they meant the foyer, the wonderful labyrinth of corridors labelled A to H, the flights of steps, the little balconies, the clumsy pillars and hidden corners, all in concrete, glass and indestructible East European veneer. No, it can't stay as it is – that kind of building must have charisma, clarity, glass. You want to be seen from the street in your evening dress, so that the world will know that you are not from the streets – status does not tolerate intimacy. And so the outside of the building is peeled away, the foyers and gables disappear and everything

View of Utrecht from the cathedral.

becomes more multi-functional. The Music Centre becomes a Music Palace with a multitude of rooms contained in a cube of steel and glass, totally devoid of imagination. Fortunately its heart, the great hall, an acoustically brilliant octagonal arena, is spared. And with it the voices of poets who for the past 25 years have celebrated the annual 'Night of Poetry' with attentive audiences of over 2000. The voices of Lucebert, Annie M.G. Schmidt, Hans Faverey, Herman de Coninck, the voices of more than 200 poets live on in this place. A sacred place. After all, no-one would dream of demolishing Notre Dame in Paris or the Oracle at Delphi? Leo Vroman wrote this ode spontaneously in 1986:

I've always thought myself rather two-sided.
But my two sides were more or less parallel.
And though I still hope one of them at least
one day will cross the other,
never shall I attain that eightsidedness
with which this evening you all look at me.

E. Lange Viestraat – Potterstraat

Moving on, with all these voices in my head. There on the right Lange Elisa-bethstraat begins, and further on Steenweg, the street of Clare Lennart. '*This is a long street*', she writes at the beginning of her most Utrecht-centred book *Houses of Cards* (Huisjes van kaarten, 1938).

'*It runs all the way from C&A to the Middle Ages. One can stroll endlessly through time. But not so unruffled and unshocked as when one reads a history book. Here the years have been shuffled like a pack of cards and walking through time is like an adventurous journey through craggy mountains. The mountain peaks of 'now'* ...

Oude Gracht, Utrecht.

the deep valleys of 'then' lie cheek by jowl. The steepest precipices ... the deepest gorges ... and often the narrow path is only passable in one's dreams.'

Lennart came to Utrecht as a vulnerable but opinionated young teacher. After she was dismissed for having an affair with a married man, she managed a boarding house, wrote a voluminous oeuvre in the evenings, became a 'grande dame' of letters and is now, unjustly, completely forgotten.

Let us postpone the Middle Ages for the time being and continue into Lange Viestraat and further up to Potterstraat. Not exactly the most beautiful of streets, until dusk begins to fall and the broad vista of the urban clearance lies in splendour over Oude Gracht, shrouded in the autumnal 'violet hour', indifferent to all who are hurrying home. A sense of haste; a breath of wind; neon lights on the Neude. On the other side, above the shop-windows full of crockery and porcelain, the poet Nijhoff watered his flowers in the 1930s and wrote the most important poem in all twentieth-century Dutch literature: *Awater*. Mourning the loss of his brother and mother, the poet abandons his earlier faith, or perhaps only attempts to do so since in embracing Fate he continues to acknowledge a greater scheme of things. To this end, he pieces together a journey through the city and the poem, in the footsteps of an anonymous clerk whom he calls 'Awater'.

Suddenly Awater. Down from a landing
I see him coming, blinking both his eyes.
No mortal being, no city, no sunset glow
exists for him. With quickening pace he comes,
down sandstone stairs by gleaming snakes of copper.
It seems his eyes see a horizon, a rim
from which sheet lightning glimmers ceaselessly.
It is as though he hears what he dreams of
and sees the spot where he hopes to find it,
so he pelts past me, and I feel punched through.

The poet follows him past shop windows, past a palatial bank, a hairdresser's, a café, a restaurant, the station. In this autumnal dusk I can always sense that trail; pieces of a jigsaw puzzle, mere fragments, but it was here along these streets, amid these noises, and under the same high clear sky.

F. Janskerkhof

I'm always intrigued by the way literature converges with this city but at the same time hides in it, changes shape, gets lost. Poetry engraved in the stone-work and vice versa. Meanings rattle in loose paving-blocks. Attenuated as in a dream, it cannot be pinned down. I cannot show you in *Awater* the trees of the Janskerkhof, but I know that they are there. This square with its tall linden trees, a blaze of yellow at the end of October, and later on in December silent among the Christmas trees – look, there they come again; a man, a woman and three children beneath the street lamps, their breath forming small clouds, looking for the tree that will take them into the New Year. Shrill children's voices: what about this one? After much discussion and a few jokes with the tree seller, the tree goes into the delivery bike with the children half buried, the top just above

The Janskerkhof,
as drawn by
Isaac Ouwater
(c.1780)

the handlebars, and they disappear into the early evening laughing and ring-ing the bell. But that is December. Now there are the buses, numbers 3, 4, 53 and 135 revving up and sounding their horns, the trendy cafés and the flower stall, while on the other side F.C. Donders, cast in bronze, dares not watch the mounted Willibrord losing himself in the stream of traffic around the church.

G. Flora

'Things aren't what they used to be', says the waiter. And Flora is no longer Flora, the writers' café of the inter-war years on the corner of the Lucasbolwerk (Lucas Bastion). It was there that Cola Debrot listened to Nijhoff's doubts and observed his progress in writing *Awater*. Jan Engelman pondered his sensuous cantilenas, *Ambrosia, what flows on to me...* Outside a motorbike roars past. Gerrit Rietveld needs a pick-me-up. Whenever he felt unwell he would climb on his motorbike and race round a few blocks with his mouth wide open. 'No germs can survive that.' And there you see a small slightly stooping figure disappearing into Hieronymus Park. His bald head covered by a hat, it is C.C.S. Crone, the most Utrecht-oriented of them all. Crone's minimalist work is in fact the best guide to the city. Wandering through its streets, along canals, parks and squares he regularly noted down his observations on scraps of paper. When he had enough he would spread them over the floor at home, stick them into an account book, and use the fragments to compose his next story. It is the best way to read about and experience Utrecht, as a jigsaw of intimacy, fragments of voices and stonework. At first sight Crone's work is far from cheerful. Poverty, grime, unemployment, sickness and death flourish in riotous abundance. The main characters only manage to survive by means of countless song fragments, imagination and the city itself. *'It is the right accompaniment'*, wrote Crone later, *'for anyone who, strolling with no apparent purpose, wants to soak up the atmosphere of Utrecht's grey beauty. It lifts some of the oppressiveness that one senses in many of the neighbourhoods where all you can hear is the sound of your own muffled footsteps or the creak of a window being raised followed by the nervous fluttering of a tablecloth. Such a background accompaniment – the spirited bell tower of the Klaaskerk could play it on its lively centuries-old carillon – also lightens the gloominess of the Salvationist without which Utrecht would be unthinkable. It even suggests the possibility that along the canal that mother once showed you might some day come a ship laden with gold...'*

H. Pieterskerk

The cathedral tower.

Stop! before all the scraps of paper blow away. What is it that anchors Utrecht to the ground? Jehovah's unfathomable silence through the ages. Whoever has come this far should know about the cross of churches, an idea of Bishop

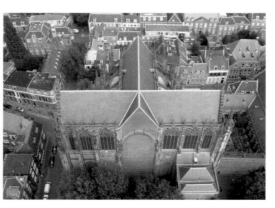

Utrecht cathedral.
The missing nave
was destroyed by
a tornado in 1674.

Bernold in the eleventh century. Property of the Lord. He dreamed of four churches built in the form of a cross around the cathedral, the absolute centre of the city where Willibrord had founded the original church in 696. To the south came St Paul's Abbey, of which only one wall is still visible in the Law Courts; to the west, the Mariakerk, of which only the cloisters remain; to the north, the Janskerk which is still intact; and to the east, the Pieterskerk.

Follow me and enter one of the most perfect Romanesque churches north of the great rivers. Inaugurated in 1048, it burnt down in 1076 after being struck by a bolt of lightning on the very day that Bishop William anathematised Pope Gregory in front of the altar. Turbulent times. A collegiate church: the priests devoted themselves entirely to worship and sang to the Lord, hidden by a screen from those who came to listen. On a good day there were 40 clergy serving 23 altars. It couldn't last. In 1580 the Protestant iconoclasm left its trail of destruction here. After that, multifunctional. Army billets, the bells sold off, a warehouse. In 1621 the choir became a dissecting room , the University's *theatrum anatomicum*. In August 1674, on the night that the Cathedral's nave was blown away, St Peter's lost its west towers. And yet the chapter was only finally

Pieter Saenredam,
Nave of the St. Pieterskerk,
Utrecht, from east to west.
1644. Panel, 59 X 111 cm.
Museum Boymans-van
Beuningen, Rotterdam.

abolished in 1811 when the church was handed over to the Walloon Reformed community. During its restoration in the 1960s four Romanesque reliefs dating from 1170 were rediscovered, together with painted sarcophagi and the grave of Bernold himself. He now lies in the crypt of St Peter's, the most easterly point of his cross of churches, peacefully awaiting the Day of Judgement.

Silent treasures. In summer when the café terraces are overflowing and the heat of the sun paralyses activity, one can go 'Looking at Churches' with guides who will tell you everything about their city's stoically floating monuments. Collegiate halls, monastic gardens; the window through which the Pope had to climb to gain access to the papal quarters unseen when he visited Willibrord's labyrinthine legacy.

Kromme Nieuwegracht,
Utrecht.

A. Nieuwegracht

*(It was here that the 14-year-old Rosa Mettelstrauch (anagram of the writer
Charlotte Mutsaers), her head buried deep between the bare knees of her dangling
legs, decided that there was after all such a thing as beauty. 'Suddenly I understood
everything. Of course beauty still existed: to the eye, to the ear, to the heart, too
much to list it all. The curse was that there were always people who would stop at
nothing to undermine it and make it impossible to experience.)*

I was a guide here once through the latter part of the summer. I immediately
recognised what would be my fate, even in love: nothing I see will I ever possess
unless it is meandering and singing. And so I follow the canal, the dead water
sleeps, murmuring lines from the poet Marsman in its bronze bed between the
wharves, the trees silent, the leaf holds its breath from the translucent lisp-
ing tale that it will repeat endlessly to itself, because yes, you are here again
walking by my side, and we talk and talk about nothing, the tale wants to be
retold, whether I, what flows on to me, could be your girlfriend, and you with
me, too near, too interwoven, so it is our voices still meandering like magnets
chattering, here, quicksilver, their joys, their ricocheting short-circuits, until
– Nieuwegracht with its stately houses, streetlights and leaves overhanging the
water and the carillon of the Klaaskerk sympathetically scattering his tinkling
over the evening are my witnesses – until I kissed you without warning – there
are girlfriends who do this – praise be! That immortal feat – geography blended
with time equals destiny – made up our unique date, that was October nineteen
eighty eight.

B. The Sonnenborgh Observatory

Stars, wait! One night, on the roof terrace of the Sonnenborgh fortress and its observatory I stood face to face with Jupiter. Somewhat nearer on the other side of the water, the sound of the level crossing, with in the distance, for those who can see it, a glimpse of the Maliebaan station where, it is said, Awater ended his meanderings. It is now the Dutch Railway Museum. The street widens. Dew drips from the trees. Directly in front of us is the station. Would one really hold a meeting here at midnight? Awater watches a Salvationist giving an address. *'We are living the whole of our life wrongly'*, she says, go on then, and *'love is never offered in vain'*. Awater remains, but I walk on quickly as if I had to catch a waiting train. I still believe, however, that in Nijhoff's imagination there floated another station, the white, slender Central Station designed by Van Ravesteyn, the transparent dreamlike construction that would only be completed a couple of years later and where as a child I picked up leaflets about the Orient Express. And even less does she share your jubilation at reading the place names that are the opening chords to your adventure. She prepares for her departure without a backward glance. Because he designed so many public buildings, Van Ravesteyn became known as 'the most demolished architect', and even his masterpiece, Utrecht Central Station, was finally pulled down to make it possible to shop without a coat in Hoog Catharijne. The circle is complete. The tale that will be endlessly retold. Prepare for your Demise. Suddenly a shower of lines from Leo Vroman:

Translated by Chris Emery
Poetry excerpts translated by Tanis Guest

Still that same observatory   just 1 observatory
Of all the universes   and in that
that link up around us   just 1 autumn night
ours is the one and only   and in that for so long now
and in this universe   your one and only left
of all the many   cheek
inhabited planets   first cold because
our earth's the one and only   of the cold rain
and on its surface   then hot
just 1 Netherlands   because
and in it 1 Utrecht   That was November
in which   nineteen thirty eight

Central Station, Utrecht.

October-November 2004
This text is interwoven with many lines from authors who have lived in or written about Utrecht; I thank them all, because without them I could not express my love for the city.

STAN: Repertory Theatre with a Breath of Fresh Air

[LUK VAN DEN DRIES]

I am meeting the Flemish theatre company STAN on the road, more specifically in Lyon, where they are performing the play *Tout est calme* (All is Quiet – Alles is rustig) by their favourite writer Thomas Bernhard. This is more than the hundredth time they have done so. It has been in their repertoire for five years and they have toured the Netherlands, Germany, France, Portugal, Switzerland, Austria and Italy with its French and Dutch versions. Five years is a long life for a production. At least it is in Flanders, where most of them are dropped after a few weeks. STAN has opted for a repertory system. Their plays remain available to anyone who asks for them. That evening shows how productive this can be. The actors know Bernhard's play better than the contents of their pockets. Over time they have developed an easy familiarity with the words. The script is at their fingertips, often cherished, much used. You can sense and hear this intimacy. STAN creates theatre that's close up. Close to the scripts. Close to the authors. That evening in Lyon they win over the audience entirely. Bernhard can sometimes sound so monotonous, almost nagging. STAN makes music of him. The actors let fly at each other with pomp and circumstance in their lives.. The pockets are turned inside out. In their hands, the whining Bernhard becomes a razor-sharp piece about history and how it still affects the present day.

The performance is followed by a discussion with the audience. The French still see Belgium as a land of oddballs. The STAN actors are perfect examples of this. By French standards they produce extremely eccentric plays. French theatre is built on acting codes; it is a vocal theatre that wallows in tremolo, effect and rhetoric. But the rhetorical theatre STAN performs is of a completely different class. The rhetoric of these Flemings has far more layers. It is based on contrariness. The emotions in the script are not reiterated on stage. STAN is practised in counter-readings. Rubbing a script up the wrong way. Looking for the development of an argument in a seemingly neutral fragment of material. French audiences are astounded to hear that an actor can act independently in this respect. That while on stage he himself can choose how he will perform the script. Evening after evening. That theatre is not repetition, but action. That a script is an open score that allows a great many interpretations. That no strict arrangements are needed before the acting can start. That the theatre's vitality gains from a reduction in the number of prior arrangements. That it is neces-

sary to continue amazing and surprising each other and that you can take this
a very long way. As long as you are free.

    And of course there is that obligatory question. How come they can do it just
as easily in French? After all, surely they speak some other language up there
in 'La Flandre'? STAN's answer is very sweet and kind.

STAN, *All is Quiet*
(Alles is rustig).
Photo by Thomas Walgrave.

Foreign body

STAN's European breakthrough, including a positive presence at the Festival
d'Automne and the Théâtre de la Bastille in Paris and the Théâtre Garonne in
Toulouse, as well as repeated invitations to Mausonturm in Frankfurt, the BIT
in Bergen, the Green Room in Manchester, the Centro Cultural in Lisbon, the
Almada festival and so on, leads us to suspect that this company is providing
the model for a new type of stage practice. Wherever the company turns up
there is an infectious enthusiasm for the way they make theatre. But it is much
harder to say what they are a model for. STAN has not made a positive decision
to develop its own style. It has no aesthetic programme. Artistic labels and

STAN, *Poquelin*.
Photo by Bernaded Dexters.

genre definitions (intercultural, visual and suchlike) fail entirely in the face of their principle of diversity.

In fact you could call STAN a foreign body. Their practices clash with the customs of the repertory genre. This genre is burdened with a great many premises. There is the problem of remaining faithful to the script – a problem that has been dragging on for decades and has given rise to fierce debate. There is the question of topicality: how can you make a repertoire topical again in the present day, without constantly having to put on new plays? There is the matter of direction: more than any other genre in the performing arts repertory theatre appears to have thrown in its lot with directors. Directors who have a clear view of a play and put forward a new interpretation that is intended to make short work of all previous versions.

STAN does not carry on such discussions. Faithfulness to the script is not a problem. They are able to stay very close to the script. If you love a particular play very much, why would you start cutting it up? No, they prefer to stay very close to the original and so the discussions are all about words, details, nuances. But they may just as easily take a knife to it. As in *Poquelin*, which is sewn together with big, rough stitches. And *Questionism* (Vraagzucht), an anthology of several short stories. Their affinity for plays also means they are constantly in search of material. The actors love reading and so accumulate masses of paper. Out of which certain plays thrust themselves to the fore. It's all a matter of appetite. Wanting to get their teeth into something. Being attracted by a certain way of telling a story. Tempted by the fascination with an image. This appetite determines the topicality of a production. And no director on earth is going to tell them how to do it. In fact they rather detest people with big ideas about a play.

But actually that is not where STAN's true individuality lies. That is at a much deeper level. The essence is to be found in a definition of acting. They see acting as being present. It is a sort of dogged immediacy. It is precisely by refusing to work to a programme, and, on the contrary, by again and again starting from a situation in the here and now, that they create an unrepeatable stage practice. This is essential. Night after night their principle is that it has to happen *now*. In essence every theatre-maker does this, but the STAN actors take it to its consequential extreme. They do not make any strict arrangements about blocking, what they are going to do and how they are going to say things. This is all decided at the moment itself. This gives a tremendous openness and directness to the quality of the acting.

Mouth to mouth

STAN has been around for fifteen years. During that time the company has made history. First of all in terms of attitude. It advocates a form of theatre in which the members' individual responsibility defines the structure of the group. Everyone who works for this company (from actors to technicians) helps determine the direction it takes. In other words there is no set course, neither in the form of a management office that provides continuity nor of a hierarchy that chooses and maps out a course. STAN is thus not an institution. It is a collective name for people with theatrical plans and the appetite to develop them

STAN, *Oftheoathofthe-writerofthekinganddiderot* (Vandeneedevandeschrij-vervandekoningendiderot). Photo by Thomas Walgrave.

collectively. Steps are taken and a direction chosen depending on the degree to which each one stands up for their own plans. They are consistent in not using a director. STAN outsources nothing, but does everything itself, from choice of play to sales, not because they think they can do everything better, but from the conviction that by applying themselves to every level of theatre activity this will also reflect on the theatrical product itself. So what the audience gets to see has passed through STAN's hands and has been given a life of its own, and

STAN, *Questionism*
(Vraagzucht).
Photo by Bernaded Dexters.

since this occurs at every level of production it possesses that characteristic STAN vigour. For this company theatre is not mass production, not specialised work, but the quest for a common affinity and the painstaking attempt to give it shape. It is a matter of a product passing by hand from a maker (the performer) to a consumer (the audience). It is the conveyance of this breath of life 'mouth to mouth' that gives the theatrical event its added value.

One of the constants in the life of this company is talking about acting. No one can define it, no one has any nameable method up their sleeve, but it's always about the same thing: how ought one to act?

The production entitled *Oftheoathofthewriterofthekinganddiderot* (Vandeneed evandeschrijvervandekoningendiderot) is perhaps the one result of this actors' conversation that makes the most lasting impression. It is a hilarious piece which at the same time goes to the heart of the complexity of acting. Rarely has so flawless a manifesto of what acting today may signify been expressed in a performance. An actors' comment on Diderot's well-known propositions. A demonstration of 'lessons in acting'. Illusion and reality, emotion and rationality, the two poles of Diderot's paradox are played off against one another. The performance can be seen as a synthesis of a view in which theatre is seen in terms simultaneously of real and unreal. Diderot suddenly becomes a comedy. A play like *Questionism* shows the other side of the actors' discussion. Not about how to act, but why. This discussion is about relevance, topicality and politics. About social contexts in urgent need of an answer. About the ongoing neo-liberalisation of the world. About the necessity of doing productions which in terms of temperament go completely against this.

Questionism fits into the series of pieces by STAN made under the pressure of current events: *It's new moon and it's getting considerably chillier* (Het is nieuwe maan en het wordt aanzienlijk frisser, 1992) and *One 2 Life* (1997) are its immediate predecessors. It is a new sort of documentary theatre based on a highly personal view. This is because one is allowed into the theatre-makers' minds so that they can show what motivates them, which issues they are wrestling with and which plays have stuck in their minds. You find yourself right in the middle of an extremely intimate and equally personal mental and physical world. And through this thunders the current political situation in the form of preparations for the war against Iraq. The documentary element lies not so much in the critical analysis of a particular point in time or political event, but in letting a specific moment loose on you. You are awash with questions. You are battered by propaganda. You stumble from the small and fragile to the oversized and unimaginable. In this loss of direction, in this excess, the actors' fury becomes palpable. All the images and ideas that come together in one mind in a single day now explode. It's documentary overload, but unaccompanied by any political instruction book. Because in this case the spectator has to figure it out for himself.

Clear air

In reviews of their plays, STAN's acting is often regarded as an extension of Brecht's views on the subject. And this is partly justified. The extreme openness and the clear air Brecht sought with his actors also applies to the STAN actors. All the magic has vanished from this profession. They have nothing up

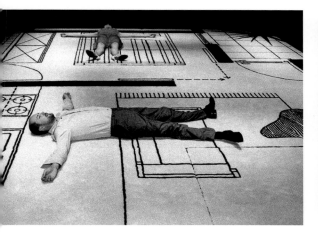 

STAN, *The Monkey Trial*.
Photo by Bernaded Dexters.

their sleeve, nothing in their pockets. They behave like labourers on a stage demonstrating how they have to operate a machine. In this case, a language machine.

In STAN's hands language is always a form of refined warfare. It may sometimes be about relationships. In plays such as *Lucia Melts* (Lucia smelt, 2003) and *See and See* (Zien en zien, 2004) love stories are laid on the dissecting table. In plays like these language is a wasteland full of painful memories. Conversations are extremely laborious; every word hurts a little. Talking becomes a minefield where something might explode at any moment. So people are constantly restraining themselves. This is STAN at its quietest: highly-refined chamber music. In their productions language is always linked to ideology. They are concerned with a demonstration of rhetoric, and with showing that all speech is essentially determined by power. This is made very clear in *The Monkey Trial* (2003), a courtroom drama on a leading ideological topic: does man originate from God or is he an ennobled primate? The actual trial in Tennessee in 1925 was taken as the basis for a reconstruction with prosecutors , lawyers, witnesses and accused. This well-tried format proved to have lost none of its appeal.

STAN, *Lucia Melts*
(Lucia smelt).
Photo by Bernaded Dexters.

Translated by Gregory Ball

STAN takes the immediacy of theatre very seriously. The repertoire is tested for its powers of contemporary expression. Molière, for example. In *Poquelin* (an adulterated collage taken from several plays by Molière) this classical French author is reduced to his hysterical obsessions with sex and adultery. This is immediately and abundantly clear from the very beginning of the performance. While the audience is coming in the actors are already standing waiting with their parts exposed. Trousers are stripped off and blouses lifted up. The argument is thereby already put forward and is developed hilariously in the rest of the play. Not a trace of classicism left. The hard core. Molière with his buttocks bare.

In this repertoire, what is most conspicuous is the attention paid to bourgeois society. STAN's favourite authors, Chekhov and Bernhard but also Ibsen, Wilde and Shaw, show up the fat on the bourgeois mentality. There is an edge of greed and intolerance on the propriety, languor and fussy boredom found there, and this is painstakingly brought out in STAN's interpretation. No one escapes the lucid sharpening of their knives. Even the kindly likeable ones appear not to be entirely blameless. Yet this is clearly not a social analysis (after all there is no other, better social class), but a scraping taken from each one of us. This theatre makes you very much aware of your own layer of fat. They hone your awareness of your own attitude till it's razor-sharp. That which only a minute ago tickled – since STAN's theatre verges on the hilarious – now suddenly stabs beneath your calloused skin. ■

STAN will tour until the beginning of May 2005 in Great Britain, Portugal, Norway and Sweden with their production of *Bérénice*. It's one of the most famous plays by the seventeenth-century dramatist Racine – and his only tragedy that doesn't end in a bloodbath. *Bérénice* tells the story of an impossible love: the Palestinian queen Bérénice is sent back to Palestine by her lover, the Roman emperor Titus, because the Roman people doesn't want him to wed a foreign ruler.

www.stan.be

A Great Language

Why Do Foreigners Learn Dutch?

If you want to study Dutch you no longer need to travel to the Netherlands or Flanders. All over the world, interest in the Dutch language is growing. Today Dutch is being taught at approximately 220 universities in more than 40 countries. An estimated 10,000 students are taking Dutch as a main subject at a university outside the Netherlands or Flanders. If you count the number of students taking Dutch as a minor subject or a practical language course, the total is much higher. There are more than 600 teachers of Dutch based in universities as far afield as Aruba, Australia, South Africa and Sweden. Since 1970 they have been represented by the Internationale Vereniging voor Neerlandistiek (IVN), an international association that aims to promote 'extramural' Low Countries studies, i.e. teaching at universities outside the Dutch-speaking regions. The IVN does this in a number of ways, including the organisation of a three-yearly colloquium where teachers and students of Dutch from all over the world can meet and exchange information. The association also publishes a journal, *Neerlandica Extra Muros*, which keeps teachers in departments of Dutch outside the Netherlands up-to-date on recent research in the wide-ranging discipline of Low Countries studies. The *IVN-krant* is a newsletter, which is posted on its website. Since March 2004 each issue of the newsletter has included a contribution from a student of Dutch (who is about to complete a course or has just done so) describing his or her introduction to the language.[1]

The Dutch Language Union (*Nederlandse Taalunie*) is an umbrella organisation within which the Netherlands, Belgium and Suriname co-operate on issues relating to Dutch language policy, language teaching and literature. It supports Dutch teaching abroad in various ways; for example, universities where Dutch is taught may be eligible for a special grant. The emphasis is on regions bordering Flanders and the Netherlands, i.e. Lower Saxony and North Rhine-Westphalia in Germany, the Nord and Pas de Calais departements in France and the French-speaking community in Belgium. The Dutch Language Union also runs summer courses every year in Zeist, Gent and Hasselt. Each course lasts three weeks and is designed to introduce foreign studdents to the Dutch Language, culture and society. The courses are highly succesful. In addition, the Dutch Language Union co-ordinates the examinations for the Certificate in

[BART VAN DER STRAETEN]

Japanese women dressed like Dutch flower girls, saying 'cheese' to the camera in the now bankrupt Holland Village.

Dutch as a Foreign Language (CNaVT). In 2004, 2,111 students registered for the examinations and 1,455 were awarded the coveted Certificate.[2]

So Dutch Studies is flourishing, and that would not be possible if no-one was interested in Dutch. Every one of the many thousands of students who learn Dutch has a specific reason for doing so. I made a 'virtual' tour of the world and asked as many university teachers and students as possible why people want to learn Dutch, the language with 22 million native speakers that is an official language in three countries (the Netherlands, Belgium and Surinam) and ranks 37th in the list of, in total, some 6,500 world languages.[3]

Long live the linguaphiles!

In many cases the answers to the 'why' question are obvious. Many of the respondents have family or friends in the Low Countries, or know people with a Dutch background. They like to be able to wish their friends or relatives *'Prettige verjaardag'* instead of *'Joyeux anniversaire'* or 'Happy Birthday'. Secondly, in the countries bordering on Flanders and the Netherlands, and in countries to which Dutch-speakers have emigrated, people study Dutch because their roots are in the Low Countries and they want to learn about their heritage. In the United States, certainly, this has been one of the main reasons for studying Dutch. More recently, the number of students in this category has fallen. The children of the last generation of Dutch immigrants from the 1950s now have children of their own who have grown up in America and therefore feel less affinity with the Netherlands. A third category is those who study Dutch purely for pleasure: they simply enjoy learning languages, so why not learn Dutch? These students – the 'linguaphiles' – often achieve more in terms of promoting the language than governments can achieve with a whole series of promotional campaigns. *'Long live the linguaphiles!'*, as one teacher of Dutch in America enthusiastically put it.

The fourth category of students could be described as opportunists. They believe or hope that a knowledge of the Dutch language will look good on their CV and give them an advantage in the job market. This is certainly the case in what President Bush still referred to in 2004 as 'the new Europe', the former Eastern Bloc countries that joined the European Union in May of that year. Countries such as Poland and Hungary are keen to attract new investors, and the new member states open up a dreamed-of new market for Dutch and Flemish companies. But the presence of Flemish and Dutch companies in any country will have a stimulating effect on the Dutch language. In Sweden, for example, people who work for the Dutch electronics company Philips sometimes feel the need to learn Dutch. Translators and interpreters are aware that a qualification in Dutch is essential for those who want to succeed in the small but specialised market for Dutch translation. A student from Italy notices that a good many books are translated from Dutch into Italian, and believes it will be easier to find work with a qualification in Dutch than with a qualification in another language. A student in Germany openly admits to studying Dutch because he wants to 'benefit from the economic advantages'.

It is no coincidence that this remark was made by a student from Germany, one of the regions bordering the Netherlands in which Dutch is increasingly being taught in secondary schools. This is a result of the Euroregions, officially defined as 'transfrontier co-operation bodies'. Career prospects are therefore good for Dutch speakers who want to go into teaching. At universities in Lower Saxony and North-Rhine Westphalia, the regions on which the Dutch Language Union is focussing its efforts, the rapid rise in student numbers for Dutch can only be controlled by the introduction of tuition fees for students in certain categories, and by the recently introduced *numerus fixus*, i.e. a limit on the number of places available.

Very few students cited an interest in literature and culture as the reason for learning Dutch. Although art historians sometimes learn Dutch because they want to study the paintings of the Golden Age, many of the students I contacted emphasised their interest in contemporary Dutch culture. A Spanish architect is learning Dutch because she admires Dutch architecture and wants to learn more about it. A student in Vienna comments on the powerful impact of Dutch design. The Netherlands, she thinks, has a strong tradition in graphic design. When it comes to Dutch literature, opinions differ. Someone from Cambridge finds modern Dutch literature from the nineteenth century on very interesting. Others are of the opinion that the Dutch-speaking regions have produced at least a few exciting writers. But there was one individual who finds the *belles lettres* of the Low Countries 'quite mediocre – well, apart from Harry Mulisch'.

The Low Countries' international reputation is, then, probably a better ambassador for the Dutch language. The Low Countries as a haven of tolerance, freedom and openness: this image is still uppermost in the minds of students abroad. In Hungary, people look up to the Netherlands with its 'free' (i.e. tolerant and multicultural) mentality that is 'unique in the world'. Explaining why he decided to study Dutch, an American student referred to the 'very laid-back' mentality, particularly with regard to the drug enforcement laws, which are evidently still attracting world-wide attention. A student in Germany replied that his fellow students study Dutch 'because they want to smoke good dope'. So the cliché still prevails, much to the frustration of the Austrian student who visits the Netherlands regularly: 'Some people associate the Netherlands with marijuana and coffeeshops. I'm not into that at all, and I've never met a Dutch person who goes to coffeeshops regularly.' It is nevertheless true that many people learn Dutch in order to study legislation on drugs, euthanasia and gay marriage. Although the impression of freedom has faded somewhat since 9/11 and the murders of Pim Fortuyn and Theo van Gogh, legislation in the Netherlands and

Belgium still incorporates enough exceptional 'freedoms' to ensure that people in other countries continue to take an interest in Dutch and Flemish culture.

A 'soft' language

Many students have a positive perception of Dutch and Flemish people. A student from Poland who had visited the Netherlands found the people 'polite and always willing to help'. Someone from Vienna described the Dutch as 'open and easy to talk to'. Students of Dutch in Belgrade referred to the Dutch as businesslike, well organised, tolerant and self-reliant, but somewhat on the frugal side. Their impression of the Flemish was quite different: sincere, cheerful, optimistic and friendly nationalists – in other words, like the Serbs themselves. This identification is apparently an important reason for learning Dutch.[4] Many students and teachers find it very useful that they can use the same language in two European countries. In that respect, Dutch has an advantage over Spanish and Italian. Moreover, the differences between the Dutch spoken north and south of the border provide some interesting points for comparison. An Austrian student drew a comparison with German as it is spoken in Germany and Austria. Others are aware of the need for 'political correctness' when using terminology relating to the Low Countries. Someone in Hungary found it 'difficult to know how to refer to Flanders, Holland or Belgium without offending anyone.' The interest of the majority of students is oriented towards the Netherlands. A teacher from Strasbourg replied that his (French) students are barely aware of the fact that Dutch is also spoken in Flanders. And, to many people, Amsterdam still sounds much more exotic than drab Brussels, which is often regarded – wrongly, I might add – as a dull city full of bureaucrats. Some respondents have first-hand experience of the complex language situation in the Belgian capital. During a visit to Brussels, a student from Poland had problems shopping because he did not speak French. Officially, Brussels is a bilingual city and every shopkeeper should be able to serve customers in Dutch. The reality is often different, although the situation has improved considerably over the past twenty years. A student from Wallonia complains: 'I wish everyone was bilingual.' Many Dutch speakers in Brussels would agree with him.

There are still a number of students who favour Belgium, in spite of its language problems. A student from Germany described Belgium as 'a nice place', and a respondent from Hungary prefers Dutch as it is spoken in Belgium to the Dutch spoken north of the border. Many students appreciate the variation in the language: 'with all the different dialects, the language is a culture in itself', someone remarked. Yet this can also cause problems. Dutch dialects are difficult for a non-native speaker to understand. And they cause a great deal of confusion: which variant is the standard?

Learning Dutch and German at the same time can also be confusing. 'The language itself isn't difficult to learn with German, but after a while it's confusing because I don't know whether a word is used only in German or only in Dutch', one student confessed. Students who have chosen to learn Dutch because they think it is 'easy' to learn in combination with German are often disappointed. Linguists often refer to the interesting position of Dutch as a Germanic language. In addition to its own particular features, the language also has features of English and German. This intermediate position leads to some interesting comparisons for students of Germanic languages. Someone from Portugal commented: *'You're learning something new, but there are elements that you recognise.'* A student from Slovenia found Dutch *'softer and more melodious than German'*. One German-speaking student explained that she sometimes finds Dutch difficult *'because it is easier than German'*. The Dutch language has peculiarities that cause problems for foreign learners. The definite article is a good example: when do you use *de*, and when do you use *het*? Many non-native speakers wrestle with this problem. Another problem is the difference between spelling and pronunciation, particularly the use of different spellings for a single sound. When do you use the *ij* spelling, and when do you use the *ei* spelling? Why is *controle* spelled with a c, and *kolibrie* with a k? Other students of Dutch have problems with prepositions, the use of *er*, word order, and with the pronunciation of the 'g' and the 'h'. It is difficult to master the rhythm of Dutch sentences. Moreover, someone commented, the Dutch speak much too fast!

Paradoxically, foreign students experience the greatest problems when they actually visit the Low Countries. They make every effort to speak Dutch but are often rebuffed, as a somewhat dismayed student from Sweden explained: *'I really wanted to speak Dutch when I was in Amsterdam, but everyone spoke such good English.'* A German student had the same experience, and was very unhappy about the fact that *'you don't need to know any Dutch in the Netherlands because everyone prefers to speak German'*. The Flemish and Dutch should be more confident about using their own language. Because they are keen to demonstrate their own language skills, they deprive people of the opportunity to practise speaking Dutch in everyday conversation, something that is very important for foreign learners. This was confirmed in an internal study commissioned in 2004 by the Institut Néerlandais, the Dutch cultural institute in Paris.[5] The institute's Dutch courses attract some 230 students every semester. It began to notice that many students did not complete the course, and commissioned a survey of students' wishes. The study revealed that students would prefer more day-to-day conversation in their lessons.

Another conclusion from the study was that, even during language lessons, students want to learn more about culture and everyday life. The replies I received from university students of Dutch indicated the same thing. They too are keen to learn about contemporary culture in Flanders and the Netherlands. From the students' point of view, the most successful courses are those that go beyond the bare language itself. They think it very important to experience Dutch and Flemish culture for themselves. Some students even choose to learn Dutch because they have heard that the teaching staff are very active in this respect and make their lessons interesting.

Students are quick to realise that, by learning Dutch, they can also learn a great deal about the rest of the world or about themselves. A German student, for example, appreciates the fact that, by studying Dutch, she has also learned more about the Second World War. Others are enthusiastic because, via Dutch, they have been introduced to the history of colonialism and the overseas possessions.

A number of students suggested some logistical improvements. Two students from Germany complained about the lack of good textbooks for learning Dutch. There is also a lack of good Dutch-German/German-Dutch dictionaries designed for foreign learners. According to one student, the dictionaries that are currently available do not contain the information that non-native speakers need, such as how a particular word or expression is used in sentences.

So how does the future look for extramural Dutch Studies? Good, in many cases, but we need to remain vigilant. In English-speaking regions, interest will remain limited to a small group of specialists whose work requires highly advanced literacy skills. In the United States, the cultural centre of our globalised world, there is relatively little interest in Dutch – or any other foreign language, for that matter. But we still need to make sure that Dutch becomes more established in this centre of global culture (which has at least 100,000 Dutch speakers). Extra efforts are needed to achieve this. In South Africa, too, the position of Dutch is difficult and socio-political developments are working against it. But a university teacher from South Africa remains optimistic: *there is a lot going on, and a lot will be done in the future, too.* In former colonies such as Indonesia and Surinam, which, like South Africa, have special ties with the Dutch Language Union, the interest in Dutch will continue. After the Netherlands and Belgium, Surinam is the third country in the world where Dutch is an official language. The country joined the Dutch Language Union in December 2003, which means that there will now be greater emphasis on the Dutch language in education. This should boost the number of students studying Dutch. In Indonesia, a knowledge of Dutch is important for those who want to work in tourism and for those who want to study Indonesian history or law.

Within the European Union, the question of where Low Countries studies is heading received a mixed response from teachers. In the regions that border on the Dutch-speaking areas, interest in the discipline is increasing. This is also the case at universities in the new EU member states. But this trend is also having a negative impact on Dutch: the languages of the new EU member states – some of which have more native speakers than Dutch – are providing attractive opportunities for translators and interpreters, particularly now that those languages are used in European institutions. In cities such as Trieste, located just where the Romance, Germanic and Slavic language areas meet, Dutch is facing strong competition from the 'new' European languages. It is also suffering because German is becoming less popular in the other Western European countries. Because students of German are often required to study another Germanic language too, fewer students of German may also mean fewer students of Dutch.

Increasing student mobility in Europe is also endangering extramural Dutch programmes as more and more students spend only one or two years at the home university before leaving to complete their studies in the Low Countries. If this trend continues, the number of people studying Dutch outside the Low Countries may well decline, and cash-strapped universities may then start to consider whether the department can justify its cost. Over the last few years cutbacks have already claimed some victims; the Dutch department at the University of Hull has been closed, and from 2007 it will no longer be possible to study Dutch as a main subject at Leipzig. On a more positive note, the Dutch department at Sheffield is expanding, and a full teacher-training programme for Dutch will be developed at Oldenburg.

European students are apparently becoming more and more aware of the fact that they will be living in a united Europe. Some hope that studying Dutch will help them to become *a true European citizen*. Many are even considering moving to the Netherlands or Flanders when they have completed their studies.

Nevertheless, as one university teacher of Dutch in England pointed out, it is still important to continue promoting Dutch because *'it will never be the first subject that springs to mind when people are deciding what to study.'* A teacher in Portugal also explained that a proactive approach is needed to stimulate interest in Low Countries Studies. Perhaps it would be a good idea to involve enthusiastic students who are learning Dutch as a foreign language. Some of them are already acting as ambassadors for the Dutch language. *'Dutch is a great language'*, according to a student from Sweden. *'My heart is orange!'* added an enthusiastic student from Vienna. But the most remarkable reactions came from Russia and Slovenia. *'In Dutch you can express your thoughts using only a few words'*, a Russian student explained. *'If you choose the right words, the result will always be clear and coherent.'* One student from Slovenia has an even stronger reaction to hearing such lucid and coherent language: *'It still gives me goose bumps to hear journalists and presenters speaking perfect Dutch on television.'*

You can experience this too. Wherever you live, you will be able to join a Dutch course somewhere in your area. If you learn the language properly, you will always be able to express yourself clearly and succinctly. So do it! It will give you goose bumps – it's a great language. ■

Translated by Yvette Mead

NOTES

1. See www.ivnnl.com

2. See www.taalunieversum.org and www.cnavt.org

3. I would like to thank all the teachers and students for taking the trouble to answer my questions. Without their help, this article would not have been possible.

4. Jelica Novakovic-Lopusina & Irena Ajdinovic, 'Tussen hemels en aards' in: *Nieuwsbrief van de Orde van den Prince* (to be published).

5. Dreville, Delphine (sous la direction de Mme Valérie Haas), *Les interruptions de parcours en formation linguistique: un système de formation en décalage avec les besoins de son public'* Mémoire présenté pour l'obtention du DESS 'Ingénierie en Formation d'Adultes', Université de Picardie – Jules Verne, Faculté de Philosophie – Sciences humaines et sociales, Département des Sciences de l'éducation, Chemin du Thil, Amiens, 2004.

SEE ALSO:

Amft, Sabine , 'Een 'opdringerige' taal of een geleidelijk gegroeide vriendschap'. In: *IVN-krant*, vol. 9 (2004), no. 3.

Hermans, Theo, 'Studying 'Single Dutch'? What Next?! Dutch Studies in the Anglophone world'. In: *The Low Countries. Arts and Society in Flanders and the Netherlands*, vol. 1 (1993-4), pp. 204-211.

Krol, Martin, 'Een grenssituatie en de taal van de buren. Verhaal van mijn ontmoeting met het Nederlands'. In: *IVN-krant*, vol. 9 (2004), no. 3.

Liberati, Alessandra, 'Het verhaal van een boeiende ontmoeting'. In: *IVN-krant*, vol. 9 (2004), no. 1.

Marynissen, Ann, 'Nederlands studeren in Duitsland: mogelijkheden en motieven'. In: *Nieuwsbrief van de Orde van den Prince*, vol. 24, no. 1 (Sept/Oct 2004).

Salverda, Reinier, 'Wat doet een neer-landicus in Londen?'. In: *Vaktaal*, October 2004.

Talasi, Zsofia, 'Diep in de Nederlandse kaas. Een onvergetelijke (zoek)tocht in het Nederlandse taal- en cultuurlabyrint'. In: *IVN-krant*, vol. 9 (2004), no. 2.

Internationale Vereniging voor Neerlandistiek (IVN), Van Dorthstraat 6, 2481 XV Woubrugge, The Netherlands, tel. +31 (0)172 518 243, fax +31 (0)172 519 925, bureau@ivnnl.com, www.ivnnl.com

De Nederlandse Taalunie (Dutch Language Union), P.O. Box 10595, 2501 HN The Hague, The Netherlands, tel. +31 (0)70 346 95 38, fax +31 (0)70 365 98 18, info@taalunie.org, www.taalunieversum.org

American Association for Netherlandic Studies (AANS), c/o Amy Golahny, Lycoming College, Art Department, Williamsport, PA 17701, USA, golahny@lycoming.edu

Association Française d'études néerlandaises (AFEN), c/o Dr. P. de Klerk, Université Stendhal, Grenoble III, Département d'études allemandes et néerlandaises, B.P. 25X, 38040 Grenoble, France

Association de Néerlandistes de Belgique Francofone (ANBF), Inez de Valck, Université de Liège, Place Cockerill 3, Bâti A2, 4000 Liège, Belgium, idevalck@ulb.ac.be

Association for Low Countries Studies in Great Britain and Ireland (ALCS), Department of Germanic Studies, University of Sheffield, Sheffield S10 2TN, United Kingdom, tel +44 (0)114 222 43 96, fax +44 (0)114 222 21 60, alcs@sheffield.ac.uk, www.shef.ac.uk/alcs

Canadian Association for the Advancement of Netherlandic Studies (CAANS), c/o Basil D. Kingstone, French Department, University of Windsor, 401 Sunset Avenue, Windsor, Ontario N9B 3P4, Canada, bkinst@uwindsor.ca

Certificaat Nederlands als Vreemde Taal (CNAVT), c/o Sonia de Becker, Blijde Inkomststraat 7, 3000 Leuven, Belgium,tel. +32 (0)16 32 55 16, fax +32 (0)16 32 55 12, cnavt@arts.kuleuven.ac.be, www.cnavt.org

Comenius, Association for Dutch Studies in Middle and Eastern Europe, Universität Wien, Institut für Germanistik/Nederlandistik, Dr. Karl Lueger-Ring 1, A-1010 Vienna, www.ned.univie.ac.at/CMS/comenius

Fachvereinigung Niederländisch, Haus der Niederlande, Alter Steinweg 6/7, 48143 Munster, Germany, fax +49 (0)251 83 285 30, geschaeftsstelle@fachvereinigungniederlaendisch.de, wwwhein.uni-muenster.de/

Steunpunt Nederlands als Vreemde Taal (Dutch as a foreign language), Spuistraat 210, NL-1012 VT Amsterdam, tel. +31 (0)20 525 31 52, fax +31 (0)20 525 30 52,, snvt-fgw@uva.nl, www.snvt.hum.uva.nl.

Suider-Afrikaanse Vereniging vir Neerlandistiek, R. Marais, Departement Afrikaans, Universiteit van Pretoria, Pretoria 0002, South Africa, rmarais@postinfo.up.ac.za

Werkgroep Docenten Nederlands in Azianië (Teachers of Dutch in Australasia, Hans Groot, Erasmus Taalcentrum, Via Koeriersdienst BuZa, P.O. Box 20061, 2500 EB The Hague, The Netherlands, erastaal@indo.net.id

Other links to websites of interest to those wanting to know more about Dutch and Dutch studies can be found at www.ivnnl.com and www.taalunieversum.org.

High and Dry

Media-Friendly Dutch Droog Design
on the International Winners' Podium

In the last decade of the twentieth century, Droog Design was one of the most talked-about cutting-edge movements in the world of design. The young force that first presented itself under the name of Droog Design in April 1993 at a group exhibition in Milan rapidly succeeded in gaining international attention for its new design mentality. With its emphasis on clear concepts, its sober, 'dry' approach, its 'dry' sense of humour (all encompassed by the one short word *'droog'*, 'dry', which also evokes all the relevant Dutch historical stereotypes), Dutch design was suddenly on top again. All at once it was back on the world map.

However, the sounds of celebration on the occasion of its recent tenth birthday weren't exactly deafening. At least not on the home front, where Droog Design came under fire. For it was in 2003 that the Dutch people started a great debate on the *'crisis in Dutch design'*, or, more specifically, *'the diminished influence of Dutch design'*.

It must be said that this *'diminished influence'* is not always so clearly apparent outside the Netherlands itself. It even seems significant that *No Design No Style Droog Design*, the first retrospective to mark ten years of Droog, was held at the Art Museum in Seoul and was the brainchild of curator Kim Sang Kyu. Then the 'official' retrospective, *Simply Droog. 10 + 1 Years of Avant-garde Design from the Netherlands*, was held first in Munich and Bremen. Only afterwards (from 18/12/2004 to 13/02/2005) did the exhibition come to The Hague. The pervasive influence of the Droog Design way of thinking was also obvious at the design events held as part of Lille 2004, Cultural Capital of Europe. The prestigious Italian magazine *Domus* devoted 18 whole pages of its October 2004 issue to the *Droog Event: Open Borders*. Even the people at Design Flanders, the Belgian design organisation, were strongly influenced by Droog Design in their Design Triennial *Imperfect by Design*.

The Dutch platform for conceptual design is still decidedly flourishing on the international stage and in the media. So what's the problem in the Netherlands? Is this a typical case of prophets being without honour in their own country? Lucas Verweij, project manager of Premsela, the Dutch Design Foundation, has expressed his criticism forcefully; in his words: *'Art magazines, design magazines, colleagues and the culturally-minded may all sing the praises of Dutch*

Droog Design,
Open Borders:
Overview 19. Lille, 2004.
Photo by Fendry Ekel;
courtesy of Droog Design.

Design, but industry and ordinary consumers aren't impressed. You have to realise that for Wanders' chairs[1] the ratio of editorials to sales is about a thousand to one. Dutch top design consists mainly of media products; there's hardly any connection to industry and the market.'

Revolution as design

Predictably, Droog Design's poor financial performance is viewed more criti-cally in the current economic climate than during the boom of the mid-1990s. Nowadays, the principle that *'conceptual design mainly (stimulates) the imagina-tion and not so much the desire to buy'* sounds like a gibe. Ten years ago things were different. The innovators of 1993, after all, weren't interested in increasing the numbers of even better or even more functional products; it was all about a different, more considered attitude towards design, and making inroads into our living environment and society. *'Form follows concept'* was the new bat-tle cry. The *'form follows function'* of the modernists, which had come about as a reaction to elitist and extravagant ornamental styles, had proved its useful-ness; but the market had long ago become saturated with design products that were admittedly functional, but much too boring, cold, clean and characterless. Already in the 1980s the radical Italian group Memphis had violently rebelled against that modern, functional rationalism. Riotous use of colours, busy pat-terns and tumultuous decoration, kitschy excess, a cheerful blending of incom-patible cultural and historical references, parody, pastiche, irony, fragmenta-tion, ambiguity, self-reference, ideological criticism... In short, Memphis had already unleashed the whole post-modern repertoire upon the field of design.

With their emphasis on a sober, clear approach, Droog Design decisively fol-lowed a different course, interpreting the spirit of the 1990s, the decade that saw the rediscovery of the minimalist ideal of 'less is more'. But in many respects Droog Design, as a non-conformist avant-garde platform, is also a continuation of Memphis, even though they may be said to practise a more northern, maybe even a more Calvinist version of postmodernism. With Droog Design the theory is often considerably more interesting than the practice; the idea behind the object much stronger than the object as such. (It should be noted that Droog Design has never been a fixed group or school of designers, but that the founders, the design critic Renny Ramakers and the (jewellery) designer Gijs Bakker describe Droog Design as a mentality. Over the years the collection of products bearing the Droog Design seal of approval has grown to more than 150).

The question, of course, is not just one of whether playing with concepts in this way can boost the Dutch economy (though economic factors are inevitably more decisive in design than in autonomous art, however much Droog want to emphasise the crossovers). Another interesting question is whether, ten years on, most of those clever, ironic, thought-provoking social comments go beyond the level of frivolous entertainment. If design spends too much time hanging around (and looking too smug?) in museums, subsidised promotional shows and art galleries, if it doesn't end up in our living rooms because not one single manufacturer is able or willing to produce it at an affordable price, then does it have that everyday relevance that the anonymous designer of

Droog Design,
Knitted Maria coffee-pot.
Coffee-pot and casy in one,
porcelain and varnished cotton.
Designed by Gijs Bakker, 1997.
Photo by Hans van der Mars;
courtesy of Droog Design.

sound, functional, ecological, attractive and reasonably priced mass-produced articles can and should be able to claim? After all, Aaron Betsky, the director of the Nederlands Architectuur Instituut (Nai), in 're:droog', his contribution to the book *Simply Droog. 10 + 1 years of creating innovation and discussion*, describes the greatest merits of Droog Design as follows: '*For all the critical rhetoric, irony and high design that characterises Droog Design, this is perhaps their most lasting and important contribution: that they have institutionalised political and social criticism as a lifestyle – the hippie way of revolution – into design and thus into at least some small part of our daily lives'*.

It's not quite fair to try and assess the impact of Droog on our daily lives by counting the number of functional objects that they have actually brought into the average household. It would, of course, demonstrate more understanding of the new philosophy to try to establish the extent to which they have

Droog Design,
Chest of drawers. All drawers
are collected from the street and
re-used in this chest.
Each chest is unique.
60 x 110 x 120 cm.
Designed by Tejo Remy, 1991.
Photo by Bob Goedewagen;
courtesy of Droog Design.

introduced their ideas in a successful and enduring way. To what extent has Marcel Wanders' aversion to a society with what he calls a 'baby-face fixation', where everything has to be young, new, smooth, taut, flawless and unwrinkled, prompted people to enter into a more profound and lasting relationship with functional objects? Have we – in imitation of Tejo Remy – dared to kit out our interiors with DIY rag chairs or milk-bottle lamps? Or have we been inspired by that other icon of his, the legendary chest of drawers made out of twenty individual second-hand drawers randomly piled up and held together with a long strap? In other words: have we learned to reflect more on the never-ending stream of newfangled mass-produced articles and tried to give new life to our old, worn-out possessions, which have so many memories and emotions attached to them?

Particularly for the first generation of Droog designers in 1993, readymade and recycling were obvious themes. Not only materials, but also ideas, memories and emotions were subjected to recycling. Gijs Bakker designed his *Peepshow* wallpaper in 1992. Round peepholes of various sizes allow something of the decorative patterns on the old underlying layer of wallpaper to remain visible.

Jurgen Bey's cocoon furniture also counts as a distinctive recycled product. He patches up old-fashioned tables and chairs by wrapping them in a PVC cocoon. Logically, his implicit comment on the consumer society goes hand in hand with an incompatibility with industrial mass production. In the long run, such a position becomes untenable.

Over the course of time the emphasis has changed. Ramakers and Bakker

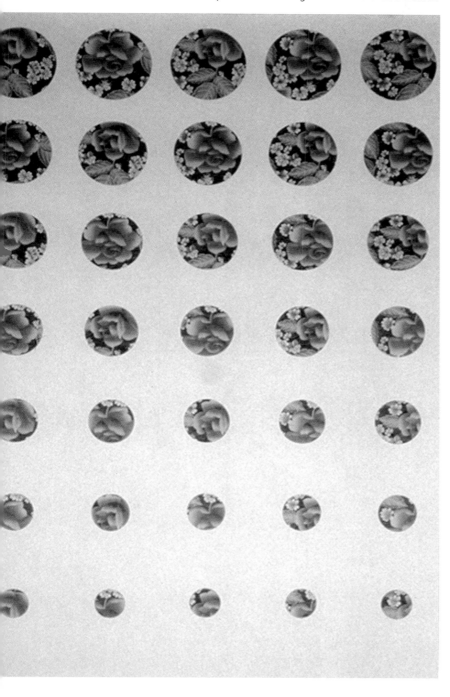

Droog Design,
Peepshow wallpaper.
Giving a new look to
'old wallpaper'. 65 x 320 cm.
Designed by Gijs Bakker, 1992.
Photo by Hans van der Mars;
courtesy of Droog Design.

Droog Design.
Knotted chair.
Soft material used in an
unconventional way.
Carbon and epoxy.
50 x 60 x 100 cm. Designed
by Marcel Wanders, 1996.
Photo by Hans van der Mars;
courtesy of Droog Design.

encouraged thematic diversity and started new projects and joint ventures. For
example, in 1995 and 1996, together with the Aerospace Engineering department
at the Technische Universiteit Delft, they carried out the projects 'Dry Tech I and
II'. The purpose was to give selected designers the opportunity to experiment with
new composite materials. One of the results was Marcel Wanders' world-famous
and inspired *Knotted chair* (1996). The amazing combination of high-tech materials and low-tech manufacturing processes is characteristic of his work. From
a rope made of carbon and aramide fibres a macramé chair is 'knotted' manu-
ally. Once it hardens, the chair is ultra-light and surprisingly strong because of
the carbon. Wanders says of this futuristic example of technology that he wanted
something *'with a traditional feel, so that you can see it has been made with love'*.

Ten different themes were presented at the *Simply Droog* exhibition: *'Use it again'*, *'Familiar – Not so Familiar'*, *'Open Concept'*, *'The inevitable Ornament'*, *'Simplicity'*, *'Irony'*, *'Tactility'*, *'Experience'*, *'Hybridisation'* and *'Form follows Process'*. It's all about subjects such as recycling, ways of giving brand-new industrial products

a feeling of age and familiarity, interaction with the user, who has a more active role and to a certain extent helps to design the product, the comeback of decorative touches, structure and texture that invite us to touch and physically experience them, the combination of different functions in a single object, and experimentation with imperfections, flaws and random elements in industrial production processes that ensure that the products become unique rather than identical.

What all Droog products have in common is that they are *'clear concepts carried out in an equally clear manner'*, to quote Renny Ramakers and Gijs Bakker. Yet it can be maintained with equal certainty that they are all strongly paradoxical, so the message is not that simple at all. Simple and clear would, after all,

Droog Design,
Cocoon furniture (table+chair).
PVC coating completely
changes an existing chair or
creates a union of different
furniture pieces.
Designed by Jurgen Bey, 1997.
Photo by Bob Goedewagen;
courtesy of Droog Design.

Droog Design, *Rag chair*.
Re-use of clothing makes
for a comfortable and
individually unique chair.
Rags, steel strips,
60 x 60 x 110 cm. Designed
by Tejo Remy, 1991.
Photo by Hans van der Mars;
courtesy of Droog Design.

mean that a chair has four identical legs, not that you have to prop the fourth leg up with a pile of books in order to get it to balance, as in Jurgen Bey's *Do add 'short leg'* (2000). And not everyone thinks that it is clear why someone would ask a company that is well known for its perfectionist culture to apply its high standards to the production of a deliberately distorted product, or to making a brand-new manufactured product look botched and unfinished, like *Soft Urn* (1993), Hella Jongerius' intriguing polyurethane vase, and much of her other work. The typical Droog attitude to design is layered, experimental, self-referential and altogether rather complex. Its paradoxical character is made abundantly clear, for example, by the famous slogan that designer Richard Hutten uses to describe his design method: '*No sign of design*'. As an 'anti-designer', Hutten was asked to create a design academy in Seoul named after him, along with the course programme and even a sponsoring shopping centre. So much for 'diminished influence'! However strongly their conscience objects to it, eventually designers cannot escape the essence of their trade, which is to continue making new products and thereby adding to the existing profusion. It goes without saying that Hutten's new assignments will not just lead to constructions that are conceptually strong, but also technically feasible, sturdy, safe and functional.

Several things point to the fact that brilliant young Dutch designers are increasingly keen to leave the experimental laboratory and gain access to the 'real world of design'. Functionality is, for example, clearly the focus of one of Droog's most recent showpieces, Joris Laarman's radiator, a functional object with a strikingly decorative appearance. But the baroque floral interplay of shapes is not just some trendy style feature. It turns out that the intertwined concrete tubes circulate warmth much more efficiently than the simple, minimalist radiators that we're used to. So, in this case, decoration improves performance.

Droog Design, Radiator.
A radiator element in an
unusual style that can best
be named neo-rococo.
Concrete and plumbing
parts, various sizes.
Designed by Joris
Laarman, 2003.
Photo by Anita Star;
courtesy of Droog Design.

Laarman's radiator, his graduation piece from Enthoven Academy, was also widely featured in all sorts of magazines, from Tokyo and Seoul to Milan and New York. A conversation with this twenty-something designer reveals that he's far more interested in the possibilities of production than he is in the over-whelming media attention that almost inexplicably has come his way. He admits how upset he was when he discovered that Italian industrial design companies, in spite of a genuine sympathy and enthusiasm for his idea, make absolutely no secret of the fact that as a rule they don't take Dutch designers seriously. And that's in spite of the fact that you can warm yourself up so much better in front of his radiator. ■

NOTE

1. *Knotted chairs* by Marcel Wanders, one of the Dutch design stars who originally owe their reputation to Droog Design.

www.droogdesign.nl

Translated by Laura Watkinson

Nice Boys in a Cold World

The Literary Works of Nescio

'Nescio': who on earth would hide behind a peculiar name like that? But that's just what the businessman Jan Hendrik Frederik Grönloh did in 1911. 'Nescio' is a Latin verb form that literally means 'I don't know'. It's my guess that in choosing the name he meant to say, 'Reader, don't expect any certainties from me. I hold everything in doubt.' I also think he chose his pseudonym in imitation of the author he so admired, Multatuli, who in real life was the civil servant Eduard Douwes Dekker. Dekker published the novel *Max Havelaar* in 1860 under the pen name 'Multatuli', Latin for 'I have suffered much'. Multatuli's book is now one of the classics of Dutch literature. It has been translated into many languages and in 1987 was given the honour of being included in the *Penguin Classics* series. The other Dutch author with a similarly strange pseudonym, Nescio, produced a small and very Dutch oeuvre whose subtle irony and finely tuned style is also fully deserving of a place in the literature of Europe.

God's throne, little boulders and great nostalgia

For many years Nescio was the author of only one book: the collection of stories entitled *Little Poet, The Sponger, Young Titans* (Dichtertje, De uitvreter, Titaantjes), first published in 1918 by the Haarlem art dealer J.H. de Bois. *The Sponger* and *Young Titans* (both previously published in magazines) are set within a circle of young bohemians in the years leading up to the First World War. *The Sponger* is the story of Japi, a likeable *bon vivant* whose goal is '*to wither away, to become indifferent to hunger and sleep, to cold and damp*', but who is also quite capable of fully enjoying the good things of life, especially if somebody else is footing the bill. A quote: '*Painting was all right, he thought, if you were good at it. He wasn't good at anything, and that's why he didn't do anything. You couldn't reproduce things as you experienced them anyway. He had only one wish: to wither away, to become indifferent to hunger and sleep, to cold and damp. Those were your great enemies. You were forever having to eat and sleep, to get out of the cold, forever getting wet and miserable or tired. A stretch of water like this has it easy. It throws up a few waves and reflects the clouds, it's always different and yet it's always the same. Not bothered by anything.*'

The painter Bavink introduces him to his Amsterdam friends, where Japi, because of his idiosyncrasies, soon acquires the nickname 'sponger' which he manages to twist into a title of honour. But he can't keep up that free life. He develops socialist sympathies and does his best to change the world. But *'the world had kept on turning, it turned just as it always had. It would probably keep on turning without him. (...) He was wiser now. He washed his hands of it all.'* The story ends in a mood of resignation with the sponger's suicide. *'His journey to Friesland was never fully explained'* reads the last sentence of the story. It seems to be saying: you may know what the outcome is, but that doesn't tell you everything.

Young Titans is about the same circle of friends minus Japi: five young men of nineteen or twenty fired by a vague idealism. All the introductions are swallowed up in the opening sentence: *'Boys we were – but nice boys. Even if I do say so myself. We're much wiser now, wise and pathetic, that's what we are – except for Bavink, who's gone crazy. Didn't we want to make something of the world, though. We were going to show them how things ought to be done. We, that's who we were, the five of us. Everybody else was "them". "Them", who didn't understand anything and didn't see anything. "What?" said Bavink, "God? You're talking about God? Their next hot meal is their God."'* In scene after scene we watch what happens to these *'nice boys'*. They dream of accomplishing *'great things'*, but after a couple of years it is clear they have had to abandon their ideals. Only Bavink is *'defeated by those "God damned things"'* and goes insane. The last paragraph of *Young Titans* raises the story to a higher plane and gives us a clear idea of Nescio's philosophical take on life and of his masterly style: *'God's throne remains unshaken. His world just goes its own way. Every now and then God smiles a little at the gentlemen of consequence, who think they're so important. New Young Titans are already at work, stacking up little boulders to knock him from his exalted position and then organise the world to their own liking. He just laughs and thinks, "Very good, boys, crazy as you are, you're still dearer to me than all those fine men of wisdom. Sorry that you've got to break your necks and that I've got to let the fine gentlemen prosper. I'm only God, after all." And everything just keeps on going, and woe to him who asks the question: Why?'*

The story *Little Poet* takes place mainly in the year 1917 and has to do with the same problems, but this time within the context of marriage. The little poet is happily married, but *'if you're a poet, the prettiest girls are always on the other side of the canal'*, and you keep longing irrationally for things you don't know. *'And being married forever is such a long time.'* He falls under the spell of his sister-in-law, who reciprocates his love. This story, too, has a dramatic conclusion and ends with the death of the little poet. It is the most literary story of the three because – as in Goethe's *Faust* – God and the Devil both become involved in the little poet's life. At the same time there's also a God of the Netherlands walking around representing middle-class Respectability: *'The God of your auntie who said you must always tip your hat whenever you go past your boss's house, in Delft or Oldenzaal (where was it again?), even if nobody saw you. You never knew who was watching.'*

The 'plot' of the stories is compelling. The writer shows that sensitive young people are no match for the world they face (especially if they don't have any money), and any attempt to resist or to ponder the great existential questions will only destroy them, for *'woe to him who asks the question: Why?'* The stories also provide a splendid glimpse of life in Amsterdam at the beginning of the twentieth century, and they testify to a great love for the Dutch landscape. But the most extraordinary aspect of the work is Nescio's writing style. It is a miracle that this voice, from the years before the First World War, still strikes us as so human and modern. The transcendent simplicity and the originality of his way of writing go hand in hand with a great mastery of such literary conventions as humour, irony, understatement, sentiment (never sentimentality or self-pity), all marvellously held in balance. Nescio's world view is complicated, and as a true romantic he prefers to express it by means of opposites: freedom versus constraint, longing for eternity versus the awareness of mortality. The characters' vicissitudes are both humorous and tragic; they themselves are both great and small. In Nescio's hand this almost principled dualism results in sentences such as *'We were above the world and the world was above us and weighed heavy on us'*. This is the voice of someone who can assume different points of view, someone who chooses 'Nescio', 'I don't know', as a pseudonym, which does not alter the fact that he has more sympathy for one point of view than another. And all this is permeated by a nostalgia for the irretrievable past.

Recognition takes patience

The writer who chose the unusual pseudonym Nescio in 1911 was in everyday life Mr J.H.F. Grönloh, 'Frits' to his family and friends. He was born in Amsterdam in 1882 and spent practically his entire life in that city (*'You an Amsterdammer?'* is a question Japi the sponger is asked, and he answers from the bottom of his heart, *'Yes, thank God'*). The young Grönloh was the eldest son of a plumber-shopkeeper, which means he grew up in the milieu of the lower middle class. He was allowed to continue his studies at the three-year non-classical secondary school and the two-year business college, but when school was over it meant his freedom was over as well, just as it was for Japi the sponger: *'Then your old man sticks you in some office. Then you discover that you learned all that stuff at school to spend your time dampening paper with a wet brush.'* During those years, he and a few friends bought a small piece of property with the idea of starting an agricultural colony – an idealistic enterprise that quickly failed due to lack of money and experience. Later he gave a sympathetic account of this period of his life in *Young Titans*.

In 1904 Grönloh took a job with the Holland-Bombay Trading Company in Amsterdam. He was promoted to deputy manager and then to joint manager. He married and became the father of a lively family of four daughters. Running a trading company during the Depression was not easy and in 1937 he stepped down for health reasons, but continued to work for the company as an advisor until he reached pensionable age. It was then that he rediscovered the freedom to do whatever he wanted (*'I'm free. After forty years I'm free. And I can get my hair cut whenever I feel like it and then just let it grow,'* thinks one of his characters). He made regular trips to the Dutch landscapes of which he was so fond, as he had in his youth: het Gooi, Waterland, the rivers, Limburg, Zeeland. But in 1956 he suffered a stroke, which put an end to his expeditions. He died in 1961.

Only a few people knew he had written a book, and Gronlöh himself kept his distance from the literary world. *'I always kept as quiet as possible about my writing,'* he said one of the few times anyone ever came to interview him, *'because I spent my entire life in an office, and in places like that if they find out that you have such inclinations they think you'll be no good at your work.'* But he was grateful that he had had the chance to say what he wanted to say, and he knew that his work was worth something. '*They don't recognise me now,*' he told his family when he was getting on in years. '*But we must be patient. You'll see that I'm right.*' During his lifetime his work was mainly valued and admired by other authors, so he can rightly be called a 'writer's writer'. In articles about his work he was characterised as '*the most re-read writer around*' and '*the writer of whom it is most often said that he doesn't get enough attention*'.

The writer Nescio and his book *Little Poet, The Sponger, Young Titans* were favourably received by the critics in 1918, but the print run of five hundred copies did not sell quickly. It was not reprinted until 1933. Because his work was being persistently attributed to someone else, J.H.F. Grönloh felt compelled to reveal himself formally as the work's author. In 1956, when the fourth printing came out, a slim bundle of sketches entitled *Mene Tekel* was added to the three stories, so in some sense Nescio remained a one-book-author. That did not change until 1961, which saw the publication of *Above the Valley, and Other Stories* (Boven het dal, en andere verhalen), a collection of mainly unfinished stories, thanks to the efforts of family and friends. Fifty years after his first volume, and just before his death at the age of 79, Nescio had become the author of an oeuvre. The new book, and the writer's death, produced a torrent of articles, most of which dealt with the entire oeuvre. Interest in his work went up, and reprints followed each other with increasing speed. The collection *The Sponger, Young Titans, Little Poet, Mene Tekel* is now in its 35th impression, and the collection *Above the Valley* in its 24th.

Master of the unfinished

The long-awaited *Collected Works* – which I had the pleasure of editing – appeared in 1996 in two volumes and received a great deal of media attention. This edition, too, has already been reprinted several times. The first volume contains the works published during the writer's lifetime, together with a great deal of unfinished work from the author's literary estate. In a writer like Nescio, however, for whom literally every sentence is of value to the reader for its own sake, being unfinished is totally irrelevant. The second volume, *Nature Diary* (Natuurdagboek), was a big surprise. It contains notes from the journeys that Nescio took between 1946 and 1955, mostly in the immediate vicinity of Amsterdam. The notes begin as a perfunctory record, but as time passes they take on a more personal and sometimes distinctly lyrical character. At such times the diary becomes a hymn, with almost every page glorifying the Dutch landscape, lovingly observed in the ever-changing Dutch light. The observations sometimes border on the mystical as Nescio applies himself to creating an immaterial world from the things he sees, where time, place and name lose their meaning ('*The landscape lay beyond all place and time*').

In the introduction to *Above the Valley* Nescio wrote that he wanted to tell '*a simple story*' in his work, thus '*capturing in passing some clouds etc. for a couple of centuries, which is what it's all about to me.*' The story's sole purpose is to '*capture readers*'. This is such an evocation: '*And the many gilded tips of the summer trees and the autumn trees, and all those clouds. I wish they were alive, that this transience lived as long as thoughts do, all this fragility, that I myself would live as long as Dutch was being read, a simple little man like me,* that's *what I wish. Or perhaps it should be translated into a language that will be read longer, and so on, as far as I can think. In the same way I see a woman, living, and I see her eyes. She's already been dead for maybe five hundred years, but I stand before the painting and her smile lives. And the grass lives and the little leaves on the willows and the little flowing river and the beeches on the grass in front of the white house, and the clouds live, and I'm standing beside the same water that happened to be flowing there and reflecting the sun, just as the painter stood there, in England, let's say in June 1750, and I am that painter. Who still remembers the wars that were waged in all those centuries?'*

Nescio's small, nostalgic voice will soon make its way to the body of European literature. Gallimard is including the work in the series *Du monde entier*. The website of the Pen American Center is also recommending *Young Titans* and *The Sponger* for translation; Nescio is the only Dutch candidate: *'These two long stories detail the minor victories and defeats that make Dutch middle-class life so bleak and comical. The details are all tiny, exquisitely understated and dry'*. And indeed there is much to experience in this highly original work. Nescio is essentially a lyricist, a poet writing in prose. He's a cynic too, as well as a mystic in his own way. Like Chekhov and Turgenev, he is able to say complicated things with simple words. That for all that his work is so light and playful, so tender, moving and witty, is nothing short of miraculous. ■

An Extract from *Young Titans*

by Nescio

III

It was a curious time. Come to think of it, that time must still be going on – it goes on as long as there are young men around who are nineteen, twenty years old. But for us it is long gone.

We were above the world and the world was above us and weighed heavy on us. Deep, deep down we saw the bustling world and felt contempt for those in

Cover of the 2002 edition of *Young Titans*, by Joost Swarte for Nijgh & Van Ditmar publishers.

it, especially the gentlemen of consequence – those who are always busy and believe that they really have come a long way in the world.

But we were poor. Bekker and I had to spend most of our time in an office doing what those gentlemen said, listening to their stupid opinions when they spoke to each other and putting up with the fact that they thought they were far cleverer and smarter than we were. And if they thought it was cold, all the windows had to be shut and in the winter the lights had to be switched on much too early and the curtains drawn, so that we never saw the red sky or dusk falling in the street outside, and we couldn't do a thing about it .

And we had to live in streets, very cramped, with a view of the lancaster curtains on the other side with their tasselled fringes and the aspidistra in a pot with an impossible flower on top.

Oh, we took our revenge, we learned languages the names of which they had never heard of and we read books of which they could understand nothing; we experienced emotions the existence of which they did not suspect. On Sundays, we walked for hours and hours along roads where they never came, and in the office we thought of the ditches and the meadows we had seen, and while the gentlemen ordered us to do things we could not see the use of, we thought of how the Sunday-evening sun had set behind Abcoû. And how we had reflected wordlessly on the universe, how God had filled our heads, our hearts and our spinal cords and how foolishly they would gape if we were to tell them that. And how they, with all their money and their trips to Switzerland and Italy and God-knows-where and with all their cleverness and industry, would never be able to experience that.

But in spite of all that we were in their power; they laid claim to most of our time, they kept us away from the sun and the meadows and the water's edge. They forced us to constantly occupy our minds with their incomprehensible affairs. But that was as far as it went. And they used to tell us off; in the office we were mere nobodies. 'Oh, Bekker,' they would say to each other. They were well-educated, those gentlemen; the woman from two-up used to say 'that half-baked one' – but the gentlemen were too well-bred to say anything like that. And they were clever, far cleverer than the woman from two-up, whose husband was a lamplighter, a nice job that doesn't call for all that much learning. My boss asked me whether I wrote poetry. Bekker said that such a man really shouldn't utter that word, it oughtn't to be allowed. 'What did you say to him?' I had said nothing; I had just stared him in the face and it had struck me that he had a turnip for a head and I had thought: 'He doesn't know who he has in front of him; he's too stupid for that.' And they paid us badly, those gentlemen.

IV

And we were in love. For months, Bekker used to walk every morning along the Sarphatistraat where he had no business to be. He was in love with a schoolgirl who was about seventeen, and he used to walk about fifty paces behind her or on the opposite side of the street and look at her. He never found out what her name was and he never spoke a word to her. In the Christmas holidays he was miserable. In February, he took an afternoon off to wait for her when she came out of school. There he was, standing by a quiet little canal in the snow when a bloke rode past on a white horse, wearing a blue smock and a straw hat. How strange to see something as crazy as that on precisely such an afternoon. But at five minutes to four Bekker left – he didn't dare keep on standing there. He slowly strolled off and on the Weteringschans she caught up with him. She was laughing loudly to a female friend of hers. I don't believe she ever knew Bekker existed.

Bekker wanted to know from me how it was all going to end, as things couldn't go on like that. And it didn't go on like that either, for she didn't come back any more after the summer holidays.

'Girls,' Bekker said, 'a waste of time... She bounced when she walked.' He turned the lamp up a bit and flicked over a page in the book he was reading. 'Where would she be now? Would she be kissing someone?' An ember from his pipe fell onto the book. He put it out with a match-box. 'Dammit, a hole, that was stupid of me.' 'It's better this way, girls are a waste of time, you don't get anywhere, they just distract you. They're nice at a distance, for writing poetry about.'

He went on reading. After a little while he looked up again... 'Do you know what was strange about it? When she caught up with me that afternoon, she brushed past me. There was virtually nothing between us, a bit of her clothes and practically none of mine.' (Bekker used to wear a shirt with nothing under it summer and winter.) 'That's not much, is it?' I didn't feel it was much; between Naarden tower and Bekker's room, for example, there was much more. 'Between Naarden tower and this mustache,' Bekker said, 'there's much less, much less than there was then between her shoulder and mine. Nowhere near, Koekebakker.' He turned another page, looked at the light, and said: 'That's how it is,' and went on reading.

V

That's how it was: God revealed and concealed his countenance alternately. You didn't get anywhere, even though you admired the girls only from a distance and let their pretty faces be kissed by others, by the gentlemen of consequence that they generally rated more highly than they did us. For they were far sprucer and spoke so nicely. And we were down-and-outs.

There was nothing to be hoped for from God, he goes his own way and doesn't have to account for his doings. If we wanted something, we would have to do it ourselves. But we felt that it was all very well for Bavink and Hoyer – they could do something, could show how it ought to be done, but the rest of us, Bekker and Kees and me, at best we could become 'socials' and that seemed pretty poor, when you had sat at God's table, to end up writing addresses for printed matter or become a member of the 'free group Kastanjeplein and environs'. And the plan to live out on the heath would never come to anything either, for as soon as Bekker had scraped together a few cents, his shoes needed repairing. We could perhaps have joined Van Eeden's colony, but when we had gone there one Sunday – a four-hour walk – a man was strolling around there in a peasant's smock with expensive yellow shoes, eating little sponge cakes out of a paper bag, bareheaded, in deep communion with nature, as it used to be called, his beard full of crumbs. Then we didn't dare go any further and walked all the way back to Amsterdam, following each other along the Naarden canal and singing. And a peasant girl said to a peasant boy: 'Been nowt about that in the paper, lad, what d'you make of that? You know anything about it?'

VI

So we just did nothing. Well, not quite, for it was then that Bekker wrote his first poem.

I still remember it well, it was on a Sunday, of course. If anything ever happened, it was on a Sunday. For the other six days of the week three of us were shackled from nine to six.

I had been out looking for a job in Hillegom at a bulb dealer's, a man with podgy, red, close-shaven cheeks. And the others had promptly turned it into a day out. Bavink, Hoyer and Bekker had all been wanting to visit the museum of antiquity in Leiden for ages, and now was the time to do it. And Kees had to come along; he always did what the others did. I was to meet up with them in Leiden.

It was December. I stood at the back of the tram, right on the balcony. The tram just trundled through the countryside, stopped and trundled on again. This went on for hours, the fields stretching out endlessly. And the sky got bluer and bluer and the sun shone as if flowers would start sprouting from the country yokels. And the red roofs in the villages and the black trees and the fields, many of them covered over with rushes, basked in the warmth, and the dunes stood in the sun with their heads bare. And the highroad lay there white and painful in the light and could not bear the sun and the panes of the village lamps glinted; they too found it hard to put up with the glare of the light.

But *I* got colder and colder. And as long as the sun shone, the tram trundled on. It's a long ride from Hillegom to Leiden, and the days are short in December. And finally a corpse stood in the tram staring at that silly great cold sun that blazed as if the revolution was about to begin, as if they were busy in Amsterdam demolishing the offices, and it could not bring a spark of life to my cold feet and numb legs. And the sun got bigger and bigger and colder and colder and I got colder and colder and stayed the same size. And the blue sky looked at me terribly seriously: 'What on earth was I doing on that tram?'

That afternoon Bekker wrote his first poem. And when I arrived in Leiden as the gas lamps were being lit and found the immortals sitting next to each other on a long bench in the third-class waiting room of the station, close to the stove, I also had to be subjected to the poem. It was really beautiful. Didn't it have a title? Bekker shook his head. But Bavink and Hoyer screamed that they had seen something at the top. A respectable gentleman said: 'Show-offs' to the man clipping his ticket at the door. Bavink grabbed hold of the piece of paper. What did it say? Of course. 'To her.' I'd known all along, of course.

Bavink felt the stove needed a shovelful of coal, but couldn't find the shovel. In those waiting rooms they always take the shovel with them; otherwise the public would keep piling on the fuel.

Then Bavink threw the lumps of coal on the stove with his hands and got into trouble with a bloke in a white coat.

It was very amusing that evening. Kees and Hoyer fell asleep in the train. Bavink sat talking to a young lady from the Hague, sniffing at the heliotrope fragrance that rose from her lovely limbs.

Then Bekker began to talk about the heath again. He wanted to live there quietly and just wait for whatever God had in store for him. You couldn't do anything. He was very melancholy. I had my objections to the heath: it's too dry there. And I asked Bekker what he was going to live on, that for office staff country-dwelling normally didn't work all that well, except in America, where there were all sorts of lying promises about it. But he wasn't worried about that. He didn't need anything.

Now he knows better. Only God doesn't need anything. And precisely that is the great difference between God and us.

And so it never came to anything, that heath.

From *Young Titans* (Titaantjes, 1915). In: *Collected Works* (Verzameld werk; ed. Lieneke Frerichs). Amsterdam: Nijgh & Van Ditmar, 1996. Vol. 1, pp. 48-53.

Translated by John Irons

Rudy Kousbroek and the Art of Memory

Rudy Kousbroek was born in 1929 in Pematang Siantar on the island of Sumatra in the then Dutch East Indies, present-day Indonesia. After the war years, which he spent with his father in a Japanese internment camp, he came to the Netherlands and began to study mathematics, Japanese and Chinese in Amsterdam. In 1950 he went to live in Paris, where he met his wife, the American writer Ethel Portnoy, whose work he translated into Dutch (see TLC 12). After a few years in The Hague in the seventies he moved back to Paris in 1978, and finally settled in the Netherlands in the mid-nineties. Today he lives and works in Leiden, the author of an oeuvre of mesmerising richness and diversity, ranging from poetry and language, photography, the archeology of motorcars, travel, literature, children, cats and other animals, through memory, emotions and the study of the human mind, to critical scrutiny of the Dutch colonial past and the modern history of Indonesia and Japan.

As a poet but also a translator and critic of poetry, Kousbroek's central preoccupation is with language. Very early on, with his friend the poet Remco Campert, he set up the poetry magazine *Braak* (1950-1951), which made a leading contribution to the experimentalist revolution in post-war Dutch literature. As recently as 2003 his *Animal Languages* (Dierentalen) brought together in a single volume the poems he had published over many years on the children's page of a leading Dutch newspaper. In between, in 1987 he published a study on the Greek poet Konstantinos Kafavis of Alexandria, and in 2001, with Hans Teeuw, a Dutch translation of the pre-war poetry of Indonesia's greatest poet, Amir Hanzah.

Beyond this there is his original study of the language of cats of 1983 and *The Logological Space* (De Logologische Ruimte, 1984), a collection of essays about language, which opens with a scintillating 'Hommage à Georges Perec'. One of my favourites in this volume is his 'Memorandum on Scientific Language Renovation' of 1977, a wildly successful April Fool's joke on Dutch spelling reform. The book is full of language games, puns, anagrams, palindromes, Tom Swifties and other jokes which mark him as an external Dutch member of the Oulipo Laboratory, the international writers' collective established in Paris in 1960 by Raymond Queneau, whose *Exercices de style* (1947) Kousbroek translated into Dutch in 1978. The same pleasure in shifts and transpositions shows itself in Kousbroek's fairytales for children, collected in *The Empire of Yes-Bear* (Het rijk van Jabeer, 1984), every one of them as cruel and irresistible as anything that Angela Carter ever wrote.

But Kousbroek is best known for his essays. In the sixties, writing under the pen name Leopold de Buch, he reported from Paris on the upheavals of 1968 in the leading progressive weekly *Vrij Nederland*. Under his own name he published many more essays, in journals and magazines such as *Hollands Maandblad*, *De Gids* and *NRC-Handelsblad*. From 1969 onwards, the most important of these have been collected in a long and often reprinted series of volumes, beginning with *Anathemas* and *The Strokeability Factor* (De aaibaarheidsfactor) and continuing to the present day. In 1978 he was awarded the highest honour in Dutch literature, the P.C. Hooft Prize, but in a sense this was only the beginning, since his most important works were yet to come.

Central to Kousbroek's writing is his running battle against superstition and the irrationalism of those who feel more attracted to incomprehensible 'deep' ideas than to disciplined abstract thought. As an antidote Kousbroek offers analysis and criticism – in his playful and taboo-breaking essays of the sixties, on the discovery of sexuality, on sexual freedom and toleration, and on the rhetoric of pornography, just as much as in his fiery polemics against the obscurantist tendencies of fellow Dutch writers such as Gerard Reve and Harry Mulisch. The former is taken to task for his bourgeois sentimentality and his bigotry, the latter for the scientific ignorance that underpins his philosophical system. Like a second Voltaire, Kousbroek is taking the moral temperature of the nation, and his essays – whether they attack the Dutch lack of a sense of their own history, the imbecility of children's TV, or the disappearance of a basic human emotion such as *misericordia* from the Netherlands – amount to a sustained critique of the cultural poverty of Dutch society today.

The same sharply critical approach also informs his many contributions on the history of Dutch colonialism. In 1992 the most important of these were collected in *The East Indies Camp Syndrome* (Het Oostindisch kampsyndroom). The centrepiece of this volume is a comparative study of Studs Terkel's *The Good War* (1986), the searching French war documentary *Le chagrin et la pitié* (1970) by Marcel Ophuls, and the silences and clichés surrounding the Dutch actions during the Indonesian war of independence (1945-1950). Other case histories expose the tissue of myths and fictions that holds sway in Dutch colonial historiography. Here again, we find many fiercely polemical exchanges with other writers such as Jeroen Brouwers, whose account of life in a Japanese internment camp, in his novel *Sunken Red* (Bezonken rood, 1981; tr. 1992), was comprehensively demolished by Kousbroek. Both because of its critical approach and its documentary value, *The East Indies Camp Syndrome* is required reading for anyone trying to understand the colonial culture and society of the former Dutch East Indies which came to an inglorious end under Japanese and Indonesian attack.

On a more personal note there is his *Return to the Lan of Ori Gin* (Terug naar Negri Pan Erkoms, 1995), an account of a journey back to the land of his early youth. Some of the most haunting memories in this book revolve around his time in boarding school in Sumatra before the war, compared to which, as he once remarked, the Japanese internment camp was almost a holiday. Ever since the war Japan has been one of Kousbroek's most central interests, and one can only hope that his essays on this subject will soon be collected into one volume too. What we do have, in his travelogue *In the Time Machine through Japan: the Court Journey of 2000* (In de tijdmachine door Japan: De Hofreis van

2000), is a fascinating reconstruction, in text and on film, of the lengthy official journey which Dutch colonial officials had to undertake almost every year between 1609 and 1858, from their trading post at Deshima near Nagasaki to the court of the shogun at Edo.

But ultimately, whatever the subject matter, Kousbroek's essays are dedicated to the art of memory. They are the work of a rationalist who explores this domain while in full possession of his intellectual powers, and who knows only too well that memory is deeply fraught with emotion, desire and imagination. This shows clearly in *The Lake of Remembrance* (Het meer der herinnering, 1984), where he describes his mother's curious menagerie of Indonesian pets – cats, dogs and rabbits, of course, but also squirrels, mouse-deer, badgers, pigs, snakes, chameleons, tropical birds and monkeys – on their plantation in Sumatra. At the same time, the volume contains an essay on Stendhal's analysis of emotion and make-belief in his autobiographical *Vie de Henri Brulard*, and an elegiac study of a ninth-century painted Chinese chronicle of the city of Kaifeng and the deep longing of its exiled citizens after it had been destroyed. In each case, what Kousbroek does is to describe as exactly as possible the details that matter, and then to explore with great lucidity the emotions they evoke. This technique was perfected in his writings about travel in the colonial era, such as *A Passage to East India* (Een passage naar Indië, 1978), and his essays about the lost harbours of Genoa and Alexandria. There is a pervasive sense that this era is now all but gone forever. As he put it himself, '*the saddest feeling I have ever had is to know your way around in a house that no longer exists*'.

Few authors can write as precisely as Kousbroek does about memory, emotion and longing. Very often his memories are triggered by seeing an image, a picture, a landscape, in a photograph or a dream. Images also play a central part in his novel *Vincent and the Secret of his Father's Body* (Vincent en het geheim van zijn vaders lichaam, 1981), a surreal love story written to accompany a series of 241 old engravings which he took at random from the nineteenth-century French illustrated periodicals he had bought in a Parisian flea market in the 1950s. The uncanny narrative in this novel reveals the internal logic that connects those engravings. It is a logic of irreality that is as strange and fantastic as that of the writer Raymond Roussel and his republic of dreams. The same goes for Kousbroek's recent *Recovered Miracles: Photosynthesis* (Opgespoorde wonderen: Fotosynthese, 2003), in which he presents a series of almost seventy extraordinary photographs, each accompanied by a single page of text in the most witty, dream-like and erudite prose, which elucidates not just the miracle we can see before our eyes on the facing page, but also its hidden meanings and the forgotten longing it evokes. ∎

'When will it be 1960 again? - Never'

The most beautiful part of *Bébert, le chat de Louis-Ferdinand Céline* by Frédéric Vitoux is the section with photographs in the front. Bébert, as you can see from these photos, was a cat the way Steinberg drew them: strict but fair, a patron of the birds, retriever of balls of paper, guardian of mice, Keeper of the Fridge – proud wearer of the striped uniform of field marshal in the cats' army, impressively bewhiskered but with the hint of an unmilitary readiness to lie on his back and have his stomach stroked.

Sighing with love I gaze at these photos. What is it about cats that calls up in people this curious mixture of enchantment and longing? Is it hereditary? How long has it existed? In my darkest moments I sometimes think about all that purring, millions of years of it, that cats did before there was anyone there to hear them. Nature is so very wasteful.

The same goes for that feeling of longing. Longing for what?

I think it is for the great, ultimate communication. When all the obstacles separating us – cats and people – finally fall away. It is a feeling that the time will come when we will be able to tell each other everything, without difficulties, without misunderstandings. Later, later.

When? I think this is a version of what Donald Schon once described as *the stable state*. 'For as long as I can remember,' wrote Schon, 'I have always believed in a hereafter *during* my life, a time of peaceful stability which would be reached after a period of care and turmoil. When I was a child the hereafter meant being adult. As I grew older its contents became vaguer but the idea behind it clung stubbornly on. This picture of a hereafter during life itself is a belief in what I would call *the stable state*, a state of stability.'

The belief in this stable state, Schon continues, is integral to our social institutions and the notion of social change itself: the striving for and anticipation of a stable final state. Which, as I hardly need add, does not exist. There is plenty to say about it though, and Schon does so, under the heading 'The Loss of the Stable State'; but what interests me about it is what exactly happens at the point at which one's idea of a hereafter-during-one's-lifetime starts to become 'vague', while the idea itself is still 'clinging stubbornly on'.

This is a phenomenon which is quite familiar to me, if I have understood Schon correctly: a feeling that 'everything is temporary', that everything that happens, literally everything I do and everything that happens to me 'does not count' because it will happen again later, or rather it will only happen for real later.

Denying this has a curious effect on remembering.

It resembles the process of scientific observation, but with the certainty of never being able to come back and repeat the observation. Like walking around in Atlantis, half an hour before it was engulfed by the waves. You hear rumbling, but nobody suspects a thing. You cannot warn anyone, you are an invisible observer. You make notes like mad – the language, the architecture, the flora, fauna, agriculture, animal husbandry – and in the frenzied rush to note down as much as possible you start using all kinds of abbreviations, more and more radical, relying on your memory. The half hour is over, the country begins to tilt like an enormous torpedoed ocean liner. Atlantis is sinking! It grows dark, rain is falling.

Back home to work out your notes, and what transpires? They are incomprehensible. On the pages there are only cryptic abbreviations; impossible to know what you meant by them. My memory let me down, I didn't look properly, paid too much attention to the notes themselves; them I know perfectly, but they are useless, clarifying nothing.

And this in turn is related to something else that I have tried to describe before: the feeling that my memories do not refer to events that I have myself experienced but to something that I only know from having been told, from a description or, even more precisely, from a deduction. Let us take as an example a good, clear memory – my daughter on the roundabout on the boulevard Brune, on her birthday. I remember it perfectly, I know what she was riding on: a wooden swan, slowly rising and falling, with a pole through its back. How she looked. The February sun. That I was present – it sounds like a foregone conclusion. I must have been, how else could I know these things? The thought: later, when she goes on that roundabout again, *then* I must look, look as I have never looked before, devouring, so that only darkness remains.

But that is just it, she won't ever sit there again. I know perfectly well that it won't happen. It is another way of saying that there is no going back. When will it be 1960 again? – Never – QED.

The hereafter doesn't exist, the 'stable state' is an illusion and that so impatiently awaited moment when we will finally be able to tell each other what it was like, the time when you were dressed as a cat and I as a person, that moment will never come.

The question of what happens to animals after death troubled me already when I was a child; it was one of the main reasons why I decided that religion could only be a kind of fairy tale. I believe the church seriously underestimates the effect on children of animals being excluded from the proceedings. After persistently asking about it and getting the unqualified final answer that animals had no 'soul', that we would never see them again in the hereafter and that there was nothing left of them after death, I was filled with the overwhelming certainty that it must be the same for people.

The only thing you can do, with animals as well as people, as I was already aware, is to look at them while they are still alive, look at them and hold them tight; not later, but now, now.

Preface to *The Strokeability Factor* (De Aaibaarheidsfactor).
Amsterdam: Uitgeverij De Harmonie, revised edition 1978.

The Oldest Face in the World

This is the oldest human face that I know. It dates from before our era, it is more than 22 centuries old. Some human heads even older than this have been preserved but they look more like crumpled balls of paper, dessicated birds' heads or mythical sculptures from a fantasy world called 'the past'.

This, on the other hand, is the face of an ordinary real person, so real that you can almost predict how he would move and what his voice would sound like. It is strange that one can hardly say that about any historical figure. Christ, for example, with whom many people have a personal relationship, even that of bride – nobody would recognise him on the street.

The face on this photo belongs to a man of about thirty-five, found in a peat-bog in Denmark in 1950 and known since then as the 'Tollund Man'. Twelve years earlier, in 1938, and not far from there, also in peat, the body of a woman aged about thirty was found. She is known as the 'Elling woman'. They both died by strangulation, perhaps even together, some time in the third century B.C. Both bodies are now in the Silkeborg Museum. The Elling head was originally in the same perfect state of preservation, there are photos to prove it, but through lack of expertise it dried out and became mummified.

Why were Tollund and Elling executed? The traditional explanation is that they were guilty of adultery. Reference is made to Tacitus who, in *De situ, moribus et populis Germaniae*, describes how in the frozen North those found guilty of adultery were strangled and their bodies thrown into the bog.

I hope this is the correct explanation; it is highly significant that the oldest face in the world should be that of an adulterer. Unfortunately the museum's most recent publications say that this was not a case of punishment but a ritual sacrifice to the god or gods of peat. The fact that some 600 peat bodies have been found in Denmark alone, and more than 1500 in the whole of North-West Europe, would seem to confirm this.

But it was the original explanation that I found so stirring: it suggested that adultery was a favourite pastime in our Nordic regions. Of course the punishment was cruel and inhuman, but the mere fact that people knowingly took that risk, that they were ready to die for love, is something that gives a divine dimension to the human heart. It restores faith in the authenticity of our natures, which is in my opinion denied by references to some kind of religious ritual.

'Sacrifices to the peat gods' – great despondency overcomes me on reading this. Whenever the past sets us some riddle there is always that talk of religion, which can explain everything from prehistoric cave-drawings to Bach fugues.

What a pity they let Mademoiselle Elling's body dry out. I would have liked to see them in each other's arms, intact. Reunited at last, after 2250 years. My treasure, my angel, my darling, where have you been all this time? I have been waiting for you.

I imagine them during their lives, madly in love and terrified. Shall we? What if we're caught?

All extracts translated by Sarah Hart

Yes, I call out to them, do it! It will make you immortal and give hope to people living twenty-two and a half centuries later. But it is easy for me to talk, I'm not going to end up in the peat with a plaited leather rope round my neck. Mademoiselle, no, not Mademoiselle: Madame Elling, I was pleased to discover, also appealed to the imagination of the Irish poet Seamus Heaney, who saw the peat-bodies in Silkeborg in about 1970:

Little adulteress,
Before they punished you
you were flaxen-haired,
undernourished, and your
tar-black face was beautiful.
(Seamus Heaney, *North*, Faber & Faber, 1975)

From *Recovered Miracles: Photosynthesis* (Opgespoorde wonderen: Fotosynthese).
Amsterdam/Antwerp: Uitgeverij Augustus, 2003, pp. 40-41.

The Artist as Sharpshooter

The Visual Precision of Liza May Post

The oeuvre of Liza May Post consists of images that you can never forget, but which are difficult to describe. They are vivid and concise, but they operate on ambiguous levels of reality. Photographed or filmed with great visual precision, the scenes engender confusion and emotional agitation. In a bit over ten years, Post has created a compact series of works. They all bear her unique artistic signature, yet there's no question of thematic repetition. Every piece encompasses a stand-alone world. The oeuvre speaks the language of a young woman and although it's not explicitly autobiographical, the feminine condition is a determining factor.

The lightness of an elephant

One of her most light-footed works is *Trying* (1998), a short 16-mm film, 2.16 minutes in length.

We see an elephant filling the whole screen, filmed from the side from a fixed camera position. The animal is standing still; the one visible eye is the only evidence that something's happening to it. A simple leather strap over its back ends in a stirrup, about a metre above the ground. A woman is trying to get her foot into it. She's put down her handbag for a moment, close to those broad feet, with complete confidence that the elephant will stand still, and is completely absorbed in her attempts to climb onto its back, just as she is absorbed into the animal, becoming one with it, with her grey dress and her grey wig made from a horse blanket. Her light shoes match the bag.

Most people know elephants from children's books, zoos or the circus. So it's not difficult to return to that childish desire to touch the animal, to achieve some kind of understanding with it. Or even to balance on top of it wearing an elegant suit. So it's very easy to identify with *Trying*. But it's also a little odd. It is clear at a glance that the attempt to climb up will always be a futile one. On her own, it's an impossible task. The woman stands with her back to the viewer, assesses her chances, but doesn't go for help. Calmly, she explores how it might be possible. She touches her hand to the animal's hide and tries once more to get her foot into the stirrup. The attempt doesn't end in triumph, but remains

only an attempt. The film shows moving images, but, uncinematically, there is very little dynamic and no plot. It is a film by a visual artist, which uses visual methods to sketch a meaningful staged reality.

Liza May Post, *Trying*. 1998. 16-mm film transferred to dvd, 2.16 min. Photo courtesy of Annet Gelink Gallery, Amsterdam.

The out-of-place fire

Post's other films are also based on concise and rather static scenes. In *Sigh*, a 16-mm film just over a minute long, which she made in 1994, we see a dark room. The only light comes from a log fire. The room is bare, with only the bed revealing anything about the nature of the room. On the bed there's a satin bed-spread, with a hanging flounce. The young woman sitting on the ground with her back leaning against the bed is watching the fire. She is immaculately dressed. She's wearing high-heeled shoes and on her head she's wearing something that represents a tonsure, as a metaphor for stress-related premature hair loss. The white blouse lights up in the flickering light, as does her face, upon which it is difficult to make out any emotion. For a moment you think that this upper-crust girl has left the party downstairs to come and sulk for a while in her own room in front of her own fire. Until you notice the absurd position of the fire: it's not burning in the open hearth, but right there on the floor of the room, on the carpet of all places. It immediately becomes clear that this is not a normal situation, but one that is removed from reality. Something's not right, there's something else hidden beneath the calm and neatness of the protagonist – loneliness, contrariness, mental desperation? *Sigh* is one of the works in which the scenario is so self-evident and understated that no meaning imposes itself. Viewers feel completely free of the content and gradually develop their own interpretation.

Fire, says a Gothic specialist, plays a role in the Gothic's function of breaking open social patterns, rational decisions and accepted emotions in order to create new perspectives. Houses are consumed by fire, or even more strangely, furniture is burnt as a charming domestic fire, awkwardly placed in the centre of the room, as we read in Eve Kosotsky Sedgwick's *The Coherence of Gothic Conventions* (1980).

The idea of merging with the ground, said the well-known psychoanalyst

Liza May Post, *Sigh*. 1994. 16-mm film transferred to dvd, 1.04 min. Photo courtesy of Annet Gelink Gallery, Amsterdam.

D.H.Winnicott when discussing the difference between 'a figure-ground relationship and an ego-world relationship, expresses *'the ego's desire to dissolve itself into a more generalised type of being, on the remembered model of the infant's sleep on its mother's breast'*. But simple visual associations also present themselves. Fire is one of the 'artist's materials' that were often used in artists' initiatives, in spaces that artists appropriated in the 1980s, where they carried out daring performances. Seen in that light, the out-of-place fire is not weird, but amusing, a comment on the work produced by the extravagant young artists of that time. At the same time it's also a fascinating source of moving, indoor light, reminiscent of the mystical atmosphere of the paintings of Georges de la Tour. But where Mary plays a significant role, the girl in *Sigh* is a spectator, just like us.

The short film *Place* (1996) evokes similar feelings of loneliness. This time the action takes place outside in the street, on the earth around a tree, where a young woman has laid out a tea set. She's kneeling and leaning slightly against the tree, which gives structure to the image as a central, vertical element. She's

wearing her light-blue towelling suit in a very precise way: the zip of the top lines up exactly with the skirt. Only the most observant viewer will notice that the tea set is also covered with the same towelling material. Who's she waiting for, this young woman? The cups must be there for a reason. She goes and sits down, pours the tea, we hear a blackbird singing, it's spring, but apart from that nothing actually happens. It seems that our expectations will be nipped in the bud, evoking feelings of naivety and failure in the viewer.

Here, Winnicott's '*ground*' is literally earth. He would undoubtedly refer to the earliest days of childhood, perhaps to the habit that toddlers have of sucking water out of the wet flannel. Is this scene a flashback? A dream, an image from the subconscious?

Liza May Post, *Place*. 1996. Video transferred to dvd, 1.04 min. Photo courtesy of Annet Gelink Gallery, Amsterdam.

It's the artist herself who acts in this piece, just as in *Sigh*, but in *Place* she shows only her back and the back of her head. The face that is turned aside, hidden or eclipsed appears quite often, particularly in her early works, which seem to coincide seamlessly with the private life of a young woman who is exploring her existential space. It began in 1992 with her participation in a group exhibition at an artists' initiative. Liza's class exhibited at W139 in Amsterdam and she took

Liza May Post, *Table*.
1992.
Photo courtesy of
Annet Gelink Gallery,
Amsterdam.

part in the opening with a performance: sitting at a school desk, she kept her head hidden under the desktop, in the 'cupboard' part, which had been made a fraction larger for the purpose. The act of hiding made her presentation into a non-presentation; she was there, but didn't show herself. Her clothing, a classic flowered dress and boarding-school-style knee socks and shoes, revealed the careful attempt to create a well-considered image. She didn't isolate herself from the group in a disloyal or a physical sense, but she certainly did in a psychological sense. She wrapped herself up in an immaterial cocoon, as though she wanted, once and for all, to denounce the whole business of exhibiting, of revealing, of opening up to the public, actions that are intrinsically linked to the visual arts. As though she were entering upon a rite of passage with the aim of reconciling the conflict between the desire to protect your intimate identity and the necessity of placing your creative identity in the spotlight.

After the opening, the photo of the performance, which had lasted two-and-a-half hours, took the place of the actual performance. It is a powerful image and certainly appears to have gained quite a following. Other female artists of the 1990s, such as Marlene Dumas and Rineke Dijkstra, achieved prominence with a strong form of ambiguous vulnerability.

Liza May Post,
Z/T Untitled. 1994.
Photo courtesy of
Annet Gelink Gallery,
Amsterdam.

An outfit for every role

The performance that Liza May Post contributed a few years later at the opening of *Exchange/Dacha*, an exchange with Russian artists the second part of which took place on the new polder near Almere, was different in character, though there were parallels. The photo *Z.T./Untitled* again has an iconic power: Liza May Post stands at the window of the dacha building, as still as a wax dummy. There are white curtains hanging at the window, which only turn out not to be transparent when you take a closer look at them. Instead of outwards, the gaze is directed inwards. The introspective statement this time is undoubtedly also a reaction to her working visit to Moscow. She had wanted to do a project with curtains there and involve the mothers of the Russian project assistants. But in the local context she realised that her intention was inappropriate, so she changed her plan. At the same time the curtains form a barrier, in the same way as she had earlier talked about her body as a barrier in connection with the photo *The Perfume Department* (1992). In that work the artist lies stretched out on the ground, in the middle of the luxury realm of make-up and nail polish, without the other people present taking any notice of her. In *Z.T./Untitled* the face is partially hidden by a long blonde wig, whilst her girlish clothing (which is midway between something innocent and the outfit of a junkie hooker) radiates

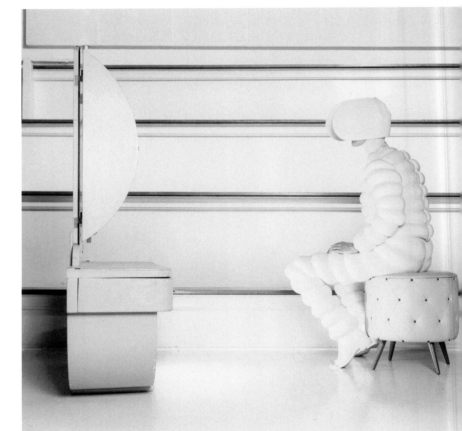

Liza May Post, *Bound*.
1996.
Photo courtesy of
Annet Gelink Gallery,
Amsterdam.

an atmosphere of '*noli me tangere*'.

Liza says that her father's family would sometimes put on performances, complete with costumes, and that some 8 mm films of these have been kept. This is reminiscent of the pioneering photographer Julia Margaret Cameron, who used to devise tableaux in which her family and friends (who included Charles Darwin) were allocated a role. She produced her art in the England of the Pre-Raphaelites and has only recently been rediscovered. In the first instance, the enigmatic *Bound* (1996) evokes associations with a fancy-dress party, albeit a quiet and private one. The photo is on the cover of the catalogue *Jan Nelson & Liza May Post*, which accompanied the 2004 exhibition of the same name at the Museum of Contemporary Art in Sydney. The work is virtually monochrome white, bright white, with a few accents of wood and skin – a line of toes, a hand, the chin, are exposed. There is little depth to the setting, which has a back wall with conspicuous horizontal sections. In the foreground there are two vertical elements to the image: to the left is a sixties dressing table with its side mirrors parallel to the back wall, in such a way that no reflection is visible. To the right, almost completely camouflaged in the white, sits a girl in an immaculate futuristic suit made of puffed-up strips off padded material. She's wearing headgear that's somewhere between a space-helmet and a wimple. The semicircular sides end in blinkers that visually echo the side panels of the mirror. Her gaze is fixed on the mirror. But the viewer cannot see anything of what she sees; there is no trace of a reflection and just as little sign of a face or eyes. So they remain private, the mirror image and the facial features, withdrawing from the public eye and pulling together in a silent denial of the impression that the image makes as a whole: the painstaking early stages of a lively, showy spectacle.

However, Liza May Post wasn't attempting to make a theatrical statement. She wanted to create a photo that was reminiscent of an engraving, taking her inspiration from Dürer's famous copperplate *Die Melancholie*. Her personification of melancholy, though, is situated in a more futuristic environment, but the direction of the gaze is the same, combining with the gaze of the viewer to form a triangle.

What is striking about these sets is not only the terrifying precision (she selects the one and only correct camera position, piece of furniture, the right wall, floor, clothing, pose, colour, lighting), but also the very feminine line of approach. Of course there are references to identifiable images from film or fashion magazines, but each piece of clothing is packed with her own inventions and all the accessories appear to be selected or designed with passion. This shows her personal fascination both with the feminine and with clothes.

The incomplete, uninjured body

Prompted by the film *Trying*, Liza May Post says that she used to want to be a dancer on an elephant. She's got a childhood drawing of that scene. Dancing in a spangled costume on the back of an elephant! You have to be tough to do that and she really wanted to be tough. But she wouldn't want to give up her feminine side to do it. So she wants to be tough in a feminine way.

Liza later explained that, as an up-and-coming artist, using *Table* to draw a line between herself and her classmates was about the fact that she had a different experience of life than they did, which made it difficult for her to conform to the group expression. She comes from an artistic family. Her father, Waldemar Post, is a gifted portrait artist; his drawings are prominently placed in daily and weekly publications. For a time, her mother made installations that filled whole walls, based on repeating elements from fabric and other materials. This was after her successful career as a leading Dutch model. The early death of her mother when Liza was nine years old has greatly influenced her life. A number of her artistic decisions have undoubtedly been a result of this. The importance of photos of someone after their death. The significance of clothing and hairstyle in different identities. Or the emphasis on girlishness, in an evident attempt to delay or deny adulthood. The fact alone that at a certain point her father became both father and mother to her changed her vision of such things as role-division and gender issues. The absence of her mother, as Liza explained to Camiel van Winkel (the interview is included in the Sydney catalogue) 'has become second nature, ingrained in who I am. (...) Still, for a long time I have believed in the adaptability of the mind – as if one could neutralise the sense of loss just by trying hard. I have looked for ways to reduce the symptoms as much as possible.'

This was the first time she spoke candidly in public about the effect of her mother's death. But the suppressed state of desperation and alarm is also apparent without any concrete biographical knowledge. 'The impaired body is the site and symbol of all alienation' said David Cronenberg, talking about his film *Crash* (1996). 'It is psychic alienation made physical. The contorted body is the final progress and statement of a painful mind'. It's the other way round here: the body is intact, there's no external sign of pain, but that 'painful mind' is heading straight for the body. So it's far from being intact. It is wilfully held together in immaculate clothes and secured within bourgeois parameters of neatness and order. So that everything will be normal.

Psychological inversion

Liza May Post, *Under*.
2000.
35-mm film transferred
to dvd, 4 min.
Photo courtesy of
Annet Gelink Gallery,
Amsterdam.

In the short film *Under* (2000), that control disintegrates. In a cramped basement there are some figures, one of which is a girl sitting immobile on a stretcher, whilst another is acting the freak. He's a tall man – he can't stand up properly because of the low ceiling. But still he walks around, sluggishly, standing still, stereotypically, in a robe that's too long so that the hem is becoming more and more stained. He seems like a toothless giant from the old legends, who has degenerated in a forgotten niche. (Giants are always on the move, I read somewhere, unlike the minipeople that folk mostly like to keep in cages). Although a second man looks much better adjusted and more civilised, he's not able to neutralise the oppressive feeling. Incidentally, there's absolutely no mutual contact. When the young woman, who is wearing a flowered coat and sitting in the foreground so that we see the scene mainly from her perspective, stands up at the end of the film, this movement hardly demonstrates that she is free to act. The spell of unpredictable and uncontrollable relationships remains unbroken.

At first sight *While*, the film that Post made for her solo at the 2001 Venice Biennale, is much less grotesque. There's nothing strange about the four protagonists, who all have their place in a waiting-room-like setting, on chairs which are connected to each other, yet still separated from each other. No-one here is moving and rendering the room unsafe. This time it's a spacious, neutral public space of some (dated) grandeur. Here too, though, the reference to the carnivalesque, to a theatrical archetype based on the exorcism of fear, is unmistakable. Although it's done in a subtle way, like an imploded exaggeration. With absolute regularity, confetti falls through the air, dropping onto the people, the empty chairs, the floor. The confetti is black. And this spells out the people's breathing space, the space between them, the atmosphere surrounding them, permeating it with doom. The emotionally charged shadow is brought about simply by inverting the connotation of celebration that is attached to coloured confetti, and turning it into its black counterpart.

Liza May Post,
Lifting up. 1994.
Photo courtesy of
Annet Gelink Gallery,
Amsterdam.

This predilection for psychological inversion also crops up in other works, primarily in the interaction between physical attraction and the desire to keep one's distance. The idea of lifting up a lover, for example, occurs in the photo *Lifting up* with such grating exaggeration that it results in a confusing and ambiguous image. Velcro, a textile that was designed to fasten things by sticking them together, rather than buttoning them up, is used to stick two people together in *Bros.* (6 min., 1999). This gives their battle something of a courtship display, whilst at the same time the striped material of the suits plays an independent pictorial role. During the same period, Liza May Post shocked theatregoers in Amsterdam by basing her contribution to the stage piece *Post coitum omne animal triste est* exclusively on the act of sticking. Her acting was extremely passive: she was literally stuck to a wall and could only move if someone pulled her off the wall, carried her to a new place and stuck her on again. The noise was horrifying and the display of passivity was disconcerting. Was it an expression of reluctance to go along with the theatrical friends who also feature in her work? She's too loyal for that. Her role was reminiscent of her

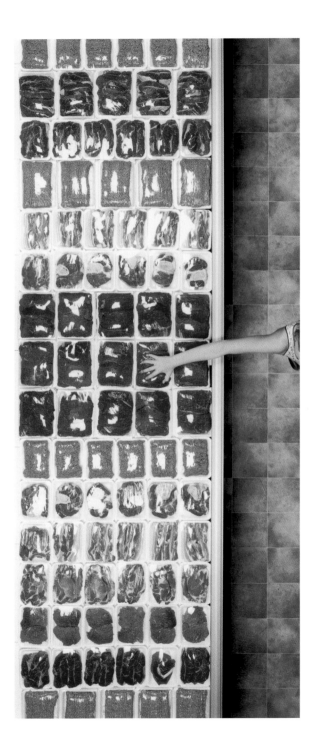

Liza May Post, *Push*.
1994. Colour photograph
mounted on aluminium,
139 x 196 cm.
Photo courtesy of
Annet Gelink Gallery,
Amsterdam.

camouflaging performances: now, in the real theatre, amongst real actors, it was possible to take to the extreme the idea of merging with the surroundings, of making oneself disappear.

The tenderness of dead meat

Liza May Post chose the adhesive material as a metaphor for the Other. She lived for some time in New York and was sensitive to the masses of people moving over the broad pavements there. It was, she said then, as though you picked up something from those people who passed, as though something about them stuck to you.

On the other hand, she made costumes like armour, like the Freud carpets which were made into clothes in the film *Visitors* (4.14 min., 1997). Even the flowery coat of the girl in *Under* is made from a stiff, plasticised material. But whilst the carpets are furry and have associations of receptivity, the plastic repels even water. The material reinforces the idea that a vulnerable girl can remain psychologically strong by making herself an 'iceberg' in a threatening environment. In all these works, touch (or the avoidance of touch) is expressed and supported by the texture of the material, which usually has a protective power.

There is one work that breaks through the intrinsically defensive atmosphere: the photo *Push* (1994). This shows an outspread hand actively and wilfully pushing into flesh – admittedly flesh that is dead and sealed in plastic. It's about one single touch in the midst of an exaggerated quantity of prepared cuts of meat. This makes the work humorous and also surprising. The usual labels are missing, so thoughts of consumption and supermarkets just don't occur. The image is raw and red, starkly realistic and, at the same time, full of poetry and painterly qualities. The geometric rhythmicality of the tiled floor and the packs of meat is reminiscent of works of art from the Zero movement. In this visually rather accessible work, something that applies to all of Post's work comes explicitly to the fore: her flawless sense of composition and colour. It is natural to speak of this oeuvre in psychological terms, something which Kate Bush did excellently in Liza May Post's Venice Biennale 2001 catalogue. However, the ability of the works to remain fascinating in all their details is to a great extent down to the felicitous hand of this visual artist. Not only does she know how to structure the light, outside as well as indoors, in such a way as to create an intimate focus of attention, but her palette is often largely restricted to the monochrome, the individual elements being placed within the image plainly and with no incidental intrusions. Small details can be important for the right balance or for a contrast in composition. For example, the tea-pouring scene in *Place*, which is filmed from above (from the window of Liza's studio, in fact) called for a dark accent next to the central tree. To achieve that, the hair of the character was accentuated a little and a dark, stringy wig was selected.

Her extreme visual precision and effectiveness in terms of content mean that there is not one mediocre link in this oeuvre. Liza has taken a break because of the birth of her daughter. It remains to be seen whether this will have an effect on her new work. What is certain, however, is that it will be pictorial, painstaking and unsettling. ∎

Translated by Laura Watkinson

Unmodern Architecture
in the Netherlands

[HANS IBELINGS]

Almost unnoticed among the controversial projects and ideas from firms such as Rem Koolhaas's Office for Metropolitan Architecture, MVRDV and UN Studio, a completely new style of architecture has evolved in the Netherlands in recent years: a contemporary traditionalism that can best be described as 'unmodern'.

Unmodern architecture in the Netherlands has been shaped by the work of a relatively small group of architects who work together in ever-changing partnerships: Soeters Van Eldonk Ponec, Gunnar Daan/Doeke van Wieren, Molenaar & Van Winden, Scala, Mulleners & Mulleners, Rapp+Rapp and foreign architects such as Charles Vandenhove, Krier & Kohl, Kollhoff und Timmermann and Adolfo Natalini.

Characteristic of most of the Dutch architects in this group is that they regard adherence to a particular style as a constraint rather than a positive quality. Almost every contemporary traditionalist draws on a wide range of styles, ranging in time and appearance from Neoclassicism to the Amsterdam School, from traditional to entirely contemporary. This eclecticism is the outcome of what Sjoerd Soeters refers to, by analogy with NATO's Cold War strategy, as a *'flexible response'*. By comparison, the work of exponents of unmodern architecture from outside the Netherlands has a stronger personal signature. It is these foreign architects who, through working on commissions in the Netherlands from the beginning of the 1990s, have paved the way for contemporary traditionalism in this country. Moreover, they have convinced several of their Dutch contemporaries that there is an alternative to the modernism that is and has been so prominent in all its forms in Dutch architecture, even when postmodernism was causing a stir elsewhere in the world.

Contemporary traditionalism has its roots in that postmodernism or, to be more precise, in the European postmodernism that evolved from the end of the 1960s, notably in Italy, France, Germany, Luxemburg and Belgium. In the 1970s and 80s, Brussels was a focal point for the renewed appreciation of the traditional city, one of the central themes of European postmodernism. This manifested itself in the drive to reconstruct the (European) city and in a desire to return to the coherence and order of the traditional city.

In 1980 this was the subject of the Brussels Declaration published by the AAM (Archives d'Architecture Moderne), one of the two organisations in Brussels in

which Maurice Culot was a key figure. In 1968 he had been one of the founders of the AAM, the aim of which was to collect architectural archives, organise exhibitions and produce publications. This resulted in increased historical awareness and attempts to revise modernist historiography by focusing on many lesser-known and neglected movements and designers. In that same year, 1968, Culot was involved in founding the ARAU (Atelier de Recherche et d'Action Urbaine), an organisation which, through its research and designs, took a stand against massive modernisation resulting from demolition to make way for major traffic routes, redevelopment and city formation in the Belgian capital. From the end of the 1960s, the ARAU produced sixty counterproposals, which demonstrated that there were alternatives to ever-encroaching modernism. The ARAU's activities in this field can be compared to the way in which, in the Netherlands for example, architects supported residents' organisations that were protesting against demolition and redevelopment plans in their neighbourhoods. Here too alternatives were sought for modernist 'clearances', although the outcomes showed less architectonic imagination and a more pronounced orientation towards history.

The preference which the ARAU revealed for the restoration and, where relevant, the reconstruction of the pre-modern, pre-industrial city undoubtedly contains an element of nostalgia, but also of the revolutionary spirit of 1968: the advance of modernisation was no longer blindly accepted, but subjected to critical assessment. This critical approach sprang not so much from conservatism, but rather from a resistance to the degeneration of high-tech society. In that sense, the traditionalist basis of European postmodernism is indisputably a product of the revolutionary year of 1968.

Helmond has become the centre of unmodern architecture in the Netherlands. The Brandevoort district plan was drawn by Krier & Kohl in 1996, together with landscape architect Paul van Beek. Brandevoort has been designed as a contemporary interpretation of a traditional small town. The cast-iron market hall is a Krier & Kohl creation.
Photo by Hans Ibelings.

Architecture and ethics

Early postmodernism bypassed the Netherlands, but took hold the second time around when it was experiencing a revival everywhere else. It is not only traditionalist architecture in the Netherlands (and elsewhere in Europe) that is rooted in European postmodernism, but also the architecture that is evolving in the United States under the banner of New Urbanism and is currently being exported to Europe (where New Urbanism is following the same path as Starbucks, which has been trying for several years to find a niche in the European market for its American interpretation of the European coffee house).

Traditionalist architecture is like organic food. In the past all food was organic, so we didn't need the adjective. But not any longer. It is no longer safe to assume that something is continuing a tradition or has been produced in an eco-friendly way. In today's world, creating something traditional – or something organic – means shunning all the modern resources and technology that are now available, in other words: adopting a deliberately unmodern approach.

Traditionalism in contemporary architecture is not a style that can be precisely defined, but a broad classification for the work and philosophy of designers for whom conventions, customs and traditions are the basis for architectonic development. Their aim is neither to innovate nor to break with the past, but to establish an organic continuity with what exists and has existed.

Lovers of traditionalist architecture are like lovers of organic products, in that there is no one reason for their preference. At one end of the spectrum we have an ethical rationale: producers and consumers of organic food object to the inhumane methods of intensive farming and to agricultural practices that damage the environment. Similarly, those who commission and design traditionalist architecture sometimes have moral objections to the destruction of town and country and the (real or imagined) short lifespan of non-traditionalist products.

At the other end of the spectrum we have the lifestyle variant. Organic vegetables might appeal to us mainly because they taste better than non-organic alternatives, or perhaps because we like the idea that they were grown without using chemicals. In the same way, traditionalism can be preferred for aesthetic reasons, either for its appearance or because we like to think that this type of building could have existed centuries ago, or will still exist for centuries to come.

How should we categorise the devotees of organic products and traditionalist architecture? Does a preference for 'slow food' (as the traditional, natural alternative to 'fast food') reflect conservatism or progressiveness? Do the champions of organic food yearn to return to a time before food became a processed industrial product? Are they the precursors of a new age in which man will take better care of his world? Or are organic products simply meeting a growing demand for gourmet foods?

The same questions can be asked of contemporary traditionalist architecture. Is it fulfilling a need to return to a past in which the streets were not choked with cars and not every square metre was built on? Is it the beginning of a re-evaluation following a century of architectonic innovation? Or is contemporary traditionalism simply serving a niche market, in the same way as 'slow food'?

The radicalism of the traditionalist

In a broader context, traditionalist architecture and organic products can be regarded as a response to what the American sociologist George Ritzer calls 'the globalization of nothing'. In the book of the same name (London/New Delhi: Thousand Oaks, 2004) Ritzer describes the massive spread of various forms of nothing. Fast-food restaurants, self-service, branded clothing and call centres. In his view these are all examples of the 'globalization of nothing', and are the opposite of *real* places, *real* service, unique objects, and personal attention. Ritzer's underlying argument is that, under the influence of globalisation and market liberalism, more and more is leading to less and less. The overwhelming spread of all this nothingness has provoked a reaction: a new appreciation of the unique, the specific and the authentic. The furore caused by traditionalism in architecture in today's world is one expression of this.

But traditionalism in architecture is more than a by-product of globalisation. Its popularity is also related to our current pluriform and in many respects fragmented culture. Within that culture tradition and innovation, new trends and retrotrends can easily co-exist; they are not mutually exclusive and sometimes even coincide (e.g. cars that are designed to resemble a model from decades ago, but are based on the latest technology). In today's world, it is often difficult to distinguish between modern and old-fashioned, progressive and conservative – and even between old and new.

Contemporary traditionalism in the Netherlands cannot be considered in isolation from changes in the Dutch housebuilding sector. For many decades, housebuilding was synonymous with public housing, and the decision-makers tended towards modern architecture for economic, technocratic and/or ideological reasons. This situation changed when the free market – which, inciden-

Soeters Van Eldonk Ponec, De Parade shopping mall, Nootdorp 1997-2003. A mall with a parking garage at its core, ingeniously subdivided housing on top and a village atmosphere. Photo by Hans Ibelings.

Scala, housing project, Amsterdam 1998-2001. This project in the city centre has been designed so as to make it fade discreetly into the urban tissue. Photo by Hans Ibelings.

Molenaar & Van Winden,
housing project,
Lelystad 2000-2003.
These detached houses are
a contemporary interpretation of the comfortable
typical houses of the
1920s and 1930s.
Photo by Hans Ibelings.

Translated by Yvette Mead

tally, is not as free as its protagonists claim – took over from the public housing officials. The housebuilding industry has become increasingly oriented towards the demands of the market, personified by the housing consumer. One of those demands was for architecture that looked like what was, or could have been, there already.

While traditionalism undeniably answers the wishes of a mass market, its practitioners are regarded by their peers as rather non-conformist. In the past it was considered radical to break with tradition. In the course of the twentieth century, however, innovation became the norm to such an extent that it became a new tradition. Today, it takes more determination to be a traditionalist than to ride the successive waves of what remains of avant-gardism. Contemporary traditionalists are therefore considerably more radical than their familiar – and sometimes frankly dated – architecture would suggest, precisely because they are resisting the tradition of innovation. This tradition of innovation is so power-ful that almost all the contemporary traditionalists were trained, and in many cases started out, as innovators, only to become traditionalists later in their careers. ∎

FURTHER READING

Hans Ibelings, *Unmodern Architecture. Contemporary Traditionalism in the Netherlands* (Fascina-tions, 15). Rotterdam: Nai Publishers, 2004 (www.naipublishers.nl)

Felix Bonfils, pillars of the Baalbek sun temple, c.1865.
Albumin print. Collection FotoMuseum, Antwerp.

Tales of the Invisible City

As the capital of the then Belgian Congo, Kinshasa occupies an important place in the history of Belgian architecture and urban planning. The development of the capital was an outstanding project of Belgian Modernity; but nowadays that modernist quality is only one of the many realities of Kinshasa. *Kinshasa. Tales of the Invisible City* deals with the complex reality of Kinshasa as a post-colonial Central African city.

The motivation behind the book's publication is

KINSHASA
TALES OF THE INVISIBLE CITY

BY FILIP DE BOECK & MARIE-FRANÇOISE PLISSART

LUDION

worth exploring. Anthropologist Filip de Boeck and photographer Marie-Françoise Plissart, together with architect/curator Koen van Synghel, put together an exhibition on this theme for the Belgian pavilion at the International Architecture Biennale in Venice (2004). Held in the beautiful surroundings of the Giardini, the Biennale sometimes resembles an interesting, but rather respectable world exhibition, where countries can display the best of their archi-

tectural ability. Contributions such as the one about Kinshasa, on the other hand, call the nationalistic understanding of architecture into question. With its examination of the unique urban nature of the modern-day Central African metropolis, it even calls into question the organisational capacity of architecture and urban planning. For those reasons the exhibition attracted a considerable amount of criticism. There was also the fact that Flanders alternates with the French-speaking Community of Belgium and only gets a chance in Venice every four years, so an important opportunity for the international promotion of Flemish architecture was lost. However, the whole controversy suddenly died down when it was announced that the Golden Lion, the first prize in the Biennale competition, had been awarded to the Belgian pavilion. A stroke of luck for the Flemish Architecture Institute, which had organised the exhibition, but on the other hand this success meant that the debate over the statements made by the exhibition was nipped in the bud.

'It is not, or not primarily, the material infrastructure or the built form that makes the city a city,' argues Filip de Boeck, 'The city, in a way, exists beyond its architecture.' According to the traditional western philosophy of town planning, it is possible to use physical additions to the environment, such as buildings or public infrastructure, not only to give shape to a city, but also to determine its identity. In large Central African cities like Kinshasa, however, that no longer holds true. In order to describe the real identity of Kinshasa, De Boeck begins with three mirrors that reflect the city. First there's the mirror of the colonial origins. Whilst colonisation has been over and done with since 1960, the foundation and development of the modern Kinshasa naturally still has an impact on urban life. The integration of this inheritance is a laborious process, as can be seen from the new names that are given to the city, the streets and the neighbourhoods with each new regime. A second mirror is that of the village, the hinterland, the bush. Kinshasa defines itself on the basis of contrast with the village, which is depicted as primitive. However, the urban identity of Kinshasa is in fact continually infiltrated by the traditions, the customs and the heritage of village life. Gangs of youths mark out their territory in the streets in the same way as the hunter does in the bush. The diaspora of Kinois throughout Western Europe and the United States forms the third mirror. Myths about the lively lifestyle in the Brussels area of Matonge, where Congolese immigrants have concentrated, were cultivated for a long time, but are increasingly being dispelled. The diaspora has turned out to be not some heavenly existence, but a tough and difficult one.

Kinshasa is *'a city in which the spoken form regularly seems to dominate the built form'*. In the city there is a constant and ubiquitous flow of rumours, accusations, fabrications and stories that hold the town spellbound. If we really want to understand the urban nature of Kinshasa, this invisible city is at least as important as the tangible city of built architecture, says De Boeck, restating his basic assumption. For example, there's the dramatic phenomenon of the occult stories about bewitched children. A link may perhaps be demonstrated between the increase in accusations of witchcraft in the Congo over the past decade and the rising numbers of street children in Kinshasa. Children who are seen as bewitched are usually turned out of the house and end up on the streets. The occult stories claim that the bewitched children – sometimes scarcely four years old – lead a second life. At night they're supposed to have a secret, hedonistic existence in which cannibalism, flying, and adult romantic relationships are the rule. Death, sickness or other misfortunes in the immediate surroundings of the families of these children are associated with them and for that reason they're turned out or given refuge in churches. De Boeck has brought together actual stories and testimonies that are extremely moving. The understated portrait photography of Marie-Françoise Plissart makes the effect all the stronger. The phenomenon of the bewitched children dominates the whole book not only on an emotional level, but also in terms of content. This phenomenon corresponds to De Boeck's assertion that different realities co-exist in Kinshasa and reflect each other. The first world of the children dur-ing the daytime and the second world at night represent such a pair. They seem to correspond to the contrast between the physical reality and the imaginary dream, between the visible and the invisible. But, argues De Boeck, this duality in the Central African urbanism of Kinshasa demonstrates something else at work, something much more interesting. The mechanism that unites these simultaneous, different worlds, but also distinguishes between them, is changing. If the invisible world of the 'bewitched children' stories has such effects on the visible world of family structure, of life on the streets and of the church communities, then the two worlds have become drastically entangled. *'Today, the two sides of the mirror have not only become entangled, but they have radically collapsed into each other. It is at this very point that the mirror has lost its power of reflection'*.

Kristiaan Borret
Translated by Laura Watkinson

Filip de Boeck & Marie-Françoise Plissart, *Kinshasa. Tales of the Invisible City*. Ghent: Ludion, 2004. 285 pp. ISBN 90-5544-528-2. (www.ludion.be)

How European is Dutch Culture?

On 28 October 2004 a series of books entitled *Dutch Culture in a European Perspective* was launched at deBuren, the Flemish-Netherlands House in Brussels. I was honoured to have been asked to address the audience on so weighty a topic as the place of Dutch Culture in a European Perspective, the more so as I was not quite sure that the credentials ascribed to me by Prof. Fokkema, general editor of the series, really sufficiently qualified me to do so. It is true that I have some first-hand experience of things Dutch by dint of having taught and lived there for almost twenty-five years before moving on to a position at Leuven, in my native Belgium. Perhaps, too, my present position at Leuven as Director of a Centre for European Studies may be thought to have provided me with the necessary insight, or authority, to hazard any and all rash pronouncements on the matter. The truth is, though, that any ideas I might have on the subject would not transcend the level of the personal and the mundane if not backed up by research such as that displayed in the volumes of *Dutch Culture in a European Perspective*. At least, they do so in English, because the original Dutch title is somewhat different; translated literally into English, it is *Dutch Culture in a European Context*. Though ostensibly minor, this terminological shift seems to me still significant. The original Dutch title emphasises the unity, the solidity of Dutch culture, its 'identity' in the sense precisely of its being 'unique'. The English title allows for greater flexibility, adaptability, malleability even, in response to changing circumstances. The subtle difference between these two titles, then, to me suggests an equally subtle shift in perceptions of the position of the Netherlands within Europe over the period between the original inception of this project in the early 1990s, and the translation of its results. I myself am inclined to interpret this shift as a confirmation of how 'Europe', in the guise of the European Union, but also in terms of the re-adjustment in horizons political, economic and cultural that the development of the European Union entails, has gained ever greater 'visibility' in the Dutch per-

ception. On the downside, I would hazard that this same phenomenon leads to a diminished sense of security in what was hitherto, at least until recently, perceived as an unassailable national identity. Still, such re-adjustments are not new in the history of the Netherlands, nor indeed in the history of most other European countries. The volumes of this series are eloquent testimony to that.

The answer to the question in my title, then, is easy. Of course, Dutch Culture is European down to its very roots. After all, the country to which this culture pertains is squarely located in Europe, the majority of its population is of European origins, and for the last twenty centuries it has participated in most of the major political, economic and cultural developments on the Continent. The question therefore needs rephrasing in the sense of: in which way, and to what extent does, or did, Dutch culture interact with its European neighbours, near and far? And this both in a passive and an active sense. So not only with regard to what the Netherlands stole, borrowed, or gleaned from other European nations, but also what they contributed to a wider European commonality of acting and thinking, a more encompassing European sensibility, or – why not use the term – identity? From this point of view, the original question in the title might perhaps even be recast as: how Dutch is European culture? After all, these are questions that become ever more pressing as the European Union grows, not only in numbers, but also in degree of integration. Elsewhere in the world, the EU is even now often regarded as a single entity, if not culturally, nor perhaps politically, then certainly economically. If the old adage that culture follows trade still holds, we might speculate that before too long some common sense of European identity will emerge. Of course, this identity will never be cast in stone. Rather, it will be a mutable and ever-changing thing. And Dutch culture, like that of all other European countries, will have contributed to this 'European' identity, as these books amply prove.

Questions such as those I have hitherto raised immediately surface when we ask to what extent the Republic of the United Provinces considered itself, or was considered by its neighbours and rivals, to be a separate entity at the time of the Treaty of Munster (or Westphalia) in 1648, the event which officially marked the country's independence. After all, the United Provinces went by various names at the time, and were represented under those names in the work of the most famous cartographers of the period: Leo Belgicus, Belgium, Leo Hollandicus, Olanda, Nether Germany, Paesi Bassi, Nederlandt. It is likewise fitting to ask to what extent perceptions of the age correspond with actual reality. Both the Dutch historian Johan Huizinga and his British counterpart Simon Schama suggest 'internalist' explanations for Dutch culture in the seventeenth century. Huizinga sees the Dutch Republic as a creation *sui generis*, rooted in the specific circumstances of its genesis and its already fundamentally middle-class make-up, which ultimately gave rise to a people characterised by *'simplicity, frugality, cleanliness'* as well as *'sobriety, a prosaic attitude, and commonness'*. Schama sees the specificity of Dutch culture in the Golden Age as the result of an act of self-invention by what was in essence a newcomer on the European scene. Yet one may well wonder whether more 'internationalist' explanations would not do more justice to what really happened in the Netherlands in that fabled seventeenth century.

Indeed, in 1650 a number of developments that had marked the period from the earliest rebellions against the Spanish down to the Peace of Westphalia have worked themselves out: the emergence of Holland, and to a lesser extent Zeeland and Friesland, as the dominant members of the Republic of the United Provinces; the successful assimilation of successive, and sometimes massive, waves of immigrants, from the Southern (and still Spanish) Netherlands, but also from many other surrounding regions, as well as a substantial number of Jews fleeing persecution in Spanish-held territories, and even already from Central Europe; the creation of a national language; the cementing role of a belief in liberty, the importance of faith, the preservation of hard-won rights and privileges, and a measure of self-respect. Still, the Republic remained very much a house under construc-

Johannes Vermeer,
The Cartographer (detail).
c.1668-1669.
Canvas, 52 x 45,5 cm.
Städelsches Kunstinstitut,
Frankfurt am Main.

tion, and this was abundantly clear to outsiders. This actually contributed to the smooth working of society, politics, and the economy. In fact, the metaphor of the market may well be most apt for the United Provinces in the seventeenth century. The Republic acted as a market, or perhaps rather an 'exchange', for all manner of products, material as well as cultural; it was a land of 'diffusion', of import and export, a place of trade and mediation, characterised by neutrality in the public sphere, voluntarism in most matters political, religious, philosophical and cultural, and essentially middle-class. As such, it served as a model for much of what would happen later, to a greater or lesser extent, in much of the rest of Europe.

The books in this series are not only highly informative, they also make for thoroughly enjoyable reading. The scholarly discourse is regularly leavened by striking anecdotes, whether from the everyday life of the common man or the life of the nation in its official celebrations. Long-standing stereotypes are debunked, or at least re-evaluated, often in dialogue with the works of the most reputed historians of Dutch culture: Johan Huizinga, Jan Romein, Geoffrey Parker, Simon Schama, Jonathan Israel. All in all, I know of no other such sharp and varied portrait of four centuries of one national European culture against the backdrop of the other European cultures that surround it. Though written by the most renowned scholars in the field, these volumes wear their learning lightly, and succeed in not only surprising, but at times even amusing, the reader with their wealth of quotations from the most diverse sources, their superbly chosen illustrations, and their judicious use of anecdotes. Even if only in this, Dutch culture here makes a substantial contribution to European culture. These books are a superb illustration of how Europe's various constituent cultures continually, and fruitfully, interact within the wider space of what ultimately can only be called a shared European culture.

Theo D'haen

Dutch Culture in a European Perspective. The Significant Moments in the History of the Netherlands: 1650, 1800, 1900, 1950 and 1650 – 2000 (ed. D. Fokkema). Assen: Van Gorcum. 2004 (Vol. 1 – 1650: *Hard-Won Unity*. ISBN 90-232-3963-6, 764 pp. / Vol. 2 – 1800: *Blueprints for a National Community*. ISBN 90-232-3964-4, 630 pp. / Vol. 3 – 1900: *The Age of Bourgeois Culture*. ISBN 90-232-3965-2, 630 pp. / Vol. 4 – 1950: *Prosperity and Welfare*. ISBN 90-232-3966-0, 560 pp. / Vol. 5 – *Accounting for the Past*: 1650-2000. ISBN 90-232-3967-9, 420 pp. (www.vgorcum.nl)

Death of a Polemicist
On Theo van Gogh (1957-2004)

On 2 November 2004 in Amsterdam-Oost three Theo van Goghs were murdered. First, we mourn the loss of one of the Netherlands' most talented, productive and independent-minded filmmakers. Second, a gifted television interviewer passed from our midst, someone who coaxed private revelations from the mouths of countless well-known Dutch personalities in the programme *Een prettig gesprek* (A Nice Chat). This is probably the Theo van Gogh that his family and friends knew: open-hearted, generous and inspiring. And then there is the third Theo van Gogh: the provocateur who in his columns fiercely lashed out at everything he opposed and found no insult too coarse when engaging in controversy. Van Gogh waged his own war against hypocrisy, against politically correct thinking, against people who sought to curb freedom of speech and against anyone who made the slightest effort to thwart his film career.

Theo van Gogh was brutally killed by the radical Muslim Mohammed B. out of vengeance for the short film *Submission I*, which Van Gogh had made in the summer of 2004. *Submission I*, based on a screenplay by the Dutch-Somali politician Ayaan Hirsi Ali, was meant as an indictment of the Muslim religion. The film shows veiled, abused women with texts from the Koran written across their bodies. The filmmakers used this means to draw a direct connection between the abuse of women and Islam. Hirsi Ali, who herself had been raised in a strict Islamic environment, has been under threat for quite some time because of her views on Islam. It is clear from the letter that Van Gogh's murderer left on his body that Hirsi Ali was the real target.

A death threat in the form of a ritual murder – events that had been considered unimaginable in the Netherlands up to now. The attack created a climate of great agitation in the Netherlands. It was followed by bold public debates. Politicians had to go into hiding and mosques and Islamic schools were attacked. In the meantime, Van Gogh was honoured both at home and abroad as a martyr for free speech and a

Theo van Gogh (middle)
on the set of *06/05* (2004).

great political filmmaker. The BBC even called him the Dutch Michael Moore.

But to come to a deeper understanding of the life and work of Van Gogh, it's important that his three guises be kept carefully separated. The scathing views on Jews and Muslims (not racist, but certainly meant to be offensive) with which he filled his columns are completely absent from his films. Indeed, in most of the thirteen feature films and a number of the television series that Van Gogh left behind there wasn't a scrap of political or social ideology. The provocations that are so prominent in his columns are reduced in his films to a few sick jokes or a vicious dig at people with whom he had a bone to pick in his own everyday life.

Theo van Gogh, the son of an official in the Domestic Intelligence Service, was self-taught and made his debut in 1982 with *Luger*, a film in which a simple-minded millionaire's daughter is held hostage by a psychopath. His sardonic sense of humour is evident in the scene (created by special effects, of course) in which young kittens are put in a washing machine. Although the film went unnoticed by most of the movie-going public, Van Gogh immediately earned a reputation as an self-willed, controversial filmmaker.

Yet even that reputation is undeserved in view of most of the films that followed. He made a number of quite respectable film versions of Dutch novels: *Back to Oegstgeest* (Terug naar Oegstgeest, 1984), *A Day at the Beach* (Een dagje naar het strand, 1987) and *False Light* (Vals licht, 1991). When major film companies and conventional producers lost interest in his projects, he decided that from then on he would finance his work himself, or seek outside backers. *1-900 (Sex without Hangups)* (06, 1994), *Blind Date* (1996), *The Rack* (De pijnbank, 1998) and *Interview* (2003) were all produced this way: on a minimal budget, with a small cast and at a very limited number of locations.

For a long time he seemed to be entirely in his element with such projects. In *1-900 (Sex without Hangups)*, perhaps his best film, he expresses the view that love is a great battleground, and lying is the most important weapon in the struggle. In this film version of a play by the Dutch theatre maker Johan Doesburg, a man and a woman engage in telephone sex. As their conversations continue a bond begins to grow, but because they cannot see each other and are otherwise unknown to each other it is easy for them to lie about themselves.

In the more recent *Interview*, too, the truth plays

a game of hide-and-seek: a soap opera star (played by the former soap opera star Katja Schuurman) is interviewed by a journalist from a quality newspaper (played by the illustrious Pierre Bokma), whom she keeps misleading in order to confront him with his own prejudices.

Many of Van Gogh's films are intimate *Kammerspiele*, perfect vehicles for showing off his outstanding skill as a director. Only in his last projects did he extend the relational and emotional battle beyond the space of four walls, and the outside world began to make its way into his films and television series. In the much-praised television series *Najib and Julia* (2002), a Moroccan pizza delivery boy falls in love with a girl hockey player from The Hague, thus bringing the perils and dilemmas of the multi-cultural society to the surface. His last feature film but one, *Cool* (2004), has to do with a number of prodigal youths – most of them from ethnic minority groups – who commit a bank robbery that goes very wrong and end up in the Glenn Mills re-education camp (Glenn Mills being one of the film's financial backers). And then there's his posthumous work and swan song, *06/05*, a political thriller about the murder of politician Pim Fortuyn.

In these films, Van Gogh waded into the sphere of current social events that he inveighed against so strongly in his columns. But as a film director he is primarily interested in plot and drama, not in unvarnished opinions. *06/05*, for example, is not an uncritical tribute to the *'divine baldy'*, as he referred to the politician in his columns, but a successful and exciting *JFK*-like conspiracy film in which a photojournalist discovers that the Dutch secret service, the AIVD, were aware of the plan to murder Fortuyn. Nothing is done to thwart the attack, however, because Fortuyn was opposed to the acquisition of the costly Joint Strike Fighter.

The film begins when Fortuyn is murdered in the Hilversum media park. The politician is not featured as a character; he is not played by an actor with a shiny false pate. Nevertheless, Fortuyn is omnipresent in *06/05*. Throughout the entire film we see the archival images that dominated Dutch television during those days: how his opponents stood there groping for words during debates with him, and how he was pushed into an extreme right-wing corner by politicians and journalists – unjustly, Van Gogh believed. This successful collage is a good demonstration of how the image of Fortuyn developed during those confusing months of 2002. And it's impossible to look at the images of the sea of flowers left at the spot where Fortuyn was shot down without thinking of the similar honour that fell to Van Gogh after his own murder.

Perhaps the point where Van Gogh's work as a polemicist intersects with his work as a filmmaker is his great love of sarcasm. His sometimes coarse insults and scornful characterisations of Jews and Muslims were never really serious; he loved to bait his opponents and make them look foolish. And all his films are peppered with a sardonic sense of humour that infuses even the motives of his characters with a taste of irony. For no matter how fiercely and emotionally they may struggle for love and recognition, they are never without a certain cynicism.

It is precisely that sarcasm that is absent from the film that spelled his doom. *Submission I* is a rather histrionic film in which kitschy symbolism and a pamphleteer's message jostle each other. There's not a single comic note, no attempt to put things in perspective, no mocking details. Van Gogh himself always said that one of the big problems with Muslims is that they haven't got a sense of humour. An Islamic variant of Monty Python's *Life of Brian* is therefore inconceivable. That makes sense. But on the other hand, Van Gogh was never threatened because of his columns, and perhaps *Submission I* hit the Muslim world as hard as it did precisely because of its unambiguously political character. It was courageous of Van Gogh and Hirsi Ali to make the film, but the mocking intelligence that was so finely crafted in Van Gogh's work is sorely lacking in *Submission I*. Which makes it all the more ironic that Van Gogh was murdered because of this film in which, for once, he refused to play the fool.

Pieter Bots
Translated by Nancy Forest-Flier

Infection Welcome!
Het muziek Lod

Het muziek Lod in Ghent presents itself as a platform for all-round musicians who take a very broad view of their own domain and are open to music theatre and other art forms. Het muziek Lod currently has four music and music-theatre makers in residence: Dick van der Harst, Kris Defoort, Jan Kuijken and Dominique Pauwels, who each have the freedom to develop their own work. They work on a wide variety of productions in ever-changing but frequently recurring partnerships (with Karine Ponties, Guy Cassiers, Eric de Volder...). Het muziek Lod was recently honoured with the Océ Podium Prize, and Defoort's opera *The Woman Who Walked into Doors* also received a nomination. During a fifteen-year voyage of discovery, Het muziek Lod has established a unique place for itself in the world of Flemish – and international – music and music-theatre. Without fear of the new, the old, the alternative or the unknown, the composers are developing their own individual oeuvres which do not fit into any one category, and which are increasingly characterised by a sense of social engagement. Music is blended with dance, theatre, text, video. This blending occurs not only between the disciplines, but in the music itself. The credo is 'Infection is not a danger but a must', and this is borne out by the work of the resident composers.

Dick van der Harst has worked at Het muziek Lod as a musician, arranger and composer since it was founded in 1989. His instrument, the bandoneon, is the common element in all his compositions. The accordion is also important, for example in the evening-long concerto for accordion and ensemble *Non vides sed audis*. His most recent music-theatre productions include *Deep in the Woods* (Diep in het bos), *Black Birds in the Trees* (Zwarte vogels in de bomen) and *Vadria*, all three with Eric De Volder, and *Cara mia*, a song cycle that was originally written for the dance show *Chers Amis* and has since become well-known in its own right. In 2004 he presented the Banda Azu-faifo, a combination of classic brass band and folk instruments. He also performs with his own trio Audible Life Stream, consisting of bandoneon, bass clarinet and percussion.

Van der Harst uses jazz, classical music and folk music in his compositions, along with a healthy dose of improvisation. The result is 'contemporary global music'. He is always in search of the meaning of authenticity today. *Nineteen Books with Songs and Dances* (played on a large street organ, with arrangements of traditionals, anonymous medieval pieces, Dowland, Bach and even – briefly – James Ensor) and *La Casa de las musiquillas ocultas* (The House of the Hidden Music, with musicians from as far afield as Ireland and Galicia, using Mozart, Machaut, Poulenc and troubadour melodies) show Van der Harst as an 'authenticist'. He goes in search of the most diverse forms of folk music and incorporates them unpretentiously into his own arrangements. Depending on the project he is working on, he works with folk musicians, specialists in early music, and jazz players or classically trained musicians. His interpretations and creations based on folk music reveal a sensitive and at the same time discerning engagement with its roots. Van der Harst's approach is a daring one:

The Soul of the Ant
(Die siel van die mier, 2004).
Photo by Herman Sorgeloos
(courtesy of Het muziek Lod).

using his innovative musical language he is able to blend a disruptive and slightly chaotic polyphony with the popular vernacular. His music has a surprising and refreshing unpredictability.

And then we come to Kris Defoort: 'When I was younger I wanted to be a "jazz musician" but I've come to realise that it isn't possible. I don't have the background and I don't lead that sort of life. Making the music I want to – and can – make, here, with my background and the way we live, that's what it comes down to.' Kris Defoort reached this decision at the end of the 1980s, after three years studying jazz and, more importantly, living in New York's jazz milieu. While in the United States he became aware of his European identity and European musical background. Before this he had studied jazz at the music academies of Antwerp and Liège. In Liège he formed the quintet Diva Smiles (an anagram of Miles Davis) and the group won the Liège provincial jazz competition in 1984. The CD Sketches of Belgium (1993), recorded by KD's Basement Party, the ensemble that Defoort set up after returning to Belgium, includes two Monk arrangements by Defoort, as well as his own compositions. Defoort: 'The name "Basement Party" is a metaphor for "dissident understanding". Our band ("Party") thinks underground ("basement") about musical renewal. Out of this opposition, instinctive and intellectual, arises the second meaning of "Party" – namely a feast.'

In the fusion of jazz with 'new music', Defoort focuses on communication: 'I want to make music that, to a much greater extent than written material, is based on the verbal interaction with the musicians I work with.' Music then becomes 'something natural, that comes from inside'. Music should bring together extremes: 'Something that is at the same time collective and highly individual, in a fairly clear-cut and rigid form, but a form that we can interpret very freely.' This worked extremely well in his work for the choreographer Fatou Traoré. They successfully based their collaboration on 'the permanent tension between form and freedom'. In Passages, six dancers are confronted with ten musicians in a game that is played out at the interface between harmony and chaos; a pendulum swinging from the individual and the individualistic towards the collective. The tension can become extreme, an 'overstretching' in which everyone involved departs from and loses the points of reference.

An even greater challenge for Defoort was his collaboration with Guy Cassiers on The Woman Who Walked Into Doors, based on the novel of the same title by the Irish author Roddy Doyle. On the set, the audience sees the 'outside world' as a video screen. The characters' dialogue is 'neutralised' because it appears in text form on the screen. The audience sees only the female lead on the otherwise empty stage, and they see double, as it were: she appears as a singing actress as well as a speaking actress. Guy Cassiers and Kris Defoort have created a new type of music theatre that is free of all operatic conventions. It is a successful and well-balanced blend of various branches of art that explicitly invites the audience to form their own interpretation.

Kris Defoort's recent productions include his new jazz CD Sound Plaza and the 'fusion' piece Conversations with the Past, commissioned by the Filharmonie. Defoort builds on and explores the confrontation between past and present in a most unique way in ConSerVations/ConVerSations with the musicians from Het muziek Lod, with jazz musicians and with the Danel String Quartet. This piece is a conversation between classical music and jazz which is, however, based on Renaissance music.

Classical music brings us to the third composer, Jan Kuijken, who had a classical training as a cellist and pianist, but decided early on that he did not want to pursue a career in classical music. He soon made a name for himself on the Brussels musical scene, in which fusion and cross-over are central. He worked on a series of very diverse projects: Urbanised by Luk Mishalle and Trevor Watts, The Soluble Fish (De Oplosbare Vis) by Peter Vermeersch and Josse De Pauw, The Sands of Time by Dick van der Harst, Passages by Kris Defoort and Fatou Traoré. It is no surprise that the names of his fellow resident composers at Het muziek Lod feature so prominently. Kuijken's work as a composer includes Louise Avenue (Let's take one more...) in light jazz style, music for various dance productions including *Kreuset* by Karin Vyncke and the dance video *Tristitia* by Vyncke (which won an award in Paris), two 'classical' string quartets and the *Farewell Symphony* (Afscheidssymfonie) for the Oxalys Ensemble. He has been a resident composer at Het muziek Lod since 2000. He earned considerable acclaim with the music-theatre production *The Flood* (De Overstroming), based on a play by Peter Handke and directed by Peter van Kraaij. In 2004 he enjoyed great success as a composer (and live performer, in collaboration with George van Dam) in the production *The Soul of the Ant* (Die siel van die mier) with Josse De Pauw, to a script by David Van Reybrouck.

From the perspective of style fusion, Kuijken sees his music-theatre scores as 'organically interwoven with the actors' performance'. His music must therefore be idiomatically linked to the instruments and, for dance *performances*, organically linked to the art of dance. A recent example is his music for the new solo *Brutalis* by the choreographer Karine Ponties, in which 'one cannot exist without the other'. In short: 'A dialogue between theatre, dance and his music. A search for the point at which the different languages connect.'

The fourth composer is Dominique Pauwels. Pauwels was fascinated by multimedia, the interaction between composer, performer, scholar, computer and technology, and has studied the style of the French Spectralists (computer analysis of the harmonic spectra of single sounds, the results of which are used as the basis for new compositions). Pauwels has developed into a very versatile and adaptable composer.

His oeuvre includes extremely diverse genres. Unusually for a composer, he makes a distinction between functional and non-functional compositions. Functional compositions include title music for television programmes, scores for films and documentaries, theatre music, and music for children's theatre and dance productions. The 'functional' category also includes a whole string of compositions for publicity and advertising purposes. Non-functional compositions include classical genres, for example piano music and a string quartet (with electronics, naturally), along with algorithmic pieces and a concerto for piano and computer. He likes to rework his own compositions into other styles, as in *Variation 1 on Come and Went* for piano, hip-hop and lead guitar. Pauwels again broke away from existing concepts with *Nocturne or Procession for Piano and Max*, which takes four days to perform. He later reworked this into a thirty-year variation, whatever that may mean. This combination of non-functional and functional work allows Dominique Pauwels to make a living as a composer – which is not so easy to do in Flanders. This is yet another example of the fusion that is so characteristic of Het Muziek Lod.

Yves Knockaert
Translated by Yvette Mead

www.hetmuzieklod.be

Leine and Roebana: Explorers of Music and Dance

In 1993 *Suites (Dances for the Queen)* marked the international breakthrough of the Dutch choreographer couple Andrea Leine and Harijono Roebana. With this work the duo won prizes in Italy and France and put themselves at the forefront of today's modern dance. The subtitle 'Dances for the Queen' is just an ironic addition to the title. The couple could never have dreamed that it would ever become a reality. But at the première of *Les Indes Galantes* in April 2004 Queen Beatrix was actually sitting in the theatre balcony, watching with a smile (or was that just our imagination?) Leine and Roebana's courtly dance.

For those who have kept an eye on the couple's choreographic career, the move from modern experimental dance to participation in a prestigious international project to put on an historic opera will have come as no surprise. In their search for an ideal language for dance, music is both their basis and their guide. Along with intractable twentieth-century music, the particular timbre of early music has become a guiding principle in their choreographic oeuvre.

It was director Jeroen Lopes Gardozo who had the idea of involving the couple in this historic production. It was created to mark the accession of the new EU member states, one of which, Poland, was involved as co-producer. After all, Jean-Philipe Rameau's opera ballet of 1735 has peace in a war-hungry Europe as its theme. The Goddess of Love (Amour) calls upon young men to look for untainted love in faraway places: in Turkey, Peru, a Persian flower garden and in America among the noble, savage Indians.

Dance was originally an indispensable feature of the opera ballet genre of which *Les Indes Galantes* is a superb example. In the overture Hébé, Goddess of Youth, calls for the dawn to be greeted with song and the day begun with dance: '*Vous commencez avec le jour, Les jeux brillants de Terpsichore*'. In the original version, the dance was choreographed by Louis Dupré, who himself performed with, among others, the lyrical Marie Sallé. Dreamy minuets, rustic rigaudons and lively gavottes garlanded the allegorical ballet and gave the scenes the requisite local colour. Also included were expressive dances to accompany the action and symbolic Italian figure dance. *Les Indes Galantes*, with its expressive music and the Enlightenment ideas expressed in it, was the most successful French opera ballet of the eighteenth century.

It is also an important work for the history of dance. In 1758 the Viennese choreographer Hilverding turned the second act of *Der Grossmutige Türke* (*The Noble Turk*) into an independent exotic drama which with its expressive gestures typified the *ballet d'action* (that is, a ballet in which the storyline predominates). The Romantic Movement then ignored the work , but in the course of the twentieth century *Les Indes Galantes* attracted renewed interest. Maurice Lehmann's new production at the Paris Opera in 1952 has become legendary. Various contemporary artists (such as the choreographer Lifar and the painter Wahkevitch) collaborated to bring it to the stage.

Recently the Paris National Opera gave Rameau's opera ballet a makeover. Director Andrei Serban and conductor William Christie, leader of Les Arts Floris-

Leine and Roebana, *ditto* (2004). Photo by Deen Van Meer (courtesy of Leine and Roebana).

sants, asked the modern choreographer Blanca Li to take care of the dance elements. And in Zurich the choreographer Heinz Spoerli recently ventured on a reconstruction.

The version by director Jeroen Lopes Cardozo, in collaboration with Frans Brüggen's Orchestra of the Eighteenth Century and Capella Amsterdam, was a mixture of the authentic and the contemporary. The plot was retained and the singing is to all intents and purposes identical to the original. But the staging looked modern and full of life, and the music absolutely sparkled. The contemporary aspect came from the dance and the overall design – Melle Hammer had designed a fanciful and ingenious stage-set for the production. One eye-catching feature was her design for 'The Persian Garden' with large pastel-coloured inflatable flowers which were as reminiscent of the Rococo paintings of Watteau and Lancret as they were of 'flower power'. The costumes by fashion designer Aziz Bekkeaoui were also a delight to the eye, with extravagant and fantastic costumes, attributes and wigs in a wild mix of Baroque, Rococo and the 2004 catwalk.

The relationship between early music and Leine and Roebana's contemporary dance was less obvious. Sometimes the dance adds nothing where you would expect it to, and in *Les Sauvages* – where Rameau even had an authentic Indian dance in mind – it was missing altogether. The dances sometimes illustrated the action, as did a whirling dance accompanying the gathering storm in Act three. More often the dancers circled sensually but aimlessly around the soloists and chorus. The most successful characters were those portrayed by Tim Persent and Ty Boomershine as alter egos of Bellone (War) and L'Amour (Love, and in this case Peace as well). The latter was dressed in a fire-red costume and with graceful and serene steps performed a balanced game with a sparkling white ball, as if playing with the entire world. By contrast Persent demonstrated – in low, twisting movements – the dark, capricious side of international power politics.

Leine and Roebana have said with reference to *Les Indes Galantes* that they see history as a living part of the present, and in it they display a dynamic approach which had found expression in their earlier work as well. The duo regards opera as '*a statement of contemporaries*'. That unbiased attitude – which could as well be called naïve as poetic – did not work very well within the strict framework of an allegorical ballet. Their connection with early music was more

successful in their own work, in the direct dialogue between dance and music.

In *Suites* (*Dances for the Queen*), by using Beethoven's 'Rasumovsky String Quartets' they already indicated that they were not choosing easy music to work with. Their uninhibited choice of music is equally striking in *Tales of Eversion* (1997), with its combination of compositions by John Zorn, Gavin Bryars and Edgar Varèse. Their participation in the international summer course on composition and choreography in the English town of Wakefield in 1998 deepened their exploration of music and dance. There they met the composer Yannis Kyriakides – a former student of Louis Andriessen – who like them was fascinated by the combination of old and contemporary. This meeting led to a composition being commissioned. In *Byrd* (1999) Kyriakides revived a song from *Lady Nevells Booke* by the Renaissance composer William Byrd. The song was played on the virginals. Another composition by Kyriakidis, played half live and half on tape, formed a second layer. A direct consequence of this is *Cantus firmus* (2000). In this the medieval principle of an extremely slowed down music line was translated into video images of old people, which provided a framework and a point of departure for the dance. The conceptual framework is less easily discernible than the echoes of medieval melodies and 'sounds of the future' reworked by Kyriakides.

In *S/he* (2001) the duo turned their attention to the viola da gamba, attracted by its soft and personal sound which could well be compared to the human voice. Baroque music (in *S/he* that of, among others, Marin Marais and the Master of Sainte Colombe) appeals to Leine and Roebana particularly because of its reconciliation of strict form with emotionality, combining detachment and passion. In a similar way they want to make emotions resonate through formal dance. It is a vision they share with the Flemish choreographer Anna Teresa de Keersmaeker, whose favourite composer is Béla Bartók because of his combination of emotion and structure.

In *S/he* Leine, Ty Boomershine and Tim Persent entered into a dialogue with violists da gamba Freek

Borstlap and Ivanka Neeleman. They twined playfully around the musicians. The circles and ovals which the dance trio traced with their supple upper body, swinging arms and whirling legs created a curlicue calligraphy which went wonderfully well with the Baroque music. But there were also sharp and angular movements which left scratches on the overall dance – as a sign of the present.

The next production, *Eye in All* (2002), showed a much more dynamic rapport with the music. It was danced to sharp, snappish and bare percussion by Pierre Boulez, Yannis Xenakis and Steve Reich, powerfully played live by the percussion group Amsterdam. The simultaneous collaboration with Ton Simons and Dance Works was outstanding. Set against his long-drawn-out and balanced style, the dance of Leine and Roebana seemed even more earthly, rounder, more fluent and sensual than it actually is.

The duo continued their quest for synergy between music and dance in *Türings Tijgers* (2003). Here the dancers shared the stage with nine musicians from the Maarten Altena Ensemble. In an unusual ensemble that included, among other instruments, electric guitar, xylophone, recorder, trombone and voice, the musicians performed modern work by Altena, Kyriakides, Gilius van Bergeijk and Steve Martland. The singer Noa Frenkel performed a song by William Byrd, the composer who comes close to being a leitmotif in the work of Leine and Roebana. Frenkel's rarefied voice was accompanied by its equivalent in subtle dance solos. In *Sporen* (2004) the duo recycled dance fragments from their existing work and added new (early) music to it, played by Freek Borstlap and Ivanka Neeleman on the viola da gamba. In the opening solo to Purcell's song *O Solitude*, Tim Persent added even more resonance to the voice of countertenor Joseph Schlesinger. In such moments Leine and Roebana's contemporary chamber dance achieves the perfect synthesis of music and dance

In the recent production *ditto*, the integration of dance and music is again to the fore. But with the provocatively theatrical performance by the Canadian composer Krista Vincent and the electronic sound engineering and disorganised video images of Palin-drome, a German new media collective, Leine and Roebana embarked, startlingly, on a completely new chapter. However, the atmosphere of their serious, humane dance did not fit in with the irony of these young conceptual artists with their interactive gags and fun. Only Tim Persent and Ederson Rodrigues Xavier, in their dance solos, managed to bring together these two divergent visions. *ditto* would appear to be no more than a daring excursion in an otherwise coherent body of work.

Isabella Lanz
Translated by Brian Granger

www.leineroebana.com

In their new dance production *Terts*, which premiered on 7 April 2005 in the Utrecht Stadsschouwburg, the collaboration with the Maarten Altena Ensemble is intensified. The choreographers and the Ensemble have found common ground in their use of capricious contrasts; contrasts, however, which reinforce each other and thereby emphasise an underlying unity and continuity.

The End of the Nineteenth Century in 1914
On Gas Attacks, Poetry, Cruelty and Increased Mobility in WW I Belgium

'The attack of last Thursday evening was preceded by the rising of a cloud of vapor, greenish gray and iridescent.' This is how Will Irwin, correspondent for the *New York Tribune*, described the German offensive at Ypres on 22 April 1915. It was a historic moment: the first successful gas attack in military history, instantly resulting in 1,200 dead and 3,000 wounded. The French had already used tear-gas grenades, but that wasn't an illegal weapon, because it wasn't deadly. Strictly speaking, the Germans were also 'safe' as far as the Hague Convention was concerned, because that prohibited only the use of *'projectiles, the sole object of which is the diffusion of asphyxiating gases'*. And on 22 April the Germans simply released the gas from cylinders and let the wind carry out the destructive work. Later the British would significantly improve the diffusion technique. In spring 1916 they introduced the Livens projector, a sort of grenade launcher that could fire projectiles with 13.6 kg of pure phosgene. As Christ's catchy phrase about turning the other cheek isn't all that popular in wartime, every country involved in the war soon began to regard the use of gas as legitimate. In total around 112,000 metric tons of gas were employed by all the warring parties during World War I.

1915 was the year of the first gas attack and of the Second Battle of Ypres, but it was also the year that John McCrae wrote his poem 'In Flanders Fields', on the night of 2 May at the Essex Farm dressing station, just to the north of Ypres. On 2 May 2005 a new monument is being unveiled there. In conjunction with this, there will be a small exhibition about McCrae and the significance of his one world-famous poem at the In Flanders Fields Museum in Ypres, which took its name from the celebrated poem by this Canadian military doctor. The museum is also commemorating the 90th anniversary of the fifteen famous lines with a number of activities focusing on the literature of the First World War. For example, at the end of March

The residence of the Belgian
Amicitia Society in Dulwich,
London, c.1917.
Photo Aartsbischoppelijk
Archief, Mechelen.

2005 you could follow, text in hand, in the footsteps left by the most important war poets left in the fields of Flanders, a trip culminating on 3 April at Wilfred Owen's grave at Ors. On 30 April 2005 five speakers are giving introductions to literature from and about the First World War written in English, German, French, Italian and Dutch.

However, the Great War was about more than gas attacks and the despair of the poet-soldiers in the muddy trenches. During the first weeks after the German invasion of Belgium it was largely a mobile war. The Belgians had been living in peace for some generations and now they were suddenly confronted with the pandemonium of modern warfare: rattling machine guns, exploding shells and droning aircraft. Added to this was the German strategy of *Schrecklichkeit* and the associated bloody reprisals against the civilian population. In 2001, the American historians John Horne and Alan Kramer published an extensive study thoroughly documenting the German war crimes against the Belgian population. Their *German Atrocities, 1914* has the subtitle 'A History of Denial'. Their contentions are supported by Larry Zuckerman in his more recent *The Rape of Belgium: The Untold Story of World War I* (2004): just as the Germans had made efforts between 1914 and 1918 to play down the atrocities in Belgium, so 'poor little Belgium' suddenly became considerably less pitiable to the British, French and Americans during the peace conference in Versailles. This meant that Belgian demands for German reparations could be tempered, thus providing a larger share of the cake for France and Great Britain. And so the executions, rapes, burnt-out villages, looting, demands and deportations were erased from history, and even the Belgians have come to believe over the years that it's all part of the Myth of the Cruel Hun. Zuckerman wants to expose the wartime suffering of the Belgians once again. For him, the nineteenth century stops in 1914: not only did Europe rip itself to pieces in that year, but an end also came to the ideas of honesty, beauty, progress and the possibility of improving humankind.

The German acts of violence and the – admittedly – often embroidered rumours about those crimes certainly served to foster a climate of mass hysteria: at one time no fewer than two million Belgians were fleeing the country. Following the fall of Antwerp, a million Belgians found themselves on Dutch territory. The other half of the refugees sought refuge in France and England. After the fall of Ostend, the number of Belgian refugees on English soil increased dramatically, although that number decreased somewhat when a substantial number of them left for France.

So France was the only nation to see the number of Belgians within its borders increase up until 1918.

In France and England, the necessary humanitarian relief measures were immediately put into effect, as they also were in the Netherlands. This happened through official channels as well as through private initiatives. In England, aristocratic ladies fought to get the few wealthy refugees into their houses. In Chelsea there was even a residence for 'First Class Belgians'. But it was also a privilege for the less well-to-do to have a Belgian in their home. A worker wrote to the War Refugee Committee: '*I've got five of them myself, but I would still like to have another Belgian*'. However, there was of course the occasional disappointment. For example, there's a letter from a Mrs Lovatt, who was complaining that the Belgian child she had taken in not only had lice, but – to top it all – might also be Jewish.

The war lasted much longer than everyone had expected, and now and then the well of charity did indeed dry up. Fortunately, the refugees themselves rolled up their sleeves and got to work. In France they could work in the agricultural sector, and in England in the war industry. There was a dire lack of munitions, and the first Belgian factories in England started up as early as 1914. In 1916, there was even a sizeable Belgian industrial zone in Birtley, with a Belgian town-within-a-town for the employees of the National Projectile Factory. Elisabethville was a sort of mini-Belgium: the streets had Belgian names, there was a *chef du village* and Belgian gendarmes (although they were replaced by British police following riots). The social and cultural life was in the hands of a Vlaamsch Verbond, a Cercle Wallon and Les Amis de Luxembourg. This Belgian linguistic-social stratification was also apparent in another area: the management and assistants in the factory were mainly French-speaking, whereas the workers were almost exclusively from Flanders.

As the war progressed, a kind of weariness developed, and the initially charming idiosyncrasies of the Belgians suddenly became irritating characteristics. People began increasingly to perceive the refugees as a burden and xenophobia reared its ugly

head. In the suburbs of London there were disturbances directed against the refugees in 1916; in 1917
a couple of Belgians in the Netherlands were beaten
up because they were suspected of having eaten a
loaf of bread that was reserved for Dutch people; and
in 1916 the home for First Class Belgians in Chelsea
closed its doors, because the Belgians' occupancy of
the house had become *very difficult'*. In this context
it's not surprising that Elisabethville was closed off
from the outside world by an iron fence. As far as
possible, the Belgians were kept away from the local population, one consequence of which was that
the number of British-Belgian marriages remained
remarkably low. In *The Birtley Belgians* Schlesinger
and McMurtrie mention the fact that *'the segregation
of Belgian workers in their own village was a deliberate
policy aimed at great productivity'*. But they also add:
*'the question arises how much was lost in terms of mu-
tual understanding between the two communities'*. The
author J.B. Priestley described Elisabethville in his
English Journey (1934) as a noxious haunt of apartheid,
*'a nightmare place that seemed to have been con-
structed out of small army huts and unwanted dog ken-
nels'*. Although Schlesinger and McMurtrie believe
that this should be taken with a pinch of salt, as *'the
huts had flush toilets, this at a time when most locals
had open sewers or middens.'* The nineteenth century
really was over.

Filip Matthijs

Translated by Laura Watkinson

www.inflandersfields.be

John N. Horne & Alan Kramer, *German Atrocities, 1914:
A History of Denial*. Yale University Press, 2001.
Larry Zuckerman, *The Rape of Belgium: The Untold Story of
World War I*. New York University Press, 2004.
J. Schlesinger & D. McMurtrie, *The Birthley Belgians*. (4th
revised edition, ISBN 1- 870268-07-5). Information: The History
of Education Project, Durham University School of Education,
Leazes Road, Durham DH1 1TA, United Kingdom.

'Nuts', Hunger and Cold
The Last Winter of War

*'It's just as comfortable here and we feel just as safe as
we did when we were in England,'* the English soldier
Joe Schectman wrote to his parents on 15 December
1944 from the area around Bastogne. He didn't have
long to enjoy this peace and quiet, though, because at
half past five on the morning of 16 December the last
German offensive on the Western Front began.

The plan, devised by Hitler himself, was to launch a
large-scale attack across the Maas with the aim of re-
taking Antwerp and driving a wedge between the advancing Allied troops. According to the Dutch historian
Lou de Jong, Hitler's objective was chiefly political. The
Führer was presumably hoping that this attack
would lessen the Allies' will to continue the war and
that British and American differences of opinion about
military and political strategies would increase.

This German plan has been given different names:
the Ardennes offensive, the Battle of the Bulge, and
sometimes it is mistakenly called the Von Rundstedt
offensive. Field Marshal G. Von Rundstedt was the
commander of the Western Front. He realised that
Hitler's plan was insane, but he didn't dare contra-
dict the Führer. The Germans called the plan 'Wacht
am Rhein' (the Watch on the Rhine), with the intention of creating the impression that it was more of a
defensive plan designed to stop the advancing Allies
at the Rhine. A strict timetable was drawn up for
the attack: 16 December: D-day; 18 December: the
Maas is reached; 19 December: the Maas is crossed;
23 December: Antwerp is captured. To implement
this plan a military force of around 220,000 soldiers
was assembled . They had enough fuel to reach the
Maas; after that the German troops would make use
of captured Allied depots. Liège and Antwerp were
bombarded with V1 and V2 bombs. The assault was
to be supported by two special units: a group of para-
chutists and a group of German servicemen dropped
behind Allied lines and operating in American uniforms. This unit was under the command of Colonel
Otto Skorzeny, the *'most dangerous man in Europe'*.
Many of his men were unmasked because their

23 January 1945: a small
unit of the US 7th Armored
Division reaches St-Vith.

Small mercies during the hunger winter
of 1945 in the Netherlands.
Museum van de Twintigste Eeuw, Hoorn.

American English wasn't good enough or because they turned out to be wearing German underwear beneath their American uniforms.

Over a front of 125 kilometres, from Monschau to Echternach, the German military force faced a total of 85,000 American soldiers. Initially the German action had some success and the American troops came under very great pressure. However, their indomitability was best characterised by the Battle of Bastogne. On 21 December the Germans surrounded the town. But when German officers came to demand surrender, the American commanding officer General Anthony McAuliffe answered 'Nuts'. Or at least that's how the story goes, because in fact the general hesitated over his answer for a long time and the German officer who had to communicate the answer didn't quite understand what the general meant by it. Four days later General Patton relieved the town.

On 24 December the German offensive became stuck at the Maas. Weather conditions also improved, which meant that the Allies were able to use their air power. By 27 January 1945 the battle was over. It had lasted five weeks, cost fifty thousand lives and had changed the front line hardly at all.

Sixty years on, the Battle of the Bulge still fires the imagination. Heroic combat encounters, in exceptionally bad climatic conditions, have given rise to many stories and myths, which are reflected in eleven museums in Belgium and Luxembourg.

Cold and hunger played a major role at the end of the war. The first things that the German soldiers took from their American prisoners of war were not weapons, but provisions. Hunger and cold also played a major role in the Netherlands. From September 1944 (after the Battle of Arnhem) a genuine crisis arose in those parts of the Netherlands that had not yet been liberated. Three factors played a part in this: the supply of coal from the mines in the already liberated South Limburg was cut off; the railway strike imposed from London by the Dutch government; and finally the actions of the German occupiers. As a response to the railway strike, transport by water was prohibited, supplies and machines were taken away and the transport of foodstuffs to the west of the country was banned for six weeks. On top of all this misery came a particularly harsh winter, with 26 days of frost in January 1945. In the western Netherlands rationing had already been introduced in October 1944: 1 loaf of bread and 1 kilo of potatoes per week. For the first time since the Middle Ages the Netherlands was experiencing a real famine. Long queues shuffled along at the central soup kitchens. The average ration, which in October 1944 still contained 1,300 calories a day, sank to 340 calories a day in February 1945. City-dwellers went to the countryside to obtain produce direct from the farmers. During this period an estimated 50,000 Dutch people a day were searching for food. Tulip bulbs and sugar beet regularly featured on the menu. And there was no fuel either. In the towns, abandoned houses were demolished for wood. In Amsterdam alone 20,000 trees were felled and even the timbers between the tramlines were torn up. More than ten thousand Dutch people certainly died as a direct result of the famine. Many also succumbed to all manner of diseases, to which they had very little resistance.

Towards the end of the war, large-scale food aid could finally be provided. Allied planes dropped food parcels. In total more than ten million tons of food were dropped and more than 5,000 flights were made. Flour was brought in from Sweden via the ports in the North and this was used to bake 'Zweeds Wittebrood' (Swedish white bread).

For Dutch people who experienced the famine winter, the liberation still tastes of white bread.

Dirk van Assche
Translated by Laura Watkinson

Air and Emptiness, says the Preacher (from now on)
The New Bible Translation

At the end of October 2004, the long-awaited New Bible Translation (*Nieuwe Bijbelvertaling* or NBV) was presented in Rotterdam and Antwerp. Like other language areas, the Low Countries too now have an ecumenical church Bible. With its inclusive nature and the translation strategies employed (it is faithful to the source text and focused on the target language), the New Bible Translation is to some extent comparable with the Revised English Bible, although the New Bible Translation appears to be more ecumenical (with Catholics involved from the beginning) and organised in a more consistent fashion. Just as Protestants in English-speaking areas have had to free themselves from the King James Bible, so Dutch-speaking Protestants, almost exclusively to be found in the Netherlands, have had to defy the authoritative power of the 1637 *Statenvertaling*, or States' Translation. On the other hand, what most distinguishes this new version from the majority of English translations is perhaps that for the first time the translators have taken into account the literary character of the Bible without being influenced by an 'Authorised Version' and have sought to reproduce this in their translation. A most daring undertaking.

Dozens of translators, exegetes and Dutch language experts worked on the translation for more than ten years. The interdenominational project was given the working title NBV; now it's called the '*Nieuwe Bijbelvertaling*' and is supported by over twenty denominations. It is the Low Countries' first ecumenical church Bible; the *Groot Nieuws Bijbel* (Great News Bible) was indeed also an interdenominational initiative, but it was primarily intended for people who don't go to church very much. This time the intended readership was mainly the church community of practising Christians.

Yet this translation is also looking to reach an audience outside church circles. After all, the Bible is also a cultural text, perhaps *the* cultural text of West-

European society. Without some knowledge of the Bible it is impossible to look at paintings, read poetry or, more generally, to understand the Western value system. Nowadays the Bible can increasingly count on interest from outside the church, from intellectuals and in education; for example, through the debate with Islam. Within the church in Flanders there are also hundreds of family groups and dozens of reading circles where the Bible is studied as a source of spiritual inspiration.

In addition to this, in the field of exegesis but also elsewhere, people have started to read the Bible as a literary text. More than ever before, people have come to appreciate its special literary power. You no longer have to be a believer to appreciate the Bible: secular people in the twenty-first century read the Bible as they read Homer, Dante or Shakespeare, for literary enjoyment and general cultural education. Lay organisations such as the Dutch Bible Society (Nederlands Bijbelgenootschap) and the Catholic Bible Foundation (Katholieke Bijbelstichting), which with their Flemish counterparts are responsible for the dissemination of the Bible, have found the literary and cultural aspects a good starting point for making the Bible better known to more people. So the New Bible Translation is being published not only on the traditional church publishing circuit, but also as part of Athenaeum's literary series, the Gouden Reeks. This means that in Dutch-speaking regions the Bible now belongs to the canon of world literature, alongside Boccaccio and Cervantes.

The cultural significance of the Bible and of this Bible translation is particularly great in the Dutch-speaking area. In the Netherlands the New Bible Translation is replacing the now outdated NBG translation, which still relies heavily on the seventeenth-century States' Translation (*Statenvertaling*). In Flanders and the Catholic areas of the Netherlands the translation sits alongside the Willibrord Translation (*Willibrordvertaling*), a new, complete translation from the source languages published in 1995. The two translations, the New Bible Translation and the Willibrord Translation, used similar translation principles. Both attempt to reproduce the source text as

Detail from a *Vanitas* painting by Cornelis de Vos, 17th century. Herzog Anton Ulrich Museum, Braunschweig.

faithfully as possible in modern Dutch. In practice this means that every translation is based on close textual analysis and interpretation and that not only exegetes, but also experts on the Dutch language, have played a role in the translation process. But the New Bible Translation has taken more account of the literary character of some books of the Bible than the Willibrord Translation did. The work was also more systematic and carried out with more input from expert readers, so-called 'supervisors' and literary specialists. Each individual translation is the result of teamwork, firstly between an exegete and an expert on the Dutch language, and then also with as great a contribution as possible from revisers. In addition to this the Dutch Bible Society, which set up the project together with the Catholic Bible Foundation, provided impressive financial support to fund the professional organisation of the whole translation project. Finally, a Flemish readers' panel ensured that the Dutch of the translation could also be used in Flanders.

All these differences mean that the New Bible Translation, with its consistently high exegetical and linguistic quality, should come across as more consistent than the Willibrord Translation, and so become the standard Dutch translation of the Bible. In practice, of course, every translation has its own place, because each is always also an interpretation of the original text. Rather than making other translations redundant, the New Bible Translation adds something not only to our understanding of the Bible, but also to the Dutch language.

To give some impression of this literary approach and the relationship to the Willibrord Translation, I would like to take as an example a well-known passage from the Bible: the beginning of the Book of Ecclesiastes. The King James Version reads as follows: 'Vanity of vanities, saith the Preacher, vanity of vanities; all is vanity,' and the traditional Dutch translation of the key phrase has likewise been 'ijdelheid der ijdelheden' (vanity of vanities). The Willibrord Translation has: 'IJl en ijdel, zegt Prediker, / ijl en ijdel, alles is ijdel' (empty and vain, says the Preacher, / empty and vain, all is vain). The New Bible Translation says: 'Lucht en leegte, zegt Prediker, / lucht en leegte, alles is leegte' (air and emptiness, says the Preacher, / air and emptiness, all is emptiness). Both these Dutch translations have replaced the traditional translation; the new translations are more literal and at the same time more in keeping with Dutch language use. The original Hebrew 'havel havalim' literally means something between 'vapour of vapours' and 'fleetingness of fleetingnesses'. The Dutch 'ijl' and 'lucht' clearly refer to the literal meaning of the Hebrew, but the Hebrew way of expressing a superlative, which was imitated in the earlier

translation, has now been replaced by a more usual Dutch formulation. Not as Aart Schippers' recent translation did, by giving only the figurative sense and turning it into a superlative: 'uiterst absurd' (most absurd), but by adding a word that alliterates with the previous one: 'ijdel' (vain) in the case of the Willibrord, and 'leegte' (emptiness) in the New Bible Translation. The alliteration is intended to retain the suggestion of the superlative. It would have been just about possible to use the formulation 'uiterst ijl', but not 'uiterst luchtig'.

'IJdel' can still mean 'vain' in the sense of 'futile' in modern Dutch, but like the English 'vain' it is more often used to describe a self-important show-off. That is a moral connotation that doesn't feature in the original. The New Bible Translation takes a radical approach and goes for a completely different translation: 'leegte' (emptiness). This word fits seamlessly (almost tautologically when it has the meaning 'nothing, nothingness') with the word 'lucht' (air) and has at most an existential connotation which is consistent with the contents of Ecclesiastes. The reason the translators give for their choice of 'lucht' is the context: in the verses that follow there is reference to the sun, the wind and the rivers. So 'lucht' (air) fits in perfectly with those nature metaphors. In addition to this, it turns out that the translation can be inserted without difficulty in the many places where it occurs in the text. In short, the choice of 'lucht en leegte' (air and emptiness) is rather more sophisticated, daring and ultimately more efficient from a literary point of view than 'ijl en ijdel' (empty and vain). And a glance at a number of English Bible translations shows that from an international perspective too the New Bible Translation can well be described as innovative.

Paul Gillaerts
Translated by Laura Watkinson

Bijbel: Het Oude Testament, De deuterocanonieke boeken,
Het Nieuwe Testament (3 vols.). Amsterdam: Athenaeum -
Polak & Van Gennep, 2004. (www.denieuwebijbelvertaling.nl
and www.denieuwebijbelvertaling.be)

Speaking Dutch – Past, Present and Future

All around the world today, English, as the language of globalisation, is rapidly spreading everywhere. China already has 200 million English speakers, Chile has just decided to make English an obligatory second language after Spanish, Germany has instituted 500 new MA courses that are taught in English, and even if the European Union (EU) is officially multilingual, in reality we may well be heading – as Robert Phillipson has suggested – towards an English-only Europe.

In a number of EU member states this develop-ment has triggered debate about the future of their own national language. French, for example, which is in a very strong position with 350 million speak-ers worldwide, is steadily losing ground to English in international communications, trade, entertainment and scientific publishing. In these domains the fu-ture of French may well depend on whether, and how effectively, the EU's multilingualism can be made to work. This situation – coming as it does after centu-ries of a single national language policy imposed by the French state – of course involves a major cultural change for the French.

The language issue has also come up in the Low Countries, where Dutch, with 22 million speakers, ranks number seven among the official languages of the EU. Both in Flanders and the Netherlands – just as in France – the language has the active support of the state, and it is well-established in the me-dia, politics and the education system. In contrast to French, however, Dutch is a polycentric language, with two main centres, the Holland/Randstad area in the Netherlands and the Flanders/Brabant area in Belgium. While the two centres share the same standard language, they also – as Robert Howell has pointed out – represent two sharply contrasting kinds of nationalism. In Flanders and Belgium, for example, as in France, the language is enshrined in the constitution, whereas in the Netherlands, as in Britain and the USA, it is not.

The difference between the two centres is clearly apparent in two recent books on the history of the Dutch language, respectively *The Story of Flemish* (Het verhaal van het Vlaams, 2003) by Roland Wille-myns and Wim Daniels, and *Language is Made by People. The Making of General Standard Dutch* (Taal is mensenwerk. Het ontstaan van het ABN, 2004) by Nicoline van der Sijs.

Willemyns and Daniels start with the Middle Ages, when the cities of Flanders formed the hub of the European economy until the Spanish sack of Antwerp in 1585, when some hundred thousand Flemings fled to Holland. Amongst them was the mathematician Simon Stevin (1548-1620) from Bruges, who exerted a major influence on the development of the Dutch language in the north. For the southern Netherlands, however, this was a major cultural, intellectual and economic disaster. Ruled from abroad – first from Madrid, then Vienna, then Paris – they fell prey to the onslaught of French, especially after 1750. Later, in the nineteenth century, when Belgium had gained its independence, again French was the dominant lan-guage.

The history of Flemish offered by Willemyns and Daniels is laced with all kinds of new and surpris-ing data, for example about the continuing use in the eighteenth century of the vernacular in administra-tion, the courts and the schools; about the low levels of literacy in Dutch and the widespread use of local dialect; and about the cultural tradition kept alive by Flemish writers such as Willem Verhoeven and Jan Baptist Verlooy. For the nineteenth century too they report some interesting discoveries. For example, at the time there were more Dutch-speaking people living in Flanders than up north in the Netherlands. And during the brief reunion with the Netherlands between 1815 and 1830, the Dutch language policy of King William I (1814-1840) was actually far more successful than previously thought. By the end of his fifteen-year rule the use of Dutch in Flanders had be-come quite widespread, and this in turn provided the foundation for the Flemish Movement and its long and difficult but ultimately successful struggle for linguistic and cultural rights in Belgium.

As Willemyns and Daniels conclude, '*Flanders to-day is a monolingual state within federal Belgium; Dutch is the official language of the majority of the population and of the wealthiest part of the country. All the things that determine the prestige of a language can be found in Flanders today, and as long as this situation does not change, there is nothing that can threaten the status, the function and the prestige of Dutch in Belgium.'*

Van der Sijs, by contrast, takes as her starting point the seventeenth-century Dutch Republic, and keeps her focus throughout on the development of the standard language in the North. Her book contains a series of solid chapters on the historical development of Dutch spelling, pronunciation, morphology, grammar and lexicon, and on the many people (*'Dramatis Personae'*) who over the centuries have shaped the modern Dutch standard language. Amongst the illustrations there are a number of good language maps.

Of particular interest are the data she presents on migration and the demography of the past. In the seventeenth century, half the population of Amsterdam consisted of immigrant speakers of Low German, and these have exerted a major influence on the further development of Dutch. It is true that many other languages were in use in Amsterdam at the time – Latin in academic, legal and theological circles, French by the Huguenot refugees, Spanish, Portuguese and Hebrew by the Sephardic Jews, Italian in the domains of commerce and music, Malay in the printing works of the East India Company (VOC) – but the demographic factor has been decisive. A large majority of the people in Amsterdam spoke Dutch, and the extensive diphthongisation which was then common in the backstreets and which was definitely not the norm for civilised pronunciation has since become the common standard throughout the Netherlands. As Van der Sijs shows with many interesting details, Dutch then also became the main language of the Bible and the Protestant church, of the schools, politics, the law, science and literature.

However, developments in neighbouring Flanders are mentioned only when Van der Sijs gives a comparative review of the differences between Dutch as spoken in the Netherlands and Belgian Dutch. Her list of *Dramatis Personae* mentions a fair number of Flemings, but these are almost all different from those mentioned by Willemyns and Daniels. Her account of Simon Stevin is much more detailed than theirs, but that is because he played such an important role in the formation of the Northern Dutch standard. King William I, however, is not mentioned in her book.

These differences reflect the general relationship between the Flemish and the Dutch. They may be neighbours in Europe and they may speak the same language, but centuries of history have left a legacy, and here the two books testify to the lively and often productive tension between the two main centres within the Dutch-speaking area. However, as the books also demonstrate, the national border, although in theory abolished under the Schengen Treaty of 1995, continues to represent an important socio-cultural reality. European unification here offers an opportunity for the Netherlands and Flanders to (re-)discover each other as Dutch-speaking neighbours. This is not a simple and straightforward matter, though, and will require a certain toleration for the existing north-south differences within Dutch, as well as an active and effective cooperation in language matters over the longer term. Over the past quarter-century this process has been set in motion and is now well under way, through the Dutch Language Union and the Dutch-Flemish Cultural Treaty, through all kinds of cross-border cooperation, cultural as well as economic, and via deBuren, the joint centre for Dutch and Flemish culture in Europe that opened in Brussels in June 2004.

As for the future, both books take a cautious look at how the twenty-first century may affect the Dutch language. Both expect further change, but again with interesting differences in emphasis. Alongside the uniform standard language of today, Van der Sijs expects an increasing range of variation in Dutch, due to pressure from regiolects, informal group languages, the ethnic Dutch of immigrant minorities, and English (which is being used more and more in the Dutch education system). She is optimistic about the vitality of the language. Dutch will definitely not disappear; it will become different, of course, but no less strong. And again, just as in the seventeenth century, demography will be the key – the fact that so many people today are speaking Dutch. Willemyns and Daniels too are confident that the Dutch language in Belgium is not under threat, at least not from the inside. They expect a further divergence between the North, where the new 'Polder Dutch' (*Poldernederlands*) will grow and expand, and the South which will see more and more 'Beautiful Flemish' (*Schoon Vlaams*). To counterbalance this, they add, a large-scale language planning effort will be needed for the longer term.

In this context it is really extremely interesting to see that neither of the books spends much time on English. English may have become an unofficial second language in both Flanders and Holland today, but there appears to be no need to discuss this, since it is used predominantly with English-speaking foreigners and not by the Dutch and Flemish amongst themselves. There is a simple but crucial message here for language policy makers – the future of the Dutch language is going to be determined by the millions of people who speak it and want to speak it.

Reinier Salverda

Howell, Robert B., 'The Low Countries: a study in sharply contrasting nationalisms'. In: Stephen Barbour & Catie Carmichael (eds.), *Language and Nationalism in Europe*. Oxford: Oxford University Press, 2000, pp. 130-150.

Phillipson, Robert, *English-Only Europe? Challenging Language Policy*. London: Routledge, 2003. 240 pp.

Treffers-Daller, Jeanine & Roland Willemyns (eds.), *Language Contact at the Romance-Germanic Language Border*. Clevedon: Multilingual Matters, 2002. 149 pp.

Van der Sijs, Nicoline, *Taal is mensenwerk. Het ontstaan van het ABN*. The Hague: Sdu Uitgevers, 2004. 718 pp.

Willemyns, Roland & Wim Daniels, *Het Verhaal van het Vlaams. De Geschiedenis van het Nederlands in de Zuidelijke Nederlanden*. Antwerpen/ Utrecht: Standaard/Het Spectrum, 2003. 399 pp.

An Intractable Cathedral of Language
The Poetry of Kees Ouwens

The first poem in the collection *Dream* (Droom, 1988) by the recently-deceased Dutch poet Kees Ouwens (1947-2004) opens by speaking of a journey, a journey into the past. '*A good twenty years we had to travel back in time.*' The reference is to the beginning of his career as a writer, the year 1968, which saw the appearance of his poetic debut, the collection *Arcadia*. It is the period when he shuts the door on his youth and leaves his home village of Zeist, a community situated in the centre of the Netherlands on the border between well-wooded sandy country and the archetypal clay plains of Holland with their polders, meadows and farms, a landscape that is omnipresent in Ouwens' work.

The world of his youth underlies the whole of Ouwens' writing. This is certainly true of his poetry, but applies equally to a number of his novels. Both *The Strategy* (De Strategie, 1968) and *Loneliness through Pleasure* (De eenzaamheid door genot, 1987) are set in and around the castles and country houses found in Ouwens' native region. In an interview Ouwens put it as follows: '*There are lovely stretches of country around Zeist, where I come from. When I started writing poems I became susceptible to their beauty. Between the ages of eighteen and twenty-one I visited a number of places in that landscape very regularly either on foot or by bike. In those years my emotional life was shaped, and I acquired a sensibility. They are an important source. Looking back, it was a mythical period.*'

When he was about seventeen Ouwens broke with the Catholic tradition in which he had been brought up, and in which he had risen to the position of altar boy. There is some irony in the appearance of the Virgin Mary in Ouwens' first collection as '*the chubby mother*' and the '*merciful whore*'. The break with his childhood faith and the loss of a self-evident meaning to life is the principal driving force in Ouwens' creative work. The conferring of mythical status on nature and landscape in his writing can be seen as a surrogate for the loss of faith. In the collection *Stuck* (Klem, 1984) the sense of a lost Arcadia, a past that

Kees Ouwens (1947-2004).
Photo by Klaas Koppe.

Linguistically *Stuck* pulls out all the stops as a defence against the futility of youth and the condition of being *'lost in dreams'*. The last verse of the poem 'Detention' ('Detentie') puts it in a way that for Ouwens is exceptionally simple and in a tone that seems to point forward to the more sober orchestration of the collection *Dream*:

I remembered the day I bade home farewell;
showing my stature
turning my back on my street
outgrowing my district
abandoning my village;
planning to clothe myself;
being irrevocably my footwear and
insurmountably my appearance.

The style of this poetry and the size of the oeuvre – the cumulative collection *All the Poems So Far* (Alle gedichten tot dusver, 2002) contains over 500 pages of poetry – suggest a huge rocky massif, whose intransigent form is intriguing but which seems barely accessible. An extraordinary body of work, certainly when seen against the background of the fairly flat landscape of Dutch-language poetry in the last two decades of the twentieth century. Despite its somewhat hermetic quality the work has always enjoyed ample critical attention, especially because of its exceptionally driven and 'authentic' nature. Ouwens has the reputation of being mainly a poets' poet. His work also suggests an intractable cathedral of language, constantly under construction, composed in countless different styles to the design of a monomaniac architect, cutting things down to the poetic bone, in search of a sacred space to celebrate the rites of his poetry. An oeuvre like a temple, referring only to itself, without a god or a doorway admitting a wider public.

The collection *Dream* (1988) can be regarded as Ouwens' most accessible. It is one of the principal pillars supporting the mythical edifice of his poetry. Its content represents the result of a poetic investigation of the purport of the poet's own lot, in which connections are made with broad social, ecclesias-

has shut itself off, also becomes a prominent theme. It confronts the poet with the question of a possible future and a possible justification of his own existence. The option of withdrawing completely from the visible world is restricted by the presence of one's own body, which links the ego to reality and brings with it the promise of youth. In the poem 'Robe' Ouwens formulates this as follows:

and I could be nothing but the repetition of
myself under the roof beams of the youth of this body,
I could be nothing but the utter destruction of what
my father destined me for in the glorious light of
progression
and of the unfolding of a final goal, yes, I married
myself, for I was completely ignorant of the materiality
and the inescapability of my choice.

tical and economic developments in the post-war Netherlands.

In a sense *Dream* represents a pivotal point in Ouwens' development as a poet. It is also his most 'committed' collection, with a striking use of the 'we' form that makes the poems appear to tell the story of a generation: the generation that grew up in the period of post-war reconstruction in an ideologically polarised society and in the 1960s became socially active in a relatively prosperous, secular welfare state. In some ways there is a close thematic connection between these poems and Michel Houellebecq's *The Elementary Particles* (Particules élémentaires). In *Dream* Ouwens depicts a generation for whom the abandonment of traditional religious, philosophical and moral structures led to personal upheaval. The empirical life style embraced by individualism did not produce an existential solution that was felt to be meaningful. *'I was a man, not a boy any more'*:

So I was a product of the final year of the war and grew up during reconstruction
Later I dwelt in abundance's house of cards
Beneath the roof of illusion I took shelter
In the lee of the affluent state I frittered away my time till I wasn't a boy any more but a man and although I rejected the latter state the cards were shuffled once more the house was demolished and my mature self grew desolate

After *Dream*, which was a merciless commentary on the poet's own existence, Ouwens' poetry gradually moved beyond the sensory fixations characteristic of the poems in *Intimate Acts* (Intieme handelingen, 1973), *Like a Stream* (Als een beek, 1975) and *Stuck* (1984). In later collections Ouwens' poetry moved markedly in the direction of a kind of earth-centred mysticism, in which 'light' often makes it possible to experience reality as transcendental and to behold the sublime. It is poetry that in a supra-personal way tries to lift a corner of

'Maya's Veil' ('Maya's sluier'), the title (taken from the philosopher Schopenhauer) of a poem from the collection *Of the Loser and the Light Source* (Van de verliezer & de lichtbron, 1997).

The fact that all Ouwens' later work, from the collection *Dismissals* (Afdankingen, 1995) onwards, centres on saying the unsayable, uttering the unutterable and describing the indescribable has not made his poetry any easier to understand. On the other hand, many poems can be traced back to primeval images, deriving mainly from the Bible, such as the image of the river of life. *'On the bank of the ego, the self rests,'* runs a line from the collection *Mythologies* (Mythologieën, 2000), which speaks of a kind of *'knowing that blinds me'*, of a *'foretaste'* of the *'other'*, which remains invisible until it is suddenly revealed in the late sunlight at the mouth of the River Scheldt, *'brilliantly broken on Vlissingen's roadstead / and with a sweetness we cannot attain'*.

Nevertheless, in Ouwens' later collections the imploding formulations, the fractured verse forms, the line breaks, the white spacing, the fragmenting typography and the 'dismissive' quality constantly give the impression that this is poetry that seeks to negate itself, strives to dissolve into the inimitable, like scaffolding that is no longer required.

Kees van Domselaar
Translated by Paul Vincent

The collection *All the Poems So Far* (Alle gedichten tot dusver, 2002) was published by Meulenhoff, Amsterdam. (www.meulenhoff.nl)

'Becoming the part you are playing'
Marek van der Jagt aka Arnon Grunberg

Like his alter ego Arnon Grunberg (1971-), the young Dutch novelist Marek van der Jagt (1967-) writes life stories. His 2000 debut, *De geschiedenis van mijn kaalheid* (lit. – as in the American translation – 'The Story of My Baldness', but widely translated as *Amour fou*, after its main theme), could be seen as a novel of adolescence or *Bildungsroman*. His second novel, *Gstaad 95-98*, which appeared in 2002, goes further, following a life far into adulthood.

This resulted in the unique phenomenon of a writer being honoured twice in his lifetime for producing the outstanding debut of the preceding two years, since Grunberg had received the award for his own first novel, the masterly study of adolescence *Blue Mondays* (Blauwe maandagen, 1994).

Actually the latter book is the only one of his novels to be set entirely in his own country, in the prosperous Jewish world of South Amsterdam, the Greenwich Village and Long Island of the Dutch capital. If there is one striking feature of the rapidly growing oeuvre of this master-narrator, it is its cosmopolitan character. *Silent Extras* (Figuranten, 1997), for instance, is set mainly in New York, where the author has lived for the past ten years, as is *Phantom Pain* (Fantoompijn, 2000), which in 2001 won the Netherlands' main annual fiction prize, sponsored by a Dutch bookshop chain. In his most recent large-scale novel from 2004, The *Jewish Messiah* (De joodse messias), Basel is the principal location for the complex lives of his characters. This Swiss city close to the border with France and Germany is also where the main characters of Van der Jagt's *Gstaad 95-98* find a temporary refuge, at a midway point in their sinful course through life. As Marek van der Jagt the writer has positioned his characters in Central and Western Europe respectively.

It will consequently come as no surprise that the literary roots of Grunberg/Van der Jagt are to be found much less in Dutch literature than in the Jewish American and Central European novel tradition. In *The Low Countries 9* Frans de Rover pointed, for example, to the link between Grunberg's first novel *Blauwe maandagen* and Salinger's *The Catcher in the Rye*. The tragicomic approach in substance and style that is Grunberg's hallmark is equally evident in the two novels of Van der Jagt. The author shows an affinity with writers of international stature who explore the world of Jewish immigrant families in the US – writers like Philip Roth, whose *Portnoy's Complaint* is definitely among Grunberg's favourites, Saul Bellow, the chron-

icler of the oversexed Jewish-American intellectual in crisis (in *Herzog*), or Bernard Malamud. In the work of Grunberg/Van der Jagt the father is a failure, the mother a hysterical nymphomaniac, and all the members of the household go their own headstrong way. Harmony is nowhere to be found. Grunberg thoroughly explores the picture of Jewish togetherness. In addition he shows some of the same boldness with which the Czech master of *The Unbearable Lightness of Being*, Milan Kundera, records the ways his characters enter into sexual relationships and regard life as a task that they must somehow fulfil. Van der Jagt/Grunberg's main characters are acutely aware of the role they play on the stage of life.

As an essayist Grunberg pondered the '*consolation of slapstick*' and that phrase, which he attributes to Buster Keaton and others to Woody Allen, brings us to the heart of the work of Grunberg / Van der Jagt, whose greatness lies in its humour and in the author's ability to expand the tragic developments in which his characters become entangled because of their apparently directionless lives, into full-blown tragicomedies. Almost every page of Van der Jagt's two novels triggers hilarity, although the facts described are as gruesome as the final outcome, particularly in *Gstaad 95-98*.

An obsession

'*At the age of fourteen I read about* amour fou. *A few weeks later I had made my decision; man's vocation is* amour fou. *Exactly what it was, I did not know;* amour fou *came without a beginner's manual.*' In Van der Jagt's debut Marek, the main character and narrator, looks back on his life. He tests out his theory on a maid. Don't try it again, she says, it'll pass of its own accord. *Amour fou* becomes an obsession. '*Like comparing a twenty-volume encyclopaedia with a piece of toilet paper*', is how Marek experiences the qualitative difference between his own diminutive penis and the member of his elder brother Pavel. He might have an eternal smile on his face, but his prick was useless. This is the obsession which with its tragic-comic consequences preoccupies him throughout the story. Two girls from Luxembourg, whom he picks up in a bar, make it clear just how modest his obsession with *amour fou* will have to be. What a contrast with his nymphomaniac mother, a Viennese opera singer who claims the scalp of one artist after another! This woman is something of an oddity among the many that feature in Grunberg's and Van der Jagt's stories, a woman with lots of money, in an environment that generates money. Whatever the narrators, alter egos of the writer, may do, they are never short of money, they are awash with it, and never need to earn any. Giving out-of-school coaching to Max, the victim of a traffic accident, is simply an attempt by Marek to see if he can do it and so gain some self-respect. Older women are constantly falling for the youthful protagonist. He puts up with this in a detached way and is seldom really involved in what happens to him.

Marek's family is just as chaotic as Arnon's is in Grunberg's first novel. Everyone lives in their own little world. All the characters in this work are essentially lonely, egocentric individuals, who wherever possible exploit other individuals. Grunberg does not have a high opinion of humankind. For example, none of Marek's family react to his announcement that he is in the grip of an *amour fou*. So Marek decides *'to be a dwarf trapped in the body of a medium-sized giant'* – and those who know their literature can take this as a wink in the direction of Günther Grass' *Die Blechtrommel*, whose hero Oskar decides at the age of three to remain a dwarf as a protest against hypocrisy. A hilarious image: *'To understand what it feels like to be a dwarf, I started walking on my haunches at home. And not long afterward I summoned the courage to walk about in public in a squatting position.'*

His mother is the dominant presence in his life. *'Anyone who knew no better would think that promiscuity was mama's sole aim in life. But she was not a slave to her lust, nor was she driven by money worries. She was simply looking for something that was nowhere to be found in this world. Mama wanted to be resplendent and awaken desire. But those whose sole aim is to be resplendent do not exist when the other person is not looking.'*

The unmistakable climax of this book is the moment when the protagonist realises that his obsession was a huge mistake. *'All that remained of* amour fou *at this moment was a desire for vengeance'*, vengeance directed at everything and everyone that has previously claimed his attention, from his genitals and his mother to the French teacher who introduced him to the surrealists and *'to the civilisation I didn't believe in'*.

From now on all that remains for him is the imitation of an amour fou, experienced with an older lady, by whom he feels deflowered. He exclaims pathetically: *'I'm the jamming station and all of you are the silence, I rattle the gates of you family graves, I bring the dead back to life with my whip.'* That has a New Testament ring, as if Christ himself were cleansing the temple! His imagination is more powerful than reality, Marek realises; in fact, he sees only his own creations. He is obsessed by the thought that his genitals will disappear completely and even a plastic surgeon cannot convince him otherwise. Only when his now terminally ill mother forces him to take to the mountains with her does the obsession disappear. After she has revealed mockingly to Marek that his father is not his biological father, he shakes himself free of the woman who for so long has kept him under her thumb. *'With all the strength I possessed, I pushed her away from me. Because she was laughing. At a moment when I saw nothing to laugh about.'*

Marek is subsequently given penis-enlarging homeopathic remedies by a woman he had met in a pub at the start of the novel, and this introduces the story of his baldness, which provided a title for the novel's original version. In this woman Marek does unexpectedly find his great *amour fou*, but also loses all his hair. Whereupon the woman dumps him. End of *amour fou*. The grotesque wheel has come full circle.

Chronique scandaleuse

Even more than *Amour fou* Van der Jagt's second – in fact Grunberg's seventh – novel has the character of a picaresque epic-cum-*chronique scandaleuse*. The main characters are the narrator and his mother

Mathilde. A product of the hasty copulation of this woman with a French down dealer travelling through Heidelberg, François Lepeltier learns from his mother how to steal like a magpie. He is not only her accomplice in crime, but throughout his life is her only true lover. The two are an inseparable pair of rogues. As a baby he hides the booty acquired by his mother as a chambermaid in hotels and boarding houses under his soiled nappies. From Heidelberg the action moves to Baden-Baden. There mother and son enter the service of an elderly Italian couple; the wife seeks sexual satisfaction with the mother, while the son endures the advances of the husband. This episode ends with the electrocution of the Italian woman by a heater placed in her bath, after which mother and son come under the protection of her husband. When the latter sexually assaults the boy, Mathilde skewers him with the bread knife. This is followed by episodes where the son practises as a phoney dentist among illegal Turkish immigrants in Stuttgart and presents himself as the ski instructor Bruno Ritter near Basel, where he concentrates on the peaceful deflowering of young ski pupils. The story, as shocking as it is hilarious, climaxes with the murder of a young girl by Bruno Ritter, now working as a wine waiter in the Palace Hotel in Gstaad, who has meanwhile entirely lost touch with normality. He is universally denounced as the Monster of Gstaad. Despite all the hilarity it soon becomes clear to the reader that Ritter's infantile fixation will end in disaster. Every aspect of his behaviour, particularly as evoked in his physical contact with his mother, points to his sexual frustration, his inability to progress beyond the anal phase.

As in Van der Jagt's first novel the last period of a life gives its name to the whole book, since Gstaad is only the place where François' life takes its decisive turn. For three years as a wine waiter at the Palace Hotel he will play the gigolo before meeting his final downfall. Actually no one and nothing matters here except his mother, but life has to be acted out. And the main character proves incapable of doing so, at least when it comes to finding the right way. Again the neurotic falls prey to obsessions and compulsive

behaviour. These are his undoing. *'My Mathilde. She was real, I was imitation. When she died, a life came to an end, when I died only a game would end.'* Having assumed this role, he flies kites that he has made himself in his bachelor home. *'In the superfluous world my kites provided a pleasant distraction.'*

'I had become the person I had at first only been playing,' says François later when he has passed himself off as a dentist. *'And that is the essence of happiness. People who can't be anything have to become the part they are playing.'* Here *Gstaad 95-98* also touches on the dominant theme of the oeuvre of Grunberg / Van der Jagt. In his books he puts into practice Sartre's assertion that *'to be is to be seen'*, and in so doing, for all the larger-than-life effects used by the author, often to the great amusement of the reader, he comes very close to the everyday reality of our TV society. *'Identity is closely bound up with how other people see you'* says Grunberg in a recent interview. That one can control this is proved by the main character of *Gstaad 95-98*. I would also refer to what one could call the *Blechtrommel* effect to explain the determination of the protagonist to create his own identity: *'I stared back with those eyes behind which I had always hidden and behind which I can still hide, the eyes of a backward child that heard everything but understood nothing, that saw everything but retained nothing.'*

Wam de Moor
Translated by Paul Vincent

www.grunberg.nl

The Story of my Baldness was published by The Other Press, NY (tr. Todd Armstrong). 264 pp., 2004. ISBN 1-59051-122-0 (www.otherpress.com). In this article the translations of quotes from that novel are Paul Vincent's.

Music

The Brussels Jazz Orchestra: from Local Substitutes to Big-Timers

The end-of-year issue (Dec.1979/Jan.1980) of the French magazine *Jazz Hot* was devoted entirely to big bands. As well as providing a nostalgic retrospective of the golden years of the rhythmic swing machines, it also looked at some of the hopeful new developments taking place within the large jazz orchestras. This was something of a novelty, given that a quarter of a century ago it was fashionable in some sections of the jazz press to claim that the big bands were ailing anachronisms. As the great stars disappeared from the scene and their orchestras disbanded – Duke Ellington, Count Basie, Woody Herman, Kenny Clarke-Francy Boland, Thad Jones-Mel Lewis and Buddy Rich – it was easy enough to conclude, quite wrongly of course, that the big bands had had their day. In the meantime Gil Evans, George Russell, Toshiko Akiyoshi/Lew Tabackin and others went on creating first-rate music in the USA, while in Europe and surrounding countries numerous public radio big bands enjoyed loyal audiences – WDR Big Band (Cologne); BB Danish Radio; the Belgian Radio and Television corporation's BRT Jazzorkest, together with prominent privately funded bands, such as the Dutch Willem Breuker-Kollektief, the Peter Herbolzheimer Big Band, the Vienna Art Ensemble and Chris McGregor's Anglo-South African band. Soon after that, the Orchestre National de Jazz de France was launched thanks to a state subsidy made available under the French Minister for Culture Jacques Lang. And anyone who attended a concert by the European Community Youth Jazz Orchestra in those days could judge for himself the sort of artistic potential that was around.

So the survival or creation of 'great' jazz orchestras was more a question of enlightened subsidisation, based on a longer-term vision. After all, according to the rhetoric of the number-crunchers, it did not make economic sense to keep these ensembles in being for a mere handful of fans. In such a climate, an orchestra like the BRT Big Band had to go. On March 22nd 1991 they recorded their very last song – an arrangement by vibraphonist Sadi featuring trombonist Marc Godfroid – in the multi-track recording studio in the Flagey building in Brussels. And that was it. No flowers, no accolades. An ensemble which under the inspiring leadership of Etienne Verschueren had made its artistic mark and scored triumphs over the years was laid to rest. But among younger jazz musicians who, as occasional 'substitutes', had had a taste of this orchestra, the flame was far from extinguished. In their view, the big band had certainly not had its day.

In that same year saxophonist Frank Vaganée, trumpeter Serge Plume and trombonist Marc Godfroid, three young and enthusiastic trained musicians with big band experience, came up with the idea of filling the gap and starting afresh with a professionally-run, twenty-four carat big band. With a group of like-minded people they found a temporary rehearsal and concert hall in The Sounds (Ixelles, Brussels) where they held their intensive open rehearsals on Monday evenings, which invariably resulted in a concert (1993). All these young musicians, who were highly skilled both instrumentally and technically, were beginning to reap the benefits of a changed relationship between 'the jazz world' and music education, which had recently opened its doors – albeit very cautiously – to a jazz curriculum encompassing music theory and practice, taught by qualified jazz musicians. This new approach more than illustrated E. Verschueren's adage that a jazz musician can only really express himself freely when he has a very high degree of technical skill. The belief that maximum freedom and successful personal expression could only be acquired after a period of hard slog sounded like a paradox only to a handful of hardcore advocates of unconditional – and now dated – free jazz.

In 1994 the new Brussels Jazz Orchestra (BJO) came up with a basic repertoire that left nobody in any doubt as to its ability, tastes and direction. They made their intentions clear from the outset and resisted any temptation to churn out redundant stock arrangements.

The very first concert recording by what was then Radio 3 comprised highly exacting charts by

The Brussels Jazz
Orchestra.
Photo courtesy of BJO.

(among others) Bill Holman, Thad Jones and Bob Brookmeyer, *the* big band composers of the time, played with spunk and a commitment that was contagious. Things were getting serious; something was definitely in the air. But without financial backing the BJO would not make it, that much was certain. The BJO founders were holding on by their fingernails when at the last minute the Flemish Community granted them a short-term project subsidy. It was a start.

Where there's a will there's often a way

Jazz Middelheim 1995 has to have been one of the BJO's finest moments. It had considerably expanded its repertoire, not least with works by Belgian composers (F. Vaganée, M. Herr, B. Joris, E. Vann). The orchestra's homogeneity was also a talking-point. The enraptured public reactions were reminiscent of the loud applause the BRT -J.O. had received on the

same stage years earlier. Once the band's file had done the lengthy rounds of government offices, its brilliant performances and growing fame finally resulted in a structural four-year subsidy (1999). But even before that (1996) the big band had made a substantial contribution to the historical re-play of an important composition by Louis de Meester, who had integrated an exhilarating jazz episode into his magnum opus *The Temptation of St Anthony* (1957).

Gradually recognition and the financial scope provided by the subsidy gave the BJO momentum and access to a wider circle. The band's first CD, recorded live in the brand-new Cultural Centre in Roeselare during 'Radio 3 in Roeselare', was an immediate success (1997). Scarcely any technical adjustments needed to be made, the quality was amazing, and the reactions in the press (albeit still only local) unanimously favourable.

Middelheim 1997 was another milestone in the BJO's career: Jean Warland, the former bass player from the prestigious WDR Big Band, was wildly enthusiastic about the orchestra's virtuosity and potential, which had come as a real revelation to him, and he was determined that together they should pay homage to that other Belgian monument to big band composition, his friend Francy Boland. The sound of the brilliant charts once performed by the historic Clark-Boland Big Band filled the tent in a memorable Middelheim 1997 concert. The applause is still ringing in the ears of all those lucky enough to be there.

The structural subsidy awarded in 1999 not only enabled the big band to pay for advertising, legal, accounting and technical support, it also meant that musical director Frank Vaganée could at last concentrate on the music. Moreover, the subsidy provided some – limited – scope for inviting famous soloists from abroad for a series of concerts. Pianist-composer Ken Werner (USA) flew over for Middelheim '97. Immediately after the ovation he faced the audience and clearly sounded the praises of this orchestra during an impressive, eight-minute eulogy: this really was a godsend, particularly in terms of the band's future prospects. So now we had heard it from the mouth of an American and the band could cast off that 'second-hand' feeling. The era of legitimate artistic self-respect seemed to have dawned. A couple of months earlier congratulations had been sent from just about every jazz department of the ERU (European Radio Union), each of which had made a live contribution to a jazz day devoted to Duke Ellington, simultaneously broadcast in fourteen countries, the USA and Canada included. At the Spinoy Cultural Centre in Mechelen the BJO had recreated the intriguing Far East Suite (Ellington-Strayhorn), based on (incomplete) photocopies of the Ellington charts hastily dispatched by the Smithsonian Institute.

Shortly after the Middelheim concert with Ken Werner, the BJO began to record its second CD at Studio Toots (VRT), with compositions by (among others) Michel Herr, Bert Joris, Erwin Vann and conductor Frank Vaganée: 'The September Sessions'. The CD came out in 2000, and during the Mechelen Jazz Day the public was treated to a thrilling live performance with Bert Joris as the guest artist (June 2000). With the catchy final number of the show Warp 9, a stunt for the saxophone section, Joris gave the orchestra real credence, which could serve as a metaphor for their rapid development: an unstoppable bolide.

After this, what could prevent this orchestra from joining the ranks of award-winning big band composers and leaders like Bill Holman (Nacht Radio 3 – DeSingel Antwerp, Dec. 1999), Maria Schneider (Middelheim 2001), Bob Mintzer and soloists like Jeanne Lee (2000), Toots Thielemans (Middelheim 2001), David Liebman and Philip Catherine?

Transatlantic, etc.

The year 2001 was a particularly busy one for the BJO. January brought its first performance at the annual jazz musicians' fair, the IAJE (International Association for Jazz Educators) in New York, where Ken Werner had proved an energetic promotional pace-setter for the BJO, then still an unknown quantity in America. By the time they returned they were famous and showered with praise and invitations for festivals. At Middelheim 2001 Maria Schneider made no attempt to hide her admiration, and coming from a composer and very demanding conductor who is pretty much the touchstone of every contemporary big band within the imaginary first division, that was praise indeed. Even Toots Thielemans, not really a big band habitué, was clearly delighted to have shared a stage with them. The virtuoso compositions of Bert Joris, combined with his increasingly regular collaboration as guest soloist, raised the BJO's profile to dizzying artistic heights. Once again the biennial Middelheim act proved to be a crucial event for the BJO; indeed, the band can even take much of the credit for setting the tone for the festival. After that the organisers of the gigantic North Sea Festival in The Hague could hardly be indifferent to the BJO's reputation, and the band was invited to play there in 2001 and 2002. Offers of concert tours to Ireland, Luxembourg, France and Spain followed.

The next step was inevitable: Bert Joris' outstanding compositions provided the material for a third CD (a double), again recorded live over two evenings, this time in the jazz-friendly De Werf in Bruges.

For the last couple of years the BJO has also cooperated in the prestigious Hoeilaart competition for young jazz groups. By agreeing to perform live a number of big band scores selected by a professional jury, the BJO does its bit to promote jazz composition. There can be no doubt that when the music is expertly written, it sounds at its best on an instrument like the BJO.

On the basis of his positive experiences to date with the BJO, Ken Werner was keen to undertake a more lasting project with the band; this eventually resulted in CD no 4. Recorded in 2002, *Naked in the Cosmos* was dedicated to and produced by Ken Werner.

A fifth CD with Philip Catherine and Bert Joris is planned for 2005. And among many other commitments, the BJO recently took part in a live multimedia project: *BJO versus the Big White Screen*, in which the orchestra played specially composed pieces to accompany early twentieth-century silent films: a feat of atmospheric creation and synchronisation. There can be no doubt that the BJO is alive and kicking! This superb machine deserves to be challenged, promoted and fostered.

Johan Vandenbossche
Translated by Alison Mouthaan-Gwillim

www.brusselsjazzorchestra.com

Mountaineers of Dutch Pop
(The) Nits: Thirty Years of a Unique Sound

The Nits are a pop group from Amsterdam that was formed in 1974. It was a somewhat confusing year for pop music. Rock had been 'dead' for several years following the Beatles split and the death of a number of 1960s pop icons such as Jimi Hendrix, Janis Joplin and Jim Morrison. The charts were full of shrieking men with lacquered hair, lipstick and mascara, clad in glitter suits and platform boots. Bubblegum rock and glam rock heralded the return of the 'throwaway' single. The first seeds of Dutch-language pop music were germinating in the Netherlands, and Flanders had just discovered its future hero Raymond van het Groenewoud. The anti-commercial bands were rock-

ing in the pubs of Great Britain, and pub rock was elevated to a genre in its own right.

This was the period during which the founder members of The Nits, Hans Hofstede (who changed his first name to Henk in 1993) and Alex Roelofs, were studying at the Rietveld Academy. Rob Kloet joined the group later. The first Nits single, 'Yes or No', was released in 1977, the year in which punk made its breakthrough on the international music scene. From that moment it was clear: The Nits were not punk, but an arty band influenced by the New Wave scene (Television, Blondie, Talking Heads) that was evolving at CBGB's in New York. The Nits took the charts by storm in 1979 with 'Tutti Ragazzi' and the British pop magazine NME named the album *Tent* as runner-up in the category Best Foreign Album. The group's ability to make the most of its commercial potential without following well-trodden paths and making concessions to greedy record companies is largely due to the talents of producer Robert Jan Stips, who joined the group in 1981 as a keyboard player and stayed with them for many years. After *Tent*, The Nits decided to turn professional. By the time they celebrated their 30th anniversary in 2004, they had been professionals for almost twenty-five years. This is an enormous achievement, given that they haven't had many hits. But they have written and sung so many songs that 'everyone' knows, and at least one of those songs will always be remembered: 'In the Dutch Mountains', with 'Adieu, Sweet Bahnhof' and 'Nescio' coming a close second. An appearance at the Roskilde rock festival in Denmark in 1983 launched the group's impressive European career. It is no easy task to win over the highly critical Scandinavians, but The Nits managed it, purely on the strength of their uniqueness and character: the combination of Henk Hofstede's Dutch-English accent and his unique voice is unmistakeable. The Nits have been a constant factor in the pop scene of continental Europe. They sing in English, but it comes out as a sort of euro-Esperanto, a jumble of words from many languages. This is a highly individual solution to the language problem. The group has had to cope with its fair share of disruption as

a succession of producers and group members came and went. Michiel Peters left in 1985. Bass player Joke Geraets made her own mark on the Nits sound. She was with the group during its commercial hey-day from 1986, but had to leave for health reasons in 1990. The group enjoyed international success with *In the Dutch Mountains* (1987), a prime example of their talent that earned them the BV Pop Prize. This was followed by a tour of the Soviet Union and the United States. In 1988, *In the Dutch Mountains* even topped the charts in Austria. In 1989 the band shortened their name to Nits. In the 1990s they established themselves in the world of alternative pop, and in 1991 they opened the New Music Seminar in New York. Hit singles were almost a thing of the past. In 1995 the group made an unexpected comeback with Dutch-language interpretations of Nits numbers combined with old cabaret songs by Freek de Jonge, who translated 'In the Dutch Mountains' as 'Dankzij de Dijken' (Thanks to the Dikes). They worked with De Jonge under the name Frits. Frits 2 followed in 2004, with songs from Freek de Jonge's theatre marathon *The Ageing* (De Vergrijzing). Dutch pop

music made a definitive breakthrough at around this time, thanks to Marco Borsato's huge hit 'De meeste dromen zijn bedrog' (Most Dreams are Deceptions). Nits didn't pursue their Dutch-language experiment, but returned to their familiar world of melancholic skilfulness (and sometimes affectation). Robert Jan Stips parted from The Nits in 1996. His departure was marked with a live concert on television, in collabo-ration with Freek de Jonge and a Finnish shouting choir. This was followed by a period of 'radio silence', and the group appeared to have lost its way. But in 1997 Hofstede and Kloet performed again as Nits in their beloved Finland. In 1998 this revival resulted in *Alankomaat* (Finnish for the Netherlands), a col-laboration with guest musicians from Finland. With Arwen Linneman and Titia van Krieken, the group was complete again. They took the concept of the theatre tour to the whole of Europe in an exhaust-ing series of performances. In 2000 the group per-formed in Japan to help commemorate 400 years of Dutch-Japanese relations. Nits are without doubt among the most remarkable and most tenacious of the Netherlands' cultural ambassadors.

In recent years, the Nits have been doing all the things established bands usually do: reissues, celebrating the usual milestones, combi-tours, solo projects and commissioned compositions. No more struggles now they've reached the top. In 2003 Hofstede released his first solo record in Dutch: *Het draagbare huis* (The Portable House). Robert Jan Stips is the most well-grounded musician of the group, and according to some he is a genius. He is an incredibly active pop musician who has long been involved with other projects and solo activities; among other things, he is Freek de Jonge's composer and accompanist. Stips' commitment to Nits was still strong enough to go on tour with them again. In its current formation (Hofstede, Kloet, Stips, Van Krieken), Nits still performs regularly in the Netherlands and abroad. So anyone who was not around thirty years ago, or has never seen the band perform, still has the opportunity to get to know their work. It is a good sign that, although the group have been with us for so long, their music has not stood still. They are not simply churning out the old favourites for ageing fans. Their music is current and fresh, without losing its Nits trademark. For example, all the material on the 'jubilee' album *1974* is new. This individualistic approach and adventurous sound is an inspiration to talented pop musicians such as the Flemish group Zita Swoon, who always name Nits as one of their greatest influences. For the Nits, Flanders was the obvious place to branch out, and that goes for other distinctive Dutch groups too.

Pop musicians in English-speaking countries usually do not welcome foreign bands that try to compete and encroach on their territory, although informal collaborations are sometimes possible. Kevin Hearn of Barenaked Ladies (from Toronto in Canada) happened to meet Nits when he was in Switzerland. He said they were '*amazing*'. In July 2003, the Barenaked Ladies organised a double concert in Toronto, with Nits as the main act. '*[Their music] has a rare charm and the kind of really good craftsmanship you may not see any more these days*', Hearn explained. The critic Ira Robbins of *Trouser Press* is equally impressed. His characterisation of Hofstede's style as '*Lennonish*

Costelloisms' is spot-on. He qualifies this elsewhere: '*but dreamier, more vulnerable, less venomous*'. The Nits phenomenon is part of a disappearing country: the Netherlands.

Lutgard Mutsaers
Translated by Yvette Mead

www.nits.nl

1978 *The Nits*/1979 *Tent*/1981 *New Flat*/1982 *Work*/1983 *Omsk*/ 1983 *Kilo*/1984 *Adieu, Sweet Bahnhof*/1985 *Henk*/ 1987 *In the Dutch Mountains*/1988 *Hat* (mini-album, 6 tracks)/ 1989 *Urk*/1991 *Giant Normal Dwarf*/1992 *Hjuvi, a Rhapsody in Time* (composer: Robert Jan Stips; Nits with the Radio Symfonie Orkest), live recording/1992 *Ting*/1993 *dAdAdA*/1995 [as Frits, with Freek de Jonge] *Dankzij de dijken*/1996 *Nitsbox: Nest; Vest; Quest* (compilation of old hits, new numbers, studio material and self-produced video clips)/1998 *Alankomaat*/2000 *Nitshits* (compilation cd)/2000 *Wool*/2002 *Songs from Wool* (live) – dvd/ 2003 *1974* + dvd

Comfort without Hope
The Topicality and Relevance of Spinoza

There can be little doubt about the relevance of
Spinoza's thinking. It is reflected in the fact that societies like the Dutch-International Spinoza House
are flourishing, and by the continuing world-wide interest in Spinoza's philosophy in various media and
the arts. The reason for this interest is not hard to
find. Spinoza's thinking is attractive to those who are
trying to make sense of life but who are not, or no
longer, satisfied with traditional religion and find the
alternative varieties of esoteric irrationalism even
less attractive. Spinoza's work seems to succeed in
reconciling a robust acceptance of scientific ideas
and attitudes with sensitivity to the deeper issues of
our existence, such as the desire for a good life and
for salvation. His philosophy has the advantage that it
can be interpreted in two ways, depending on whether one emphasises its rationalism or its more mystical aspects. The *Ethica* can indeed be read either as
a guide to a rationalistic therapy for the good life or
as a description of a contemplative route to true salvation – even though that route is typically Western,
mediated through a Western understanding of nature
and the human psyche.

The enduring appeal of Spinoza's philosophy is
undoubtedly also linked to the *enigmatic* nature of his
thinking, which reflects his personality and vice-ver-
sa. There are few other philosophers who can rival
Spinoza in this respect: Socrates, Nietzsche perhaps,
Kierkegaard or Wittgenstein. There is a paradox in
Spinoza's attempt to combine strict scientific thinking with his powerful commitment to what today we
would call existential questions. Also paradoxical are
his extremely impersonal philosophical method and
its unique and idiosyncratic style and content.

Philosophy has become fashionable again. Trendy
thinkers regularly feature in life-style magazines.
Managers read Seneca or Marcus Aurelius, and
Plato is a substitute for pills. As the religious basis
of our world view has weakened, philosophy in general has moved in to take its place. However, the fact
that Spinoza has played a prominent role in this trend

Rachel Baes, *Les Tics de Spinoza*
(L'Etique) ou cogitata metaphysica. 1967.
Canvas, 81 x 65 cm. Private collection.

is not obvious and can be partly attributed to misunderstanding. His thinking is far more radical than the
de-Christianised humanism that currently prevails.
George Santayana described Spinoza as a purely
Jewish thinker who, in contrast to Christian thinkers,
was free of any Platonism or any conception of participation. His God – but this is a radically anti-anthro-
pomorphic God – is the *only* power, who determines
absolutely *everything*. That is the intellectual truth of
Judaism, stripped of all its inessentials and perfectly
expressed by Spinoza. Or as Spinoza put it, echoing
St Paul: *'We are as clay in the hands of the potter who
makes of us what He will'*. The divine laws through

which and according to which God acts have absolutely *nothing* to do with the moral desires of human beings, they are simply the laws of science. Although Spinoza's philosophy concerns itself with salvation there is no hint of religious fervour or fanaticism. Its message is too paradoxical for that: we have not been planned and nature has no purpose. Salvation consists in realising this and in that insight finding peace and an acceptance of life. *Comfort without hope*. If there is any divine transcendence it is not the transcendence of *Someone* (who cares about us). It is only a trans*descendence*: an in-being of the human in the Non-human. Spinoza's wisdom is wisdom without illusion. It is built on the negation of what, even today, many consider to be absolute truths: free will, the existence of evil, the immortality of the soul and a universal purpose.

Spinoza's philosophy is a modern philosophy. It would be unthinkable without Galileo. Its relationship with modern science is one that calls on science to search for a truth that will liberate us from all kinds of virtually unavoidable illusions. Modern science reveals a reality that is indifferent to our dreams and it is therefore able to contribute to a genuinely illusion-free life. Again this is not obvious. For modern culture has evolved in a direction where science is forced into the service of anthropocentric desires and ideas. In the form of technology it has become a slave to the pursuit of wealth, honour and pleasure. Combined with the illusion of spontaneous anthropocentrism it leads alternately to hubris or cynicism: the hubris of believing that anything can be achieved (or manipulated), or the cynical realisation that – as Isaac Bashevis Singer says – we are no more than a temporary fungus on the surface of a planet doomed to extinction. Spinoza's philosophy is exceptional in the sense that it does not harness science to the pursuit of power or pleasure, but attributes to it a spiritual function that leaves it completely free. Although it takes the brutal insights of science completely seriously, this does not lead to cynicism. On the contrary; the human body, for instance, becomes an object of wonder and admiration that stimulates further study; the human mind

is conceived of as an extremely complex part of God's Intellect, of the 'Mindedness' in which we participate – a part that is capable of unique insights and even of mystical experience.

How can there be 'salvation' without the hope of (personal) immortality? What does a love of God, *amor Dei*, and an enjoyment of one's own glory in the realisation of God's majesty (*gloria*) signify if God is nothing but an impersonal Substance or *Natura Naturans*? My question is not whether or how particular statements about this can be proved: for that one can consult part V of the *Ethica*. My question is whether one can even imagine what it is all about if one has not yet achieved that *amor* or that *gloria*. Perhaps a kindred spirit, not a scientist-philosopher but a scientist-poet, can help us out. The following quotation is from the poem 'Understanding' ('Begrip') from Leo Vroman's 1989 collection of poems *Precious Indivisibility* (Dierbare ondeelbaarheid; a substance precious and at the same time indivisible; how very Spinozist):

When I come to the limits of my powers
Suddenly my soles are flattened drastically
I feel an itch above my elbows and
I understand: now I understand something.

Then tears will sometimes come into my eyes.
Not from what's understood but rather because
I realise how childishly excited
I am again by what I've never possessed.

Beloved nature by nature deceived
I embrace nature and I keep on trying
To bathe in her whom I have long adored.

Here the scientist sees his own activity and his own emotions as a part of nature, a part in which nature becomes a paradoxical self-reflection. A self-reflection that shares in the joy of understanding but at the same time recognises it as inevitably somewhat illusory (is all of it actually produced behind our backs by nature's mechanisms?) But through this recognition he comes to a tender acceptance of himself (beloved nature) and a love for that of which one is a part (I embrace Nature). Insight into an initially harsh truth (I am *only* this) combines with the joyful experience of one's own activity and leads to tender feelings for oneself and love for that which makes *everything* possible, including these paradoxical experiences.

It would be doing Spinoza less than justice to confine his relevance to questions of ethics and the proper way to live. He is rightly being appreciated more and more as a political philosopher; and a political philosopher, moreover, who raises questions that nowadays it is increasingly difficult to avoid, such as the relationship between politics and religion, between politics and science. It is no accident that the subtitle of his *Tractatus theologico-politicus* describes the theme of the work as an investigation into the mutual relationship between peace (politics), piety (religion/ethics) and the search for truth (science and philosophy). This means that in his political thinking Spinoza also develops a theory of religion and science (including philosophy) as *social* realities that impact on politics. At the same time it is clear that the work also seeks an answer to the question of how (Western) politics should deal with its Judaeo-Christian heritage. Unquestionably an issue of great current importance.

I have already pointed out that Spinoza's philosophy is critical of the delusions of anthropocentric humanism; which of course, as Theo Zweerman has rightly observed, does not make him an anti-humanist. One might indeed argue that, one way or another, a basic assumption of true humanism should be that Man is not the measure of all things. Just as present-day thinking in general is strongly anthropocentric, so present-day political philosophy with its emphasis on human rights is strongly humanistic. But again one hears a dissenting voice from Spinoza. Just as religion and the churches do not stand above or outside the state, the same can be said of human rights. That is because no meaningful right exists that is not based on power. Rights, including 'human rights', can only exist where there is a sovereign power to impose them, even upon itself. Once again Spinoza warns against delusion: human rights are pious

hopes, perhaps even dangerous lies, if there is no political power to uphold them. Again, this does not mean that Spinoza is a supporter of tyranny. He is only sceptical about international sovereignty and doubts whether it is really possible. And he also seems to be saying: beware of those, particularly those in power, who claim to speak on behalf of the fundamental rights of man.

My concluding thought may be somewhat far-fetched. Some time ago I read an interesting article, which argued that Spinoza's metaphysics becomes much clearer if one regards him as a modern Avicenna. It is a convincing argument that suggests to me that research on Spinoza should investigate the Arabic roots of Spinoza's thought with the same thoroughness that it has traced his scholastic-Cartesian and Jewish roots. It looks as if in the new century, whether we like it or not, we in Europe will once again be confronted with the Muslim world-view and everything that that entails. There are many who look forward to seeing the development of a modern Islam that will openly and confidently confront modern science, hermeneutics and the like. It may be important that, in their own way, non-Muslims also participate in this development. It seems to me that Spinozism, with its specific intellectual legacy and its partly Arabic-Jewish background, is particularly well suited not only for coming to terms with our Judaeo-Christian heritage, but also for playing a fruitful role in the philosophical-ideological dialogue with Islam.

Herman de Dijn
Translated by Chris Emery

BIBLIOGRAPHY

John Carriero, 'Spinoza's Views on Necessity in Historical Perspective'. In: *Philosophical Topics* 19 (1990), pp. 47-96.

Herman de Dijn, *Spinoza. The Way to Wisdom*. West Lafayette, IL: Purdue University Press, 1996.

George Santayana, 'Introduction'. In: Spinoza, *Spinoza's Ethics and 'De intellectus emendatione'* (Everyman's Library). London /New York: Dent/Dutton, s.d. [1910].

Isaac Bashevis Singer, *Op zoek* (tr. Joop van Helmont). Amsterdam: De Arbeiderspers, 1985, p. 93.

Leo Vroman, *Dierbare Ondeelbaarheid*. Gedichten. Amsterdam: Querido, 1989.

Theo Zweerman, 'Spinoza en de hedendaagse kritiek op het humanisme als ideologie'. In: *Mededelingen XXXIV vanwege Het Spinozahuis*. Leiden: E.J. Brill, 1975.

Marcel Minnaert and the Lacework of Nature

Marcel Minnaert (1893-1970) was a Flemish activist, an astrophysicist, a professor, an educational reformer, a social and scientific pioneer, and an advocate of Esperanto. In the hefty biography that Leo Molenaar has devoted to Minnaert, this last point is only mentioned sporadically. Yet it meant a lot to Minnaert. His magnum opus, the *Photometric Atlas of the Solar Spectrum* (1940), was published not only in English but also in Esperanto, as *Fotometria Atlaso de la Sunospektro*. And that's really rather odd. Esperanto, after all, is a litmus test for unworldly idealists. Anyone who believes that this constructed, unemotional language is capable of bringing world peace even a step closer understands nothing about the nature of language and communication and the uncertainty of human life. Yet on the face of it Minnaert was not in the least unworldly. On the contrary, his life was an extremely successful one and he enjoyed worldwide recognition for his scientific work. And yet it always seems as though there is something that stands between him and the reader, something that prevents us from coming any closer to him. Maybe the key to this really does lie in that firm faith in Esperanto.

There are all sorts of reasons for writing a proper biography of Minnaert. In his youth he played an active role in the Flemish Movement, which he took to its ultimate conclusion in 1916 by accepting a position at the University of Ghent, which had been made Dutch-speaking by the German occupiers. At the end of 1918 he fled with his mother to the Netherlands and made a new and brilliant career for himself in Utrecht as an astrophysicist at the physics institute of W.H. Julius and L.S. Ornstein. He developed a standard measure for the intensity of the Fraunhofer lines in sunlight (equivalent width), became professor of astronomy in 1937 and just before the onset of World War Two, together with two colleagues, he completed his photometric atlas of the solar spectrum. In addition to this, he worked to reform the teaching of physics and became a celebrated populariser of science. The three volumes of *De natuurkunde van't vrije veld* (published in English as *The Nature of Light and Colour in the Open Air*) are still read nowadays. After the war, during part of which he was detained in a camp in Sint-Michielsgestel, North Brabant, he received many accolades from home and abroad and devoted himself, without taking sides, to controlling the arms race and to promoting the concept of social responsibility amongst researchers. He was also tireless in his efforts to popularise science and did a great deal (together with the historian of science, E.J. Dijksterhuis) to keep alive the memory of Simon Stevin, a fellow citizen of Bruges, by publishing his *Principal Works*. A packed, rich and multifaceted life, in which science and politics continually came into contact and which was not lacking an element of drama and tragedy, such as the disappearance and (suspected) suicide of his eldest son Koen in 1963.

Molenaar, a chemistry teacher from Delft who had previously written about ground-breaking scientists in the Netherlands following the Second World War, has now turned this life into a marvellous biography. He had access to plentiful documentation, spoke to many dozens of people, went through hundreds of publications and finally turned it all into an epic work that is compelling in parts. There are moments when he misses the mark. When he discusses Minnaert's involvement with the debate about education in the field of mechanics in 1920-1940, contrasting Minnaert's experimental approach with Dijksterhuis' mathematical approach, he unfairly dismisses Dijksterhuis as a representative of the traditional way of thinking. This is not right, because Dijksterhuis' rigorous abstract approach was just as revolutionary as Minnaert's, if not more radical, and most teachers liked it just about as much as Minnaert's DIY didactics. Molenaar has also apparently not understood the importance of the role of A.A. Nijland, Minnaert's direct predecessor as astronomer in Utrecht, in the advancement of research into solar physics at the university. It was Nijland who, back in 1899, focused research in Utrecht on the sun, and Julius followed in his wake. And finally Molenaar's description of Minnaert's married life is unsatisfactory. He notes the chill that entered the marriage, but doesn't consider the possibility that this came about because his wife discovered at a certain point that she was a lesbian. But these are small points in comparison with the rest. No, Minnaert could not have had a better biographer than Molenaar.

Yet even in Molenaar's biography Minnaert ultimatel remains a stranger. The causes are to be found partly in the personality of Minnaert himself. He was an only child and demonstrated all the possible forms of egocentrism associated with that. He was extremely helpful to others and fought like a lion for his social ideals, but from an emotional point of view it was always one-way traffic. He knew no doubts, thought he was the centre of the universe and was heedless of the emotional confusion that other people could sometimes find themselves in: his wife, his children, his daughter-in-law when her husband (his son) suddenly disappeared (all Minnaert did was go off on a trip round the world, visiting fellow astronomers in Australia and then getting in touch from Bangkok to find out if there was any news about Koen).

But it's not just his personality that makes him remain a stranger to us; it's also down to the nature of his work. Minnaert was a scientist and scientists only have biographies written about them when they've achieved something special in their academic field. That was certainly the case with Minnaert – there's no doubt about that. But when it comes down to it, what we want to read in such biographies is not a brief summary of their scientific work, but what they did with it, how they elevated or transformed their specialised work into a vision of humankind and the world. This can also certainly be said of Minnaert. He developed a rationalist philosophy of life, based

Marcel Minnaert at work during the 1926 eclipse expedition on Sumatra.

on the total rejection of religion and mysticism, on the glorification of the beauty of nature and on striving for the salvation of humankind through reciprocal acts of service. But that relentless fight against religion and mysticism also made him indifferent to the elements of symbolism and play, whilst his fanatical enthusiasm for such an abstract, empty category as 'humankind' always has something unpleasant and uncompassionate about it when viewed in the context of his own emotional failure. As a thinker on these sorts of issues Minnaert sometimes cut a sorry figure. He was of the opinion that human self-awareness was no more than the higher stage of development of a capacity that – even though it may be in a rudimentary or latent form – is also possessed by all lower forms of life and even so-called dead nature. It was his older friend and colleague Anton Pannekoek, a more sharply analytical philosopher, who had to point out that the continuity principle that Minnaert was employing was a sophism. Minnaert also argued time and again that free will was a fiction and that morals and conscience are no more than products of evolution, without seeing that, at the *moment suprême*, when the salvation of humankind was proclaimed as the highest aim of human activity, he was suddenly and inexplicably introducing a moral necessity into a line of reasoning that professed to be only about 'being'.

So it's no surprise that at a crucial moment Minnaert came up with precisely the wrong imagery to illustrate his point of view. In 1963, in a lecture on the unity of the cosmos at a meeting of the Royal Netherlands Academy of Arts and Sciences, he fell back on an experience from his own youth in Bruges: *'From my childhood I remember the lace-makers in the streets of old Bruges, sitting in front of their doors, bent over their lace pillows. They'd wind and twist together the single threads that formed the basis of their work, whilst an endless variety of fantastic flowers, tendrils and festoons came into existence under their rapid fingers. Our task is to detect the threads in the wonderfully intricate lacework of nature that make up the essence of this infinite beauty, this cosmos. Maybe it's just one single thread.'*

Did no one ask him back then who, on a cosmic level, was the equivalent of the lace-maker who had devised those beautiful patterns?

Klaas van Berkel
Translated by Laura Watkinson

Marcel Minnaert, *The Nature of Light and Colour in the Open Air*. Dover Publications, 1948.

Leo Molenaar, *De rok van het universum. Marcel Minnaert, astrofysicus 1893-1970*. Balans: Amsterdam, 2003, 602 pp. (see also: www.leomolenaar.nl for information on literature and internet sites about Minnaert, most of which are in English)

Digital Clusius

In the botanical world of the sixteenth century Carolus Clusius (1526-1609) played a key role. Some fifteen hundred letters testify to the scale of his international contacts. This slightly anarchic network is now being opened up with the aid of digitalisation.

'You can see the watermarks!' Cambridge says. *'So much more definition than the microfilms,'* is Budapest's comment. Lund: *'This is going to save me a lot of travelling.'* But then Oxford adds: *'Technical ingenuity might be self-defeating.'* The twenty Clusius scholars who were introduced to the digital correspondence of the botanist Carolus Clusius on 24 September 2004 in a computer room at Leiden University Library were enthusiastic about the quality of the scans (600dpi). At the same time they considered what would be the best way for them, as European Clusius specialists, to increase the value of such a database by the addition of headwords, annotations, transcriptions, translations, illustrations and links. The visitors gave us some sensible advice: consider the digital maintenance and avoid making it too labour-intensive.

In the second half of the sixteenth century botany began to be studied more and more for its own sake. Before that attention had focused on plants as symbols or on their practical use as food or medicine, but from 1550 on the plants themselves also became the object of study. At the universities of Padua, Pisa, Leiden, Bologna, and Basel botanical gardens were established together with the first professorial chairs. Explorers brought exotic plants back to Europe, and gardening and the propagation of plants became extremely popular both at the various royal courts and among 'ordinary' people, while the empirically-minded undertook botanical expeditions to extend their knowledge through field work. Large collections were assembled to fill *Kunst-und Wunderkammern* – cabinets of curiosities – and newly acquired knowledge was made public in illustrated botanical encyclopaedias.

In this dynamic botanical world Carolus Clusius

Batatas.

The sweet potato (*Batatas*), illustration in:
Carolus Clusius, *Rariorum Plantarum*
Historia, Antwerp, 1601.
Plantin-Moretus Museum, Antwerp.

The story of the introduction of the potato illustrates the way Clusius's network functioned. In the mid-sixteenth century the *conquistadores* had brought the potato to Europe from the Andes, and in 1565 had presented it to Philip II of Spain. Because of its presumed medicinal value the Spanish king sent some to the ailing Pope Pius IV. Subsequently, in 1588, a cardinal sent two tubers and some potato seed from the Southern Netherlands to Clusius who was then at the imperial court in Vienna. Finally the botanist took the potato with him to Leiden in 1593 and planted it in his Hortus Botanicus. In 1601 Clusius published his first scientific treatise on the potato, *Rariorum Plantarum Historia* (The History of Rare Plants), and was thus in at the start of the most important source of popular nutrition in the Low Countries.

In the history of science Clusius has up till now failed to receive the attention he deserves. The lion's share of his correspondence, i.e. 1,100 letters addressed to him and 300 from him to others, is in Leiden, while Erlangen in Germany possesses 200. The correspondents (many of them doctors and apothecaries) came from the whole of Europe, from England to Hungary, from Italy and Greece to Sweden and Poland. Most of these letters, from a total of 300 writers, have never been studied and only a limited number have ever been published. The Scaliger Institute, which was originally set up to stimulate research into special collections owned by Leiden University Library, therefore initiated a Clusius project under the name *Clusius in a New Context*. The project got under way in September 2004 with a three-day conference attended by a select international gathering of Clusius scholars. The purpose of the project is an analysis of Clusius's life, work and network, not only from the (traditional) angle of botany and medicine, but with a good deal of attention to the socio-cultural context in which he operated.

An important objective of the project is to make the Clusius correspondence accessible worldwide. Clusius corresponded extensively with many scholars all over Europe and in many languages – Latin, French, Italian, Spanish, Dutch and German. Hence, a considerable number of the letters are not writ-

was the leading figure. Born in Arras as the son of a nobleman, he studied law in Leuven and medicine and botany in Wittenburg. He travelled the length and breadth of Europe, introduced the tulip and the potato into the Low Countries and advised princes and aristocrats, among them Emperor Maximilian II in Vienna. He spoke eight languages, was the author of important botanical publications and corresponded with hundreds of people from all walks of life. In 1593 Clusius settled in Leiden, where as professor of botany he established the Hortus Botanicus.

First picture of the potato,
with a note written by Carolus Clusius.
1588. Watercolour.
Plantin-Moretus Museum, Antwerp.

of their sex, class or geographical origin.

Unlike the correspondence of Hugo Grotius and Antoni van Leeuwenhoek, the Clusius correspondence is going to appear not in print but digitalised on the Internet. This opens up extra opportunities, and the size of the collection makes Clusius an attractive pilot project. The conference in Leiden was also intended as a first move towards a present-day reconstruction of the Clusius network: the formation of a team of experts from the countries where Clusius was active, experts who by working together over the coming years should add further information to the database of letters. This added value can vary from elementary key words and biographies of correspondents to links to transcriptions of letters (but how trustworthy are these?), botanical watercolours and editions of letters from other humanists. It is the task of the Scaliger Institute, and in particular of its Director Paul Hoftijzer and Fellow Florike Egmond, to keep an eye on things and see to it that the project does not get out of hand. The intention is for the database to be made accessible to the public in five years' time.

By then the research planned as part of the Clusius project should also have been concluded. This will involve three PhD students, while Florike Egmond will be responsible for a comprehensive monograph. The three doctoral students who should start work in September 2005 will study Clusius's life against the background of the house of Hapsburg and the aristocratic society of the late sixteenth century, the use of French and Latin in the Clusius correspondence and Clusius's botanical research programme. The empirical approach to botany with a growing emphasis on observation, practical experience, registration and classification that took root under Clusius's guidance was a forerunner of the scientific revolution of a century later. Perhaps *Clusius in a New Context* will upgrade his role to that of mastermind.

Dirk van Delft
Translated by Elizabeth Mollison

ub.leidenuniv.nl/bc/scaligerinstitute/clusius

ten in Latin, the language of the humanists, because much practical botanical knowledge came from non-scholarly circles. As a result, the tone of the correspondence is conspicuously lively and characterised by a touch of anarchy. All sorts of subjects are aired: patronage, the postal service, the exchange of gifts, complaints, gossip, travel stories and, it goes without saying, a great deal of botany. The botanical community owed its free-wheeling manner to its diversity: it was a community of experts whose practical knowledge was held in esteem regardless

'Europe, your Time has Come'

Sometimes the world can take on the appearance of an airport, with metal detectors, private security firms and patrolling Alsatians. That was the scene as I joined the queue outside the Van Nelle factory in Rotterdam, its twinkling lights making it look for all the world like a fairytale castle, a wonderful icon of modernity dating from the late 1920s; a Titanic on the quayside, eager to set sail from Fortress Europe. The Tilburg-based Nexus Institute had chosen this former coffee, tea and tobacco factory as the venue for the final conference in a series of international gatherings of 'thinkers and decision-makers', entitled *Europe. A Beautiful Idea? European Intellectual Summit.*

The Dutch government had asked the Nexus Institute to organise a series of international conferences during the Dutch presidency of the EU in the second half of 2004, focusing on the values that Europe embraces, the values that it should embrace, European citizenship, the *'European civilisation ideal'* and how that might be *'cultivated'*. In an interview for the regional newspaper *Brabants Dagblad* the director of Nexus, Rob Riemen, revealed that Dutch Prime Minister Jan Peter Balkenende originally wanted the conference series to focus on *'norms and values'*, but that he subsequently *'to all intents and purposes gave the Institute a free hand'*. The series began with the first conference in the stately surroundings of the ancient Ridderzaal in The Hague in the presence of Queen Beatrix. This was followed by meetings in Warsaw, Berlin and Washington. Politicians, scientists, historians, lawyers, philosophers, opinion leaders and writers from Europe, the United States, Canada, Russia, Iran, Iraq and Israel were all in attendance. In the more than ten years since the Nexus Institute was founded, Rob Riemen has built up an international network of thinkers, writers and artists who regularly make the journey to Tilburg. The network was expanded further for the conferences.

I will briefly summarise what was discussed in Rotterdam.

No-one is prepared to die for Europe. The sole exception to this view was a Syrian, who described himself as a *Wahleuropäer*, a European from free choice. He saw a lack of *esprit de corps* in Europe, a lack of commitment. Those are notions that suggest passion and a willingness to make sacrifices – both of which, he believes, are absent in Europe. Others felt that loyalty to a constitution (and thus constitutional patriotism) was more important than the feeling of belonging. The European Union, so I am told, was created for political reasons using economic means, but a unified currency and market are not in themselves enough to create that loyalty.

One delegate described Europe as an admirable invention and called for the tensions ('Montaigne *and* Pascal'), the dualities and contradictions of Europe to be embraced (the continent has produced both the best and the worst; some described themselves as *'fascinated and shocked'* by this). Europe cannot and must not ever be so arrogant again. A historian who was born in Riga but lives in Canada sang the praises of that now modest, humble Europe which cultivates its historical consciousness and doubts, and which after 1945 created something of historic global significance. Europe is a fragile power which – fortunately, in his eyes – stays well away from grandiose 'visions'; fortunately, because this speaker believed that visions are associated with visionaries and can therefore be dangerous. Others praised what they described as Europe's *'tragic wisdom'*.

In the closing speech, Prime Minister Balkenende reminded those present that the 'European' values of freedom, solidarity and equality are currently under fire from small groups of radicals. He repeated the message that was scrawled on a note pinned by a knife to the chest of the murdered filmmaker Theo van Gogh: *'Europe, your time has come'*. He described Europe as an inclusive project, which is neither anti-Islam nor anti-United States. He talked about leadership and social cohesion (*'holding it all together'*); about decency and honesty; about a balance between freedom of speech and responsibility. During the course of the day, the rule of law and tolerance were added to the list of *'inviolable basic European values'*. But are they exclusively European values?

I went home with mixed feelings. I would not have

Euromast Tower in
Rotterdam.

wanted to miss this day. But something was gnawing at me. A few hours later I was cleaning my teeth and thinking about Wittgenstein, who argued that moral statements are like the water that was now running over the rim of my tooth mug: full to the brim with statements about reality. Because ethical statements cannot be empirically verified. More than that, the uncompromising Wittgenstein argued that it is not possible to say anything constructive about ethics. Ethical behaviour is something that can only be demonstrated. That took me back to those *'norms and values'*. Norms are rules. They can be imposed.

Values cannot. Whingeing about the decline in values does not bring them any closer. I do not doubt the integrity of the devoutly religious Balkenende, whose final words at the conference were that he wanted to build a bridge between *'values'* and *'politics'*. The man meant it. He wants to break through *'the conspiracy of silence'*, turn Europe into *'a powerhouse of ideas'*. But Balkenende is not an *'intellectual'*. Unlike the Nexus Institute, which is. It publishes a journal which opts resolutely for essay and reflection from the authors it draws from all over the world. It has a nose for the great voices of the cultural debate (who are often not afraid to embrace the pessimistic cultural mantra *à la* Steiner and Scruton) as well as for unknown and interesting thinkers. The journal really is worth reading, though I have to confess that I often do not finish the articles. That is because of the kind of language in which the debate is often conducted: lofty values are described in the journal using lofty words. Rob Riemen, in his essay 'Talking of Europe. A reflection' ('Over Europa gesproken. Een nabeschouwing'), writes sentences like these: *'Only culture, the work of poets and thinkers, prophets and artists can teach us values, provide us with understanding, refine our tastes, help us to cultivate the human soul and spirit, so that human beings may become more than what they are: beasts.' 'Thanks to his spirit every human being has a knowledge of freedom, peace, justice, compassion, love and beauty; he knows the difference between good and evil, truth and lie.'*

Culture! Soul! Spirit! Love! Beauty! These are container concepts. Even Erasmus has become such a concept: you can pile so many meanings into them that they eventually mean everything and therefore nothing. The nominalist in me says: these are *nomina*, pure names, empty shells, mere movements of air, *flatus vocis*. 'Culture is the key' is one of the pieces of advice given to Barroso by Nexus. He was clearly in full agreement with it, because at the conference he asserted roundly that culture should be given more prominence than the economy in the Union. I could not believe my ears.

There is a gigantic confusion of meaning pervading this continent, between 'Europe' and the European

295

Union which, with the enlargement that took place in 2004 and the further enlargement that is in the pipeline for the future, is doomed to become nothing more than a free-trade zone. That other 'Europe' is a sort of background to everything that we do, think, dream and remember. Perhaps it only exists if it is not mentioned. It is the bookcase that stands 'behind us' – in both senses of the term: it is forgotten yet continues to protect us. Milan Kundera once wrote that religion was the factor that bound Europe together in the Middle Ages; later it was culture, cultural creation, and later still there was no longer anything to bind Europe together, unless we count the market or brilliant technological achievements. Which we do not. Kundera does not believe in the democratic ideal or the principle of tolerance as a binding element: ' (...) if that tolerance no longer offers protection to rich creation or great ideas, does it not then become empty and useless?' Kundera believes that culture has already relinquished its position. A European, he ends, is 'someone who is nostalgic about Europe'.

Europe has won everything and lost everything. Today it cultivates doubt and caution, chooses authority above power, irony above belief. Yet Europe will have to demonstrate great resolve if it wishes to retain all of that; and therein lies the paradox. Liberal democracy has always been exceedingly fragile and needs constant attention and protection. And what will bind Europe in the future? I cannot help thinking of the precocious 17-year-old Dutch girls in a documentary shown at the Nexus conference: they felt closer to the United States than to Italy, and a French film was an unbearable trial for them. Education has evidently failed when it comes to foreign languages, literature and history. 'European citizenship begins with education in the spirit of Europe', runs another recommendation by Nexus, which would like to see Montaigne and Aristotle's *Ethica* being taught in schools.

In conclusion, while English (the language used at the conference) is clearly necessary, it is not enough: if the 91-year-old, almost blind classicist Jacqueline de Romilly had been allowed to speak in French, something more of the much-vaunted European diversity would have shone through, and her plea for Greek and Latin to be taught in secondary schools would have sounded more impressive – and above all more precise and more elegant. But Europeans know too little of each other's languages (the Dutch don't know French any more, that's for sure). Do something about that, Barroso and *tutti quanti*.

Luc Devoldere
Translated by Julian Ross

www.nexus-instituut.nl

The Importance of Being Dutch

'The Dutch do not like the sea.' 'The Netherlands is not a football nation, it's a football-fighting nation' (the players brawl among themselves). As for the famous cleanliness, 'the Dutch male in particular stinks'; he has 'foul crotch creases' in his ubiquitous jeans and 'lots of dandruff' on his collar. Gay schoolteachers can have such a hard time in Dutch classrooms that they apply for sick leave, while out in the playground boys insult one another with cries of 'dirty faggot'. The Dutch don't even take many soft drugs. In April 2004 a measly 7.8 per cent of Amsterdam lit up a joint, whereas popular mythology would have the entire citizenry doing so. In the rest of the Netherlands it was only 4.8 per cent. Whatever country are we reading about?

The cultural review *De Gids* commissioned eminent Dutch intellectuals and writers to contribute to a one-off English-language issue entitled *Misunderstanding the Netherlands*, and subtitled 'Misunderstandings about the Netherlands'. The two are not quite the same thing; to have distorted or erroneous facts in one's head doesn't necessarily mean failure to appreciate the overall pattern of a society nor those features, those trends that distinguish it from others. Many of the above corrections of popular views were made, of course, in a spirit of consciously contentious impatience. Even so, at the outset of my response to this lively and thought-provoking anthology I must make two caveats. First, contradictory evidence proffered against a general perception may in fact only adulterate, or teasingly undermine it; it doesn't necessarily amount to a refutation.

Take the last two instances, concerning issues for which the Netherlands enjoys a world-wide reputation. In the excellent piece by Gert Hekma, 'The ups and downs in gay paradise', he admits as a 'given' that *'the legal situation of gays and lesbians is almost perfect in the Netherlands'* and goes on to tell us that the very term 'gay marriage' is politically *verboten*: *'We have only one type of marriage for all two-person relationships irrespective of sexual preference'*. He also relates the amusement of Dutch journalists at the hordes of foreign TV reporters arriving in Amsterdam for the city's first official same-sex marriages: call that news!! These facts alone – despite the very proper things Hekma goes on to say about the uneasy relation of freedoms to real radical expectations – give the Netherlands a most remarkable place in the history and geography of humane society. So too with drugs; Arjen Mulder here takes it completely for granted that a significant artistic achievement may owe its strengths to its creator's relationship with a congenial drug. Would this pronouncement be so gently made in the oldest review of any other nation? On to prostitution! Where in Britain is the Prostitution Information Centre advising sex-workers and customers alike to *'refrain from making hurtful comments'* if things don't work out?

The second caveat is that, even if they are clichés now, these conceptions arose for often valid and explicable reasons – e.g. the whole vanguard position of the Netherlands on certain key social issues; the Dutch gift for dissemination of knowledge and viewpoint, and perhaps too for self-advertisement. The principal harm these images do is that they eclipse other equally important features and preoccupations. Angst about the Dutch language and its future, leading to successive linguistic reforms; cultural debts to the former French occupiers; malaise about having *'lost all wars in the past three centuries'*, the top-heavy

demography consequent on the size of the economically all-important 'Randstad' (a problem top-heavy England with its huge South-East should appreciate only too well) – these are less widely understood by outsiders. Other nations – but maybe I mean the British – have been so seduced by the Netherlands in its self-created late-Sixties avatar (and just why this arose with the intensity and thoroughness it did is ceaselessly fascinating) that they are apt to deny it a proper context in their delight at its emporium of tolerance.

'Tolerance' – though I haven't done a count, this must be the most frequent word in the whole collection of essays. Almost all the writers feel obliged to use it, principally to fling it back defiantly into their compatriots' faces. 'Progressive', 'internationalist', 'non-conformist' get similar treatment. What all this self-chastisement reveals is a degree of idealism consequent on *simply being Dutch* that to me is remarkable in itself. Every piece here could be called 'Why the Dutch aren't what I, as a Dutch man/woman, once thought they both were and should be'. This itself can be legitimately rephrased as *'What I, as a Dutch man/woman, would like most (for myself, for Western civilisation) is for the Dutch really to be what I once believed they were.'* For us English, congenitally empirical, with a long history of disillusionment, this is strange: for us appeals to national virtue are confined to tabloid histrionics, with their dishonest ulterior purposes. We know – or so we think – that there must always be a gulf between ambition and achievement, between hope and human actuality, and accordingly we adopt our cynical positions.

What has inspired both this issue of *De Gids* and the tone of its articles is, of course, the ongoing Netherlands crisis of identity so dramatically manifest in the public arena itself. Were one to ascribe a specific beginning to it, surely it would be the Dutch failure at Srebrenica in July 1995, so honestly dealt with here by Abram de Swaan. This debacle - with its terrible consequences (over 6,000 Muslim dead) and unanswerable questions about warfare and international relations – led to the mammoth critical report that in turn was to lead to the eventual resignation of Wim Kok, and to lay the way open for Pim Fortuyn and his supporters. One thinks of the prolonged identity crisis in another European society with a dominant Platonic self-image, Sweden. ('Compare the "death" of the "Swedish Model" and *folkhem* with the "death" of "The Polder Model"' – a taxing but justifiable line of inquiry.) Like Sweden after Olof Palme's assassination the Netherlands is going through a kind of bereavement, in which old sorrows and guilts surface. What is often forgotten during its worst moments (as in literal bereavement) is that the sufferers are not unique, that what is being played out are particular instances of universal problems, that the Netherlands is seeing the Dutch forms of the instability, obsolescences and doubts that plague (often rightly) all Western nations today.

'Misunderstanding the Netherlands' should perhaps depress one; much of it was intended to. But it also fills one with a renewed sense of the vitality, the capacity for self-examination that distinguishes the Netherlands as much today as in its Golden Age. I much enjoyed the Maarten Asscher piece on Dutch writers and why none has won the Nobel Prize for Literature. I feel this to be a monstrous injustice, especially after learning that Johan Huizinga was passed over. That influential historian's humanism, if not now completely to our tastes, impelled him to show exemplary integrity and courage at a time of unprecedented international barbarism. Today's Dutch writers – whether they get the Nobel Prize or not – testify to an energy of spirit, where most Western societies are enervated – Harry Mulisch, Cees Nooteboom (I agree with Asscher; the Prize should be his!), Gerrit Kouwenaar, Gerard Reve, Margriet de Moor, Adriaan van Dis, Marcel Möring, Arthur Japin, Connie Palmen, Rutger Kopland. I end the list with Kopland because his quiet concentration of mind and sensibility seems, taking a long view, exceedingly Dutch, and I think this quality not enough stressed in this publication. Perhaps the Dutch – lucky people! – really do take this attribute of theirs for granted. Says Kopland (as rendered by the, sadly, late English poet, James Brockway, long resident in the Netherlands because of its inclusive sexual attitudes): *'Go now into the garden, dear, and lie/ in an empty spot where the grass grows tall./That's what I've always wanted to be,/ an empty spot for someone, to stay.'*

Paul Binding

De Gids, May/June 2004. (www.uitgeverijbalans.nl)

FotoMuseum: Photography Rehabilitated in Antwerp

There are photographic collections in many places in Belgium. The Royal Library (Albertina, Brussels), the Royal Museums of Art and of History (Brussels), the Museum of Flemish Literature (Letterenhuis, Antwerp), semi-public archives and city and municipal archives possess a wealth of photographic documents from the past. In Belgium, as elsewhere in the world, photography has entered the domain of the plastic arts and is exhibited in museums and numerous galleries. But in this country there are only two museums of photography that collect and display both images and equipment: one in each of the two language communities, as it happens, in Charleroi and Antwerp. The latter has recently taken on a new lease of life after many decades of dormancy. The FotoMuseum, as it is now called, is owned by the province of Antwerp and has a very extensive international collection of photographs, an impressive collection of photographic equipment and a library of more than 35,000 volumes and documents, and will now finally take its rightful place in the landscape of national and international museums. Thus the museum has something to offer which as regards both quantity and quality can be found nowhere else in Europe, with the exception of the United Kingdom, and from now on it is a question of making the most of that advantage.

A first obvious plus point is the building. This former warehouse, *Flanders,* built in 1911 and centrally situated on the banks of the River Scheldt, was given a thorough make-over internally by the leading Belgian architect George Baines, who was able to create a sizeable new building adjacent to the original. The coherence of old and new has been designed as a harmonious whole, with a clear infrastructure and a business-like functionality which in no way detracts from the aesthetic experience. As soon as he enters the visitor finds himself in an open space with clear signs to the FotoMuseum, the Museum Café, the bookshop, the reception desk and a first exhibition area, the gallery. Having paid the entrance fee at reception, visitors have access to the two cinemas (occupied by the Film Museum) and the core of the museum. The first floor is reserved for the library, the reading-room and a meeting-room, the collection is displayed on the second floor, and the third floor is kept for temporary exhibitions. For the time being the fourth floor remains unfinished due to a lack of financial resources, and it is as yet not clear how a putative co-operative scheme with the Antwerp Museum for Contemporary Art will develop.

A second obvious advantage is the appointment of a competent director/keeper, Christof Ruys, a young photographic historian who has grafted his personal ambitions on to the museum, which will definitely benefit greatly from the fact. In a policy plan he has drawn up a number of guidelines, which, if not revolutionary, will at least bring a breath of fresh air compared with the deadly seriousness which typified the former Museum of Photography. The museum is to become a haven for everyone who has anything to do with photography, art, fashion, photo-journalism, the better kind of amateur photographers, press-photographers, in short, everyone who handles the medium of photography in a sensible manner. To ensure an exhibition policy that also appeals to the younger generation, monthly portfolio days are organised when anyone can show his/her work to the curators, and which may form the basis of an exhibition in the gallery. To make sure that the regular collection does not outstay its welcome in the museum and so create an impression of *déjà vu*, as was the case in the past, every four months a guest curator is charged with making a selection from the entire holdings (images and equipment). In this way the whole patrimony is displayed to the public turn and turn about. The other exhibitions also change every four months, so that the public is kept on the qui vive. According to Ruys interest in the museum has to be stimulated in various ways and on different levels. So parts of the collection are being shown in different cultural institutions all over the country and abroad. Universities and polytechnics must find an anchorage there through workshops, colloquia and study days, amateur-photographers must have a sounding-board there, the many and varied activities of the

FotoMuseum, Antwerp.
Photo by Guy Voet.

Education department must enable young people to learn to discover and use the medium.

The *FotoMuseum Magazine* (following on from the periodical *Obscuur* started by Ruys), is becoming a unique Dutch-language publication for photography in general and the activities of the museum in particular. There is now a fully-fledged catering department and, finally, the museum is continuing the initiative for commissioning its own photographs.

The history of the FotoMuseum is one of ups and downs. Its origin is in the initiative of Karel Sano, who was working at the time for the then Gevaert Photographic Products, and his colleagues Dr Laurent Roosens and Marcel Gruyaert. They wanted to create within the company a historically interesting collection of equipment, including the resultant images, to study the relevance of photography to society. Their ambition of creating a company museum failed, but in 1964 a solution was sought and found: the initiative was transferred to the province of Antwerp. Thus an official organisation was handed the task of setting up a Museum for Photography.

At first it was encapsulated within the traditional artistic/decorative crafts in the Sterckshof folklore museum, and finally, in 1984, it was able to stand on its own two feet in the former *Flanders* warehouse on the Waalse Kaai. The extensive collection (6,000 pieces of equipment, 30,000 photographs and 35,000 books and periodicals) was initially looked after by an 'academic assistant' and his helper. To make the most of its asset, for two consecutive periods the provincial council appointed managers who were to give the somewhat sleepy museum a new and modern sparkle. They failed on both occasions and the reputation of the collection, as we have said one of the best in Europe, rapidly diminished. The institution lost a lot of credibility, nationally and even locally, partly because of an incoherent exhibition policy that on the whole

A. van Besten, *Scene*.
c.1907-1910, autochrome.
Collection FotoMuseum,
Antwerp.

was not very user-friendly. The arrangement of the regular collection remained unchanged for decades and became so dated that it attracted hardly any visitors. It could not even get recognition by the Flemish Community. It became the tragic story of a museum with an exceptional collection that was not appreciated at its true worth by the authorities (in this case the provincial council) and so was treated the same as many other administrative services. This had implications for the staffing policy, financial control and infrastructural problems and hindered its effective functioning in the context of changing ideas on museums.

Christof Ruys has now been given a clear task by the provincial government: people must come to the museum, large numbers of people. The pressure of visitor statistics hangs over his head like the sword of Damocles. It is to be hoped he won't let it affect him. The constant changing of the museum displays, the

rhythm and variety of the exhibitions, the stringing together of activities are so many factors that cannot leave the public indifferent at a time when photography is almost *the* controlling element for the perception of today's society. After nearly a year the results are more satisfactory, the public (including the international public) has rediscovered the museum and is enjoying it. *Quod erat demonstrandum.*

Ludo Bekkers
Translated by Sheila M. Dale

FotoMuseum, Waalse Kaai 47, 2000 Antwerp,
tel. +32 (0)3 242 93 10
www.fotomuseum.be

Lily was Here
Temporary Installations with the Indelible Mark of Lily van der Stokker

Lily van der Stokker is a wallflower who is very much in demand. This pop star's playlist just keeps getting longer. As a solo artist or in a group. Actually, all that's missing is for T-shirts to be sold with the names of the cities that she's appeared in. But Lily van der Stokker is not a musician, but a serious visual artist and perhaps also a composer of epigrams.

Lily van der Stokker (born in 's-Hertogenbosch in 1954) has a trademark: cheerful wall paintings with flowers, clouds, doodles and statements. All of which she does in garish neon colours. Often the paintings have additional elements in the form of a lounge suite (*'coziness, sitting on my couch watching TV, it is warm, comfortable, what else do you need?'*) and/or boxes. These are the constants of the last fifteen years, which have developed in rather a natural way from the doodles of the early years. Van der Stokker said in an episode of the Dutch television programme *RAM*: *'At the end of the 1980s I made my first wall painting with a flower in it. It just appeared there. Without my thinking about it. But I probably also drew a lot of flowers as a girl, so it's something that came about naturally. But when it was on the wall in a gallery, some friends of mine said: "Lovely painting, but why'd you put those flowers in it?" It was at that moment, I think, that I decided, "Oh, that's very interesting, that one little flower like that should arouse so much opposition – then I'm going to have to get to work on them, because actually I really do like them".'*

And so from that time on she has painted stylised flowers with boundless enthusiasm. Ask a child to draw a flower and you'll get something that looks like Van der Stokker's flora. They are so abstract that they almost become pictograms. The flowers appear in practically every painting, sometimes filling the entire wall, which means that they can serve as a backdrop for an exhibition of other people's work. There's also a line of furniture now. Not for one of those huge furniture chains like Ikea, where the design (by Leo Krol) and the decoration would indeed fit in, but at the invitation of the Vijfzinnen bookshop in Gorinchem. Most of all she likes to make her flower power socially acceptable. So she's also held an exhibition at the hip design gallery VIVID in Rotterdam. The next step? Why not design fabrics for the children's fashion label Oilily (what's in a name), well-

Lily van der Stokker,
Easy Fun. 2001.
Colour pencil on paper,
21 x 30 cm.
Private collection.

Lily van der Stokker,
Easy Fun (detail). 2003,
acrylic paint on wall + couch
with textile applications.
Gallery Klosterfelde, Berlin.

Lily van der Stokker,
The Pink Building (detail).
2000. Acrylic paint on wall,
plastic and paint on roof,
45 x 50 x 70 m. Hanover,
Germany. Collection
Hannover Messe.

known far beyond Dutch borders? Oilily use a similar approach, merrily mixing patterns and materials in candy and pastel colours. They have made an accepted norm out of clashing colours and ultra-busy vacuum-abhorring designs that create a real overkill effect. (They do in fact have a range for the woman who doesn't want to get older, so there's a market for it.)

The great nothing

Is Van der Stokker's work really so simplistic, so free of meaning? She leaves the viewers to their own devices. *'What I do is glorify small things. Things that are apparently unimportant, insignificant, and I give them a larger space. Like making a piece about administrative problems such as filling in tax forms.'* The magnification of futilities, then. Very occasionally she does create the impression of a hidden agenda: '(...) it's so sweet it can kill'. But more often she'll emphasise that she's making something that 'touches you emotionally. People always start saying that my work is cynical or ironic. And then I think "where'd they get that idea?".' She doesn't like to be pigeonholed, particularly when it has too negative a connotation. So she's pleased when someone describes her paintings as 'pretty', because that's not really something that you can say about art. Her work may be called decorative, but, in her own English: 'No more I want to discuss with people who say "decorative art", meaning a negative or lower quality thing. Grow up I think. Open up your mind. Make a joke! The decorative is so fashionable now with young people. Just enjoy it! The so-called meaninglessness of the decorative is worth to be a university research project.' So, ultimately, her work is indeed about something or maybe it's better to say that the something, the discussion, is about her work.

In 2001 she staged a predominantly pink exhibition called Chatter at Galerie Van Gelder in Amsterdam. With paintings with titles such as People I know, Voebe, Twan Jansen, Kees and Me and Rob Pruitt she is quite simply indulging in artistic namedropping. A critic from the NRC Handelsblad said that it was 'devoid of substance'. Van der Stokker: 'I dare say that's true and then I think "who cares?", but it certainly was a great statement. That's really what I'm looking for, for it to be nothing. It is the duty of the artist always to work at the limits of what is allowed and what's not possible.'

Talking of pink, it's a work in a public place that may be seen as her magnum opus in that respect. For the world's fair Expo 2000 in Hanover she was asked to do something with an existing building in the immediate vicinity of the exhibition site. When all the countries were given carte blanche to create weird and wonderful temporary pavilions, Van der Stokker decided to paint the largest windowless building in Hanover (a former light-bulb factory) completely pink, covering it with ribbon-shaped festoons and flowers in the telephone-doodle style that is so peculiar to her: The Pink Building. The edifice now functions in the cityscape as a typical Lily van der Stokker installation box.

Concept

Lily van der Stokker unites two worlds with her wall paintings: the world of conceptual art and the world of pop art. She does sketches beforehand based on large numbers of ideas. She keeps her ideas and the drawings for when the right moment comes (and quite some time might go by before that happens). When she can turn a sketch into reality, the process is quite a precise one. The enlarged drawing is projected onto the relevant wall and painstakingly created. These days Van der Stokker uses assistants for this work, to whom she gives directions about the execution of the lines and the use of colour. This is where the conceptual element comes in, because however playful and impulsive the paintings end up looking, they are all thoroughly thought out in advance. The coffee-table book Friends & Family, published in 2003, gives an overview of the wall paintings and installations from the period 1983-2003, and also includes dozens of drawings. The list at the back of the book with translations from the Dutch, German and Swedish of the words and phrases that inhabit her paintings shows how seriously this book should be taken. A list of who's who is also included.

Van der Stokker may like to refer to her art as 'graffiti for girls', but she's doing nothing on the sly, at night or illegally. She shares the obsession of the paint-can sprayer, but she does it nicely with a brush and at the request of the sophisticated art world, which she supplies with her 'tags' and 'pieces'. And even if it is only temporary: Lily was here. Even if it's only on the retina and whether you like it or not. What does she care?

Frank van der Ploeg
Translated by Laura Watkinson

Lily van der Stokker is represented by Galerie Van Gelder in Amsterdam, Air de Paris in Paris and Feature Inc in New York.

Friends & Family Lily van der Stokker. Wallpaintings and Drawings 1983-2003. Dijon: Le Consortium, 2003. ISBN 2-84066-083-0. Edition in the series 'Les presses du réel', nr.6. Published to accompany the exhibition 'Friends & Family' at Le Consortium (15 June–14 September 2002).
www.featureinc.com/artists_bios/vdstokkerqa.html
For Van der Stokker's work methods and her own vision, see the *RAM* programme, which can be viewed online at www.vpro.nl/ programma/ram/afleveringen/16295151/ items/16638555

Riddles regarding Carel Fabritius

It was a Frenchman who rescued Carel Fabritius (1622-1654) from oblivion for all time. For just like Johannes Vermeer, this seventeenth-century Dutch painter was only rediscovered halfway through the nineteenth century by the art connoisseur Théophile Thoré. With surprise the latter wrote in 1859: *'I have never heard anyone in Holland mention the paintings of Carel Fabritius, and I have only ever seen one, a tiny scrap of a thing, but excellent.'* He was referring to the now famous *Goldfinch* of 1654, a deceptively lifelike painting of a goldfinch eyeing us brightly from its feeder against a white plastered wall. In the Golden Age the goldfinch was a popular domestic pet, taking its Dutch nickname of *'puttertje'* from a particular trick that it could perform skilfully. By means of a thimble attached to a chain, the bird could draw water from a drinking bowl, like drawing water from a well, for which the Dutch word is *'put'*. Fabritius' little panel belongs to the trompe l'oeil genre. The soft shadow of the bird and its feeder on the whitewashed wall and the reflections of light on the round perches create a convincing illusion, especially when you look at the painting from a distance and from below. Unlike the usual optical illusions of that period, Fabritius has not lost himself in details. With relatively broad strokes of the brush he has conjured up more than anything else the illusion of clear daylight around the bird. Small holes at the edges seem to suggest that the panel originally played just a modest role. It probably served as a door to protect another

painting. Thoré was rightly captivated and tried to acquire it for his own collection. His love for the painting was rewarded when in 1865 he received it as a gift from the heirs of the deceased owner. It was one of his most prized possessions. *'Isn't my goldfinch marvellous?'*, he used to say over and over again.

Intrigued by the painter's talent, Thoré set about looking for other work by Fabritius. At around the same time a further painting of his turned up. The restoration of a portrait of a man belonging to the Boymans van Beuningen Museum showed that the Rembrandt signature had been forged, and the top right corner revealed 'fabritius' scratched into the

Carel Fabritius,
The Goldfinch. 1654.
Panel, 33,5 x 22,8 cm.
Mauritshuis, The Hague.

Carel Fabritius,
Self-Portrait. 1654.
Canvas, 70,5 x 61,5 cm.
National Gallery, London.

wet paint. Thoré particularly appreciated the characteristic aura of the portrait, which was also admired by no less a person than Van Gogh. The coarse, thick-lipped mouth, the chiselled forehead, the shirt open at the neck showing the hairs of the chest: according to Thoré everything pointed to this being a man of the people. The unpolished style was perfectly in keeping with the subject: *'character, touch, colour, everything about it is primitive'*, according to Thoré. We now know that it is a self-portrait. From 1641-1643 Fabritius worked as a pupil or assistant in Rembrandt's studio in Amsterdam, where he must have become familiar with similar self-portraits. Following his master's example, in this instance the painter was most probably using his own reflection as the basis for a so-called 'phiz'. In such a painting

the likeness was not the most important thing, but certain characteristics in physiognomy and clothing were emphasised in order to depict a specific personality.

It appears from eulogies that the talent of the artist, who died relatively young, was highly regarded in his own time. That comes as no surprise when you see what he was capable of in his self-portraits, *The Goldfinch*, or *The Raising of Lazarus*. However, many of Fabritius' works must have been lost. There is documentary evidence that, despite his brief career, he had an extremely varied oeuvre to his name. This included phizzes and portraits as well as biblical and mythological subjects and perspective cabinets. This diversity was clearly demonstrated in 2004 at a special exhibition in the Mauritshuis in the Hague, which brought together all the artist's known works. There are only twelve of them, of which nine are signed and three have been cautiously attributed to the Dutch painter by experts. If you read the catalogue, the search for his work is as intriguing as any quest. New discoveries led to unexpected insights, which then gave rise to new options for the attribution of other works. The signed canvas *Mercury, Argus and Io* that turned up at an auction in 1985 led people to conclude, not unreasonably, that another Mercury picture was also by his hand. It shows the characteristic original approach that Fabritius used in his mythological scenes, with an eye for touching human details, such as Argus' dirty feet.

In the period after 1650, when Fabritius settled in Delft for his second marriage, he tried something new. A good example of this is the beautiful self-portrait with clouds. In contrast to the Rembrantesque lighting in the first self-portrait, this time the artist has depicted himself in a range of clear colours, against a light background. It is assumed that Vermeer, who also lived in Delft, owed his attention to light to the example of his older colleague. Fabritius painted this self-assured portrait in 1654, immediately before he perished, together with many of his fellow citizens, in an enormous explosion at a nearby powder magazine. Sources describe how at that moment the painter was busy painting the verger in his studio. For hours the painter lay crushed under the rubble, and he finally died in hospital. The disaster not only ended the life of Rembrandt's most gifted pupil, of whom it is said that had he had more time he could have emulated the master, but there is no doubt that a great deal of his artistic output was also lost in the explosion.

Juleke van Lindert
Translated by Sheila M. Dale

Frederik J. Duparc *et al.*, *Carel Fabritius 1622-1654*. Zwolle: Waanders, 2005. 160 pp.

Christopher Brown, *Carel Fabritius, Complete Edition With a Catalogue Raisonnée*. Cornell University Press, 1981. 168 pp.

Monuments to Modernism
Jan de Cock and the Spaces he Creates

Is Jan de Cock (1976-) an innovative artist? Or, as some would say derisively, a furniture-maker with pretensions? The fact that this publication has space for an article on De Cock tends to point to the first. But why is this artist, who is still only 28 years old, already such a controversial figure in the contemporary art debate? It is because he declines to let himself become part of this debate and is reviving the values of modernism in a way that is almost provocative. And also because he has a rather un-Belgian big mouth.

Over the last five years, Jan de Cock has built installations in prestigious buildings and institutions concerned with art in Belgium, the Netherlands and Germany. He alters spaces using woodwork: he pushes aside the existing space and replaces it with his own, usually wooden, construction which makes the viewer see the building, and the history attached to it, in a completely new way. In this way he creates not only a new physical space but a new mental one too. Many other artists do the same, but the difference is that De Cock treats the concept of the 'mental space' completely differently: to start with, he makes the viewer very much aware of their own prejudices regarding the concept of 'art space'. He then goes on to make it clear that the contemporary art scene has far too casually adopted a discourse in which it disdainfully, and with an obvious lack of craftsmanship, dismisses the rich history of art all the way from classical times to modernism.

Let's clarify things with a few examples. De Cock was one of the artists selected for the 2003 *Jeune Peinture* exhibition at the Palace of Fine Art in Brussels. But his work verged on blasphemy. This famous modernist building by the celebrated Belgian architect Victor Horta has in recent years been converted and transformed into the Bozar arts centre with the intention of gaining a new and international reputation. One of the steps taken was that all the rooms were more or less returned to their original state and fully opened up.

Jan de Cock, *Denkmal 23*.
2003. Bozar, Brussels.

But Jan de Cock erected a gigantic installation that turned out to be a copy of the old building. In fact he considered his copy more attractive than the state the building is now in. *'The Palace is actually a wounded animal. I filmed the building at night, using the emergency lighting and with all the doors open: you can see the wounded walls, with the holes filled up. That's how I see museums in Belgium at the present time: they have become catacombs, impoverished hospitals, occupied only with their own little networks. And yet they still ask architects: "come on, do something, camouflage our pitiful state". Places that have to be camouflaged are not worth a penny.'* It is a telling fact that almost 40 years previously, Marcel Broodthaers had taken possession of this same Palace in his own way (with a camel): not much changes.

White spaces, slumbering museums and summery green open-air locations

And this is how Jan de Cock works everywhere. He *'tackles white spaces, slumbering museums and summery green open-air locations with impressive installations built either with his own hands or with a team using a wide range of laminated woods, ranging from deep red to pale green. Like a "Cubist", De Cock assembles complex and disorientating spaces/modules in which looks passing between viewers are physically blocked by architectural obstructions, dead-ends and*

Jan de Cock, *Denkmal 9*. 2004.
University Library, Ghent.

blind arcades.' (Luk Lambrecht in *Decennium, kunst in België na Documenta IX*, Ludion/Cera Foundation, p. 65).

In 2002, De Cock's installations at the Museum of Fine Art in Ghent disoriented the viewer, who in his perfectly natural perusal of early or modern paintings found himself 'obstructed' by steps, dead-end sections of the museum circuit and other such things. At the 'Poetry Summer' in Watou in 2001 he filled a large sheep-shed so full that the viewers had to squeeze their way between the wall and the construction without being able to see anything. At the Museum of

Technical History in Grimbergen he saw to it that the nostalgic element was disrupted by his modernist interventions (2002): the antique display cases with their tools and instruments were confronted with a cool modernist approach. In the Amsterdam venues De Appel (2003) and Fons Welters gallery (2001 and 2002) he made sure the visitor ended up in completely new spaces, which very much confused them. In the former especially, where he built a library and video area that were intended to be permanent, he created a permanent shift in the architectural and artistic view of the art event, and one which made a lasting impression. And, in 2004, once again at the Palace of Fine Art in Brussels, now Bozar, he built a new restaurant in the form of a work of art, or a new work of art in the form of a restaurant (it's up to the reader to choose), with an affectionate nod to both Victor Horta and Marcel Broodthaers.

He calls his works *Denkmal* ('Monument'), a memorial to modernism, or *Randschade*, based on the idea of the military term 'collateral damage'. This is visual collateral damage, because the viewer is obstructed by the new boundaries De Cock imposes. Sometimes you are literally obstructed: the installation in the sheep-shed at Watou was even claustrophobic, so forcefully was the viewer obstructed in his view of the work in this space.

37 tons of wood in the Book Tower

In one of his latest works (2004) Jan de Cock took on the main reading room of Ghent University library, commonly known as the 'Book Tower'. He hauled 37 tons of wood into the Tower and used it to convert the bookcases, tables and shelves into miniature museums or encyclopaedias, stuffed full of knowledge.

The building is in poor condition and in urgent need of restoration; by carrying out this work, De Cock intended among other things to point out the great importance of the building and its architect Henry van de Velde (1863-1957) as milestones of modernism. It so happens that the Book Tower is close to this artist's heart: as an art student he constructed his graduation piece in the belvedere at the top of the tower. He sees Van de Velde's intention in this tower as the creation of a perfectly pure space. *'Because Henry Van de Velde had the same megalomania as I do. He himself conceived from A to Z the houses he built during his lifetime, from letterbox to door handle to teapot. He always started out from nothing, from the empty space. To him his habitat was his urge for innovation. I follow a similar course in every exhibition venue I take on. I push everything out and create my own house, my own habitat, my own formal idiom, in this case in the reading room.'*

There is another important connotation: while engaged on the Book Tower Van de Velde was also designing the Kröller-Müller Museum in Otterlo. In fact he was working on two museums at the same time. With its white walls and rounded corners, and with its great purity, the Kröller-Müller is the first museum of modern art in Europe. The Book Tower in Ghent has to be seen in the same light: for De Cock, this building is just as much a modernist museum. Like the Horta building in Brussels, from Palace of Fine Art to Bozar, it is a part of the modernist heritage that should be cherished.

Craftsmanship is mastership

Modernism turns out to be a key element in De Cock's artistic thinking. Like that other element that seems to have died a quiet death along with modernism: craftsmanship. In postmodern art the word has almost become a term of abuse. Because, it is said, craftsmanship is no longer necessary; if everyone just blunders on it's good for the democratisation of art. But De Cock considers expertise to be the basis of good art. He has made all his installations himself or in collaboration with others. And he uses simple materials. *'I deliberately use democratic material that anyone can buy in the shops, because I think the material should not outshine the work itself. Not because I think it important to make an ideological or social connection with all the building workers all over the world. No, it's just to subordinate the material to the form. That is the essence.'*

De Cock sees his craftsmanship as a form of terrorism within the discourse of contemporary art: it enables him to make these spectacular and impossible things which others would not be capable of . He sees himself as a sort of contractor offering ready-built products. Wherever he works he takes control of everything and makes and checks it all from A to Z.

This doesn't make things easy for him in the little world of art. Because in the current contemporary art world things go more or less like this: a gallery owner, conservator or curator goes in search of an artist whom he then fits into his gallery, museum or system. The way De Cock works is exactly the opposite: he adapts the gallery or museum to his own system. The others, the gallery owners and curators, have to question their principles, the way they work and set things up, and adjust them to his habits. According to De Cock this is precisely what is so pure about modernism: the institution has to adapt and not the other way round. He enters the space as a master-draughtsman. So it is not without reason that he carries out these works under the name Atelier Jan de Cock. The master plans, draws and lays the foundations, and the workshop executes the design . This was already so in the seventeenth century in the studios of Rembrandt and Rubens, it was so in modernism with Van de Velde and Horta, and it is so now in the work of Jan de Cock.

In early 2004 De Cock published a book, a little like a derivative form of Van de Velde's Book Tower: a place, a museum where all his images are stored. The book is in three parts and contains modules embedded in a timeline: each module is a cluster of images, things and experiences. The timeline suggests a reading speed. The pictures include a number of 'temps morts', images of places or sites that are also to be found in the modules, but which De Cock wanted to visit himself. Such as the places where Fellini shot his films, and where Jean-Luc Godard organised his casting in Cannes. Essential locations, from which De Cock draws inspiration.

This superbly designed book is really a work of art in its own right and is therefore of great importance: after all, little of a tangible nature remains of De Cock's work, since almost all his spatial installations are temporary. In the book everything comes together: the Denkmäler, the Randschades and the Temps Morts. It is a miniature De Cock museum in book-form.

In September 2005 Jan de Cock has an exhibition at Tate Modern in London. After the successful show by Luc Tuymans in summer 2004, this is the second time a Belgian has been invited to exhibit at this prestigious institution. Tate Modern is housed in a former power-station designed by the famous British architect Sir Giles Gilbert Scott in the nineteen-fifties. This imposing structure was nicknamed 'the cathedral of power'. The contemporary Swiss architects Herzog & Meuron adapted it to its current purpose . Gilbert Scott was not a modernist, but rather an ec-lectic architect. He was by no means averse to modernism, however; he recognised the 'negative quality of utter simplicity' in modernism, which he preferred to 'unintelligent traditionalism'. We are curious to see what Jan de Cock will do with this building and this architect.

Marc Ruyters
Translated by Gregory Ball

www.jandecock.net

Quotes taken from an interview with Jan de Cock by Marc Ruyters and Jeroen Laureyns which appeared in the newspaper *De Tijd* on Saturday 7 February 2004.

Short Takes

French fries. That's what George W. Bush found on his plate when he dined with, among others, the French president Jacques Chirac in Brussels on 21 February last. And that despite the fact that at the height of the French-American quarrel over Iraq in 2003 those chips suddenly turned into Freedom Fries on the menu of the Congress cafeterias. Or as Rep. Bob Ney, R-Ohio, chairman of the Committee on House Administration, justified the change in those turbulent times: 'This action today is a small, but symbolic effort to show the strong displeasure of many on Capitol Hill with the actions of our so-called ally, France.'

Almost two years down the line the fries can be French again (actually they're Belgian, but never mind...). Bush saw his visit to Europe as a generous gesture of reconciliation after the hard words and deep disagreements of the past few years. And the accommodating Europeans appreciated that. 'Europe and America have reconnected', said José Manuel Barroso, president of the European Commission. Among other things, the American president expects the Europeans to sign up to his mission of spreading freedom and democracy. In the Concert Noble, a salon frequented in the nineteenth century by amorously-inclined Brussels aristocrats in search of conquests, Bush declared that he wanted to open a new chapter in transatlantic relations and leave behind the past differences of opinion between the US and Europe.

Bush the charmer, then, and he could count on a considerable readiness to be charmed. During his short three-day stay in Brussels he had breakfast with British prime minister Tony Blair, attended an EU meeting, called briefly on NATO Secretary-General Jaap de Hoop-Scheffer and had a meeting with the newly elected Ukrainian president Victor Yushchenko. He was received at the royal palace and had a chat with the Belgian premier Verhofstadt which lasted longer than officially scheduled: 70 minutes instead of the allotted half-hour. Afterwards Verhofstadt stressed that the importance of the meeting lay in the *change of atmosphere*. A change of atmosphere which meant that Belgium, which with France and Germany had two years before been part of the Axis of Weasel, in Bush's address was now once again *a beautiful nation*.

And as it happens, in 2005 this beautiful nation is celebrating its 175th birthday. On 21 June 1814 the Great Powers signed the 'Eight Articles of London' which made the reunification of the Northern and Southern Netherlands an established fact. On 21 September 1815 William I took the constitutional oath as 'King of the Netherlands'. But eventually the southern provinces tore themselves away and became the Kingdom of Belgium. After the so-called Belgian Revolution the Provisional Government proclaimed independence on 4 October 1830. On 20 December 1830, after a conference in London, the Great Powers recognised the divorce between the Netherlands and Belgium.

By now it is well known that some Belgians are Flemings, and others are Walloons, and that the two groups have never been able to live together in total harmony. In 1980 changes to the constitution gave greater autonomy to the communities and established the different regions. Only the status of bilingual Brussels was still a source of disagreement. But

it quickly became apparent that the reformed constitution left a lot of problems unresolved. After a further constitutional reform in 1993 Belgium became a truly federal state and the powers of the state, the communities and the regions were officially laid down.

So this is a double anniversary, in the true spirit of Belgian compromise: Belgium is celebrating 175 years of independence (construction!) and 25 years of federalism (deconstruction!). The country's various entities, the federal government, Communities and Regions, are working together to organise a special programme of festivities. On the four-language website www.175-25.be we read that *'this festive year, which looks firmly to the future, offers opportunities for meetings. (...) Meetings between cultures, between generations, between the political, economic and social worlds, between citizens.'* All kinds of activities are planned: concerts, congresses, exhibitions etc.

Wim Delvoye,
Cloaca – Quatro. 2005.
Mixed media.
Photo by Dirk Pauwels.

One of the high points will certainly be the exhibition *Visionary Belgium, C'est arrivé près de chez nous*. Its creator Harald Szeeman worked for two years on this exhibition with its over 500 works of art. It is the last flourish of this internationally-known curator, who died in February 2005. In a triptych, together with utopian and original artists he displays a surprising and idiosyncratic image of Belgium. He brought together works by great names such as Ensor, Magritte, Rops, Delvaux, Khnopff, Broodhaers, but also by contemporary artists like Charlier, Jan Fabre, Luc Tuymans, Wim Delvoye (with a new and improved Turbo-cloaca!) and Panamarenko. Along with these there are unexpected projects which raise more questions than they give answers, like the model of the flint tower by paleontologist Robert Garcet, a scale model of the demolished Horta Volkshuis, the futuristic view of the Central Station and the TGV of architect Luc Deleu and the garden gnomes of Johan van Geluwe... It is an ambitious cultural portrait of a country, and if we can believe the climatologists of the Catholic University of Leuven it's now or never. At the end of 2004 they published a new report which suggests that by the end of the century most of the Belgian coast will have been swallowed up by the sea. And by 3000 a tenth of the country will be below sea-level. A bit less of that *beautiful nation*, then.

Enough of Belgium for now. How are things with the Netherlands? Not good, if we're to believe President Bush. During his address in the Concert Noble the world 'Netherlands' crossed his lips just once. He impressed upon his audience that we must reject antisemitism in all its forms and condemn violence such as we have seen in the Netherlands. According to Bush we must all ensure that minorities can play their full part in the community and that each new generation learns the value of tolerance.

It's not entirely clear what he meant by this, but probably he was referring to the wave of fear and intolerance that swept the Netherlands immediately after the murder of the film-maker Theo van Gogh, famous and notorious for his often crude remarks about Jews and Muslims. Following his mur-

der there were lively debates in the Netherlands on how to curb Muslim extremism. In the short film *Submission 1* Van Gogh and VVD politician Ayaan Hirsi Ali had drawn attention to the most anti-feminist texts from the Koran. In her book *Factory for Sons* (De zoontjesfabriek, 2003) Hirsi Ali had already pointed to that hostility to women as one of the main causes of the failure of the multicultural social model in the Netherlands.

But the Dutch image of tolerance had come under pressure even before this. When in early 2004 the Cabinet approved the proposals of Minister for Alien Affairs and Integration Rita Verdonk, Andrew Mueller wrote in *The Independent on Sunday*: *'Holland's government is shipping home 26,000 asylum seekers. What's happened to Europe's most tolerant nation?'* Foreigners entering the new Netherlands must, according to one of Verdonk's recent proposals, sit two examinations. First, after taking a course in their country of origin they are tested on their basic knowledge of Dutch and Dutch society; the second exam, taken after a course in the Netherlands, decides whether or not they are granted a residence permit. In early 2005 the British press reported rather cynically on this entrance exam; the newcomers themselves had to foot the bill for the teaching package and for an exam with such questions as *'how many wheels has a car?'* and *'where can you sunbathe topless in the Netherlands?'*.

But despite all the caricatures and the upheaval there is still the opposing voice of nuance and toleration. In *Doomed to Vulnerability* (Gedoemd tot kwetsbaarheid) Geert Mak, author of the impressive book *In Europa* (which will also be published in English) has written a pamphlet attacking the *'trafficking in fear'* which he has observed in the Dutch media and politicians since 2 November 2004, the day of Theo van Gogh's murder in Amsterdam: *'Anyone who followed the media in those weeks saw a country that seemed to have come adrift from international ties, cut loose also from all its historical roots, focused only on itself.'* The scientific facts regarding immigration and Islam barely got through to the public debate. What Mak is concerned with is to rescue rare and important qualities such as 'our pacification, with as a side-product our famous tolerance'. The intolerance of Islam must be combatted, but equally the humanist forces within Islam must be embraced. There is no future for either Europe or the Netherlands as a fortress: they are doomed to be vulnerable, and that is as it should be if they are to take on the challenges of the twenty-first century. Hardness is necessary in dealing with those who want to attack Europe's foundations, but in so doing it is necessary to work with care and precision. Nobody is served by what Mak describes as a 'trafficking in fear' in today's Netherlands.

So in this way the Netherlands has another chance to become a guide-country. In the *Financial Times Magazine* Simon Kuper commented: 'Once a bastion of liberal values, the Netherlands is struggling to accept its large Muslim population. And the world is watching.'

On www.condoleance.nl under the name 'Theo van Gogh' we read: 'Theo....life goes on, but it is so different. Half the world is rotten already, and now the Netherlands is going that way too, unless... perhaps another one like you will come? Sleep softly dear Theo, you are unforgettable.' And also: 'You were a great asset to our Dutch culture.'

Another great asset to Dutch culture, according to some people at least, was the Amsterdam folk singer André Hazes, who died of a cardiac arrest on 23 September 2004. Hazes, the Number 1 Dutch Folk Hero, lived what he sang and sang what he lived: sadness, loneliness and drunkenness. While not everyone agreed about his musical qualities, there was no disputing the man's street cred. Four days after his death 50,000 fans bade farewell to their idol in the Amsterdam Arena. The television coverage was watched by more than 5 million people.

But although some would say that music in the Low Countries has been decapitated, it is very far from being dead. The Fleming Adriaen Willaert, one of the sixteenth century's top composers, got his own Adriaen Willaert Foundation in 2004, and on top of that at almost the same time the rights to his work were bought by the American A.R. Editions. Rita Reys, the Dutch 'First Lady of Jazz', was 80 in 2004, and she still sings with the same velvety erotic hoarseness that caught the attention of George Avakina of Columbia Records and Art Blakey back in the fifties. The proof can be heard on the new cd *Beautiful Love* and the boxed set *Songs of a Lifetime 1953-2000*. And in February 2005 the Flemish conductor René Jacobs won a Grammy in the 'opera' category for *Le nozze di Figaro*, a Mozart recording from 2004.

And for those who prefer something rather more cross-grained: in 2004 the Dutch group The Ex celebrated 25 years of existence with a festival in both Amsterdam and Brussels; *A Beautiful Frenzy* twice provided 'an ecstatic day with music, poetry, movies, performances'. For The Ex (www.theex.nl) is so much more than just a punk band. Originating among the squatters of Amsterdam, the group gradually swapped the messy post-punk for what eventually became known as 'Ex-music': added to the basic punk were ethnic influences, jazz improvisations, headstrong drum patterns and a characteristic guitar sound. The lyrics of singer G.W. Sok are spiked with social criticism, but slogans are shunned like the plague. The group's 25th birthday was marked by the double cd *Turn*, produced by Steve Albini, of which a reviewer for *Pitchforkmedia* wrote: 'To me, The Ex make vital music. They're not just shouting about trade unionism, materialist greed, and the inherent contradictions of modern free-market societies; they can bring the noise, too, and their polemics come wrapped in a blistering package of smouldering art-punk informed by free jazz and global folk. On their latest album they elevate their craft to near perfection over the course of two wild, unpredictable, and unforgettable discs.'

'We need poets, we need painters!', sings G.W. Sok in 'Listen to the Painters', the opening track of *Turn*. Social commitment and the need for art and knowledge: these were also important to the Dutch writer Theun de Vries, who died on 21 January 2005. For a long time De Vries' communist convictions kept the doors of the Dutch literary world closed against him. With around 150 titles to his name he was one of the Netherlands' most prolific authors, and also one of the most varied. He wrote poetry (including some collections in Frisian), stories and novels, essays and biographies, plays for the stage and for radio, film scripts, and on top of all that more than fifty translations. Some of his work bears the stamp of his communist views, but he is never doctrinaire. De Vries wrote about social justice, racism and freedom, and this brought him the prestigious P.C. Hooft Prize in 1962 and in 1979 an honorary doctorate at the University of Groningen for 'the expertise and integrity with which he has served the discipline of history'.

In 1956 he published The Girl with the Red Hair (Het meisje met het rode haar) about the resistance fighter Hannie Schaft, which was filmed in 1981. At first the novel was not rated very highly, but over the years it has become a classic for successive generations of Dutch schoolchildren. Despite this, on www.condoleance.nl Theun de Vries has to make do with a sparse personally listed page while Hazes, Theo van Gogh and even 'Pistolen Paultje' (Paul Wilking, the uncrowned king of the Amsterdam underworld) have jam-packed nationally listed pages. But luckily that solitary page does contain a very concise assessment of De Vries: 'a great red writer'.

'A master between light and dark' is the subtitle of the novel De Vries published in 1931 about Rembrandt. The book deals with the period between 1650 and 1669, the year in which the Amsterdam Master shuffled off this mortal coil. The British director Peter Greenaway, who is currently making a film in connection with the Rembrandt Year 2006, will also zoom in on the the painter's final years. Nightwatching is set before, during and after the painting of The Night Watch. During that time Rembrandt lost three children and his wife. There then followed many other, often younger, women, who did the painter little good. On top of which the artist started living above his station, which eventually led to his bankruptcy.

Greenaway will also be responsible for an installation in Amsterdam's Rijksmuseum (www.rijksmuseum.nl) which will cast light upon the individuals who appear in the world-famous painting. Actually the Rijksmuseum has been closed for over a year now for alterations and renovation and will not reopen until 2008. In the meantime its finest seventeenth-century works – including The Night Watch – will still be accessible to the public under the title The Masterpieces in the newly refurbished Philips Wing.

So we need painters, poets and writers, but we can't do without architects either. On 27 April 2004 the Serpentine Gallery in London announced that the Rotterdam-based firm of architects MVRDV (www.mvrdv.nl) would be designing the next temporary pavilion in the gallery's garden. For years now the Serpentine Gallery has been commissioning notable architects who had not previously built anything in England to design these temporary pavilions. This one was to open in 2005. MVRDV's people, famous for the hamburger-like Holland Pavilion at the Hanover World Expo in 2000, are according to connoisseurs 'the hippest Dutch architects outside the Netherlands after Rem Koolhaas'. Consequently, in September 2004 Julia Peyton-Jones, director of the Serpentine Gallery, told the Daily Telegraph: 'I think it is really audacious, really amazing and really grand. It's fab. It's so exciting.'

The pavilion was to open in 2005 and it was even to be usable in winter, which was a first. 'Was', because now Álvaro Siza and Eduardo Souto de Moura are designing the 2005 summer pavilion. Because the commissioning body refuses to make any concessions to MVRDV's design, it has been decided to postpone its implementation for a year. According to this radical proposal, in 2006 the Serpentine Gallery will be completely hidden under an enormous gras-covered mountain. This mountain is a continuation and expansion of the surrounding Kensington Gardens, a beacon that will be clearly visible from the city. But we shall have to wait for this 'pavilion with a view'.

The Dutch artist and architect John Körmeling provided a different kind of view in Toronto in June 2004. His Mobile Fun, a Ferris wheel for cars, set a lot of tongues wagging during a retrospective exhibition of his work in The Powerplant by Lake Ontario. His wheel had already been working in Utrecht in 2000, but then you could drive your own car into it and ascend into the sky like that. But in Toronto the insurance people thought that was too risky, so in the end there were just a number of Saabs fixed to the wheel. And why head for the clouds by car? Körmeling's answer is simple: *'To get away from the chaos for a bit. It's a respite'* or *'Everything's always so dead serious'*. With his stubbornly individual style of working and the startling way he looks at everyday things Körmeling wants to put our hectic existence into perspective. Why else do you think he made *square* rubber balls and exhibited those too in The Powerplant?

Rem Koolhaas too is a man of ideas. When it was announced that he had been awarded the 2004 Royal Gold Medal, the United Kingdom's greatest prize for architecture, he was still widely regarded as an architect brimming with ideas and plans, a visionary whose designs in the end *never* got built. But as Rowan Moor wrote in a major article in the *Evening Standard*, *'Koolhaas is finally becoming a prolific builder as well as a prolific writer.'* Prada's new Epicenter by Koolhaas - *'thrilling from top to bottom'*, according to a critic in *The New Yorker* - opened in 2004 in Beverly Hills, and Koolhaas' first Prada shop has been open for some time in New York. His company OMA (www.oma.nl) is now going to redevelop the site of the old covered markets in Rome.

The aim of OMA and its thinktank AMO is to keep testing ideas about contemporary society against practice. Koolhaas and his associates consistently strive to wring the last ounce out of every project, whether it be a family home in Bordeaux, the China Central Television skyscraper in Beijing, the new Dutch embassy in Berlin or the Guggenheim Museum project in Las Vegas. The house in Bordeaux was recently voted the house of the twentieth century. By no coincidence, Koolhaas collaborated on the interior with Maarten van Severen, an internationally renowned Flemish cabinetmaker who died in February 2005 after a lifetime spent in the obsessive quest for that one brilliant idea.

OMA, Seattle Public Library, 1999-2004. Photo by Ph. Ruault.

The high point so far of Koolhaas' built oeuvre, though, is to be found in Seattle. There he built a library which is remarkable for its ingenious steel construction with thousands of lozenge-shaped windows (almost 10,000 in all!). This steel structure is draped over the building like a cloak. The various layers of the library are offset, creating the extremely striking form. Nicolai Ouroussoff wrote of it in *The Los Angeles Times*: *'the stacks, arranged along a continuous spiral ramp contained with a four-storey slab, reinforce a sense of a world arranged with machine-like precision.'* Or as *The Seattle Times* put it: *'A glasshouse filled with books'*.

And that brings us to books. All manner of internet bookshops and online library catalogues ensure that today anyone can find as much as they want on every subject under the sun, but here I would like to mention a couple of 'highly recommendeds'.

Every year hundreds of books on the Dutch Golden Age are published in English. *Senses and Sins* is one such, and it offers a fine overview of *'rowdy peasants,* enraptured couples, the village school, soldiers, fashionable ladies writing letters'; in other words, of how painters recorded everyday life in the seventeenth century. Also interesting is *Selected Writings on Dutch Painting* of the eminent Vermeer expert Albert Blankaert, who here discusses not only Rembrandt and Vermeer but also less well known old masters such as Daniel van Beke and Caesar van Everdingen, and even the 20th-century painter Carel Willink.

There are books in abundance, too, for lovers of cities. Richter Roegholt has written a fascinating *Short History of Amsterdam*, in which he 'follows the successively changing political landscapes of which Amsterdam, since its founding in the 13th century, has been part'. In *Brussels* André de Vries explores a city which is continually in search of an identity, a capital on the faultline between Latin and Germanic culture, 'a place ruled by the spirit of zwanze, "self-mockery and derision", a city so down-to-earth the Bruxellois had to invent surrealism'.

And that a surrealistic and absurd sense of humour is indeed typically 'Belgian' is evident from *Hic Sunt leones*, an anthology of outstanding work by 21 young Flemish comic-strip artists and illustrators, published with support from the Flemish Literature Fund. 'Hic sunt leones (et dracones)' (Here be lions and dragons) was used on old Roman maps to indicate areas of which nothing was known and which were better avoided. Those who find themselves reading this book, though, will have no cause to regret it. Just one example: when a story starts with a one-legged man at the bar of a Flemish café musing that 'The problem with having just one leg is that you're always explaining how the other one got lost', how can you *not* want to read it?

Jan Brandes too was not one to be scared of the *leones et dracones*. A Lutheran preacher, in 1778 he travelled with his wife to the Dutch East Indies. In 1785, having amassed a modest amount of money but lost his wife, he left for Ceylon with his young son. Continuing his travels, he spent a year at the Cape of Good Hope before returning to the Netherlands. Throughout his life Brandes made drawings 'from life'. He recorded what he saw around him: his family, his house, people in the street, the church, slaves, life on board the Dutch East India Company's ships and a great many plants and animals. In *The World of Jan Brandes, 1743-1808* over two hundred of his most important drawings are reproduced in colour with accompanying descriptions. Stay home, young man, and read about those who went east.

Jeroen Giltaij, *Senses And Sins: Dutch Painters Of Daily Life In The Seventeenth Century*. Hatje Cantz Publishers, 2005 (ISBN: 3-77571-523-1 – www.hatjecantz.de / Albert Blankert, *Selected Writings On Dutch Painting: Rembrandt, Van Beke, Vermeer, and Others*. Waanders Publishers, 2004 (ISBN: 9-04008-932-9 – www.waanders.nl) / Richter Roegholt, *A Short History of Amsterdam*. Bekking & Blitz, 2004 (ISBN: 9-06109-552-2 – www.bekkingblitz.com) / André de Vries, *Brussels. A Cultural and Literary History*. Signal, 2003 (ISBN: 1-90266-947-9 – www.signalbooks.co.uk) / Ria Schulpen (ed.), *Hic Sunt Leones*. Bries, 2004 (ISBN: 9-07670-824-X – www.bries.be) / Max de Bruijn & Remco Raben, *The World Of Jan Brandes, 1743-1808: Drawings Of A Dutch Traveller In Batavia, Ceylon And Southern Africa*. Waanders, 2005 (ISBN: 9-04008-756-3 – www.waanders.nl)

Filip Matthijs
Translated by Tanis Guest

Contributors

Dirk van Assche
Deputy editor
'Stichting Ons Erfdeel'
Murissonstraat 260,
8930 Rekkem, Belgium

Michel Bakker
Archeologist / Architecture
historian
Sportparklaan 19,
Heemstede, The Netherlands

Ludo Bekkers
Art critic AICA
Eric Sasselaan 65/4,
2020 Antwerp, Belgium

Klaas van Berkel
Professor of the History of
Natural Sciences
(University of Groningen)
Oude Kijk in 't Jatstr 26,
9712 EK Groningen,
The Netherlands

Paul Binding
Writer
The House, Bull Street,
Bishop's Castle, Shropshire
SY9 5DB, United Kingdom

Kristiaan Borret
Urban planner (Technum) /
Assistant researcher (Ghent
University)
Eden City 17,
1190 Brussels, Belgium

Pieter Bots
Theatre and film critic
Frederiksstraat 17hs,
1054 LA Amsterdam,
The Netherlands

Eric Bracke
Freelance journalist
Wegvoeringstraat 115,
9230 Wetteren, Belgium

Willem Breedveld
Journalist *Trouw*/ Lecturer
in Mass Communication and
Politics (University of Leiden)
Waardsedijk 102,
3421 NH Oudewater,
The Netherlands

Ian Buruma
Writer
21 Wellington Street,
Oxford OX2 6BB,
United Kingdom

Martin Conway
Lecturer (CUF) in Modern
History
Balliol College (University of
Oxford)
Broad Street, Oxford OX1 3BD,
United Kingdom

Dirk van Delft
Science editor *NRC Handelsblad*
P.O. Box 8987,
3009 TH Rotterdam,
The Netherlands

Paul Depondt
Journalist *de Volkskrant*
Lange Violettestraat 263B,
9000 Ghent, Belgium

Luc Devoldere
Chief Editor
'Stichting Ons Erfdeel'
Murissonstraat 260,
8930 Rekkem, Belgium

Theo D'haen
Professor of American
Literature / Director of the
Centre for European Studies
(Catholic University of Leuven)
KUL English Dept.
Blijde-Inkomststraat 21,
3000 Leuven, Belgium

Marc Dierikx
Historian
Institute of Netherlands History
(The Hague)
Buskeshoeven 3,
5244 HN Rosmalen,
The Netherlands

Herman de Dijn
Professor of Modern
Philosophy
(Institute of Philosophy ,
Catholic University of Leuven)
Kardinaal Mercierplein 2,
3000 Leuven, Belgium

Kees van Domselaar
Literary critic/poet
Herenlaan 42,
3701 AV Zeist, The Netherlands

Luk van den Dries
Professor of Theatre Studies
(Antwerp University)
Universiteitsplein 1,
2610 Wilrijk, Belgium

Lieneke Frerichs
Senior Staff Member
Foundation for the Production
and Translation of
Dutch Literature (Amsterdam)
Voorhaven 120,
1135 BV Edam,
The Netherlands

Piet Gerbrandy
Poet / Critic
Prins Hendrikstraat 3,
7101 CK Winterswijk,
The Netherlands

Paul Gillaerts
Professor
Lessius Hogeschool,
Dept. for Translators and
Interpreters,
Sint-Andriesstraat 2,
2000 Antwerp, Belgium

Frank Hellemans
Lecturer in Communication
History (Katholieke Hogeschool
Mechelen) / Literary critic
(*Knack Magazine*)
Keldermansvest 23,
2800 Mechelen, Belgium

Hans Ibelings
Architecture critic
Javakade 542,
1019 SE Amsterdam,
The Netherlands

Olga van der Klooster
Researcher
(Dutch overseas architecture)
Sportparklaan 19,
Heemstede, The Netherlands

Yves Knockaert
Musicologist
Vaartstraat 61/301,
3000 Leuven, Belgium

Anton Korteweg
Director of the Netherlands
Literature Museum
(The Hague) / Poet
Wasstraat 23,

2313 JG Leiden,
The Netherlands

Isabella Lanz
Dance critic / Art historian
Binnenkadijk 306,
1018 AZ Amsterdam,
The Netherlands

Juleke van Lindert
Art critic
Roosje Vosstraat 5,
1069 RA Amsterdam,
The Netherlands

Filip Matthijs
Editorial secretary
The Low Countries
Murissonstraat 260,
8930 Rekkem, Belgium

Christelle Méplon
Freelance journalist
Kerkstraat 140,
2060 Antwerp, Belgium

Wam de Moor
Former Associate Professor of
General Arts and Literature
(Radboud University Nijmegen)
Postweg 32,
6523 LC Nijmegen,
The Netherlands

Lutgard Mutsaers
Lecturer in popular music
studies / Researcher
(Utrecht University)
Frederikastraat 16,
3572 CS Utrecht,
The Netherlands

Anneke H. van Otterloo
Staff member of
the Dept. Of Sociology and
Cutural Anthropology
(University of Amsterdam)
OZ Achterburgwal 185,
1012 DK Amsterdam,
The Netherlands

Frank van der Ploeg
Ar thistorian / Editor *kM*
Weeshuisland 54,
1541 MD Koog aan de Zaan,
The Netherlands

Tineke Reijnders
Art historian
(Sandberg Institute,
Amsterdam)
Zuideinde 116,
1121 DH Landsmeer,
The Netherlands

David Van Reybrouck
Writer / Postdoctoral research
fellow (Fund for Scientific
Research – Flanders)
Dept of History (Catholic
University of Leuven),
Blijde Inkomststraat 21,
3000 Leuven, Belgium

Peter G. Rose
Writer
27 Indian Lane,
South Salem, NY 10590, USA

Marc Ruyters
Art critic
Koning Albertlei 15,
2650 Edegem, Belgium

Reinier Salverda
Professor of Dutch Language
and Literature
(University College London)
UCL Dept.of Dutch,
Room 324 Foster Court,
Gower Street,
London WC1E 6BT,
United Kingdom

Barbara Simons
Translator / Copywriter
Bosstraat 52,
3012 Wilsele, Belgium

Bart van der Straeten
Editorial secretary *Ons Erfdeel*
Murissonstraat 260,
8930 Rekkem, Belgium

David Stroband
Art historian.
Pelsterstraat 17 G,
9711 KH Groningen,
The Netherlands

Johan Vandenbossche
Cooperator Sound Archives
Flemish Public Radio
Koningin Elisabethlaan 10,
9700 Oudenaarde, Belgium

Peter Vantyghem
Editor *De Standaard*
Gossetlaan 28,
1702 Groot Bijgaarden,
Belgium

Koen Vergeer
Literary critic/Writer
Abel Tasmanstraat 63,
3531 GT Utrecht,
The Netherlands

Marjoleine de Vos
Editor/Columnist
NRC Handelsblad
Frans van Mierisstraat 106,
1071 SB Amsterdam,
The Netherlands

Translators

Gregory Ball
Sheila M. Dale
Lindsay Edwards
Chris Emery
Peter Flynn
Nancy Forest-Flier
Brian Granger
Tanis Guest
Sarah Hart
James S Holmes
John Irons
Joy R. Kearney
Ria Loohuizen
Yvette Mead
Elizabeth Mollison
Alison Mouthaan-Gwillim
Les Murray
Julian Ross
Rina Vergano
Paul Vincent
Laura Watkinson

ADVISOR ON ENGLISH USAGE

Tanis Guest (UK)

As well as the yearbook The Low Countries,
the Flemish Netherlands foundation 'Stichting Ons Erfdeel'
publishes a number of books covering various aspects of the culture of
Flanders and the Netherlands.

NEW

Wim Daniëls
Talking Dutch.
Illustrated; 80 pp.
(September 2005)

J.A. Kossmann-Putto &
E.H. Kossmann
The Low Countries.
History of the Northern
and Southern Netherlands.
Illustrated; 64 pp.

Jaap Goedegebuure &
Anne Marie Musschoot
Contemporary Fiction of
the Low Countries.
Illustrated and with
translated extracts from
15 novels; 128 pp.

Hugo Brems &
Ad Zuiderent
Contemporary Poetry of
the Low Countries.
With 52 translated poems;
112 pp.

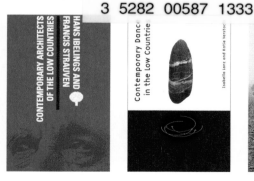  

Elly Stegeman &
Marc Ruyters
Contemporary Sculptors
of the Low Countries.
Illustrated in four colour
printing; 128 pp.

Hans Ibelings &
Francis Strauven
Contemporary Architects
of the Low Countries.
Illustrated in four colour
printing; 128 pp.

Isabella Lanz &
Katie Verstockt,
Contemporary Dance
in the Low Countries.
Illustrated; 128 pp.

Between 1993 and 2004
the first twelve issues
of the yearbook *The Low*
Countries were published.